Knowledge Management Systems in Law Enforcement:
Technologies and Techniques

Petter Gottschalk
Norwegian School of Management, Norway

IDEA GROUP PUBLISHING
Hershey • London • Melbourne • Singapore

Acquisitions Editor:	Michelle Potter
Development Editor:	Kristin Roth
Senior Managing Editor:	Amanda Appicello
Managing Editor:	Jennifer Neidig
Copy Editor:	Angela Thor
Typesetter:	Jessie Weik
Cover Design:	Lisa Tosheff
Printed at:	Yurchak Printing Inc.

Published in the United States of America by
    Idea Group Publishing (an imprint of Idea Group Inc.)
    701 E. Chocolate Avenue
    Hershey PA 17033
    Tel: 717-533-8845
    Fax: 717-533-8661
    E-mail: cust@idea-group.com
    Web site: http://www.idea-group.com

and in the United Kingdom by
    Idea Group Publishing (an imprint of Idea Group Inc.)
    3 Henrietta Street
    Covent Garden
    London WC2E 8LU
    Tel: 44 20 7240 0856
    Fax: 44 20 7379 0609
    Web site: http://www.eurospanonline.com

  Library of Congress Cataloging-in-Publication Data

Gottschalk, Petter, 1950-
  Knowledge management systems in law enforcement : technologies and techniques / by Petter Gottschalk.
    p. cm.
  Summary: " This book presents research and trends in using knowledge management to aid police activities, offering principles and practices to help law enforcement professionals find ways to use vast amounts of knowledge as a tool"--Provided by publisher.
  Includes bibliographical references and index.
  ISBN 1-59904-307-6 (hardcover) -- ISBN 1-59904-308-4 (softcover) -- ISBN 1-59904-309-2 (ebook)
  1. Knowledge management. 2. Management information systems. 3. Law enforcement. I. Title.
  HD30.2.G674 2006
  363.2068'4--dc22
                            2006012371

British Cataloguing in Publication Data
A Cataloguing in Publication record for this book is available from the British Library.

All work contributed to this book is new, previously-unpublished material. The views expressed in this book are those of the authors, but not necessarily of the publisher.

Knowledge Management Systems in Law Enforcement:
Technologies and Techniques

Table of Contents

Foreword

Crime prevention is a good example of knowledge-intensive work. Crime prevention is built upon information: gathering, analyzing, and exchanging it. Intelligence-led policing, a crime-prevention strategy that has recently gained worldwide support, has raised the significance of information. The amount of information, however, has reached a level that cannot be processed by human capacity alone. Planned information processing and tools for it are needed. Managing the cumulating amount of information and knowledge of the police is a prerequisite for success.

Crime investigation is not merely about individual competencies, although this is how it often looks in the detective stories. Crime investigation necessarily involves collaboration; working together. The new ways of gathering information in crime investigation may clash with the old structures, the way activities are traditionally organized and carried out. Crime does not obey the boundaries between authorities. Economic crime, for example, may burden authorities such as tax office, enforcement office, customs, and the prosecutor, in addition to the police. Information exchange is the minimum of collaboration, but often there is a need to work together and create new knowledge together in multiprofessional and multiorganizational groups.

The traditional mode of collaboration between agencies resembles a relay race. This *sequential collaboration* enables only the transmission of papers and information from one participant to another. The mere exchange of information does not, however, guarantee good results: *parallel collaboration*, working together and analyzing the information together, is needed. The goals of the investigation have to be defined together as well: the target has to be shared to avoid a situation in which each agency aims at its own, diverging goals. This involves negotiations, interaction, and open-minded crossing of organizational boundaries.

Knowledge management has seldom been mentioned in connection with crime investigation, although the work is highly knowledge intensive. The significance of collaboration between units within the police organization and between other agencies that may contribute crime investigation has increased not only within national borders, but internationally: Crime has globalized. Thereby, a new kind of challenge seems to have risen: How to share the information and knowledge between those who need it in the multiorganizational, possibly international, collaborative investigation process? Moreover, the mere *passing* of information from an agency to another is not sufficient: the information must also be processed together to gain accurate conclusions. The knowledge concerning the crime has, increasingly, to be *created* together, in interorganizational collaboration. The deficiencies of the existing tools and instruments make this work even more challenging. There seems to be a need for interorganizational knowledge management tools and instruments in crime investigation

All knowledge can never be explicated. There still is room for the mythical, heroic detective described in so many detective stories. Technological tools can, however, help him or her. The risk with information technology tools, especially registers, seems to be that they easily begin to lead the actors. The filling of registers takes over the power from the detective who should *use* the registers as tools for gaining better results in the investigation. Modern IT-tools can, however, give a much better base for creative investigation than the traditional registers. The detectives should be able to systematically utilize the possibilities of modern knowledge management tools. The new knowledge management technology gives an opportunity to collective learning by, for example, systematically storing and managing information about past cases, and an opportunity to utilize that information in future cases. Technology, however, will not solve all our problems. Be the tools as good as they may, the cases will be solved by objective and competent human detectives who will be able to utilize the tools.

Anne Puonti, PhD
National Bureau of Investigation
Finland

Preface

The amount of information that police officers come into contact with in the course of their work is astounding. Such information is captured within police organizations in various forms. A challenge for police organizations is how to surface information, make it into knowledge, and bring it to bear on the problems faced by police officers in a timely and effective manner. This information and knowledge challenge in police organizations is the focus of and the reason for this book.

As will be explained later, a hierarchy of terms is used in this book. The hierarchy consists of data, information, knowledge, and wisdom. Information is data that makes sense to people, while knowledge is information combined with interpretation, reflection, and context. Based on such definitions, this book argues that information can be stored in computers, while knowledge is stored in human brains. Given such distinctions, knowledge management technology supports knowledge work by receiving codified knowledge in terms of information from knowledge workers, and by supplying information that knowledge workers transform into knowledge.

This book is designed as compulsory literature for courses in management information systems and knowledge management at advanced bachelor level and at master level in all police academies and police university colleges around the world. It can be considered supplementary literature in management information systems courses and knowledge management courses in business schools in terms of knowledge work case studies.

In addition, practitioners in business and public organizations as well as the IT industry itself will benefit from insights in this book. This book is based on the premise that it is difficult, if not impossible, to manage an organization without at least some understanding of knowledge management and knowledge management systems.

Last, but not least, this book is written for law schools. Law students have a need to learn how law enforcement works. Some of them will later be employed as police lawyers; others will constantly be in contact with the police as lawyers and attorneys.

As one of the reviewers of the manuscript for this book wrote in the review:

To the reviewer's knowledge, there have not been notable efforts that systematically address knowledge management in police work; to this end, this book has an advantage of being the "sole player" in the field. The book is definitely useful for a number of audiences, starting with police staff at all hierarchy levels, who need to have an insight of the benefits new technologies may bring to their profession, best practices for obtaining them, as well as the that they may face. Lawyers and judicial workers may also benefit from the book, since they will be more efficient in their work if they have an insight of how the police is conducting its business. Finally, information technology staff that undertake knowledge management projects for police, security and similar domains, will find in this book a systematic record of issues that they will face in their projects.

This book combines knowledge management with other subject areas within the management information systems field. The subject of knowledge management is no longer a separate topic, as research and practice have moved into linking knowledge management to its uses. The scholarly value of this proposed book can be found in insights generated from the contingent approach to linking knowledge management to other IT management topics and its uses.

Governments have become increasingly focused upon the setting of targets in efforts to improve the efficacy of police performance. According to Ashby and Longley (2005), there is a lack of clarity and clear methodology in assessing the performance of policing. We argue that police investigation units have the value configuration of a value shop. Furthermore, we argue that police investigation success can be defined as the extent to which each primary activity in the value shop is successfully conducted in police investigations.

Police investigation units represent a knowledge-intensive and time-critical environment (Chen, Schroeder, Hauck, Ridgeway, Atabakhsh, Gupta, Boarman, Rasmussen, & Clements, 2002). The primary mission of any police force in the world is to protect life and property, preserve law and order, and prevent and detect crime (Luen & Al-Hawamdeh, 2001).

In response to the September 11 terrorist attacks, major government efforts to modernize federal law enforcement authorities' intelligence collection and processing capabilities have been initiated. At the state and local levels in many countries all over the world, crime and police report data is rapidly migrating from paper records to automated records management systems in recent years, making them increasingly accessible (Chen, Zheng, Atabakhsh, Wyzga, & Schroeder, 2003).

According to Manwani (2005), we know only too well the importance of information in competing in a global economy or protecting our society against terrorism. This information comes in many different forms, from a variety of sources, and has to be validated, consolidated, and presented in order to make the right decisions. We also recognize that this information has to be controlled and secured so that it is not misused. Both the public and private sector have these common challenges, even though the ultimate use is different.

Police investigations are often dependent upon information from abroad. For example, the intelligence communities of different countries cooperate and share their information and knowledge, such as the Mossad with the CIA (Kahana, 2001). According to Lahneman (2004), knowledge sharing in the intelligence communities after 9/11 has increased rapidly.

Over the past two decades, many police agencies have endeavored to implement the concepts of the "learning organization." The learning organization is characterized by the commitment of a firm to the principles of sharing, innovating, critical review, and systemic thinking. An organizational culture is nurtured, in which adherence to such principles is articulated, encouraged, rewarded, and highly regarded. In policing, this investment is based on two overarching factors. The first is that the very nature of police work necessitates officers needing access to timely, accurate, and up-to-date information. Secondly, the amount of data police officers come into contact with in the course of their work is astounding, and provides vast sources from which to collect information (Hughes & Jackson, 2004).

Information, in a policing context, covers a wide range of diverse organizational activities including crime and traffic management, budget and asset control, human resource deployment, record management, and statistical analysis. For the purpose of this book, where we will narrow our focus on criminal investigations, the term information relates to crime management data. The main sources of such data are usually the product of contacts police officers have with both law and nonlaw-abiding members of the public. This is a largely nonstructured, often tacit source of insight into crime-related events. Other data collection sources include personal and electronic observations, telephone and e-mail intercepts, registered informants, and data accessed via public and private organizations (Hughes & Jackson, 2004).

According to Pendleton and Chávez (2004), there is little evidence that the police profession is aware of knowledge management as an overall management strategy, but is involved in knowledge management activities in an incremental way. Knowledge management, as a purposeful organizational strategy, is more than an innovation in itself, but is a fundamental part of the innovation process that is essential to sustaining an organizational culture that is based in innovation. If the police profession is to sustain its position on the "cutting edge" of innovation, there is a need to integrate the various knowledge management techniques into interrelated systems based on modern information technology.

The fundamental police concern is typically with processing demand for service, not storage, retrieval, analysis, or even record management per se. Policing runs in a crisis mode and is overwhelmed with the present, impending, or possible crisis. Each information technology at first competes for space, time, and legitimacy with other known means, and is judged in policing by somewhat changing pragmatic, often nontechnical, values: its speed, its durability and weight, and its contribution to the officers' notion of the role and routines. New technologies are put into use untested and without arrangement for the maintenance that will inevitably be needed. In other words, innovations are taken up on an ad hoc, here-and-now basis, according to Manning (2003). Some IT facilities are purchased by state or local authorities for multiple purposes, and are not vetted, contracted for, nor acquired by police management or budgetary officers. The lack of understanding of IT has made police vulnerable to vendors, changes in city or county policies, and the handful of officers who have learned IT on the job and found a niche. This has increased maintenance costs, made replacement expensive, and created an array of incompatible databases and systems (Manning, 2003).

Knowledge is a fundamental asset in law enforcement. Increasingly, knowledge is distributed across individuals, teams, and organizations. Therefore, the ability to create, acquire, integrate, and deploy knowledge has emerged as fundamental organizational capability. To be successful, law enforcement departments must not only exploit existing knowledge, but must also invest in continually exploring new knowledge (Sambamurthy & Subramani, 2005).

The centrality of knowledge in organizations is reflected in the emergence of the knowledge-based view as an important theoretical stance in contemporary organizational research. Theoretical proposals indicate that advantages for a firm arise from cooperative social contexts that are conducive to the creation, coordination, transfer, and integration of knowledge distributed among its employees, departments, and cooperating agencies.

Knowledge is a complex concept, and a number of factors determine the nature of knowledge creation, management, valuation, and sharing. Organizational knowledge is created through cycles of combination, internalization, socialization, and externalization that transform knowledge between tacit and explicit modes.

Knowledge management is of particular relevance to information systems because the functionalities of information technologies play a critical role in shaping organizational efforts for knowledge creation, acquisition, integration, valuation, and use. Information systems have been central to organizational efforts to enable work processes, flows of information, and sources of knowledge to be integrated, and for synergies from such combinations to be realized.

The focus of the deployment of knowledge management systems in organizations has been on developing searchable document repositories to support the digital capture, storage, retrieval, and distribution of an organization's explicitly documented knowledge. Knowledge management systems also encompass other technology-based initiatives such as the creation of databases of experts, the development of decision aids and expert systems, and the hardwiring of social networks to aid access to resources of noncollocated individuals (Sambamurthy & Subramani, 2005).

Information systems developers have evolved several frameworks to articulate themes related to knowledge management, which will be presented in this book. There is a diversity of organizational processes through which information systems affect the management of intangible assets in and between organizations. Furthermore, technical and social processes interact in complementarities to shape knowledge management efforts. For example, although information technologies foster electronic communities of practice, there are social dynamics through which such communities become effective forums for knowledge dissemination, integration, and use.

MIS Quarterly is a leading research journal on management information systems. In March and June 2005, the journal published a special issue, in two volumes, on information technologies and knowledge management. In the introduction to the special issue, Sambamurthy and Subramani (2005) presented three types of organizational problems where knowledge management systems can make a difference:

- **The problem of knowledge coordination.** Individuals or groups face knowledge coordination problems when the knowledge needed to diagnose and solve a problem or make an appropriate decision exists (or is believed to exist), but knowledge about its existence or location is not available to the individual or group. Knowledge coordination problems require a search for expertise, and are aided by an understanding of patterns of knowledge distribution—of who knows what and who can be asked for help. Research suggests that personal, social, or organizational networks facilitate awareness about knowing entities and their possession of knowledge. Similarly, information technologies can facilitate the efficient and effective nurturing of communities of practice through which distributed knowledge can be coordinated.

- **The problem of knowledge transfer.** This problem is often faced by individuals or groups once an appropriate source of knowledge is located (generally after solving knowledge coordination problems). In particular, knowledge is found to be sticky and contextualized as a result of which it might not be easily transferable. Further, the absorptive capacity of the individuals, units, or organizations seeking knowledge might either enable or inhibit their ability to make sense of the transferred knowledge.

- **The problem of knowledge reuse.** This is a problem of motivation and reward related to the reuse of knowledge. This occurs when individuals or groups may prefer to devise a unique solution to a problem rather than reuse the standard knowledge available in repositories. Often, recognizing individuals for knowledge contributions (such as rewarding contributions to the organizational document repository or rewarding individuals for being helpful in sharing their expertise) appears to create disincentives to reuse of the knowledge, particularly when reuse involves explicitly acknowledging the inputs or assistance received.

Advances in information technologies and the growth of a knowledge-based service economy are transforming the basis of technological innovation and organizational performance. This transformation requires taking a broader, institutional and political view of information technology and knowledge management. To succeed, organizations need to focus on building their distinctive competencies (Van de Ven, 2005).

Law enforcement agencies, across the United States and other modern societies, have begun to focus on innovative knowledge management technologies to aid in the analysis of criminal information and knowledge. The use of such technologies can serve as intelligence tools to combat criminal activity by aiding in case investigation or even by predicting criminal activity.

The development of information technologies during the past few years has enabled many organizations to improve both the understanding and the dissemination of information. The development of powerful databases allows information to be organized in a manner that improves access to it, increases speed of retrieval, and expands searching flexibility. Furthermore, the Internet now provides a vehicle for sharing of information across geographical distance that encourages collaboration between people and organizations (Hauck & Chen, 2005). However, limited security and access control on the Internet often prevent law enforcement agencies from using it.

Information technology has certainly enhanced the capacity of police to collect, retrieve, and analyze information. It has altered important aspects of the field of policing; it has redefined the value of communicative and technical resources, institutionalized accountability through built-in formats and procedures of reporting, and restructured the daily routines of operational policing. The impact of technology on the habitus of policing, however, appears to be much less substantial, according to Chan (2003). The advantage brought about by technology—the capacity for a more responsive and problem-oriented approach to policing—has not been fully exploited. This is because operational police's technological frame sees information as relevant only for the purpose of arrest and conviction.

While officers are aware of the potential for smarter policing approaches, the preference is still to focus on collecting evidence for law enforcement, rather than broader analysis for crime prevention. Technologies that support a traditional law enforcement style of policing are the most successful ones. Where a more analytical approach is taken in relation to crime and intelligence, there is often a clash of cultures between police and analysts. Supervisors are aware of the capabilities that technology provides for better accountability and supervision, but these capabilities are also underutilized because they do not have time (Chan, 2003).

Introduction to Chapters

The core chapters of *Knowledge Management Systems in Law Enforcement: Technologies and Techniques* are organized according to the stages of growth model for knowledge management technology. Generally, stages of growth models have been successful in explaining and predicting organizational innovation and IT maturity. Specifically, the stages of growth model for knowledge management technology, developed by the author, has proven useful in both theoretical and empirical studies of knowledge intensive organizations (Gottschalk, 2005).

Knowledge management technology is simply defined as technology that supports knowledge work in organizations. According to the distinction between information and knowledge, computers handle information while persons handle knowledge. Knowledge management technology is technology that supports knowledge workers both at the individual level and at the organizational level. An important implication of this understanding of knowledge management technology is that word processing tools, for example, are as much knowledge management technology as case-based reasoning systems. This book focuses on technology that can improve efficiency and effectiveness of knowledge work in law enforcement, rather than advanced technology as such.

There are several benefits from applying the four-stage model for knowledge management technology. It can explain the evolution of knowledge management technology in knowledge intensive organizations. Next, it can predict the direction for future knowledge management projects in organizations. Third, it can guide the accumulation of technologies and techniques as well as infrastructures and architectures to support more sophisticated applications of information technology over time.

The stages-of-growth model, consisting of four stages, is introduced in Chapter IV. The stages are applied in this book mainly as an organizing framework for systems classification, as it is too early to tell whether Stages 2, 3, and 4 are truly observed in the real knowledge management systems in law enforcement. Furthermore, what will happen after Stage 4 is not clear; maybe a more cyclical behavior will occur involving some or all of the stages.

The first stage in the growth model, Officer-to-Technology, is concerned with information technology tools available to police officers as knowledge workers. This stage is discussed in Chapter V. It can be argued that this first stage is a computer literacy stage, which is not really a stage for knowledge management. However, from the user perspective applied in definitions of knowledge and knowledge management technology, it should be clear that the first stage represents the foundation for IT supported knowledge work.

In Chapter V, investigative thinking styles of detectives are introduced. Here, distinctions are made between police investigation as method, investigation as challenge, investigation as skill, and investigation as risk. These thinking styles based on research by Dean (1995, 2000, 2005), cause different knowledge working styles that represent variations in requirements to knowledge management and knowledge management systems. Some of these requirements can be met at Stage 1 of the knowledge management technology stage model, while other requirements have to wait until the organization matures into higher stages.

The second stage in the growth model, officer-to-officer, is concerned with communication between police officers, enabled and supported by information and communication technology. This stage is discussed in Chapter VI.

Again, to relate knowledge management systems to law enforcement work, as was done with thinking styles, this chapter describes police investigations in more detail, and exemplifies knowledge acquisition by police interviewing.

The third stage in the growth model, officer-to-information, is concerned with the electronic storage and retrieval of information that is useful to police officers. This stage is discussed in Chapter VII. Knowledge acquisition is here exemplified by knowledge derived from eyewitnesses.

The fourth and final stage in the growth model, officer-to-application, is concerned with the applications of artificial intelligence to police work to support police officers in their investigations. This stage is discussed in Chapter VIII. Knowledge application in knowledge management systems is here exemplified in terms of offender profiling, and crossing and checking in police investigations.

While Chapter IV and also Chapter III are focused on knowledge management technology, it is important to point out to the reader that the core Chapters V to VIII are less concerned with technology and more concerned with police work. The law enforcement focus should enable the reader to appreciate the linkages between policing and technology.

In Chapter V, on officer-to-technology systems, this is done by explaining different thinking styles that police officers are using in investigations. In Chapter VI on officer-to-officer systems, this is done by explaining police interviewing. In Chapter VII on officer-to-information systems, this is done by explaining the difficulties of interpreting eyewitness reports. Also in Chapter VII, the resource-based view of policing is introduced, as knowledge codified into information is stored in computer at this Stage 3 of the stages of growth model. Finally, in Chapter VIII on officer-to-application systems, offender profiling and "cross+check" are explained.

The organizing framework of the stages of growth model for knowledge management technology in law enforcement has, of course, limitations. For example, observable facts of Stages 2, 3, and even Stage 4 can occur in an IT-based law enforcement organization over time, and also at the same time. However, the main focus of knowledge management technology investments in an organization at any point in time will be found at one particular stage, rather than spread randomly across stages. Another limitation might be the sequential structure of the stage model. In reality, we will sometimes find cycles such as a return to Stage 3 after a preliminary visit to Stage 4, because the foundation for Stage 4 in terms of available information to be applied might emerge as not accessible. However, such adoption of the model to different settings and purposes should be considered a challenge rather than a weakness.

Before chapters on the stage model, the book provides background material concerning police work in Chapter I, knowledge management in Chapter II, and IT in knowledge management in Chapter III. In Chapter I, police knowledge work is described. The chapter concludes with a section on ethical issues that are exemplified by investigative interviewing by police officers.

Chapter II covers general topics on knowledge management, such as characteristics of knowledge, knowledge value levels, identification of knowledge needs, and classification of knowledge categories. For those readers unfamiliar with the topic of knowledge management, this chapter provides important background material.

Similarly, Chapter III provides important background material on the role of information technology in knowledge management. IT in knowledge management is presented in terms of knowledge management processes and knowledge management systems. Knowledge managements systems are exemplified by advanced technologies included in expert systems.

After five chapters, IV-VIII, organizing knowledge management systems in law enforcement on the stages of growth model for knowledge management technology, Chapter IX provides another framework to understand the role and importance of knowledge management systems in law enforcement.

Chapter IX describes police work by applying the value configuration of value shop to police investigations. By applying the value shop, we can discuss problem solving in terms of primary activities in police investigations. Technologies and techniques can support each primary activity in law enforcement organizations as value shops.

Law enforcement has to do with the law, and law firms are often involved on behalf of legal parties. Therefore, we take a look at knowledge management systems in law firms towards the end of this book, in Chapter X. This extension of law enforcement into law firms is included in the book to exemplify other parts of the judicial system.

This book focuses particularly on the work of police, while only marginally addressing the work of the judicial system or the penitentiary system, which might be considered important aspects of law enforcement and that also can benefit from employing knowledge management techniques. To compensate for this shortcoming, the Chapter X on knowledge management in law firms is an important extension of this book.

Law enforcement represents a variety of tasks in society. In this book, we touch upon many tasks and aspects of policing. However, as our main focus we chose police investigation, which is one of the most knowledge intensive tasks in law enforcement.

Case studies of law enforcement knowledge work in terms of research studies of police organizations are presented in the final chapter, XI. The empirical studies presented in this chapter illustrate some important dimensions of police work.

References

Ashby, D. I., & Longley, P. A. (2005). Geocomputation, geodemographics and resource allocation for local policing. *Transactions in GIS*, *9*(1), 53-72.

Chan, J. B. L. (2003). Police and new technologies. In T. Newburn (Ed.), *Handbook of policing.* Portland, OR: Willan Publishing.

Chen, H., Schroeder, J., Hauck, R. V., Ridgeway, L., Atabakhsh, H., Gupta, H., et al. (2002). COPLINK connect: Information and knowledge management for law enforcement. *Decision Support Systems*, *34*, 271-285.

Chen, H., Zheng, D., Atabakhsh, H., Wyzga, W., & Schroeder, J. (2003). COPLINK—Managing law enforcement data and knowledge. *Communications of the ACM*, *46*(1), 28-34.

Dean, G. (1995). Police reform: Rethinking operational policing. *American Journal of Criminal Justice*, *23*(4), 337-347.

Dean, G. (2000). *The experience of investigation for detectives.* Unpublished PhD thesis, Queensland University of Technology, Brisbane, Australia.

Dean, G. (2005). *The cognitive psychology of police investigators.* Conference paper, School of Justice Studies, Faculty of Law, Queensland University of Technology, Brisbane, Australia.

Gottschalk, P. (2005). *Strategic knowledge management technology.* Hershey, PA: Idea Group Publishing.

Hauck, R. V., & Chen, H. (2005). *COPLINK: A case of intelligent analysis and knowledge management.* Draft conference paper, University of Arizona.

Hughes, V., & Jackson, P. (2004). The influence of technical, social and structural factors on the effective use of information in a policing environment. *The Electronic Journal of Knowledge Management, 2*(1), 65-76.

Kahana, E. (2001). Mossad-CIA cooperation. *International Journal of Intelligence and CounterIntelligence, 14,* 409-420.

Lahneman, W. J. (2004). Knowledge-sharing in the intelligence community after 9/11. *International Journal of Intelligence and Counterintelligence, 17,* 614-633.

Luen, T. W., & Al-Hawamdeh, S. (2001). Knowledge management in the public sector: Principles and practices in police work. *Journal of Information Science, 27*(5), 311-318.

Manning, P. K. (2003). *Policing contingencies.* Chicago: The University of Chicago Press.

Manwani, S. (2005). The future of the IT organisation. *ComputerWeekly.* Retrieved October 28, 2005, from http://www.computerweekly.com

Pendleton, M. R., & Chávez, T. D. (2004). *Creating an innovation-centric police department: Guidelines for knowledge management in policing.* Seattle, WA: Seattle Police Department.

Sambamurthy, V., & Subramani, M. (2005). Special issue on information technologies and knowledge management. *MIS Quarterly, 29*(1), 1-7; and *29*(2), 193-195.

Van de Ven, A. H. (2005). Running in packs to develop knowledge-intensive technologies. *MIS Quarterly, 29*(2), 365-378.

Acknowledgment

Without the help and support from experienced police officers, this book would have been impossible for me to write. I would like to thank five scholars in particular. First, Dr. Geoff Dean at Queensland University of Technology in Brisbane, Australia, who contributed research literature on investigative thinking styles, offender profiling, and cross+check for investigations.

Second, Mr. Ivar Fahsing at the Norwegian Police University College contributed research literature on eyewitness statements and investigative interviewing. Third, I would like to thank Mr. Rune Glomseth at the Norwegian Police University College, who helped me find relevant research literature on police work, and who lets me teach executive classes in the Academy.

Furthermore, Dr. Stefan Holgersson at the Stockholm Police in Sweden has provided some very useful material from his doctoral dissertation on police officers' professional knowledge. Furthermore, Dr. Anne Puonti at the National Bureau of Investigation in Finland has provided some very useful material from her doctoral dissertation on police investigation.

Thanks to all of you!

Petter Gottschalk
Norwegian School of Management
Norway

Chapter I

Knowledge in Police Work

The public sector is turning to knowledge management, having recognized that they too face competition in funding and from alternative services. Increasingly, customers of the public sector are demanding higher service quality, particularly in the area of e-government. Services, particularly e-services, are expected to be available all the time with immediate response, simplified, and with one-stop processing. According to Luen and Al-Hawamdeh (2001), knowledge management is thus a natural solution to improve operations and enhance customer service. Large organizations around the world are implementing knowledge management.

Knowledge management is a crucial element of policing that is subject to a wide variety of laws and regulations governing crime, evidence, legal precedent, and rules of police behavior and that needs to be shared. At the same time, police forces are increasingly accountable to government at various levels and to the community at large for various aspects of their performance, and are expected to communicate with government and the public about what they are doing (Collier, Edwards, & Shaw, 2004).

The activities and work carried out by police forces are increasingly in the areas of crime prevention as well as incident management, investigation, and community policing. Crime prevention implies activities such as surveillance, patrolling, and guarding. These activities can be carried out through both reactive and proactive means. Reactive measures such as roadblocks, spot-checks, and showing police presence are routinely carried out by police officers as part of their investigative duties. Proactive measures include public education to help prevent crime. Police forces routinely use mass media as a means to convey crime prevention advice relating to current crime trends. In Singapore, police officers also reach out to the community via grassroots and community agencies to educate the public on the latest crime trends and threats (Luen & Al-Hawamdeh, 2001). Police officers, performing both reactive and proactive measures effectively, will need to know the latest legal and policy directions regarding these functions, as well the latest information on crime trends and the corresponding knowledge about the detection and prevention of crime.

In their study of the Singapore Police Force, Luen and Al-Hawamdeh (2001) found that the vast knowledge that police officers need in order to perform their normal duties required them to be proficient knowledge workers, being able to access, assimilate, and use knowledge effectively to discharge their duties.

In a UK study, five mechanisms for acquiring and maintaining knowledge in police forces were identified (Collier et al., 2004):

• Formal training and on-the-job experience
• Knowledge sharing through briefing and debriefing
• Knowledge structures including paper-based manuals and computer databases
• Hierarchical redundancy through the command structure that supports the cascading of knowledge
• Amortization through the loss of skills due to promotion, retirement, or tenure policies, and through legislative, policy, and technological change

In a study in Sweden, Holgersson (2005) found that police performance is determined by professional knowledge and motivation. Work of police officers is knowledge-intensive. Sometimes, a police officer lacks the required knowledge to be able to take action in a policing situation.

The functions of police in different countries vary. For example, the police in Norway also have administrative functions, apart from regular police work, that involve law enforcement, order maintenance, and service. This makes them similar to their counterparts on the European continent, but in contrast to the USA, where these activities are under the purview of Secretary of State offices or municipal courts. In the administrative office of the police in Norway, people apply for passports, driving licenses, pay fines, and so on (Das & Robinson, 2001).

Das and Robinson (2001) find the police in Norway exhibiting three distinct characteristics. They have unique narrative features like a flat hierarchy, strong union influence, and a system of pervasive intelligence. One can include among these features such minor matters as sharing a police gymnasium with the public, housing of police stations in rented private quarters, informal aspects of recruitment, and the role of police officers as prison guards. Except for the prison guard function, such features appear to be purely native to Norway. Like most European police, the police in Norway are directed largely by a central authority, or national government. The Norwegian police demonstrate a strong British influence in the special focus that the police have on crime prevention, the fact that they do not bear arms, and the practice of police officers as prosecutors.

Police Knowledge

It is accepted that within the crime management portfolios of policing environments, the term intelligence and intelligence-led has become an accepted term within the lexicon of modern policing. Hughes and Jackson (2004) suggest that the terms intelligence and knowledge can be used interchangeably. This suggestion is not without foundation when the two meanings are conceptualized. The overarching factor in knowledge creation is the human and social role in the application of expertise. While many definitions have been espoused to explain intelligence, the basic elements of the definitions relate to the creation of knowledge via the collection and analysis of data to inform decision making. The human and social role is, again, foremost in that an effective intelligence system requires an investment in people.

Holgersson (2005) studied the work practice of police officers and identified a variety of situations where knowledge is required. He described these situations in terms of knowledge applications. Examples of situations are showing victim empathy, prioritizing actions and resources, developing a suspicion, identifying potential suspects, communicating with persons and groups, understanding different kinds of language (i.e., people on the west and the east side of a city), handling sick people, reducing damage, solving disputes and problems, collecting and analyzing information, and using information technology.

Luen and Al-Hawamdeh (2001) find that the amount of information that police officers come into contact with in the course of their work is astounding. This and the vast knowledge that police officers need in order to perform their normal duties suggest the need for police officers to be proficient knowledge workers, being able to access, assimilate, and use knowledge effectively to discharge their duties.

Presently, such information and knowledge are captured within police organizations in various forms, ranging from computer records to documented institutional orders to the personal experiences of its officers. The crux of the issue is then how to surface such knowledge and bring it to bear on the problems faced by police officers in a timely and effective manner.

This is where knowledge management principles and practices can help. With the increased adoption of information technology within police organizations, and the increasing overall quality and IT competence of police officers, police organizations are well positioned to leverage knowledge management principles and practices. This, complemented by the enhanced skills, equipment, and empowerment given to the officers, will enable them to perform their duties at an optimal level.

In discussing the scope of knowledge management in police work, Luen and Al-Hawamdeh (2001) take into consideration two categories of knowledge within the context of knowledge management. These two categories of knowledge—explicit and tacit knowledge—give rise to different implementation approaches that are complementary rather than exclusive. Both of these implementation approaches are necessary if the organization is to reap the full benefits of knowledge management.

Explicit knowledge is used as guidance for police actions and decision making. Explicit knowledge is captured in the form of documents (e.g., doctrines, police general orders, standard operating procedures) that have been verified and ascertained to be of value to police officers. Examples of these documents include procedures of arrest, handling a fire scene, and illegal parking.

The second type of knowledge is implicit or tacit knowledge. This includes the competence, experience, and skill of police officers. Tacit knowledge is usually dynamic and fast changing as compared with documented knowledge.

Documented or explicit knowledge is normally kept as routine records in official police documents. Examples of such documented information include crime threats, crime trends and statistics, criminal records, and situational information pertaining to the incident or crisis at hand.

Regarding tacit knowledge, the scope of knowledge management in police work is primarily in the areas of creating and sharing knowledge and information. The two main issues to be addressed here are the willingness of police officers to create and share knowledge, and the ability of police officers to create and share knowledge.

According to Luen and Al-Hawamdeh (2001), the more difficult issue to tackle is that of the willingness of police officers to create and share knowledge. There is a need for a culture characterized by openness, collaboration, and sharing among police officers. This will require that police officers recognize the importance of collaboration and sharing knowledge with others.

The responsibility to surface knowledge lies with everyone in the police force, as knowledge is generated in all phases of work. In analyzing the content of the knowledge surfaced, it is necessary to check the subject matter of the knowledge as to what issues it addresses in relation to existing policies and procedures, and whether such knowledge adds value for police officers. In assessing the complexity of the knowledge surfaced, it is necessary to check whether the knowledge is mostly explicit or tacit in nature. Explicit knowledge can be documented in writing with little loss in interpretation and understanding, while tacit knowledge tends to be difficult to document comprehensively due to its scope and nature.

Effective knowledge management is dependent on a knowledge-centered culture. Organizational culture is believed to be the most significant input to effective knowledge management and organizational learning in that corporate culture determines values, beliefs, and work systems that could encourage or impede learning (knowledge creation) as well as knowledge sharing (Janz & Prasarnphanich, 2003). Therefore, an organization's culture should provide support and incentives as well as encourage knowledge-related activities by creating environments for knowledge exchange and accessibility.

In police investigations, experienced officers not only check for a more complex and integrated set of traits, but they emphasize stable, generalized clues, and actually look for fewer clues than recruits, according to Fielding (1984). Experienced officers have a more established idea of the important clues that are then linked to lower-order clues. It has also been found that, compared to appearance, behavior is much more likely to be the basis of a classification of suspiciousness.

Analysis of police competence must acknowledge that police work aggravates several factors known to limit accurate judgment, for example, sources of information vary in credibility, and the police are particularly reliant on negative information.

An interesting example of knowledge acquisition in police investigations is interrogation. Interrogation is concerned with the questioning of person(s) suspected of a crime by police. Interrogation is to ask questions of a person, especially closely, thoroughly, and formally. In most criminal justice systems there is a frequent reliance on confession evidence, and in some cases it may be the only evidence.

To understand interrogation in terms of investigative interviewing, Crawshaw, Devlin, and Williamson (1998) find it necessary to place the interviewing of victims, witnesses, or suspects in the context of the investigation. In some case, the investigator may find that the victim is dead; there are no witnesses to the offence; the witnesses are too afraid to give evidence or information; or there may be no forensic evidence. In such cases, the investigator has to rely on obtaining a confession from a suspect, and this is acceptable in those jurisdictions where a person may be found guilty by a court on the basis of an uncorroborated confession.

Since most interviews take place in private where the suspect is alone with the interviewers and there is no independent record of what happened, there is a temptation for law enforcement officials to resort to physical and psychological abuse of the detainee in many countries. Sometimes the reasons for this can be understood, but such action is never justifiable.

In most investigations, it is normally the case that there are victims and witnesses from whom information can be obtained. Rather than overrelying on confession evidence, steps can be taken to identify witnesses who may be able to provide such relevant information. Sometimes enquiries for this purpose have to be made a considerable time after the event, and a number of methods have been found to be successful in tracing witnesses. For example, "house to house enquiries," the methodological visiting of all premises in the vicinity of a crime in order to establish whether occupants are able to provide relevant information; appeals for witnesses through the news media; the distribution of leaflets giving details of a crime and appealing for information; dramatized reconstructions of a crime on television programs.

Forensic science can contribute greatly to investigations. In some countries, techniques may be basic but nevertheless sound, for example, the physical (as opposed to technological) comparison of fingerprints found at the scene of a crime with those in a collection of previously convicted criminals. Other forensic science techniques, such as DNA profiling, are sophisticated and expensive, and previously only available in well-resourced police agencies. Regardless of the degree of sophistication of techniques or facilities available, it is essential that police officials should be aware of them and maximize their use in order that they may be able to conduct an investigation that does not rely solely on confession evidence.

A fundamental flaw is created in many investigations when the investigator secures a confession from a suspect at an early stage, and then attempts to establish a case against the suspect by selectively building up supporting evidence around the confession. The key word here is "selectively," for it means that the investigator is prepared to ignore, and even conceal, evidence, that does not support the case against the accused. This can be fatal to the proper conclusion of any investigation, but especially so if the suspect has falsely confessed to a crime that he or she has not committed. If a person is convicted of a crime on the basis of evidence produced by such an "investigation," a double miscarriage of justice occurs: the wrongful conviction of any innocent person, and the avoidance of justice by the real author of the crime. It is more professional and more ethical to approach the case scientifically and with an open mind, and to gather information systematically. In order for an investigation conducted on this basis to be successful, it is essential that each step of the investigation should be documented (Crawshaw et al., 1998).

The most important asset of a law enforcement agency is personnel. There are two main reasons why. Unlike private sector business, which provides a tangible product, law enforcement provides a unique, monopolistic service. This service is reflected in the widely recognized motto that appears on many local police cars in the U.S., "To Protect and Serve." Regardless of the level of technology an agency may employ, the service performed is still delivered through interaction of agency personnel with clientele. In law enforcement, that interaction is frequently of a very personal nature (Bradford, 1998).

The second reason personnel are the most valuable asset of a law enforcement agency is that employees make the real policy of an agency by discretionary decisions made during the performance of their duties. Police officers are examples of discretionary policy makers. The argument can be made that management controls the discretionary policy making ability of officers by imposing strict guidelines through standard operating procedures and regulations. Yet, law enforcement agency administrators continually remind the troops that they are the agency, and that the agency reputation is made by their public contacts (Bradford, 1998).

The job effectiveness of police officers as human service professionals largely depends on the way in which they interact with civilians. These professionals are particularly challenged when conflicts occur with or among civilians. Dominance plays an important part in police-civilian interaction. Police officers have to cope with conflicts when civilians violate rules and regulations, and they have to maintain order. Also, police officers regularly have to intervene in conflicts between civilians. The professional challenge in these conflict situations is twofold: on the one hand it is important to prevent escalation as much as possible (including aggression), and on the other hand it is important to achieve one's professional goals, maintaining or restoring order (Euwema, Kop, & Bakker, 2004).

Dominant behavior by the police is often required, including in conflict situations. However, a demonstration of police power usually has escalating effects. Offenders feel intimidated or even provoked by dominance. For example, officers arriving at a scene where they have to interact with civilians, leaning out of their car window, directly commanding young people, or approaching people with their hands on their weapon, are experienced as highly dominant, unpleasant, and provocative. Also, in the case of intervention in conflicts between civilians, the calming down of parties is not likely to be achieved by a dominant approach of the police officer. The primary instruction in much police training, therefore, is to arrive at the scene calmly. Acting in a dominant way increases the risk of raised emotions and aggression shifting from the original parties towards the police (Euwema et al., 2004).

When one thinks about the investigation of a crime as a process of assembling knowledge, one begins to recognize the premise that police are *knowledge workers*. The basic sets of raw materials that police work with are information and interactions with people. How the police deal with these materials is determined by a variety of factors, such as the skills and education police have (Fraser, 2005).

Knowledge and Evidence

A distinction that is helpful to understanding the variety of forms that investigative practice takes is that between two basic objectives or tasks: the generation of police knowledge, and the production of evidence. This has the advantage that it draws attention to the centrality of the gathering and manipulation of information to detective work, a point stressed in much of the law enforcement literature. It also adds a new dimension to the notion of investigation as essentially a process of construction (Maguire, 2003).

Knowledge here refers primarily to the conclusions and understandings reached by the police as to what crimes have been (or are likely to be) committed, by whom, how, and why. Numerous factors can play a part in shaping this knowledge, including a host of information sources, and the perceptual lenses and prejudices of those receiving them.

Evidence refers to material that may be presented in court to help establish whether an alleged criminal offence has been committed, and whether an accused person committed it. The main forms it takes are physical traces linking a person to a particular offence, statements by victims or witnesses, and responses by suspects to questioning in interviews. Its production requires skill and care, and is surrounded by rules designed to ensure that it has been obtained fairly and is presented to the court in a valid form. Depending upon the type of inquiry concerned, the production of knowledge and of evidence has normally entailed a number of the following basics tasks (Maguire, 2003):

- **Production of knowledge**
  - Determining that one or more criminal offences have been committed
  - Producing a narrative of the circumstances surrounding offences
  - Determining the most promising lines of inquiry
  - Identifying and/or eliminating suspects
  - Exploring the backgrounds, motivations, lifestyles, and activities of suspects or known offenders and their associates
  - Gathering intelligence about planned offences
- **Production of evidence**
  - Producing evidence that specific offences were committed (or were planned)
  - Producing evidence to link suspected persons with particular offences

These tasks can be undertaken in different orders or different combinations. Investigators will sometimes start with a specific offence and seek to find out who committed it. At other times, they will start by identifying suspected individuals or groups, and seek to find out what offence they have committed. Often, the various tasks will become blurred within the same inquiry, as we will see in iterative working styles in the value shop later in this book.

Police Leadership

In February 1994, William Bratton was appointed police commissioner of New York City. The odds were against him. The New York Police Department, with a $2 billion budget and a workforce of 35,000 police officers, was notoriously difficult to manage. Yet in less than two years, and without an increase in his budget, Bill Bratton turned New York into the safest large city of the nation, according to Kim and Mauborgne (2003).

Research conducted by Kim and Mauborgne (2003) led them to conclude that Bratton's turnaround was an example of tipping-point leadership. The theory of tipping point hinges on the insight that in any organization, once the beliefs and energies of a critical mass of people are engaged, conversion to a new idea will spread like an epidemic, bringing about fundamental change very quickly. The theory suggests that such a movement can be unleashed only by agents who make unforgettable and unarguable calls for change, who concentrate their resources on what really matters, who mobilize the commitment of the organization's key players, and who succeed in silencing the most vocal naysayers. Bratton did all of these things.

Kim and Maugorgne (2003) find that in many turnarounds, the hardest battle is simply getting people to agree on the causes of current problems and the need for change. Most CEOs try to make the case for change simply by pointing to the numbers and insisting that the company can achieve better ones. But messages communicated through numbers seldom stick. Bratton (1998, p. 310) writes in his book on the turnaround in New York: "The system my team and I installed continues to bring success. New York City is a much safer place now and will remain so."

Tipping-point leaders do not rely on numbers to break through the organization's cognitive hurdles. Instead, they put their key managers face-to-face with the operational problems so that the managers cannot evade reality. Poor performance becomes something they witness rather than hear about. Communicating in this way means that the message—performance is poor and needs to be fixed—sticks with people, which is essential if they are to be convinced not only that a turnaround is necessary, but also that it is something they can achieve.

Leaders like Bratton use a four-step process to bring about rapid, dramatic, and lasting change with limited resources. Tipping all four hurdles leads to rapid strategy reorientation and execution:

- **Cognitive hurdle.** Put managers face-to-face with problems and customers. Find new ways to communicate.

- **Resource hurdle.** Focus on the hot spots and bargain with partner organizations.

- **Motivational hurdle.** Put the stage lights on and frame the challenge to match the organization's various levels.

- **Political hurdle.** Identify and silence internal opponents; isolate external ones.

By addressing these hurdles to tipping-point change, leaders will stand a chance of achieving the same kind of results as Bratton delivered to the citizens of New York. Between 1994 and 1996, felony crime fell 39%, murders 50%, and theft 35%. Gallup polls reported that public confidence in the NYPD jumped from 37% to 73% (Kim & Mauborgne, 2003).

Police Intelligence

A special branch of police work that seems extremely knowledge intensive is police intelligence. Lahneman (2004) suggests that intelligence agencies were the world's first knowledge companies. Managing knowledge has always been the primary mission of the intelligence community's leadership. Accordingly, the intelligence community can benefit substantially from knowledge management approaches.

According to Lahneman (2004), the intelligence community is now understood to have possessed several pieces of intelligence information that, in retrospect, might have warned of the September 11, 2001 terrorist attacks on Washington, D.C. and New York City. But, while U.S. intelligence agencies individually had collected considerable data on the strikes, they failed to interpret and share the information in a timely manner. In the wake of 9/11, the intelligence community clearly recognized that it needed to improve knowledge sharing among its component agencies, as well as with the new Department of Homeland Security and state and local organizations involved in the war against terrorism.

Experience so far with knowledge management indicates that two necessary conditions must prevail for improving knowledge sharing. First, given the volume of knowledge that the intelligence community must possess, the use of large-scale IT systems in handling relevant information is essential. Second, successful knowledge management depends on developing an organizational culture that facilitates and rewards knowledge sharing. In the absence of either of these components, knowledge management initiatives will fail.

The intelligence community has taken a number of steps in both areas to improve knowledge sharing. Several agencies have embarked on innovative, large-scale projects to upgrade their IT capabilities.

The intelligence community has also experienced several high-level organizational changes and proposals for organizational change. In Norway, the Police Security Service replaced the Police Surveillance Service, changing its focus from radical elements based on politics to violent elements based on religion. In the U.S., a clearinghouse for foreign and domestic terrorism analysis—the terrorist threat integration centre (TTIC)—was located at the CIA compound at Langley, Virginia, reporting directly to the Director of Central Intelligence. The centre will fuse all appropriate information, and send summary reports to the Department of Homeland Security.

Knowledge collection activities require coordination to make sure that collected knowledge gets to the right persons at the right time. They also need oversight to ensure that each agency's collection assets are so employed that the collection of potentially useful knowledge is optimized.

Optimizing knowledge sharing where intelligence analysis is concerned can be more difficult because, unlike collection efforts, coordination is increasingly interagency in nature. Analysis related to terrorism and, in particular, terrorism against the U.S. homeland, is particularly dependent on fusing knowledge from disparate sources, including the tacit knowledge of both government and nongovernment experts, into an appropriate product at the correct time (Lahneman, 2004).

Intelligence communities of different nations share information and knowledge. Intelligence activities usually remain secret, especially when the communities of different countries are involved. One known example is the cooperation between the CIA and the Mossad, where the U.S. and Israeli intelligence communities exchange information, when it serves the interests of the side providing information to the other. Therefore, providing information may at times be one-sided. According to Kahana (2001), there has been an obvious interest not to provide information, and even to block it, in several cases. For example, the United States was reluctant to provide the Mossad with satellite photographs about what was happening in peripheral Arab countries. Israel, for its part, tried to stop surveillance by the U.S.S. Liberty.

Agency Theory of Police Work

Agency theory has broadened the risk-sharing literature to include the agency problem that occurs when cooperating parties have different goals and division of labor. The cooperating parties are engaged in an agency relationship defined as a contract under which one or more persons (the principal(s)) engage another person (agent) to perform some service on their behalf that involves delegating some decision-making authority to the agent. Agency theory describes the relationship between the two parties using the metaphor of a contract.

According to Eisenhardt (1985), agency theory is concerned with resolving two problems that occur in agency relationships. The first is the agency problem that arises when the desires or goals of the principal and agent conflict, and it is difficult or expensive for the principal to verify what the agent is actually doing. The second is the problem of risk sharing that arises when the principal and agent have different risk preferences. The common element to principal-agent models is that principals are unable to monitor agents' actions or information; the heart of these models involves setting a wage for an agent without fully knowing the agent's effort (moral hazard) or ability (adverse selection).

Brehm and Gates (1993) applied agency theory to police work. They examined police supervision through an empirical analysis of the behavior of police officers with respect to their supervisor's orders. Their goal was to specify a statistical model that is appropriate for evaluation of compliance behavior in general, as long as the measure of compliance is a scale from 0% to 100% compliance. They found that some principal-agency models lead to strong predictions about the possible shape of distribution of compliance by police subordinates.

Police Performance

Police performance is a complicated construct. The police reform in the UK has developed some performance indicators for policing within an assessment framework. The policing performance assessment framework is an initiative led by the Home Office (2005a), with the support of the Association of Chief Police Officers, and the Association of Police Authorities. Here are some examples of performance indicators for 2005/2006:

- Satisfaction of victims of domestic burglary, violent crime, vehicle crime, and road traffic collisions
- Using sources such as the British Crime Survey, the percentage of people who think their local police do a good job
- Satisfaction of victims of racist incidents with respect to the overall service provided
- Using the British Crime Survey, the risk of personal crime
- Domestic burglaries per 1,000 households
- Number of offences brought to justice
- Percentage of notifiable offences resulting in a sanction detection
- Percentage of domestic violence incidents with a power of arrest
- Number of people killed
- Using the British Crime Survey, fear of crime
- Percentage of police officer time spent on frontline duties
- Delivery of cashable and noncashable efficiency target
- Average number of working hours lost per annum due to sickness per police officer

The guidance on statutory performance indicators for policing includes user satisfaction measures, confidence measures, fairness, equality and diversity measures, measures of crime level, offences brought to justice measures, sanction detection measures, domestic violence measures, traffic measures, quality of life measures, frontline policing measures, and resource use measures.

One of the resource use measures is delivery of cashable and noncashable efficiency target. A cashable gain is where a particular level of output of a particular quality is achieved for less cost. A noncashable gain is where more output and/or output of better quality is achieved for the same cost.

In 1993, there was a debate in the UK whether to allow and stimulate direct entry into police management. According to Leishman and Savage (1993), it was a fundamental fact of the British police service that everyone had to start at the bottom, at the "lowest" rank of constable, in which office all entrants must serve a minimum period of two years. On the surface, then, the police service may appear to occupy a unique position among public sector organizations as an apparently egalitarian meritocracy in which all confirmed constables could be said to have the opportunity to aspire to senior management positions.

At that time, chief constables were the first generation of completely self-made chiefs, lacking even the middle-class socialization of university, although most went to grammar schools. Leishman and Savage (1993) argue that there are two important reasons in favor of direct entry. First, direct entry offers potential for the active furtherance of equal opportunities in the British police service. Whereas in Britain, target attainment would depend on the numbers of officers remaining in the service beyond their two year probationary period, and then progressing through the rank of sergeant, this was not the case in Holland. Its system of direct entry, coupled with an explicit policy of positive action, allowed the recruitment and training of sufficient numbers of women and ethnic minority candidates directly into the rank of inspector, to achieve minimum targets within the timescale agreed.

A second argument in favor of direct entry followed, in a sense, part of the rationale for "civilianization" within the service. While much of this process had been driven by the pursuit of economies, behind it also was the question of competences and specialist skills. For example, staff with a background in personnel management have been appointed to head the personnel department in place of police officers (Leishman & Savage, 1993).

According to Jackson and Wade (2005), the understanding of police behavior, especially proactive behavior, has been pursued throughout policing history. Researchers have examined the impact of environmental factors (i.e., weapons, crime, etc.), individual factors (i.e., attitude, personality, etc.), police subculture, and organizational and departmental management on police behavior. Despite all of these research efforts, most if not all of the authors contributing to this line of research have concluded that the categorization, understanding, and predicting of police behavior is arduous (if not impossible), or that the relationship between police attitudes and their behavior is weak at best.

Researchers have examined empirically and conceptually the impact of social capital and police sense of responsibility on police behavior. For example, community social capital has been identified in the literature as having a significant impact on police behavior mainly because social capital serves as a measure of the community's ability to solve its own problems. In communities with low social capital, police may perceive themselves as the only form of social order and may, therefore, develop a higher sense of responsibility towards protecting citizens, themselves, and preventing crime.

Jackson and Wade (2005) suggest that the examination of police sense of responsibility towards the community may be important in understanding police behavior. This assertion implies that police sense of responsibility may serve as an influential variable in explaining why police may demonstrate higher levels of proactive policing in communities with low social capital in comparison to those with high social capital. Police sense of responsibility toward the community seems important for understanding how police function in areas under their command. In communities where crime is commonplace, police can become overwhelmed and may therefore focus on more serious crimes that pose a greater threat to police and citizen safety, and ignore the lower level crimes that do not.

Given these arguments, the major purpose of the study conducted by Jackson and Wade (2005) was to examine the relationship between police perception of their community's social capital and their sense of responsibility toward the provision of public safety and, in turn, to assess empirically the impact of sense of responsibility on their propensity to engage in proactive policing.

By studying police perceptions of social capital and their sense of responsibility, it was possible to not only understand why community policing is or is not successful, but more importantly it was possible to understand police behavior in environments that by their structural and demographic make-up, complicate the task of effective policing.

Jackson and Wade's (2005) findings support the hypothesis that police who indicate a more negative perception of community social capital are more likely to indicate a higher sense of responsibility towards the community. This finding suggests that as the police perception of community social capital becomes negative, they are more likely to rely upon their own resources to solve community problems. Generally, the only real resources that police possess in low social capital communities are their law enforcement powers.

Another finding was police who express a more negative perception of community social capital were more likely to indicate higher levels of proactive behavior. This finding suggests that in communities with low social capital, police may utilize their law enforcement powers more in comparison to communities that posses higher levels of social capital.

The data gathered through a questionnaire distributed among the Kansas City Police Department in the U.S., suggested that the amount of crime occurring within the community is the most important variable for the explanation of police proactive behavior. Police proactive behavior includes new patrol techniques, increased utilization of technology, the organization of specialized units, and the use of criminal profiling. By being more proactive, police are conducting more stop-and-frisk contacts, requesting proof of identification more frequently, conducting more drug sweeps, and dispersing citizens who gather to protest public policies of various kinds.

Proactive policing might perpetuate and exacerbate the social distance rift between the police and their community, and it also increases the likelihood that an officer may abuse his or her authority. In a time period of three years, Prince George's County in the U.S. paid out eight million dollars in jury awards and settlements in lawsuits that involved police misconduct and excessive force. The increasing costs resulting from payouts in police litigation cases and liability claims, coupled with increased pressure from public insurance pools to cut losses, are a few of the reasons that some U.S. law enforcement agencies are beginning to implement risk management programs (Archbold, 2005).

Risk management is a process used to identify and control exposure to potential risks and liabilities in both private and public organizations. Almost all of the basic duties of police work expose police officers to liability incidents on a daily basis. One aspect of police work that makes it unique to all other professions is the ability of police officers to use lethal and nonlethal force. This unique aspect of police work also contributes to police officer exposure to high levels of risk that could lead to litigation, liability claims, or citizen complaints (Archbold, 2005).

Police personnel face some of society's most serious problems, often work in dangerous settings, and are typically expected to react quickly and, at the same time, correctly. They must adapt to an occupation in which one moment may bring the threat of death, while other extended periods bring routine and boredom. They are expected to maintain control in chaotic situations involving injustice, public apathy, conflicting roles, injuries, and fatalities. Yet they are expected by both the public and their peers to approach these situations in an objective and professional manner, to be effective decision makers and independent problems solvers while working in a system that encourages dependency by its quasimilitary structure (Kelley, 2005).

The nature of work in police professions requires optimal mental health. When their mental functioning is compromised, police professionals can lose touch with the common sense and resilience they need to minimize stress, enjoy their work, and operate at peak performance. Over time, Kelley (2005) finds that poor mental health can dramatically increase police officers proneness to physical illness, emotional disorders, accidents, marital and family problems, excessive drinking and drug use, suicide, and litigation ranging from excessive force and false arrest, to failure to provide appropriate protection and services.

Ethical Issues

We will conclude this chapter by touching upon the topic of human rights and policing. Since 9/11 in 2001, human rights have been threatened in many societies. According to Crawshaw et al. (1998), there is still an overreliance on confession evidence in most criminal justice systems, and in some cases it may be the only evidence. The international instruments by the United Nations and other organizations are intended to provide basic protection from physical or psychological abuse. That still leaves open the question, what is good interviewing?

The specific purpose of the discussion by Crawshaw et al. (1998), presented here, is to explain the basic principles of investigative interviewing, and to describe how they can contribute to better police investigations and higher standards of professionalism consistent with international obligations.

Firstly, it is necessary to place the interviewing of victims, witnesses, or suspects in the context of the investigation. In some cases, the investigator may find that the victim is dead; there are no witnesses to the offence; the witnesses are too afraid to give evidence or information; or there may be no forensic evidence. In such cases, the investigator has to rely on obtaining a confession from a suspect, and this is acceptable in those jurisdictions where a person may be found guilty by a court on the basis of an uncorroborated confession.

Since most interviews take place in private, where the suspect is alone with the interviewers and there is no independent record of what happened, there is a temptation for law enforcement officials to resort to physical or psychological abuse of the detainee. Sometimes the reasons for this can be understood, but such action is never, ever, justifiable. The offences under investigation may be heinous and there may be pressure on officers to solve the crime quickly. This can lead to the routine use of gratuitous violence on detainees where the main means of extracting information is terror. Some victims of torture have indicated that they were willing to say anything in order to bring the torture to an end and, consequently, the information obtained from them was unreliable. Furthermore, people who are abused can become powerful symbols around which others can unite to challenge the authorities. As these situations have arisen in many countries, it is vitally important for all law enforcement officials to have a clear understanding of the principles of ethical investigation and ethical interviewing based on the respect for human rights. The mode of investigation described here is intended to promote effective investigation of crime and respect for human rights in the process, and to encourage and maintain the support of the public for the police.

In most investigations, it is normally the case that there are victims and witnesses from whom information can be obtained. Rather than overrelying on confession evidence, steps should be taken to identify witnesses who may be able to provide such relevant information. Sometimes enquiries for this purpose have to be made a considerable time after the event, and a number of methods have been found to be successful in tracing witnesses. For example, house to house enquiries—the methodical visiting of all premises in the vicinity of a crime in order to establish whether occupants are able to provide relevant information; appeals for witnesses through the news media; the distribution of leaflets giving details of a crime and appealing for information; dramatized reconstructions of a crime on television programs (in some countries there are TV programs that specialize in this).

Forensic science can contribute greatly to investigations. In some countries, techniques may be basic but nevertheless sound, for example, the physical (as opposed to technological) comparison of fingerprints found at the scene of a crime with those in a collection of previously convicted criminals. Other forensic science techniques include DNA profiling.

A fundamental flaw is created in many investigations when the investigator secures a confession from a suspect at an early stage, and then attempts to establish a case against the suspect by selectively building up supporting evidence around the confession. The key word here is "selectively," for it means that the investigator is prepared to ignore, and even conceal, evidence, that does not support the case against the accused. This can be fatal to the proper conclusion of any investigation, but especially so if the suspect has falsely confessed to a crime that he or she has not committed. If a person is convicted of a crime on the basis of evidence produced by such an "investigation," a double miscarriage of justice occurs: the wrongful conviction of an innocent person, and the avoidance of justice by the real author of the crime. It is more professional and more ethical to approach the case scientifically and with an open mind, and to gather information systematically. In order for an investigation conducted on this basis to be successful, it is essential that each step of the investigation should be documented.

In more complex or serious cases, on which a team of investigators is deployed, the senior investigating officer should set out what the main lines of enquiry are, and record his decisions on those lines of enquiry as the investigation progresses. It is also important to keep a record of all exhibits seized, and of all actions taken by the enquiry team. This means that when information is being recorded "manually" (as opposed to on a computer system), three books are required in the UK police that record "Main Lines of Enquiry and Decision"; "Exhibits," including a description of each item, and an account of who found them and where they were found; and "Actions," a record of all enquiries made and results of those enquiries.

Computerized systems are available for all of these purposes but, in their absence, the systematic and painstaking collation of information by nontechnical means is not only possible, it is absolutely essential. The methodological collection of evidence is very important for the questioning of suspects. It means that all relevant information can be available for use by the interviewer. By approaching an investigation in this way, law enforcement officials can avoid acting unethically, and avoid violating the human rights of people suspected of crime.

There are three ways in which unscrupulous investigators have brought confession evidence into disrepute. Firstly, there is violence or the threat of violence to the detainee or another person. Many of the examples of human rights abuse by police involve this type of misconduct.

This arises particularly where law enforcement and security officials, who need to respond to conflict, disorder, or tension, too readily assume that it is impossible to obtain information or confession without recourse to violence. Furthermore, because of the situation they face, they feel justified in violating the human rights of detainees and others. It is possible, and indeed it is necessary, to investigate crime successfully and to counter conflict, disorder, and tension without using unlawful violence against detainees. It is clear that the use of unlawful violence by state officials is counterproductive, and that it will almost certainly prolong and intensify hostilities. Information and confessions obtained in this way should be disallowed in any subsequent judicial proceedings.

A second way in which investigators have brought confession evidence into disrepute is by fabricating confessions. These are sometimes referred to as "verbals," that is to say, spoken or verbal confessions or damaging admissions that were never in fact said by the suspect. When this type of false evidence is presented to a court, the accused's right to a fair trial is put in jeopardy, and the rule of law is undermined. This is so because even where a confession is retracted by an accused person during a trial, a court can be influenced against the accused, and the presentation of false evidence at a trial by officials responsible for enforcing the law is corrosive to the rule of law.

A third way in which the reliability of confession evidence has been discredited is through the realization that the process of interviewing detainees can routinely create the situation where their freedom can be traded for information or money. In the latter case, the law enforcement officer is behaving corruptly, and this behavior can be described as venal.

In order to defend people suspected of crime and the criminal justice system against such abuses, some jurisdictions have introduced safeguards that are designed to ensure that what was said during an interview was recorded accurately and said freely. In other words, they require truthful records of the questions and answers, and they require voluntary confessions by people accused of crime.

According to an FBI Law Enforcement Bulletin, law enforcement has experienced both organizational and operational changes in the last several years (O'Malley, 1997). These changes, coupled with a formidable and entrenched police culture, call for fresh approaches to managing for ethics in police work. Police officers face greater temptations than they did just a decade or so ago. Many of these enticements can be traced to the explosive and lucrative illegal drug trade. A tremendous amount of illicit cash fuels this market. Potential profits for mid- and upper-level drug dealers continue to climb as criminal sanctions grow stiffer. Consequently, today's officers may be tempted by sizeable payoffs from criminals, and enticed by opportunities to steal large sums of illicit cash.

At first glance, ethics in law enforcement may appear to be a simple issue: Officers should do right, not wrong. Close examination quickly reveals that several influential factors make managing for ethics far more complex. Three of these factors—the temptations associated with the illegal drug trade, the shift toward community-oriented policing, and the barriers posed by a strong police culture—will, according to O'Malley (1997), prove pivotal in affecting the ethical health of law enforcement agencies in the years to come. Police managers must consider the relationship of these factors when formulating an ethics program. Managers also must draw information from a number of sources to understand these and the many additional factors that influence ethical behavior.

References

Archbold, C. A. (2005). Managing the bottom line: Risk management in policing. *Policing: An International Journal of Police Strategies & Management, 28*(1), 30-48.

Bradford, D. (1998). Police officer candidate background investigation: Law enforcement management's most effective tool for employing the most qualified candidate. *Public Personnel Management, 27*(4), 423-445.

Bratton, W. (1998). *Turnaround: How America's top cop reversed the crime epidemic.* New York: Random House.

Brehm, J., & Gates, S. (1993). Donut shops and speed traps: Evaluating models of supervision on police behavior. *American Journal of Political Science, 37*(2), 555-581.

Collier, P. M., Edwards, J. S., & Shaw, D. (2004). Communicating knowledge about police performance. *International Journal of Productivity and Performance Management, 53*(5), 458-467.

Crawshaw, R., Devlin, B., & Williamson, T. (1998). *Human rights and policing.* The Netherlands: Kluwer Law International.

Das, D. K., & Robinson, A. L. (2001). The police in Norway: A profile. *Policing: An International Journal of Police Strategies & Management, 24*(3), 330-346.

Eisenhardt, K. M. (1985). Control: Organizational and economic approaches. *Management Science, 31*(2), 134-149.

Euwema, M. C., Kop, N., & Bakker, A. B. (2004). The behaviour of police officers in conflict situations: How burnout and reduced dominance contribute to better outcomes. *Work & Stress, 18*(1), 23-38.

Fielding, N. (1984). Police socialization and police competence. *The British Journal of Sociology, 35*(4), 568-590.

Holgersson, S. (2005). *Yrke: POLIS—yrkeskunnskap, motivasjon, IT-system og andre forutsetninger for politiarbeide*. PhD doctoral dissertation, Institutionen för datavetenskap, Linköpings universitet, Sweden.

Home Office. (2005a). *Guidance on statutory performance indicators for policing 2005/2006*. Police Standards Unit, Home Office of the UK Government. Retrieved from http://www.policereform.gov.uk

Hughes, V., & Jackson, P. (2004). The influence of technical, social and structural factors on the effective use of information in a policing environment. *The Electronic Journal of Knowledge Management, 2*(1), 65-76.

Jackson, A. L., & Wade, J. E. (2005). Police perceptions of social capital and sense of responsibility. *Policing: An International Journal of Police Strategies & Management, 28*(1), 49-68.

Janz, B. D., & Prasarnphanich, P. (2003). Understanding the antecedents of effective knowledge management: The importance of a knowledge-centered culture. *Decision Sciences, 34*(2), 351-384.

Kahana, E. (2001). Mossad-CIA cooperation. *International Journal of Intelligence and CounterIntelligence, 14*, 409-420.

Kelley, T. M. (2005). Mental health and prospective police professionals. *Policing: An International Journal of Police Strategies & Management, 28*(1), 6-29.

Kim, C. W., & Mauborgne, R. (2003, April). Tipping point leadership. *Harvard Business Review*, 61-69.

Lahneman, W. J. (2004). Knowledge-sharing in the intelligence community after 9/11. *International Journal of Intelligence and Counterintelligence, 17*, 614-633.

Leishman, F. & Savage, S. P. (1993). Officers or managers? Direct entry into British police management. *International Journal of Public Sector Management, 6*(5), 4-11.

Luen, T. W., & Al-Hawamdeh, S. (2001). Knowledge management in the public sector: Principles and practices in police work. *Journal of Information Science, 27*(5), 311-318.

Maguire, M. (2003). Criminal investigation and crime control. In T. Newburn (Ed.), *Handbook of policing*. Portland, OR: Willan Publishing.

O'Malley, T. J. (1997). Managing for ethics. *FBI Law Enforcement Bulletin*, *66*(4), 20-26.

Chapter II

Knowledge Management

Knowledge is an important organizational resource. Unlike other inert organizational resources, the application of existing knowledge has the potential to generate new knowledge. Not only can knowledge be replenished in use, it can also be combined and recombined to generate new knowledge. Once created, knowledge can be articulated, shared, stored, and re-contextualized to yield options for the future. For all of these reasons, knowledge has the potential to be applied across time and space to yield increasing returns (Garud & Kumaraswamy, 2005).

The strategic management of organizational knowledge is a key factor that can help organizations to sustain competitive advantage in volatile environments. Organizations are turning to knowledge management initiatives and technologies to leverage their knowledge resources. Knowledge management can be defined as a systemic and organizationally specified process for acquiring, organizing, and communicating knowledge of employees so that other employees may make use of it to be more effective and productive in their work (Kankanhalli, Tan, & Wei, 2005).

Knowledge management is also important in interorganizational relationships. Interorganizational relationships have been recognized to provide two distinct potential benefits: short-term operational efficiency and longer-term new knowledge creation. For example, the need for continual value innovation is driving supply chains to evolve from a pure transactional focus to leveraging interorganizational partnerships for sharing information and, ultimately, market knowledge creation. Supply chain partners are engaging in interlinked processes that enable rich (broad-ranging, high-quality, and privileged) information sharing, and building information technology infrastructures that allow them to process information obtained from their partners to create new knowledge (Malhotra, Gosain, & El Sawy, 2005).

Characteristics of Knowledge

Knowledge is a renewable, reusable, and accumulating resource of value to the organization when applied in the production of products and services. Knowledge cannot, as such, be stored in computers: it can only be stored in the human brain. Knowledge is what a knower knows; there is no knowledge without someone knowing it.

The need for a knower in knowledge existence raises the question as to how knowledge can exist outside the heads of individuals. Although knowledge cannot originate outside the heads of individuals, it can be argued that knowledge can be represented in and often embedded in organizational processes, routines, and networks, and sometimes in document repositories. However, knowledge is seldom complete outside of an individual.

In this book, knowledge is defined as information combined with experience, context, interpretation, reflection, intuition, and creativity. Information becomes knowledge once it is processed in the mind of an individual. This knowledge then becomes information again once it is articulated or communicated to others in the form of text, computer output, spoken or written words, or other means. Six characteristics of knowledge can distinguish it from information: knowledge is a human act, knowledge is the residue of thinking, knowledge is created in the present moment, knowledge belongs to communities, knowledge circulates through communities in many ways, and new knowledge is created at the boundaries of old. This definition and these characteristics of knowledge are based on current research (e.g., Poston & Speier, 2005; Ryu, Kim, Chaudhury, & Rao, 2005; Sambamurthy & Subramani, 2005; Tanriverdi, 2005; Wasko & Faraj, 2005).

Today, any discussion of knowledge quickly leads to the issue of how knowledge is defined. A pragmatic definition defines the topic as the most valuable form of content in a continuum starting at data, encompassing information, and ending at knowledge. Typically, data is classified, summarized, transferred, or corrected in order to add value, and become information within a certain context. This conversion is relatively mechanical and has long been facilitated by storage, processing, and communication technologies. These technologies add place, time, and form utility to the data. In doing so, the information serves to inform or reduce uncertainty within the problem domain. Therefore, information is united with the context, that is, it only has utility within the context (Grover & Davenport, 2001).

Knowledge has the highest value, the most human contribution, the greatest relevance to decisions and actions, and the greatest dependence on a specific situation or context. It is also the most difficult of content types to manage, because it originates and is applied in the minds of human beings. People who are knowledgeable not only have information, but also have the ability to integrate and frame the information within the context of their experience, expertise, and judgment. In doing so, they can create new information that expands the state of possibilities, and in turn allows for further interaction with experience, expertise, and judgment. Therefore, in an organizational context, all new knowledge stems from people. Some knowledge is incorporated in organizational artifacts like processes, structures, and technology. However, institutionalized knowledge often inhibits competition in a dynamic context, unless adaptability of people and processes (higher order learning) is built into the institutional mechanisms themselves.

Our concern with distinctions between information and knowledge is based on real differences as well as technology implications. Real differences between information and knowledge do exist, although for most practical purposes these differences are of no interest at all. Information technology implications are concerned with the argument that computers can only manipulate electronic information, not electronic knowledge. Business systems are loaded with information, but without knowledge.

Davenport and Prusak (1998) define knowledge as a fluid mix of framed experience, values, contextual information, and expert insights that provides a framework for evaluating and incorporating new experiences and information. It originates and is applied in the minds of knowers. In organizations, it often becomes embedded not only in documents or repositories, but also in organizational routines, processes, practices, and norms. Distinctions are often made between data, information, knowledge, and wisdom:

- **Data** are letters and numbers without meaning. Data are independent, isolated measurements, characters, numerical characters, and symbols.

- **Information** is data that are included in a context that makes sense. For example, 40 degrees can have different meaning depending on the context. There can be a medical, geographical, or technical context. If a person has 40 degrees Celsius in fever, that is quite serious. If a city is located 40 degrees north, we know that it is far south of Norway. If an angle is 40 degrees, we know what it looks like. Information is data that make sense, because it can be understood correctly. People turn data into information by organizing it into some unit of analysis, for example, dollars, dates, or customers. Information is data endowed with relevance and purpose.

- **Knowledge** is information combined with experience, context, interpretation, and reflection. Knowledge is a renewable resource that can be used over and over, and that accumulates in an organization through use and combination with employees' experience. Humans have knowledge; knowledge cannot exist outside the heads of individuals in the company. Information becomes knowledge when it enters the human brain. This knowledge transforms into information again when it is articulated and communicated to others. Information is an explicit representation of knowledge; it is in itself no knowledge. Knowledge can both be truths and lies, perspectives and concepts, judgments and expectations. Knowledge is used to receive information by analyzing, understanding, and evaluating; by combining, prioritizing, and decision making; and by planning, implementing, and controlling.

- **Wisdom** is knowledge combined with learning, insights, and judgmental abilities. Wisdom is more difficult to explain than knowledge since the levels of context become even more personal and thus, the higher-level nature of wisdom renders it more obscure than knowledge. While knowledge is mainly sufficiently generalized solutions, wisdom is best thought of as sufficiently generalized approaches and values that can be applied in numerous and varied situations. Wisdom cannot be created like data and information, and it cannot be shared with others like knowledge. Because the context is so personal, it becomes almost exclusive to our own minds, and incompatible with the minds of others without extensive transaction. This transaction requires not only a base of knowledge and opportunities for experiences that help create wisdom, but also the

processes of introspection, retrospection, interpretation, and contempla-
tion. We can value wisdom in others, but we can only create it ourselves.

These are the definitions applied in this book. Grover and Davenport (2001)
calls these definitions pragmatic, as a continuum is used, starting from data,
encompassing information, and ending at knowledge in this book. The most
valuable form of content in the continuum is knowledge. Knowledge has the
highest value, the most human contribution, the greatest relevance to decisions
and actions, and the greatest dependence on a specific situation or context. It
is also the most difficult of content types to manage, because it originates and
is applied in the minds of human beings.

It has been argued that expert systems using artificial intelligence are able to do
knowledge work. The chess-playing computer called Deep Blue by IBM is
frequently cited as an example. Deep Blue can compete with the best human
players because chess, though complex, is a closed system of unchanging and
codifiable rules. The size of the board never varies, the rules are unambiguous,
the moves of the pieces are clearly defined, and there is absolute agreement
about what it means to win or lose (Davenport & Prusak, 1998). Deep Blue
is no knowledge worker; the computer only performs a series of computations
at extremely high speed.

While knowledge workers develop knowledge, organizations learn. Therefore,
the learning organization has become a term frequently used. The learning
organization is similar to knowledge development. While knowledge development is taking place at the individual level, organizational learning is taking place
at the firm level. Organizational learning occurs when the firm is able to exploit
individual competence in new and innovative ways. Organizational learning also
occurs when the collective memory—including local language, common history
and routines—expands. Organizational learning causes growth in the intellectual capital. Learning is a continuous, never-ending process of knowledge
creation. A learning organization is a place where people are constantly driven
to discover what has caused the current situation, and how they can change the
present. To maintain competitive advantage, an organization's investment
decisions related to knowledge creation are likely to be strategic in nature
(Chen & Edgington, 2005).

Alavi and Leidner (2001) make the case that the hierarchy of data-information-
knowledge can be of a different nature. Specifically, they claim that knowledge
can be the basis for information, rather than information the basis for knowl-

edge. Knowledge must exist before information can be formulated and before data can be measured to form information. As such, raw data do not exist: the thought or knowledge processes that led to its identification and collection have already influenced even the most elementary piece of data. It is argued that knowledge exists that when articulated, verbalized, and structured, becomes information that when assigned a fixed representation and standard interpretation, becomes data (Alavi & Leidner, 2001, p. 109):

Critical to this argument is the fact that knowledge does not exist outside an agent (a knower): it is indelibly shaped by one's needs as well as one's initial stock of knowledge. Knowledge is thus the result of cognitive processing triggered by the inflow of new stimuli. Consistent with this view, we posit that information is converted to knowledge once it is processed in the mind of individuals and the knowledge becomes information once it is articulated and presented in the form of text, graphics, words, or other symbolic forms. A significant implication of this view of knowledge is that for individuals to arrive at the same understanding of data or information, they must share a certain knowledge base. Another important implication of this definition of knowledge is that systems designed to support knowledge in organizations may not appear radically different from other forms of information systems, but will be geared toward enabling users to assign meaning to information and to capture some of their knowledge in information and/or data.

Knowledge Value Level

It is not difficult to agree with this reasoning. In fact, our hierarchy from data via information to knowledge is not so much a road or direction as it is a way of suggesting resource value levels. Knowledge is a more valuable resource to the organization than information, and information is a more valuable resource than data. This is illustrated in Figure 1. The figure illustrates that it is less the knowledge existing at any given time, per se, than the organization's ability to effectively apply the existing knowledge to develop new knowledge, and to take action that forms the basis for achieving long-term competitive advantage from knowledge-based assets.

Figure 1. Value levels of resources in the organization

Strategic value	Knowledge resources	Knowledge development
Non-strategic value	Data resources	Information resources
	Short-term value	Long-term value

According to Grover and Davenport (2001), knowledge processes lie somewhere between information and the organization's source of revenue: its products and services. This process can be generically represented in three subprocesses: knowledge generation, knowledge codification, and knowledge transfer/realization. Knowledge generation includes all processes involved in the acquisition and development of knowledge. Knowledge codification involves the conversion of knowledge into accessible and applicable formats. Knowledge transfer includes the movement of knowledge from its point of generation or codified form to the point of use.

One of the reasons that knowledge is such a difficult concept is because this process is recursive, expanding, and often discontinuous. According to Grover and Davenport (2001), many cycles of generation, codification, and transfer are concurrently occurring in businesses. These cycles feed on each other. Knowledge interacts with information to increase the state space of possibilities, and provide new information that can then facilitate generation of new knowledge. The knowledge process acts on information to create new information that allows for greater possibilities to fulfill old or possibly new organizational needs. This process is often discontinuous, where new needs and their fulfillment mechanism could be created.

In our resource-based perspective of knowledge, data is raw numbers and facts, information is processed data, and knowledge is information combined with human thoughts. Knowledge is the result of cognitive processing triggered by the inflow of new stimuli. Information is converted to knowledge once it is processed in the mind of individuals, and the knowledge becomes information once it is articulated and presented to others. A significant implication of this view of knowledge is that for individuals to arrive at the same understanding of information, they must share the same knowledge framework.

In Figure 1, we can imagine that data are assigned meaning and become information, that information is understood and interpreted by individuals and becomes knowledge, and that knowledge is applied and develops into new knowledge. We can also imagine the opposite route. Knowledge develops in the minds of individuals. This knowledge development causes an increase in knowledge resources. When the new knowledge is articulated, verbalized, and structured, it becomes information and causes an increase in information resources. When information is assigned a fixed representation and standard interpretation, it becomes data and causes an increase in data resources.

There are alternatives to our perspective of knowledge as a resource in the organization. Alavi and Leidner (2001) list the following alternatives: knowledge is state of mind, knowledge is an object to be stored, knowledge is a process of applying expertise, knowledge is a condition of access to information, and knowledge is the potential to influence action.

This book applies the resource-based theory of the organization, where the knowledge-based perspective identifies the primary role of the organization as integrating the specialist knowledge resident in individuals into goods and services. The task of management is to establish the coordination necessary for this knowledge integration. The knowledge-based perspective serves as a platform for a view of the organization as a dynamic system of knowledge production and application.

Identification of Knowledge Needs

To classify knowledge as a resource, there has to be a need for that knowledge. Hence, identification of knowledge needs in an organization is important. Three supplementary methods exist to identify needs for knowledge, as illustrated in Figure 2:

Figure 2. Methods to identify knowledge needs

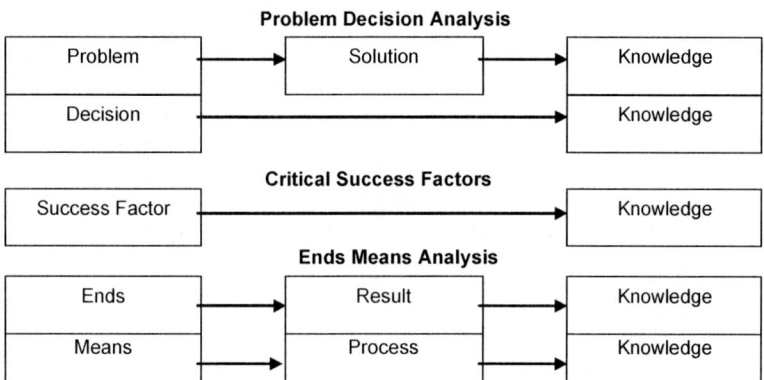

- **Problem decision analysis.** This method aims at identifying and speci-fying problems that knowledge workers have, solutions they can find, decisions they have to make, and what knowledge they need to solve problems and make decisions. For a lawyer, the problem can be an insurance claim by a client, the decision can be how to approach the insurance company, and the knowledge need can be outcomes of similar cases handled by the law firm.

- **Critical success factors.** This method aims at identifying and specifying what factors cause success. Success can be at firm level, individual level, or individual case level. For a lawyer, critical success factors at the individual case level can be quality of legal advice and service level of advice delivery. Critical knowledge in this case includes legal knowledge as well as procedural knowledge.

- **Ends means analysis.** This method aims at identifying and specifying external demands and expectations to goods and services from the firm. For a lawyer, the client expectation might be that she or he wins the case. The end is winning the case. Knowledge needs associated with winning a case includes legal, procedural, and analytical knowledge of successful cases in the past. The means for winning a case might be access to resources of various kinds, such as client documents and client funds. Knowledge needs associated with means include historical records and analysis of legal client practice.

Knowledge Categories

Many researchers have tried to define categories and dimensions of knowledge. A common distinction is made between explicit and tacit knowledge. *Explicit knowledge* can be expressed in words and numbers and shared in the form of data, scientific formulae, specifications, manuals, and the like. This kind of knowledge can be readily transmitted between individuals, both formally and systematically. *Tacit knowledge* is, on the other hand, highly personal and hard to formalize, making it difficult to communicate or share with others. Subjective insights, intuitions, and hunches fall into this category of knowledge. Tacit knowledge is deeply rooted in an individual's actions and experience as well as in the ideals, values, or emotions he or she embraces. Tacit knowledge is embedded in the human brain and cannot be expressed easily, while explicit knowledge can be easily codified. Both types of knowledge are important, but Western firms have focused largely on managing explicit knowledge (Grover & Davenport, 2001).

Tacitness may be considered as a variable, with the degree of tacitness being a function of the extent to which the knowledge is or can be codified and abstracted. Knowledge may dynamically shift between tacit and explicit over time, although some knowledge always will remain tacit. Nonaka et al. (Nonaka, Toyama, & Konno, 2000) have suggested that knowledge creation is a spiraling process of interactions between explicit and tacit knowledge. This spiraling process consists of socialization, externalization, combination, and internalization, as we will see later in this chapter.

The concept of tacit knowledge corresponds closely to the concept of knowledge with a low level of codification. Codification is the degree to which knowledge is fully documented or expressed in writing at the time of transfer between two persons. The complexity of knowledge increases with lower levels of codification. A similar distinction, which scholars frequently make, is between practical, experience-based knowledge and the theoretical knowledge derived from reflection and abstraction from that experience.

A distinction is sometimes made between codification and personalization. This distinction is related to the tacit vs. explicit concept. It involves an organization's approach to knowledge transfer. Companies using codification approaches rely primarily on repositories of explicit knowledge. Personalization approaches imply that the primary mode of knowledge transfer is direct interaction among people. Both are necessary in most organizations, but an increased focus on one approach or the other at any given time within a specific organization may be appropriate (Grover & Davenport, 2001).

Explicit knowledge is sometimes called articulable knowledge (Hitt, Bierman, Shumizu, & Kochhar, 2001). Articulable knowledge can be codified, and thus can be written and easily transferred. Tacit knowledge is not articulable, and therefore cannot be easily transferred. Tacit knowledge is often embedded in uncodified routines and in a firm's social context. More specifically, it is partially embedded in individual skills and partially embedded in collaborative working relationships within the firm. Tacit knowledge is integral to professional skills. As a result, tacit knowledge is often unique, difficult to imitate, and uncertain. It has a higher probability of creating strategic value than articulable knowledge.

Distinctions can be made between core, advanced, and innovative knowledge. These knowledge categories indicate different levels of knowledge sophistication. Core knowledge is that minimum scope and level of knowledge required for daily operations, while advanced knowledge enables a firm to be competitively viable, and innovative knowledge is the knowledge that enables the firm to lead its industry and competitors:

- **Core knowledge** is the basic knowledge required to stay in business. This is the type of knowledge that can create efficiency barriers for entry of new companies, as new competitors are not up to speed in basic business processes. Since core knowledge is present at all existing competitors the firm must have this knowledge, even though it will provide the firm with no advantage that distinguishes it from its competitors. Core knowledge is that minimum scope and level of knowledge required just to play the game. Having that level of knowledge and capability will not assure the long-term competitive viability of the firm, but does present a basic industry knowledge barrier to entry. Core knowledge tends to be commonly held by members of an industry and therefore, provides little advantage other than over nonmembers (Zack, 1999).

  In a law firm, examples of core knowledge include knowledge of the law, knowledge of the courts, knowledge of clients, and knowledge of procedures. For a student in the business school, core knowledge includes knowledge of what subjects to study this term and where the lectures take place.

According to Tiwana (2002), core knowledge is the basic level of knowledge required just to play the game. This is the type of knowledge that creates a barrier for entry of new companies. Since this level of knowledge is expected of all competitors, you must have it, even though it will provide your company with no advantage that distinguishes it from its competitors. Let us take two examples: One from the consumer electronics (hard product) business and one from Internet programming (soft product). To enter the modem manufacturing market, a new company must have extensive knowledge of these aspects: a suitable circuit design, all electronic parts that go into a modem, fabricating surface mount (SMD) chip boards, how to write operating system drivers for modems, and familiarity with computer telephony standards. Similarly, a company developing Web sites for, say, florists, needs server hosting capabilities, Internet programming skills, graphic design skills, clearly identified target markets, and necessary software. In either case, just about any competitor in those businesses is assumed to have this knowledge in order to compete in their respective markets; such essential knowledge, therefore, provides no advantage over other market players.

- **Advanced knowledge** is what makes the firm competitively visible and active. Such knowledge allows the firm to differentiate its products and services from that of a competitor through the application of superior knowledge in certain areas. Such knowledge allows the firm to compete head on with its competitors in the same market and for the same set of customers. Advanced knowledge enables a firm to be competitively viable. The firm may have generally the same level, scope, or quality of knowledge as its competitors, although the specific knowledge content will often vary among competitors, enabling knowledge differentiation. Firms may choose to compete on knowledge head-on in the same strategic position, hoping to know more than a competitor. They instead may choose to compete for that position by differentiating their knowledge (Zack, 1999).

In a law firm, examples of advanced knowledge include knowledge of law applications, knowledge of important court rulings, and knowledge of successful procedural case handling. For a student in the business school, advanced knowledge includes knowledge of important articles and books that are compulsory literature in subjects this term.

According to Tiwana (2002), advanced knowledge is what makes your company competitively viable. Such knowledge allows your company to differentiate its product from that of a competitor, arguably, through the application of superior knowledge in certain areas. Such knowledge allows your company to compete head on with its competitors in the same market and for the same set of customers. In the case of a company trying to compete in modem manufacturing markets, superior or user-friendly software or an additional capability in modems (such as warning online users of incoming telephone calls) represents such knowledge. In case of a Web site development firm, such knowledge might be about international flower markets and collaborative relationships in Dutch flower auctions that the company can use to improve Web sites delivered to its customers.

- **Innovative knowledge** allows a firm to lead its entire industry to an extent that clearly differentiates it from competition. Such knowledge allows a firm to change the rules of the game by introducing new business practices. Such knowledge enables a firm to expand its market share by winning new customers, and by increasing service levels to existing customers. Innovative knowledge is that knowledge that enables a firm to lead its industry and competitors, and to significantly differentiate itself from its competitors. Innovative knowledge often enables a firm to change the rules of the game itself (Zack, 1999).

In a law firm, examples of innovative knowledge include knowledge of standardizing repetitive legal cases, knowledge of successful settlements, and knowledge of modern information technology to track and store vast amounts of information from various sources. For a student in the business school, innovative knowledge includes knowledge of important topics within subjects, links between subjects, typical exam questions, and knowledge of business cases where theory can be applied.

According to Tiwana (2002), innovative knowledge allows a company to lead its entire industry to an extent that clearly differentiates it from competition. Innovative knowledge allows a company to change the rules of the game. Patented technology is an applicable example of changing the rules. Innovative knowledge cannot always be protected by patents, as the lawsuit between Microsoft and Apple in the 1980s should serve to remind us. Apple sued Microsoft for copying the look and feel of its graphical user interface (GUI). The Supreme Court ruled that things like look and feel cannot be patented; they can only be copyrighted. Microsoft won the case since it copied the look and feel, but used entirely different code to create it in the first place.

Many more categories and dimensions of knowledge have been suggested by researchers. The problem with most of these classifications is that they do not seem to satisfy three important criteria for classification. The first requirement is that a classification should always be complete, there should be no category missing. The second requirement is that each category should be different from all other categories, that is, there should be no overlap between categories. The final requirement is that each category should be at the same level, there should be no category including another category. Consider the following categories suggested by researchers: formal knowledge, instrumental knowledge, informal knowledge, tacit knowledge, metaknowledge, and context-independent knowledge. These categories seem to violate some of the classification rules. For example, there seems to be an overlap between informal knowledge and tacit knowledge. Maybe Long and Fahey's (2000) classification into human knowledge, social knowledge, and structured knowledge satisfy our requirements:

- **Human knowledge.** This constitutes the know-what, know-how, and know-why of individuals. Human knowledge is manifested in individual skills (e.g., how to interview law firm clients) or expertise (e.g., why this case is similar to a previous case). Individual knowledge usually combines explicit and tacit knowledge. This type of knowledge may be located in the body, such as knowing how to type touch on a PC or how to ride a bicycle. This type of knowledge may be cognitive, that is, largely conceptual and abstract.

- **Social knowledge.** This kind of knowledge exists only in relationships between individuals or within groups. For example, high-performing teams of tax lawyers share certain collective knowledge that is more than the sum of the individual knowledge of the team's members. Social or collective knowledge is mainly tacit knowledge, shared by team members, and develops only as a result of team members working together. Its presence is reflected by an ability to collaborate effectively.

- **Structured knowledge.** This is embedded in an organization's systems, processes, tools, routines, and practices. Knowledge in this form is explicit and often rule based. A key distinction between structured knowledge and the first two types of knowledge is that structured knowledge is assumed to exist independently of individual knowers. It is, instead, an organizational resource. However, to be complete, this knowledge has to be in the heads of individuals.

Figure 3. Dimensions of individual knowledge

	I know it	I don't know it
I do know	I know that I know	I don't know that I know
I don't know	I know that I don't know	I don't know that I don't know

Two dimensions have been introduced to classify knowledge. The first dimension is concerned with whether an individual knows. The second dimension is concerned with whether an individual knows whether he or she knows. This is illustrated in Figure 3. I can either have the knowledge (I do know) or not have the knowledge (I do not know). I can either be aware of it (I know it) or not be aware of it (I do not know it).

Some researchers have argued that the real tacit knowledge is found in the right upper quadrant. In this dimension, I do know, but I do not know that I know. Tacit knowledge in this sense is also called hidden knowledge or nonaccessible knowledge. In this book, we do not use this extremely limited definition of tacit knowledge. We define tacit knowledge as personal and difficult, but not impossible to communicate.

Classification of knowledge into categories and dimensions may depend on industry. For example, there are likely to be different knowledge categories in a bank compared to a law firm. At the same time, there will be certain generic knowledge categories such as market intelligence and technology understanding in most companies, independently of industry. When classifying knowledge in a firm, it is important to do the analysis without the organization chart. If you classify knowledge into technology knowledge, production knowledge, marketing knowledge, and financial knowledge, it may be because the firm, according to the organization chart, consists of a development department, production department, marketing department, and financial department. It might be more useful to introduce new knowledge categories, such as product knowledge, that include knowledge of development, production, marketing, and finance. By identifying cross-sectional knowledge categories and dimensions, solutions for improved knowledge flows in the organization will emerge.

A law firm is a good example. A law firm is organized according to legal disciplines. Some lawyers work in the tax department, while others work in the department for mergers and acquisitions. The types of knowledge involved in the practice of law can be categorized as administrative, declarative, procedural, and analytical knowledge (Edwards & Mahling, 1997):

- **Administrative knowledge**, which includes all the nuts and bolts information about firm operations, such as hourly billing rates for lawyers, client names and matters, staff payroll data, and client invoice data.

- **Declarative knowledge**, which is knowledge of the law, the legal principles contained in statutes, court opinions, and other sources of primary legal authority; law students spend most of their law school time acquiring this kind of knowledge.

- **Procedural knowledge**, which involves knowledge of the mechanisms of complying with the law's requirements in a particular situation: how documents are used to transfer an asset from Company A to Company B, or how forms must be filed where to create a new corporation. Declarative knowledge is sometimes labeled know-that and know-what, while procedural knowledge is labeled know-how.

- **Analytical knowledge**, which pertains to the conclusions reached about the course of action a particular client, should follow in a particular situation. Analytical knowledge results, in essence, from analyzing declarative knowledge (i.e., substantive law principles) as it applies to a particular fact setting.

Classification of knowledge into categories and dimensions has important limitations. For example, the classification into explicit and tacit knowledge may create static views of knowledge. However, knowledge development and sharing are dynamic processes, and these dynamic processes cause tacit knowledge to become explicit, and explicit knowledge to become tacit over time. Tacit and explicit knowledge depend on each other, and they influence each other. In this perspective, Alavi and Leidner (2001) argue that whether tacit or explicit knowledge is the more valuable may indeed miss the point. The two knowledge categories are not dichotomous states of knowledge, but mutually dependent and reinforcing qualities of knowledge: tacit knowledge forms the background necessary for assigning the structure to develop and interpret explicit knowledge.

According to Alavi and Leidner (2001), the linkage of tacit and explicit knowledge suggests that only individuals with a requisite level of shared knowledge are able to exchange knowledge. They suggest the existence of a share knowledge space that is required in order for individual A to understand individual B's knowledge. The knowledge space is the underlying overlap in knowledge base of A and B. This overlap is typically tacit knowledge. It may be argued that the greater the shared knowledge space, the less the context needed for individuals to share knowledge within the group and, hence, the higher the value of explicit knowledge. For example in a law firm, lawyers in the maritime law department may have a large knowledge space so that even a very limited piece of explicit knowledge can be of great value to the lawyers. Alavi and Leidner (2001, p. 112) discuss knowledge space in the following way:

Whether tacit or explicit knowledge is the more valuable may indeed miss the point. The two are not dichotomous states of knowledge, but mutually dependent and reinforcing qualities of knowledge: tacit knowledge forms the background necessary for assigning the structure to develop and interpret explicit knowledge. The inextricable linkage of tacit and explicit knowledge suggests that only individuals with a requisite level of shared knowledge can truly exchange knowledge: if tacit knowledge is necessary to the understanding of explicit knowledge, then in order for Individual B to understand Individual A's knowledge, there must be some overlap in their underlying knowledge bases (a shared knowledge space). However, it is precisely in applying technology to increase 'weak ties' in organizations, and thereby increase the breadth of knowledge sharing, that IT holds promise. Yet, absent a shared knowledge space, the real impact of IT on knowledge exchange is questionable. This is a paradox that IT researchers have somewhat eschewed, and that organizational researchers have used to question the application of IT to knowledge management. To add to the paradox, the very essence of the knowledge management challenge is to amalgamate knowledge across groups for which IT can play a major role. What is most at issue is the amount of contextual information necessary for one person or group's knowledge to be readily understood by another.

It may be argued that the greater the shared knowledge space, the less the context needed for individuals to share knowledge within the group and, hence, the higher the value of explicit knowledge and the greater the value of IT applied to knowledge management. On the other hand, the smaller the existing shared knowledge space in a group, the greater the need for contextual information, the less relevant will be explicit knowledge, and hence the less applicable will be IT to knowledge management.

Some researchers are interested in the total knowledge within a company, while others are interested in individual knowledge. Dixon (2000) was interested in the knowledge that knowledge workers develop together in the organization. Employees gain this knowledge from doing the organization's tasks. This knowledge is called common knowledge, to differentiate it from book knowledge or lists of regulations or databases of customer information. Some examples of common knowledge are what medical doctors in a hospital have learned about how to carry out certain kinds of surgery, what an organization has learned about how to introduce a new drug into the diabetes market, how to reduce cost on consulting projects, and how to control the amount of analysis in maritime law cases. These examples all include the how-to rather than the know-what of school learning. Moreover, it is know-how that is unique to a specific company. In the law firm example, procedural knowledge was classified as know-how.

References

Alavi, M., & Leidner, D. E. (2001). Knowledge management and knowledge management systems: Conceptual foundations and research issues. *MIS Quarterly*, *25*(1), 107-136.

Chen, A. N. K., & Edgington, T. M. (2005). Assessing value in organizational knowledge creation: Considerations for knowledge workers. *MIS Quarterly*, *29*(2), 279-309.

Davenport, T. H., & Prusak, L. (1998). *Working knowledge*. Boston: Harvard Business School Press.

Dixon, N. M. (2000). *Common knowledge*. Boston: Harvard Business School Press.

Edwards, D. L., & Mahling, D. E. (1997). Toward knowledge management systems in the legal domain. In *Proceedings of the International ACM*

SIGGROUP Conference on Supporting Group Work Group (pp. 158-166). The Association of Computing Machinery ACM.

Garud, R., & Kumaraswamy. A. (2005). Vicious and virtuous circles in the management of knowledge: The case of Infosys technologies. *MIS Quarterly, 29*(1), 9-33.

Grover, V., & Davenport, T. H. (2001). General perspectives on knowledge management: Fostering a research agenda. *Journal of Management Information Systems, 18*(1), 5-21.

Hitt, M. A., Bierman, L., Shumizu, K., & Kochhar, R. (2001). Direct and moderating effects of human capital on strategy and performance in professional service firms: A resource-based perspective. *Academy of Management Journal, 44*(1), 13-28.

Kankanhalli, A., Tan, B. C. Y., & Wei, K. K. (2005). Contributing knowledge to electronic knowledge repositories: An empirical investigation. *MIS Quarterly, 29*(1), 113-143.

Long, D. W., & Fahey, L. (2000). Diagnosing cultural barriers to knowledge management. *Academy of Management Executive, 14*(4), 113-127.

Malhotra, A., Gosain, S., & El Sawy, O. A. (2005). Absorptive capacity configurations in supply chains: Gearing for partner-enabled market knowledge creation. *MIS Quarterly, 29*(1), 145-187.

Nonaka, I., Toyama, R., & Konno, N. (2000). SECI, Ba and leadership: A unified model of dynamic knowledge creation. *Long Range Planning, 33*(1), 5-34.

Poston, R. S., & Speier, C. (2005). Effective use of knowledge management systems: A process model of content ratings and credibility indicators. *MIS Quarterly, 29*(2), 221-244.

Ryu, C., Kim, Y. J., Chaudhury, A., & Rao, H. R. (2005). Knowledge acquisition via three learning processes in enterprise information portals: Learning-by-investment, learning-by-doing, and learning-from-others. *MIS Quarterly, 29*(2), 245-278.

Sambamurthy, V., & Subramani, M. (2005). Special issue on information technologies and knowledge management. *MIS Quarterly, 29*(1), 1-7; and *29*(2), 193-195.

Tanriverdi, H. (2005). Information technology relatedness, knowledge management capability, and performance of multibusiness firms. *MIS Quarterly, 29*(2), 311-334.

Tiwana, A. (2002). *The knowledge management toolkit—practical techniques for building a knowledge management system* (2nd ed.). Upper Saddle River, NJ: Prentice Hall.

Wasko, M. M., & Faraj, S. (2005). Why should I share? Examining social capital and knowledge contribution in electronic networks of practice. *MIS Quarterly, 29*(1), 35-57.

Zack, M. H. (1999). Developing a knowledge strategy. *California Management Review, 41*(3), 125-145.

Chapter III

IT in Knowledge Management

As we trace the evolution of computing technologies in business, we can observe their changing level of organizational impact. The first level of impact was at the point work got done, and transactions (e.g., orders, deposits, reservations) took place. The inflexible, centralized mainframe allowed for little more than massive number crunching, commonly known as electronic data processing. Organizations became data heavy at the bottom, and data management systems were used to keep the data in check. Later, the management information systems were used to aggregate data into useful information reports, often prescheduled, for the control level of the organization: people who were making sure that organizational resources like personnel, money, and physical goods were being deployed efficiently. As information technology (IT) and information systems (IS) started to facilitate data and information overflow, and corporate attention became a scarce resource, the concept of knowledge emerged as a particularly high-value form of information (Grover & Davenport, 2001).

Information technology can play an important role in successful knowledge management initiatives. However, the concept of coding and transmitting knowledge in organizations is not new: training and employee development programs, organizational policies, routines, procedures, reports, and manuals have served this function for many years. What is new and exciting in the knowledge management area is the potential for using modern information technology (e.g., the Internet, intranets, extranets, browsers, data warehouses, data filters, software agents, expert systems) to support knowledge creation, sharing, and exchange in an organization and between organizations. Modern information technology can collect, systematize, structure, store, combine, distribute, and present information of value to knowledge workers (Nahapiet & Ghoshal, 1998).

According to Davenport and Prusak (1998), more and more companies have instituted knowledge repositories that support such diverse types of knowledge as best practices, lessons learned, product development knowledge, customer knowledge, human resource management knowledge, and methods-based knowledge. Groupware and intranet-based technologies have become standard knowledge infrastructures. A new set of professional job titles—the knowledge manager, the chief knowledge officer (CKO), the knowledge coordinator, and the knowledge-network facilitator—affirms the widespread legitimacy that knowledge management has earned in the corporate world.

The low cost of computers and networks has created a potential infrastructure for knowledge sharing and opened up important knowledge management opportunities. The computational power, as such, has little relevance to knowledge work, but the communication and storage capabilities of networked computers make it an important enabler of effective knowledge work. Through e-mail, groupware, the Internet, and intranets, computers and networks can point to people with knowledge, and connect people who need to share knowledge independent of time and place.

For example, electronic networks of practice are computer-mediated discussion forums focused on problems of practice that enable individuals to exchange advice and ideas with others, based on common interests. Electronic networks make it possible to share information quickly, globally, and with large numbers of individuals. Electronic networks that focus on knowledge exchange frequently emerge in fields where the pace of technological change requires access to knowledge unavailable within any single organization (Wasko & Faraj, 2005).

In the knowledge-based view of the firm, knowledge is the foundation of a firm's competitive advantage and, ultimately, the primary driver of a firm's value. Inherently, however, knowledge resides within individuals and, more specifically, in the employees who create, recognize, archive, access, and apply knowledge in carrying out their tasks. Consequently, the movement of knowledge across individual and organizational boundaries, into and from repositories, and into organizational routines and practices is ultimately dependent on employees' knowledge sharing behaviors (Bock, Zmud, & Kim, 2005).

According to Grover and Davenport (2001), most knowledge management projects in organizations involve the use of information technology. Such projects fall into relatively few categories and types, each of which has a key objective. Although it is possible, and even desirable, to combine multiple objectives in a single project, this was not normally observed in a study of 31 knowledge management projects in 1997 (Davenport & Prusak, 1998). Since that time, it is possible that projects have matured and have taken on more ambitious collections of objectives.

Regardless of definition of knowledge as the highest value of content in a continuum starting at data, encompassing information, and ending at knowledge, knowledge managers often take a highly inclusive approach to the content with which they deal. In practice, what companies actually manage under the banner of knowledge management is a mix of knowledge, information, and unrefined data—in short, whatever anyone finds that is useful and easy to store in an electronic repository. In the case of data and information, however, there are often attempts to add more value and create knowledge. This transformation might involve the addition of insight, experience, context, interpretation, or the myriad of other activities in which human brains specialize (Grover & Davenport, 2001).

Identifying, nurturing, and harvesting knowledge is a principal concern in the information society and the knowledge age. Effective use of knowledge-facilitating tools and techniques is critical, and a number of computational tools have been developed. While numerous techniques are available, it remains difficult to analyze or compare the specific tools. In part, this is because knowledge management is a young discipline. The arena is evolving rapidly as more people enter the fray and encounter new problems (Housel & Bell, 2001).

In addition, new technologies support applications that were impossible before. Moreover, the multidisciplinary character of knowledge management combines several disciplines including business and management, computer science, cybernetics, and philosophy. Each of these fields may lay claim to the study of knowledge management, and the field is frequently defined so broadly that anything can be incorporated. Finally, it is difficult to make sense of the many tools available. It is not difficult to perform a search to produce a list of more than 100 software providers. Each of the software packages employ unique visions and aims to capture its share of the market (Housel & Bell, 2001).

Ward and Peppard (2002) find that there are two dominant and contrasting views of IS/IT in knowledge management: the engineering perspective, and the social process perspective. The engineering perspective views knowledge management as a technology process. Many organizations have taken this approach in managing knowledge, believing that it is concerned with managing pieces of intellectual capital. Driving this view is the view that knowledge can be codified and stored; in essence that knowledge is explicit knowledge and therefore, is little more than information.

The alternative view is that knowledge is a social process. As such, it asserts that knowledge resides in people's heads and that it is tacit. As such, it cannot be easily codified and only revealed through its application. As tacit knowledge cannot be directly transferred from person to person, its acquisition occurs only through practice. Consequently, its transfer between people is slow, costly, and uncertain. Technology, within this perspective, can only support the context of knowledge work. It has been argued that IT-based systems used to support knowledge management can only be of benefit if used to support the development and communication of human meaning. One reason for the failure of IT in some knowledge management initiatives is that the designers of the knowledge management systems fail to understand the situation and work practices of the users and the complex human processes involved in work.

While technology can be used with knowledge management initiatives, Ward and Peppard (2002) argue that it should never be the first step. Knowledge management is, to them, primarily a human and process issue. Once these two aspects have been addressed, then the created processes are usually very amenable to being supported and enhanced by the use of technology.

What, then, is knowledge management technology? According to Davenport and Prusak (1998), the concept of knowledge management technology is not only broad, but also a bit slippery to define. Some infrastructure technology that we do not ordinarily think of in this category can be useful in facilitating knowledge management. Examples are videoconferencing and the telephone. Both of these technologies do not capture or distribute structured knowledge, but they are quite effective at enabling people to transfer tacit knowledge.

Our focus here, however, is on technology that captures, stores, and distributes structured knowledge for use by people. The goal of these technologies is to take knowledge that exists in human heads and partly in paper documents, and make it widely available throughout an organization. Similarly, Alavi and Leidner (2001) argue that information systems designed to support knowledge in organizations may not appear radically different from other forms of IT support, but will be geared toward enabling users to assign meaning to information and to capture some of their knowledge in information. Therefore, the concept of knowledge management technology in this book is less concerned with any degree of technology sophistication, and more concerned with the usefulness in performing knowledge work in organizations and between organizations.

Moffett and McAdam (2003) illustrate the variety of knowledge management technology tools by distinguishing between collaborative tools, content management, and business intelligence. Collaborative tools include groupware technology, meeting support systems, knowledge directories, and intranets/extranets. Content management includes the Internet, agents and filters, electronic publishing systems, document management systems, and office automation systems. Business intelligence includes data warehousing, decision support systems, knowledge-based systems, and workflow systems.

In addition to technologies, we also present techniques in this book. The term technique is defined as a set of precisely described procedures for achieving a standard task (Kettinger, Teng, & Guha, 1997).

Knowledge Management Processes

Alavi and Leidner (2001) have developed a systematic framework that will be used to analyze and discuss the potential role of information technology in knowledge management. According to this framework, organizations consist of four sets of socially enacted knowledge processes: (1) creation (also referred to as construction), (2) storage and retrieval, (3) transfer, and (4) application. The knowledge-based view of the firm represents, here, both the cognitive and social nature of organizational knowledge, and its embodiment in the individual's cognition and practices as well as the collective (i.e., organizational) practices and culture. These processes do not represent a monolithic set of activities, but an interconnected and intertwined set of activities.

Knowledge Creation

Organizational knowledge creation involves developing new content or replacing existing content within the organization's tacit and explicit knowledge.

Through social and collaborative processes as well as individual's cognitive processes (e.g., reflection), knowledge is created. The model developed by Nonaka et al. (Nonaka, Toyama, & Konno, 2000) involving SECI, ba, and knowledge assets, views organizational knowledge creation as involving a continual interplay between the tacit and explicit dimensions of knowledge, and a growing spiral flow as knowledge moves through individual, group, and organizational levels. Four modes of knowledge creation have been identified: socialization, externalization, internalization, and combination (SECI), and these modes occur at "ba," which means place.

Nonaka et al. (2000) suggest that the essential question of knowledge creation is establishing an organization's ba, defined as a commonplace or space for creating knowledge. Four types of ba corresponding to the four modes of knowledge creation are identified:

1.   Originating ba
2.   Interacting ba
3.   Cyber ba
4.   Exercising ba

Originating ba entails the socialization mode of knowledge creation, and is the ba from which the organizational knowledge creation process begins. Originating ba is a common place in which individuals share experiences primarily through face-to-face interactions, and by being at the same place at the same time. Interacting ba is associated with the externalization mode of knowledge creation, and refers to a space where tacit knowledge is converted to explicit knowledge and shared among individuals through the process of dialogue and collaboration. Cyber ba refers to a virtual space of interaction, and corresponds to the combination mode of knowledge creation. Finally, exercising ba involves the conversion of explicit to tacit knowledge through the internalization process. Thus, exercising ba involves the conversion of explicit to tacit knowledge through the internalization process.

Understanding the characteristics of various ba and the relationship with the modes of knowledge creation is important to enhancing organizational knowledge creation. For example, the use of IT capabilities in cyber ba is advocated to enhance the efficiency of the combination mode of knowledge creation. Data warehousing and data mining, document management systems, software agents, and intranets may be of great value in cyber ba. Considering the flexibility of modern IT, other forms of organizational ba and the corresponding modes of knowledge creation can be enhanced through the use of various forms of information systems. For example, information systems designed for support or collaboration, coordination, and communication processes, as a component of the interacting ba, can facilitate teamwork and thereby, increase an individual's contact with other individuals.

Electronic mail and group support systems have the potential of increasing the number of weak ties in organizations. This, in turn, can accelerate the growth of knowledge creation. Intranets enable exposure to greater amounts of online organizational information, both horizontally and vertically, than may previously have been the case. As the level of information exposure increases, the internalization mode of knowledge creation, wherein individuals make observations and interpretations of information that result in new individual tacit knowledge, may increase. In this role, an intranet can support individual learning (conversion of explicit knowledge to personal tacit knowledge) through provision of capabilities such as computer simulation (to support learning-by-doing) and smart software tutors.

Computer-mediated communication may increase the quality of knowledge creation by enabling a forum for constructing and sharing beliefs, for confirming consensual interpretation, and for allowing expression of new ideas. By providing an extended field of interaction among organizational members for sharing ideas and perspectives, and for establishing dialog, information systems may enable individuals to arrive at new insights and/or more accurate interpretations than if left to decipher information on their own.

Although most information repositories serve a single function, it is increasingly common for companies to construct an internal "portal" so that employees can access multiple different repositories and sources from one screen. It is also possible and increasingly popular for repositories to contain not only information, but also pointers to experts within the organization on key knowledge topics. It is also feasible to combine stored information with lists of the individuals who contributed the knowledge and could provide more detail or background on it (Grover & Davenport, 2001).

According to Grover and Davenport (2001), firms increasingly view attempts to transform raw data into usable knowledge as part of their knowledge management initiatives. These approaches typically involve isolating data in a separate "warehouse" for easier access, and the use of statistical analysis or data mining and visualization tools. Since their goal is to create data-derived knowledge, they are increasingly addressed as a part of knowledge management. Some vendors have already begun to introduce e-commerce tools. They serve to customize the menu of available knowledge to individual customers, allowing sampling of information before buying and carrying out sales transactions for knowledge purchases. Online legal services are typical examples where clients can sample legal information before buying lawyer's time.

For knowledge creation, there is currently idea-generation software emerging. Idea-generation software is designed to help stimulate a single user or a group to produce new ideas, options, and choices. The user does all the work, but the software encourages and pushes, something like a personal trainer. Although idea-generation software is relatively new, there are several packages on the market. IdeaFisher, for example, has an associative lexicon of the English language that cross-references words and phrases. These associative links, based on analogies and metaphors, make it easy for the user to be fed words related to a given theme. Some software packages use questions to prompt the user toward new, unexplored patterns of thought. This helps users to break out of cyclical thinking patterns and conquer mental blocks.

Knowledge Storage and Retrieval

According to Alavi and Leidner (2001), empirical studies have shown that while organizations create knowledge and learn, they also forget (i.e., do not remember or lose track of the acquired knowledge). Thus, the storage, organization, and retrieval of organizational knowledge, also referred to as organizational memory, constitute an important aspect of effective organizational knowledge management. Organizational memory includes knowledge residing in various component forms, including written documentation, structured information stored in electronic databases, codified human knowledge stored in expert systems, documented organizational procedures and processes, and tacit knowledge acquired by individuals and networks of individuals.

Advanced computer storage technology and sophisticated retrieval techniques, such as query languages, multimedia databases, and database management systems, can be effective tools in enhancing organizational memory. These tools increase the speed at which organizational memory can be accessed.

Groupware enables organizations to create intraorganizational memory in the form of both structured and unstructured information, and to share this memory across time and space. IT can play an important role in the enhancement and expansion of both semantic and episodic organizational memory. Semantic memory refers to general, explicit, and articulated knowledge, whereas episodic memory refers to context-specific and situated knowledge. Document management technology allows knowledge of an organization's past, often dispersed among a variety of retention facilities, to be effectively stored and made accessible. Drawing on these technologies, most consulting firms have created semantic memories by developing vast repositories of knowledge about customers, projects, competition, and the industries they serve.

Grover and Davenport (2001) found that in Western organizations, by far the most common objective of knowledge management projects involves some sort of knowledge repository. The objective of this type of project is to capture knowledge for later and broader access by others within the same organization. Common repository technologies include Lotus Notes, Web-based intranets, and Microsoft's Exchange, supplemented by search engines, document management tools, and other tools that allow editing and access. The repositories typically contain a specific type of information to represent knowledge for a particular business function or process, such as:

- "Best practices" information within a quality or business process management function
- Information for sales purposes involving products, markets, and customers
- Lessons learned in projects or product development efforts
- Information around implementation of information systems
- Competitive intelligence for strategy and planning functions
- "Learning histories" or records of experience with a new corporate direction or approach

The mechanical generation of databases, Web sites, and systems that process data are good, and have the potential to take us to a higher plane in the organization, help us understand workflows better, and help us deal with organizational pathologies and problems. The data-to-information transition often involves a low-level mechanical process that is well within the domain of contemporary information technologies, though humans are helpful in this transition as well. This information could exist in different forms throughout the organization and could even form the basis of competitive advantage or information products. For example, provision of information to customers about their order or shipment status is something that companies like Baxter and FedEx have been doing for years. But unlike knowledge, mechanically supplied information cannot be the source of sustained competitive advantage, particularly when the architectures on which it is based are becoming more open and omnipresent.

IT in knowledge management can be used to store various kinds of information. For example, information about processes, procedures, forecasts, cases, and patents in the form of working documents, descriptions, and reports can be stored in knowledge management systems. TietoEnator, a Scandinavian consulting firm, has a knowledge base where they store methods, techniques, notes, concepts, best practices, presentations, components, references, guidelines, quality instructions, process descriptions, routines, strategies, and CVs for all consultants in the firm (Halvorsen & Nguyen, 1999).

Knowledge retrieval can find support in content management and information extraction technology, which represents a group of techniques for managing and extracting knowledge from documents, ultimately delivering a semantic meaning for decision makers or learners alike. This type of computer applications is targeted at capturing and extracting the content of free-text documents. There are several tasks that fall within the scope of content management and information extraction (Wang, Hjelmervik, & Bremdal, 2001):

- **Abstracting and summarizing.** This task aims at delivering shorter, informative representations of larger (sets of) documents.

- **Visualization.** Documents can often be visualized according to the concepts and relationships that play a role. Visualization can be either in an introspective manner, or using some reference model/view of a specific topic.

- **Comparison and search.** This task finds semantically similar pieces of information.

- **Indexing and classification.** This considers (partial) texts, usually according to certain categories.

- **Translation.** Context-driven translation of texts from one language into another. Language translation has proven to be highly context specific, even among closely related languages. Some kind of semantic representation of meaning is needed in order to be able to make good translations.

- **Question formulation and query answering.** This is a task in human-computer interaction systems.

- **Extraction of information.** This refers to the generation of additional information that is not explicit in the original text. This information can be more or less elaborate.

A group of computational techniques are available to alleviate the burden of these tasks. They include fuzzy technology, neural networks, and expert systems. On a more application-oriented level, there are several approaches that apply one or more of the general techniques. The field is currently very dynamic, and new advances are made continuously. One novel approach is the CORPORUM system, to be presented in the section on expert systems.

Knowledge Transfer

Knowledge transfer can be defined as the communication of knowledge from a source so that it is learned and applied by a recipient (Ko, Kirsch, & King, 2005). Knowledge transfer occurs at various levels in an organization: transfer of knowledge between individuals, from individuals to explicit sources, from individuals to groups, between groups, across groups, and from the group to the organization. Considering the distributed nature of organizational cognition, an important process of knowledge management in organizational settings is the transfer of knowledge to locations where it is needed and can be used. However, this is not a simple process in that organizations often do not know what they know, and have weak systems for locating and retrieving knowledge that resides in them. Communication processes and information flows drive knowledge transfer in organizations.

Depending on the completeness or incompleteness of the sender's and the receiver's information sets, there are four representative types of information structure in knowledge transfer according to Lin, Geng, and Whinston (2005): symmetric complete information, sender-advantage asymmetric information, symmetric incomplete information, and receiver-advantage asymmetric information. Lin et al. (2005) found that because of asymmetry and incompleteness, parties seeking knowledge may not be able to identify qualified knowledge providers, and the appropriate experts may fail to be motivated to engage in knowledge transfer.

Knowledge transfer channels can be informal or formal; personal or impersonal. IT can support all four forms of knowledge transfer, but has mostly been
applied to informal, impersonal means (such as discussion databases), and
formal, impersonal means (such as corporate directories). An innovative use of
technology for transfer is use of intelligent agent software to develop interest
profiles of organizational members in order to determine which members might
be interested recipients of point-to-point electronic messages exchanged
among other members. Employing video technologies can also enhance transfer.

IT can increase knowledge transfer by extending the individual's reach beyond
the formal communication lines. The search for knowledge sources is usually
limited to immediate coworkers in regular and routine contact with the
individual. However, individuals are unlikely to encounter new knowledge
through their close-knit work networks because individuals in the same clique
tend to possess similar information. Moreover, individuals are often unaware
of what their cohorts are doing. Thus, expanding the individual's network to
more extended, although perhaps weaker connections, is central to the
knowledge diffusion process because such networks expose individuals to
more new ideas.

Computer networks and electronic bulletin boards and discussion groups
create a forum that facilitates contact between the person seeking knowledge
and those who may have access to the knowledge. Corporate directories may
enable individuals to rapidly locate the individual who has the knowledge that
might help them solve a current problem. For example, the primary content of
such a system can be a set of expert profiles containing information about the
backgrounds, skills, and expertise of individuals who are knowledgeable on
various topics. Often such metadata (knowledge about where knowledge
resides) proves to be as important as the original knowledge itself. Providing
taxonomies or organizational knowledge maps enables individuals to rapidly
locate either the knowledge or the individual who has the needed knowledge,
more rapidly than would be possible without such IT-based support.

Communication is important in knowledge management because technology
provides support for both intraorganizational as well as interorganizational
knowledge networks. Knowledge networks need technology in the form of
technical infrastructure, communication networks, and a set of information
services. Knowledge networks enable knowledge workers to share information from various sources.

Traditional information systems have been of importance to vertical integration
for a long time. Both customers and suppliers have been linked to the company

through information systems. Only recently has horizontal integration occurred. Knowledge workers in similar businesses cooperate to find optimal solutions for customers. IT has become an important vertical and horizontal interorganizational coordination mechanism. This is not only because of the availability of broadband and standardized protocols. It is also caused by falling prices for communication services, and by software programs' ability to coordinate functions between firms.

One way to reduce problems stemming from paper work flow is to employ document-imaging systems. Document imaging systems are systems that convert paper documents and images into digital form so they can be stored and accessed by a computer. Once the document has been stored electronically, it can be immediately retrieved and shared with others. An imaging system requires indexes that allow users to identify and retrieve a document when needed (Laudon & Laudon, 2005).

Knowledge Application

An important aspect of the knowledge-based view of the firm is that the source of competitive advantage resides in the application of the knowledge rather than in the knowledge itself. Information technology can support knowledge application by embedding knowledge into organizational routines. Procedures that are culture-bound can be embedded into IT so that the systems themselves become examples of organizational norms. An example according to Alavi and Leidner (2001) is Mrs. Field's use of systems designed to assist in every decision, from hiring personnel to when to put free samples of cookies out on the table. The system transmits the norms and beliefs held by the head of the company to organizational members.

Technology enforced knowledge application raises a concern that knowledge will continue to be applied after its real usefulness has declined. While the institutionalization of best practices by embedding them into IT might facilitate efficient handling of routine, linear, and predictable situations during stable or incrementally changing environments, when change is radical and discontinuous, there is a persistent need for continual renewal of the basic premises underlying the practices archived in the knowledge repositories. This underscores the need for organizational members to remain attuned to contextual factors and explicitly consider the specific circumstances of the current environment.

Although there are challenges with applying existing knowledge, IT can have a positive influence on knowledge application. IT can enhance knowledge integration and application by facilitating the capture, updating, and accessibility of organizational directives. For example, many organizations are enhancing the ease of access and maintenance of their directives (repair manuals, policies, and standards) by making them available on corporate intranets. This increases the speed at which changes can be applied. Also, organizational units can follow a faster learning curve by accessing the knowledge of other units having gone through similar experiences. Moreover, by increasing the size of individuals' internal social networks, and by increasing the amount of organizational memory available, information technologies allow for organizational knowledge to be applied across time and space.

IT can also enhance the speed of knowledge integration and application by codifying and automating organizational routines. Workflow automation systems are examples of IT applications that reduce the need for communication and coordination, and enable more efficient use of organizational routines through timely and automatic routing of work-related documents, information, rules, and activities. Rule-based expert systems are another means of capturing and enforcing well-specified organizational procedures.

To summarize, Alavi and Leidner (2001) have developed a framework to understand IS/IT in knowledge management processes through the knowledge-based view of the firm. One important implication of this framework is that each of the four knowledge processes of creation, storage and retrieval, transfer, and application can be facilitated by IT:

- **Knowledge creation.** Examples of supporting information technologies are data mining and learning tools that enable combining new sources of knowledge and just in time learning.

- **Knowledge storage and retrieval.** Examples of supporting information technologies are electronic bulletin boards, knowledge repositories, and databases that provide support of individual and organizational memory as well as intergroup knowledge access.

- **Knowledge transfer.** Examples of supporting information technologies are electronic bulletin boards, discussion forums, and knowledge directories that enable more extensive internal network, more available communication channels, and faster access to knowledge sources.

- **Knowledge application.** Examples of supporting information technologies are expert systems and workflow systems that enable knowledge application in many locations and more rapid application of new knowledge through workflow automation.

Knowledge Management Systems

There is no single information system that is able to cover all knowledge management needs in a firm. This is evident from the widespread potential of IT in knowledge management processes. Rather, knowledge management systems (KMS) refer to a class of information systems applied to managing organizational knowledge for use at the individual, group, and organizational level. These systems are IT applications to support and enhance the organizational processes of knowledge creation, storage and retrieval, transfer, and application.

Knowledge management systems can be classified as illustrated in Figure 1. Systems are exemplified along the axis of internal support vs. external support, and along the axis of technology support vs. content support for knowledge workers. As an example of a knowledge management system, we find customer relationship management (CRM) systems in the upper left quadrant. CRM systems support knowledge exchange between the firm and its customers.

Figure 1. Classification of knowledge management systems

Tools	**Information**	
Tools for external communications such as customer relationship management services	Information for external electronic cooperation such as Web-based	**External**
Tools for internal work by knowledge workers	Information for internal work by knowledge workers	**Internal**

Despite widespread belief that information technology enables knowledge management and knowledge management improves firm performance, researchers have only recently found empirical evidence of these relationships. For example, Tanriverdi (2005) used data from 250 Fortune 1000 firms to provide empirical support for these relationships.

Knowledge management systems are becoming ubiquitous in today's organizations. Knowledge management systems facilitate the efficient and effective sharing of an organization's intellectual resources. To ensure effective usage, a knowledge management system must be designed such that knowledge workers can readily find high-quality content without feeling overwhelmed (Poston & Speier, 2005).

Requirements from Knowledge Management

The critical role of information technology and information systems lies in the ability to support communication, collaboration, and those searching for knowledge, and the ability to enable collaborative learning (Ryu, Kim, Chaudhury, & Rao, 2005). We have already touched on important implications for information systems:

1. **Interaction between information and knowledge.** Information becomes knowledge when it is combined with experience, interpretation, and reflection. Knowledge becomes information when assigned an explicit representation. Sometimes information exists before knowledge; sometimes knowledge exists before information. One important implication of this two-way direction between knowledge and information is that information systems designed to support knowledge in organizations may not appear radically different from other forms of IT support, but will be geared toward enabling users to assign meaning to information, and to capture some of their knowledge in information (Alavi & Leidner, 2001).

2. **Interaction between tacit and explicit knowledge.** Tacit and explicit knowledge depend on each other, and they influence each other. The linkage of tacit and explicit knowledge suggests that only individuals with a requisite level of shared knowledge are able to exchange knowledge. They suggest the existence of a shared knowledge space that is required in order for individual A to understand individual B's knowledge. The knowledge space is the underlying overlap in knowledge base of A and B.

This overlap is typically tacit knowledge. It may be argued that the greater the shared knowledge space, the less the context needed for individuals to share knowledge within the group and, hence, the higher the value of explicit knowledge. IT is both dependent on the shared knowledge space and an important part of the shared knowledge space. IT is dependent on the shared knowledge space because knowledge workers need to have a common understanding of available information in information systems in the organization. If common understanding is missing, then knowledge workers are unable to make use of information. IT is an important part of the shared knowledge space because information systems make common information available to all knowledge workers in the organization. One important implication of this two-way relationship between knowledge space and information systems is that a minimum knowledge space has to be present, while IT can contribute to growth in the knowledge space (Alavi & Leidner, 2001).

3.   **Knowledge management strategy.** Efficiency-driven businesses may apply the stock strategy where databases and information systems are important. Effectiveness-driven businesses may apply the flow strategy where information networks are important. Expert-driven businesses may apply the growth strategy where networks of experts, work processes, and learning environments are important (Hansen, Nohria, & Tierney, 1999).

4.   **Combination in SECI process.** The SECI process consists of four knowledge conversion modes. These modes are not equally suited for IT support. Socialization is the process of converting new tacit knowledge to tacit knowledge. This takes place in the human brain. Externalization is the process of converting tacit knowledge to explicit knowledge. The successful conversion of tacit knowledge into explicit knowledge depends on the sequential use of metaphors, analogy, and model. Combination is the process of converting explicit knowledge into more complex and systematic sets of explicit knowledge. Explicit knowledge is collected from inside and outside the organization and then combined, edited, and processed to form new knowledge. The new explicit knowledge is then disseminated among the members of the organization. According to Nonaka et al. (2000), creative use of computerized communication networks and large-scale databases can facilitate this mode of knowledge conversion. When the financial controller collects information from all parts of the organization and puts it together to show the financial health of the organization,

that report is new knowledge in the sense that it synthesizes explicit knowledge from many different sources in one context. Finally, internalization in the SECI process converts explicit knowledge into tacit knowledge. Through internalization, explicit knowledge created is shared throughout an organization and converted into tacit knowledge by individuals.

5. **Explicit transfer of common knowledge.** If management decides to focus on common knowledge as defined by Dixon (2000), knowledge management should focus on the sharing of common knowledge. Common knowledge is shared in the organization using five mechanisms: serial transfer, explicit transfer, tacit transfer, strategic transfer, and expert transfer. Management has to emphasize all five mechanisms for successful sharing and creation of common knowledge. For serial transfer, management has to stimulate meetings and contacts between group members. For explicit transfer, management has to stimulate documentation of work by the previous group. For tacit transfer, management has to stimulate contacts between the two groups. For strategic transfer, management has to identify strategic knowledge and knowledge gaps. For expert transfer, management has to create networks where experts can transfer their knowledge. These five mechanisms are not equally suited for IT support. Explicit transfer seems very well suited for IT support as the knowledge from the other group is transferred explicitly as explicit knowledge in words and numbers, and shared in the form of data, scientific formulae, specifications, manuals, and the like. Expert transfer also seems suited for IT support when generic knowledge is transferred from one individual to another person to enable the person to solve new problems with new methods.

6. **Link knowledge to its uses.** One of the mistakes in knowledge management presented by Fahey and Prusak (1998) was disentangling knowledge from its uses. A major manifestation of this error is that knowledge management initiatives become ends in themselves. For example, data warehousing can easily degenerate into technological challenges. The relevance of a data warehouse for decisions and actions gets lost in the turmoil spawned by debates about appropriate data structures.

7. **Treat knowledge as an intellectual asset in the economic school.** If management decides to follow the economic school of knowledge management, then intellectual capital accounting should be part of the knowledge management system. The knowledge management system should

support knowledge markets where knowledge buyers, knowledge sellers, and knowledge brokers can use the system.

8. **Treat knowledge as a mutual resource in the organizational school.** The potential contribution of IT is linked to the combination of intranets and groupware to connect members and pool their knowledge, both explicit and tacit.

9. **Treat knowledge as a strategy in the strategy school.** The potential contribution of IT is manifold once knowledge as a strategy is the impetus behind knowledge management initiatives. One can expect quite an eclectic mix of networks, systems, tools, and knowledge repositories.

10. **Value configuration determines knowledge needs in primary activities.** Knowledge needs can be structured according to primary and secondary activities in the value configuration. Depending on the firm being a value chain, a value shop, or a value network, the knowledge management system must support more efficient production in the value chain, adding value to the knowledge work in the value shop, and more value by use of IT infrastructure in the value network.

11. **Incentive alignment.** The first dimension of information systems design is concerned with software engineering (error-free software, documentation, portability, modularity & architecture, development cost, maintenance cost, speed, and robustness). The second dimension is concerned with technology acceptance (user friendliness, user acceptance, perceived ease-of-use, perceived usefulness, cognitive fit, and task-technology fit). The third dimension that is particularly important to knowledge management systems is concerned with incentive alignment. Incentive alignment includes incentives influencing user behavior and the user's interaction with the system, deterrence of use for personal gain, use consistent with organizational goals, and robustness against information misrepresentation (Ba, Stallaert, & Whinston, 2001).

Expert Systems

Expert systems can be seen as extreme knowledge management systems on a continuum representing the extent to which a system possesses reasoning capabilities. Expert systems are designed to be used by decision makers who do not possess expertise in the problem domain. The human expert's representation of the task domain provides the template for expert system design. The knowledge base and heuristic rules that are used to systematically search a problem space, reflect the decision processes of the expert. A viable expert system is expected to perform this search as effectively and efficiently as a human expert. An expert system incorporates the reasoning capabilities of a domain expert and applies them in arriving at a decision. The system user needs little domain specific knowledge in order for a decision or judgment to be made. The user's main decision is whether to accept the system's result (Dillard & Yuthas, 2001).

Decisions or judgments made by an expert system can be an intermediate component in a larger decision context. For example, an audit expert system may provide a judgment as to the adequacy of loan loss reserves that an auditor would use as input for making an audit opinion decision. The fact that the output supports or provides input for another decision does not make the system any less an expert system, according to Dillard and Yuthas (2001). The distinguishing feature of an expert system lies in its ability to arrive at a nonalgorithmic solution using processes consistent with those of a domain expert.

Curtis and Cobham (2002) define an expert system as a computerized system that performs the role of an expert or carries out a task that requires expertise. In order to understand what an expert system is, then, it is worth paying attention to the role of an expert and the nature of expertise. It is then important to ascertain what types of expert and expertise there are in business, and what benefits will accrue to an organization when it develops an expert system.

For example, a doctor having knowledge of diseases arrives at a diagnosis of an illness by reasoning from information given by the patient's symptoms, and then prescribes medication on the basis of known characteristics of available drugs, together with the patient's history. The lawyer advises the client on the likely outcome of litigation based on the facts of the particular case, an expert understanding of the law, and knowledge of the way the courts work ,and interpret this law in practice. The accountant looks at various characteristics of a company's performance and makes a judgment as to the likely state of health of that company.

All of these tasks involve some of the features for which computers traditionally have been noted—performing text and numeric processing quickly and efficiently—but they also involve one more ability: reasoning. Reasoning is the movement from details of a particular case and knowledge of the general subject area surrounding that case to the derivation of conclusions. Expert systems incorporate this reasoning by applying general rules in an information base to aspects of a particular case under consideration (Curtis & Cobham, 2002).

Expert systems are computer systems designed to make expert-level decisions within complex domains. The business applications of this advanced information technology has been varied and broad reaching, directed toward making operational, management, and strategic decisions.

Audit expert systems are such systems applied in the auditing environment within the public accounting domain. Major public accounting firms have been quite active in developing such systems, and some argue that these tools and technologies will be increasingly important for survival as the firms strive to enhance their competitive position and to reduce their legal and business risk.

Dillard and Yuthas (2001) find that the implementation and use of these powerful systems raise a variety of significant ethical questions. As public accounting firms continue to devote substantial resources to the development of audit expert systems, dealing with the ethical risks and potential consequences to stakeholders takes on increasing significance. For example, when responsible behavior of an auditor is transferred to an audit expert system, then the system is incapable of being held accountable for the consequences of decisions.

Expert systems can be used in all knowledge management processes described earlier. For knowledge retrieval, content management, and information extraction technology represent a useful group of techniques. An example of an expert system for knowledge retrieval is the CORPORUM system. There are three essential aspects of this system (Wang et al., 2001).

First, the CORPORUM system interprets text in the sense that it builds ontologies. Ontologies describe concepts and relationships between them. Ontologies can be seen as the building blocks of knowledge. The system captures ontologies that reflect world concepts as the user of the system sees and expresses them. The ontology produced constitutes a model of a person's interest or concern. Second, the interest model is applied as a knowledge base in order to determine contextual and thematic correspondence with documents available in the system. Finally, the interest model and the text interpretation process drive an information search and extraction process that characterizes hits in terms of both relevance and content. This new information can be stored in a database for future reference.

The CORPORUM software consists of a linguistic component, taking care of tasks such as lexical analysis and analysis at the syntactical level. At the semantic level, the software performs word sense disambiguation by describing the context in which a particular word is being used. This is naturally closely related to knowledge representation issues. The system is able to augment meaning structures with concepts that are invented from the text. The core of the system is also able to extract the information most pertinent to a specific text for summary creation, extract the so-called core concept area from a text, and represent results according to ranking that is based on specified interest for a specific contextual theme set by the user. In addition, the system generates explanations that will allow the user to make an informed guess about which documents to look at and which to ignore. The system can point to exactly those parts of targeted documents that are most pertinent to a specific user's interest (Wang et al., 2001).

Like all software, CORORUM is continuously improved and revised. The Content Management Suport (CMS) system was introduced in 2005 (http://www.cognit.no). It is based on technology that applies linguistics to characterize and index document content. The ontology-based approach focuses on semantics rather than shallow text patterns. The software can be applied for intelligent search and indexing, structure content in portals, annotate documents according to content, summarize and compress information, and extract names and relations from text.

Another software created in 2005, CORPORUM Best Practice, enables organizations to structure their business and work processes and improve value creation. It is a software tool and associated methodology to build organization-wide best practice. In operation, the Web part of the system is a work portal. It embraces an ontology-based set of templates that helps to publish work-related documentation. Company resources like check lists, control plans MS Word templates, images, and e-learning material that is relevant for any process or activity described can be linked in where it is useful and intuitive (http://www.cognit.no).

A final software to be mentioned is CORPORUM Intranet Search & Navigation (SLATEWeb), which is used for indexing and categorizing corporate information sources. Featuring language detection and find-related concept search, this tool lets companies find documents that would otherwise be hard to find. Categories are available to dynamically classify documents into a taxonomy or group structure (http://www.cognit.no).

Analysis and design necessary for building an expert system differ from a traditional data processing or information system. There are three major points of distinction that prevent expert systems development being subsumed under general frameworks of systems development (Curtis & Cobham, 2002):

1. **The subject matter is knowledge and reasoning as contrasted with data and processing.** Knowledge has both form and content that need investigation. Form is connected with the mode of representation chosen, for instance, rules, semantic networks, or logic. Content needs careful attention as once the form is selected, it is still a difficult task to translate the knowledge into the chosen representation form.

2. **Expert systems are expert/expertise orientated, whereas information systems are decision/function/organization directed.** The expert system encapsulates the abilities of an expert or expertise, and the aim is to provide a computerized replica of these facilities.

3. **Obtaining information for expert systems design presents different problems from those in traditional information systems design.** Many expert systems rely, partly at least, on incorporating expertise obtained from an expert. Few rely solely on the representation of textbook or rulebook knowledge. It is difficult, generally, to elicit this knowledge from an expert. In contrast, in designing an information system, the analyst relies heavily on existing documentation as a guide to the amount, type, and content of formal information being passed around the system. In the development of an expert system, the experts are regarded as repositories of knowledge.

Expert systems and traditional information systems have many significant differences. While processing in a traditional information system is primarily algorithmic, processing in an expert system includes symbolic conceptualizations. Input must be complete in a traditional system, while input can be incomplete in an expert system. Search approach in a traditional system is frequently based on algorithms, while search approach in an expert system is frequently based on heuristics. Explanations are usually not provided in a traditional system. Data and information is the focus of a traditional system, while knowledge is the focus of an expert system.

Expert systems can deliver the right information to the right person at the right time if it is known in advance what the right information is, who the right person to use or apply that information would be, and, what would be the right time when that specific information would be needed. Detection of nonroutine and unstructured change in business environment will, however, depend upon sense-making capabilities of knowledge workers for correcting the computational logic of the business and the data it processes (Malhotra, Gosain, & El Sawy, 2005).

References

Alavi, M., & Leidner, D. E. (2001). Knowledge management and knowledge management systems: Conceptual foundations and research issues. *MIS Quarterly, 25*(1), 107-136.

Ba, S., Stallaert, J., & Whinston, A. B. (2001). Research commentary: Introducing a third dimension in information systems design—the case of incentive alignment. *Information Systems Research, 12*(3), 225-239.

Bock, G. W., Zmud, R. W., & Kim, Y. G. (2005). Behavioral intention formation in knowledge sharing: Examining the roles of extrinsic motivators, social-psychological forces, and organizational climate. *MIS Quarterly, 29*(1), 87-111.

Curtis, G., & Cobham, D. (2002). *Business information systems: Analysis, design and practice*. Prentice Hall.

Davenport, T. H., & Prusak, L. (1998). *Working knowledge*. Boston: Harvard Business School Press.

Dillard, J. F., & Yuthas, K. (2001). Responsibility ethic for audit expert systems. *Journal of Business Ethics, 30*, 337-359.

Dixon, N. M. (2000). *Common knowledge*. Boston: Harvard Business School Press.

Fahey, L., & Prusak, L. (1998). The eleven deadliest sins of knowledge management. *California Management Review, 40*(3), 265-276.

Grover, V., & Davenport, T. H. (2001). General perspectives on knowledge management: Fostering a research agenda. *Journal of Management Information Systems, 18*(1), 5-21.

Halvorsen, K., & Nguyen, M. (1999, June 17-19). A successful software knowledge base. In *Proceedings of the Eleventh International Con-*

ference on Software Engineering and Knowledge Engineering. Germany: Kaiserslautern.

Hansen, M. T., Nohria, N., & Tierney, T. (1999, March-April). What's your strategy for managing knowledge? *Harvard Business Review*, 106-116.

Housel, T., & Bell, A. H. (2001). *Measuring and managing knowledge.* Irwin, NY: McGraw-Hill Irwin.

Kettinger, W. J., Teng, J. T. C., & Guha, S. (1997, March). Business process change: A study of methodologies, techniques, and tools. *MIS Quarterly*, 55-79.

Ko, D. G., Kirsch, L. J., & King, W. R. (2005). Antecedents of knowledge transfer from consultants to clients in enterprise system implementations. *MIS Quarterly*, *29*(1), 59-85.

Laudon, K. C., & Laudon, J. P. (2005). *Essentials of management information systems: Managing the digital firm* (6th ed.). Upper Saddle River, NJ: Prentice Hall.

Lin, L., Geng, X., & Whinston, A. B. (2005). A sender-receiver framework for knowledge transfer. *MIS Quarterly*, *29*(2), 197-219.

Malhotra, A., Gosain, S., & El Sawy, O. A. (2005). Absorptive capacity configurations in supply chains: Gearing for partner-enabled market knowledge creation. *MIS Quarterly*, *29*(1), 145-187.

Moffett, S., & McAdam, R. (2003). Contributing and enabling technologies for knowledge management. *International Journal of Information Technology and Management*, *2*(1-2), 31-49.

Nahapiet, J., & Ghoshal, S. (1998). Social capital, intellectual capital, and the organizational advantage. *Academy of Management Review*, *23*(2), 242-266.

Nonaka, I., Toyama, R., & Konno, N. (2000). SECI, ba and leadership: A unified model of dynamic knowledge creation. *Long Range Planning*, *33*(1), 5-34.

Poston, R. S., & Speier, C. (2005). Effective use of knowledge management systems: A process model of content ratings and credibility indicators. *MIS Quarterly*, *29*(2), 221-244.

Ryu, C., Kim, Y. J., Chaudhury, A., & Rao, H. R. (2005). Knowledge acquisition via three learning processes in enterprise information portals: Learning-by-investment, learning-by-doing, and learning-from-others. *MIS Quarterly*, *29*(2), 245-278.

Tanriverdi, H. (2005). Information technology relatedness, knowledge management capability, and performance of multibusiness firms. *MIS Quarterly*, *29*(2), 311-334.

Wang, K., Hjelmervik, O. R., & Bremdal, B. (2001). *Introduction to knowledge management*. Trondheim, Norway: Tapir Academic Press.

Ward, J., & Peppard, J. (2002). *Strategic planning for information systems*. Wiley.

Wasko, M. M., & Faraj, S. (2005). Why should I share? Examining social capital and knowledge contribution in electronic networks of practice. *MIS Quarterly*, *29*(1), 35-57.

Chapter IV

Stages of Knowledge Management Systems

Knowledge management systems refer to a class of information systems applied to manage organizational knowledge. These systems are IT applications to support and enhance the organizational processes of knowledge creation, storage and retrieval, transfer, and application (Alavi & Leidner, 2001).

The knowledge management technology stage model presented in this chapter is a multistage model proposed for organizational evolution over time. Stages of knowledge management technology are a relative concept concerned with IT's ability to process information for knowledge work. The knowledge management technology stage model consists of four stages (Gottschalk, 2005). When applied to law enforcement in the following chapters, the stages are labeled officer-to-technology, officer-to-officer, officer-to-information, and officer-to-application.

Knowledge Technology Stages

Stages-of-growth models have been used widely in both organizational research and information technology management research. According to King and Teo (1997), these models describe a wide variety of phenomena: the organizational life cycle, product life cycle, biological growth, and so forth. These models assume that predictable patterns (conceptualized in terms of stages) exist in the growth of organizations, the sales levels of products, and the growth of living organisms. These stages are (1) sequential in nature, (2) occur as a hierarchical progression that is not easily reversed, and (3) involve a broad range of organizational activities and structures.

Benchmark variables are often used to indicate characteristics in each stage of growth. A one-dimensional continuum is established for each benchmark variable. The measurement of benchmark variables can be carried out using Guttman scales (Frankfort-Nachmias & Nachmias, 2002). Guttman scaling is a cumulative scaling technique based on ordering theory that suggests a linear relationship between the elements of a domain and the items on a test.

In the following main part of this chapter, a four-stage model for the evolution of information technology support for knowledge management is proposed and empirically tested. The purpose of the model is both to understand the current situation in an organization in terms of a specific stage, and to develop strategies for moving to a higher stage in the future. We are concerned with the following question: Do organizations move through various stages of growth in their application of knowledge management technology over time, and is each theoretical stage regarded as an actual stage in an organization?

Stages-of-Growth Models

Various multistage models have been proposed for organizational evolution over time. These models differ in the number of stages. For example, Nolan (1979) introduced a model with six stages for IT maturity in organizations that later was expanded to nine stages. Earl (2000) suggested a stages-of-growth model for evolving the e-business consisting of the following six stages: external communication, internal communication, e-commerce, e-business, e-enterprise, and transformation. Each of these models identifies certain characteristics that typify firms in different stages of growth. Among these multistage models, models with four stages seem to have been proposed and tested most frequently (King & Teo, 1997).

In the area of knowledge management, Housel and Bell (2001) described a knowledge management maturity model. The knowledge management maturity (KMM) model is used to assess the relative maturity of a company's knowledge management efforts. The KMM model defines the following five levels (Housel & Bell 2001, p. 136):

1. **Level one** is the default stage in which there is low commitment to managing anything other than essential, necessary survival-level tasks. At level one, formal training is the main mechanism for learning, and all learning is taken to be reactive. Moreover, level-one organizations fragment knowledge into isolated pockets that are not explicitly documented.

2. **Level two** organizations share only routine and procedural knowledge. Need-to-know is characteristic, and knowledge awareness rises with the realization that knowledge is an important organizational resource that must be managed explicitly. Databases and routine tasks exist, but are not centrally compiled or managed.

3. **Level three** organizations are aware of the need for managing knowledge. Content fit for use in all functions begins to be organized into a knowledge life cycle, and enterprise knowledge-propagation systems are in place. However, general awareness and maintenance are limited.

4. **Level four** is characterized by enterprise knowledge sharing systems. These systems respond proactively to the environment, and the quality, currency, utility, and usage of these systems are improved. Knowledge processes are scaled up across the organization, and organization knowledge boundaries become blurred. Benefits of knowledge sharing and reuse can be explicitly quantified, and training moves into an ad hoc basis as the technology infrastructure for knowledge sharing is increasingly integrated and seamless.

5. **Level five** is where knowledge sharing is institutionalized and organizational boundaries are minimized. Human know-how and content expertise are integrated into a seamless package, and knowledge can be most effectively leveraged. Level-five organizations have the ability to accelerate the knowledge life cycle to achieve business advantage.

According to Kazanjian and Drazin (1989), the concept of stages of growth is widely employed. A number of multistage models have been proposed that assume that predictable patterns exist in the growth of organizations, and that these patterns unfold as discrete time periods best thought of as stages. These models have different distinguishing characteristics. Stages can be driven by the search for new growth opportunities, or as a response to internal crises. Some models suggest that firms progress through stages, while others argue that there may be multiple paths through the stages.

Kazanjian (1988) applied dominant problems to stages of growth. Dominant problems imply that there is a pattern of primary concerns that firms face for each theorized stage. In the area of IT maturity, dominant problems can shift from lack of skills to lack of resources to lack of strategy associated with different stages of growth.

Kazanjian and Drazin (1989) argue that either implicitly or explicitly, stage-of-growth models share a common underlying logic. Organizations undergo transformations in their design characteristics that enable them to face the new tasks or problems that growth elicits. The problems, tasks, or environments may differ from model to model, but almost all suggest that stages emerge in a well-defined sequence, so that the solution of one set of problems or tasks leads to the emergence of a new set of problems or tasks that the organization must address. Growth in areas such as IT maturity can be viewed as a series of evolutions and revolutions precipitated by internal crises related to leadership, control, and coordination. The striking characteristic of this view is that the resolution of each crisis sows the seeds for the next crisis. Another view is to consider stages of growth as responses to the firm's search for new growth opportunities once prior strategies have been exhausted.

Stages-of-growth models may be studied through organizational innovation processes. Technological innovation is considered the primary driver of improvements in many businesses today. Information technology represents a complex organizational technology, that is, technology that, when first introduced, imposes a substantial burden on would-be adopters in terms of the competence needed to use it effectively (Levina & Vaast, 2005). According to Fichman and Kemerer (1997), such technology typically has an abstract and demanding scientific base, it tends to be fragile in the sense that it does not always operate as expected, it is difficult to test in a meaningful way, and it is unpackaged in the sense that adopters cannot treat the technology as a black box.

Embodying such characteristics, organizational learning and innovation diffusion theory can be applied to explain stages-of-growth models. Organizational learning is sometimes placed at the center of innovation diffusion theory through a focus on institutional mechanisms that lower the burden of organizational learning related to IT adoption. Organizations may be viewed, at any given moment, as possessing some bundle of competence related to their current operational and managerial processes. In order to successfully assimilate a new process technology, an organization must somehow reach a state where its bundle of competence encompasses those needed to use the new technology (Fichman & Kemerer, 1997).

Innovations through stages of growth can be understood in terms of technology acceptance over time. Technology acceptance has been studied for several decades in information systems research. Technology acceptance models explain perceived usefulness and usage intentions in terms of social influence and cognitive instrumental processes. For example, Venkatesh and Davis (2000) found that social influence processes (subjective norm, voluntariness, and image) and cognitive instrumental processes (job relevance, output quality, result demonstrability, and perceived ease of use) significantly influenced user acceptance. Similarly, Venkatesh (2000) identified determinants of perceived ease of use, a key driver of technology acceptance, adoption, and usage behavior.

Stages-of-growth models have been criticized for a lack of empirical validity. Benbasat et al. (Benbasat, Dexter, Drury, & Goldstein, 1984) found that most of the benchmark variables for stages used by Nolan (1979) were not confirmed in empirical studies. Based on empirical evidence, Benbasat et al. (1984) wrote the following critique of Nolan's stage hypothesis:

The stage hypothesis on the assimilation of computing technology provides one of the most popular models for describing and managing the growth of administrative information systems. Despite little formal evidence of its reliability or robustness, it has achieved a high level of acceptance among practitioners. We describe and summarize the findings of seven empirical studies conducted during the past six years that tested various hypotheses derived from this model. The accumulation of evidence from these studies casts considerable doubt on the validity of the stage hypothesis as an explanatory structure for the growth of computing in organizations.

For example, Nolan (1979) proposed that steering committees should be constituted in later stages of maturity. However, an empirical study showed that of 114 firms, 64 of which had steering committees, the correlation between IT maturity and steering committees was not significant. In practice, organizations adopt steering committees throughout the development cycle rather than in the later stages.

Another example is charge-back methods. In a survey, approximately half of the firms used charge-back systems and the other half did not. In the Nolan (1979) structure, as firms mature through later stages, they should have adopted charge-back systems. Yet, in the empirical analysis, there were no significant correlations between maturity indicators and charge-back system usage, according to Benbasat et al. (1984). Benchmark variables such as steering committees and charge-back systems have to be carefully selected and tested before they are applied in survey research.

The concept of stages of growth has created a number of skeptics. Some argue that the concept of an organization progressing unidirectionally through a series of predictable stages is overly simplistic. For example, organizations may evolve through periods of convergence and divergence related more to shifts in information technology than to issues of growth for specific IT. According to Kazanjian and Drazin (1989), it can be argued that firms do not necessarily demonstrate any inexorable momentum to progress through a linear sequence of stages, but rather that observed configurations of problems, strategies, structures, and processes will determine a firm's progress.

Kazanjian and Drazin (1989) addressed the need for further data-based research to empirically examine whether organizations in a growth environment shift according to a hypothesized stage of growth model, or whether they follow a more random pattern of change associated with shifts in configurations that do not follow such a progression. Based on a sample of 71 firms, they found support for the stage hypothesis.

To meet the criticism of lacking empirical validity, this research presentation describes the careful development, selection, and testing of a variety of instrument parts to empirically validate a knowledge management technology stage model.

Guttman Scaling for Cumulative Growth

Benchmark variables in stages-of-growth models indicate the theoretical characteristics in each stage of growth. The problem with this approach is that not all indicators of a stage may be present in an organization, making it difficult to place the organization in any specific stage.

Guttman scaling is also known as cumulative scaling or scalogram analysis. Guttman scaling is based on ordering theory, which suggests a linear relationship between the elements of a domain and the items on a test. The purpose of Guttman scaling is to establish a one-dimensional continuum for a concept to measure. We would like a set of items or statements so that a respondent who agrees with any specific question in the list will also agree with all previous questions. This is the ideal for a stage model, or for any progression. By this we mean that it is useful when one progresses from one state to another, so that upon reaching the higher stage, one has retained all the features of the earlier stage (Trochim, 2002).

For example, a cumulative model for knowledge transfer could consist of six stages: awareness, familiarity, attempt to use, utilization, results, and impact. Byers and Byers (1998) developed a Guttman scale for knowledge levels consisting of stages by order of learning difficulty. Trochim (2002) developed the following cumulative six-stage scale for attitudes towards immigration:

1. I believe that this country should allow more immigrants in.
2. I would be comfortable with new immigrants moving into my community.
3. It would be fine with me if new immigrants moved onto my block.
4. I would be comfortable if a new immigrant moved next door to me.
5. I would be comfortable if my child dated a new immigrant.
6. I would permit a child of mine to marry an immigrant.

Guttman (1950) used scalogram analysis successfully during the war in investigating morale and other problems in the United States Army. In scalogram analysis, items are ordered such that, ideally, organizations that answer a given question favorably all have higher ranks than organizations that answer the same question unfavorably. According to Guttman (1950, p. 62), the ranking of organizations provides a general approach to the problem of scaling:

We shall call a set of items of common content a scale if an organization with a higher rank than another organization is just as high or higher on every item than the other organization.

Kline (1998, p. 75) discusses three problems with Guttman scales that may, he claims, render them of little scientific value:

1.   **The underlying measurement model.** The first concerns the fact that items correlate perfectly with the total scale score or the attribute being measured. This is unlikely of any variable in the real world. In general terms, it means the measurement model does not fit what is being measured. This is not dissimilar to the difficulty that in psychological measurement, it is simply assumed that the attribute is quantitative.

2.   **Unidimensionality of the scale.** It has been argued that all valid measuring instruments must be unidimensional. Now the construction of a Guttman scale does not ensure unidimensionality. It would be perfectly possible to take items from different scales, each item of a considerably different level of difficulty, and these would form a Guttman scale. This is because the scaling characteristics of Guttman scales are dependent only on difficulty levels. Thus, Guttman scales may not be unidimensional. The only practical way round the problem is to factor the items first, but then it may prove difficult to make a Guttman scale with so restricted an item pool.

3.   **Ordinal measurement.** The construction of Guttman scales may only permit ordinal measurement. This severely restricts the kinds of statistical analyses that can be used with Guttman scales.

These problems also occurred in the conducted empirical tests of the knowledge management technology stage model in Norway and Australia, as is evident in the book by Gottschalk (2005).

The KMT Stage Model

Stages of knowledge management technology are a relative concept concerned with IT's ability to process information for knowledge work. IT at later stages is more useful to knowledge work than IT at earlier stages. The relative concept implies that IT is more directly involved in knowledge work at higher stages, and that IT is able to support more advanced knowledge work at higher stages. The knowledge management technology (KMT) stage model consists of four stages. The first stage is general IT support for knowledge workers. This includes word processing, spreadsheets, and e-mail. The second stage is information about knowledge sources. An information system stores information about who knows what within the firm and outside the firm. The system does not store what they actually know. A typical example is the company intranet. The third stage is information representing knowledge. The system stores what knowledge workers know in terms of information. A typical example is a database. The fourth and final stage is information processing. An information system uses information to evaluate situations. A typical example here is an expert system.

The contingent approach to firm performance implies that Stage 1 may be right for one firm, while Stage 4 may be right for another firm. Some firms will evolve over time from Stage 1 to higher stages, as indicated in Figure 1. The time axis, ranging from 1990 to 2020 in Figure 1, suggests that it takes time for an individual firm and a whole industry to move through all stages. As an example applied later in this chapter, the law-firm industry is moving slowly in its use of information technology.

Stages of IT support in knowledge management are useful for identifying the current situation, as well as planning for future applications in the firm. Each stage is described in the following:

1. **Tools for end users** are made available to knowledge workers. In the simplest stage, this means a capable networked PC on every desk or in every briefcase with standardized personal productivity tools (word processing, presentation software) so that documents can be exchanged easily throughout a company. More complex and functional desktop infrastructures can also be the basis for the same types of knowledge

Figure 1. The knowledge management technology stage model

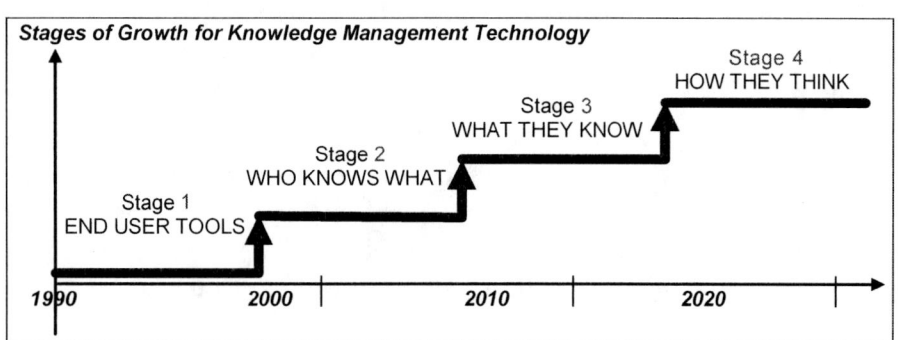

support. Stage 1 is recognized by widespread dissemination and use of end-user tools among knowledge workers in the company. For example, lawyers in a law firm will, in this stage, use word processing, spreadsheets, legal databases, presentation software, and scheduling programs.

Stage 1 can be labeled *end-user-tools* or *people-to-technology,* as information technology provides knowledge workers with tools that improve personal efficiency.

2.   **Information about who knows what** is made available to all people in the firm and to selected outside partners. Search engines should enable work with a thesaurus, since the terminology in which expertise is sought may not always match the terms the expert uses to classify that expertise.

According to Alavi and Leidner (2001), the creation of corporate directories, also referred to as the mapping of internal expertise, is a common application of knowledge management technology. Because much knowledge in an organization remains uncodified, mapping the internal expertise is a potentially useful application of technology to enable easy identification of knowledgeable persons.

Here we find the cartographic school of knowledge management (Earl, 2001), which is concerned with mapping organizational knowledge. It aims to record and disclose who in the organization knows what by building knowledge directories. Often called Yellow Pages, the principal idea is to make sure knowledgeable people in the organization are accessible to others for advice, consultation, or knowledge exchange. Knowledge-oriented directories are not so much repositories of knowl-edge-based information as gateways to knowledge, and the knowledge is as likely to be tacit as explicit.

Information about "who knows what" is sometimes called metadata, representing knowledge about where the knowledge resides. Providing taxonomies or organizational knowledge maps enables individuals to rapidly locate the individual who has the needed knowledge, more rapidly than would be possible without such IT-based support.

One starting approach in Stage 2 is to store curriculum vitae (CV) for each knowledge worker in the firm. Areas of expertise, projects completed, and clients helped may, over time, expand the CV. For example, a lawyer in a law firm works on cases for clients using different information sources that can be registered on yellow pages in terms of an intranet.

At Stage 2, firms apply the personalization strategy in knowledge management. According to Hansen et al. (Hansen, Nohria, & Tierney, 1999), the personalization strategy implies that knowledge is tied to the person who developed it, and is shared mainly through direct person-to-person contact. This strategy focuses on dialogue between individuals; knowledge is transferred mainly in personal e-mail, meetings, and one-on-one conversations.

The creation of a knowledge network is an important part of Stage 2. Unless specialists can communicate easily with each other across platform types, expertise will deteriorate. People have to be brought together both virtually and face-to-face to exchange and build their collective knowledge in each of the specialty areas. The knowledge management effort is focused on bringing the experts together so that important knowledge can be shared and amplified, rather than on mapping expertise or benchmarking, which occurs in Stage 3.

Electronic networks of practice are computer-mediated discussion forums focused on problems of practice that enable individuals to exchange advice and ideas with others based on common interests. Electronic networks have been found to support organizational knowledge flows between geographically dispersed coworkers and distributed research and development efforts. These networks also assist cooperative open-source software development and open congregation on the Internet for individuals interested in a specific practice. Electronic networks make it possible to share information quickly, globally, and with large numbers of individuals (Wasko & Faraj, 2005).

The knowledge network is built on modern communication technology. Advance in portable computers such as palmtops and laptops, in conjunction with wireless network technologies, has engendered mobile computing. In a mobile computing environment, users carrying portable computers are permitted to access the shared computing resources on the network through wireless channels, regardless of their physical locations.

According to Earl (2001), knowledge directories represent more of a belief in personalized knowledge of individuals than the codified knowledge of knowledge bases, and may demonstrate organizational preferences for human, not technology-mediated, communication and exchange. The knowledge philosophy of firms that settle in Stage 2 can be seen as one of people connectivity. Consequently, the principal contribution from IT is to connect people via intranets, and to help them locate knowledge sources and providers using directories accessed by the intranet. Extranets and the Internet may connect knowledge workers to external knowledge sources and providers.

Communication competence is important at Stage 2. Communication competence is the ability to demonstrate skills in the appropriate communication behavior to effectively achieve one's goals. Communication between individuals requires both the decoding and encoding of messages (Ko, Kirsch, & King, 2005). Lin et al. (Lin, Geng, & Whinston, 2005) found that knowledge transfer depends on the completeness or incompleteness of the sender's and the receiver's information sets.

The dramatic reduction in electronic communication costs and ease of computer-to-computer linkages has resulted in opportunities to create new channel structures, fueling interest in interorganizational systems. Interorganizational systems are planned and managed ventures to develop and use IT-based information exchange systems to support collaboration and strategic alliances between otherwise independent actors. These systems allow for the exchange of information between partners for the purpose of coordination, communication, and cooperation (Malhotra, Gosain, & El Sawy, 2005).

Stage 2 can be labeled *who-knows-what* or *people-to-people,* as knowledge workers use information technology to find other knowledge workers.

3. **Information from knowledge workers** is stored and made available to everyone in the firm, and to designated external partners. Data-mining techniques can be applied here to find relevant information and combine information in data warehouses. On a broader basis, search engines are Web browsers and server software that operate with a thesaurus, since the terminology in which expertise is sought may not always match the terms used by the expert to classify that expertise.

    One starting approach in Stage 3 is to store project reports, notes, recommendations, and letters from each knowledge worker in the firm. Over time, this material will grow fast, making it necessary for a librarian or a chief knowledge officer (CKO) to organize it. In a law firm, all client cases will be classified and stored in databases using software such as Lotus Notes.

    An essential contribution that IT can make is the provision of shared databases across tasks, levels, entities, and geographies to all knowledge workers throughout a process (Earl, 2001). For example, Infosys Technologies—a U.S. $1 billion company with over 23,000 employees and globally distributed operations—created a central knowledge portal called KShop. The content of KShop was organized into different content types, for instance, case studies, reusable artifacts, and downloadable software. Every knowledge asset under a content type was associated with one or more nodes (representing areas of discourse) in a knowledge hierarchy or taxonomy (Garud & Kumaraswamy, 2005).

According to Alavi and Leidner (2001), one survey found that 74% of respondents believed that their organization's best knowledge was inaccessible, and 68% thought that mistakes were reproduced several times. Such a perception of failure to apply existing knowledge is an incentive for mapping, codifying, and storing information derived from internal expertise.

However, sifting though the myriad of content available through knowledge management systems can be challenging, and knowledge workers may be overwhelmed when trying to find the content most relevant for completing a new task. To address this problem, system designers often include rating schemes and credibility indicators to improve users' search and evaluation of knowledge management system content (Poston & Speier, 2005).

According to Alavi and Leidner (2001), one of the most common applications is internal benchmarking, with the aim of transferring internal best practices. To be successful, best practices have to be coded, stored, and shared among knowledge workers.

In addition to (1) best practices knowledge within a quality or business process management function, other common applications include (2) knowledge for sales purposes involving products, markets, and customers, (3) lessons learned in projects or product development efforts, (4) knowledge around implementation of information systems, (5) competitive intelligence for strategy and planning functions, and (6) learning histories or records of experience with a new corporate direction or approach (Grover & Davenport, 2001).

In Stage 3, access both to knowledge (expertise, experience, and learning) and to information (intelligence, feedback, and data analyses) is provided by systems and intranets to operatives, staff, and executives. The supply and distribution of knowledge and information are not restricted. Whereas we might say in Stage 1, "give knowledge workers the tools to do the job," we now add, "give knowledge workers the knowledge and information to do the job." According to Earl (2001), this is another way of saying that the philosophy is enhancing the firm's capabilities with knowledge flows.

Although most knowledge repositories serve a single function, Grover and Davenport (2001) found that it is increasingly common for companies to construct an internal portal so that employees can access multiple, different repositories and sources from one screen. It is also possible and increasingly popular for repositories to contain information as well as pointers to experts within the organization on key knowledge topics. Often called Knowledge Yellow Pages, these systems facilitate contact and knowledge transfer between knowledgeable people and those who seek their knowledge. Stored, codified knowledge is combined with lists of individuals who contributed the knowledge and could provide more detail or background on it.

An enterprise information portal is viewed as a knowledge community. Enterprise information portals are of multiple forms, ranging from Internet-based data management tools that bring visibility to previously dormant data so that their users can compare, analyze, and share enterprise information to a knowledge portal that enables its users to obtain specialized knowledge that is related to their specific tasks (Ryu, Kim, Chaudhury, & Rao, 2005).

Individuals' knowledge does not transform easily into organizational knowledge even with the implementation of knowledge repositories. According to Bock et al. (Bock, Zmud, & Kim, 2005), individuals tend to hoard knowledge for various reasons. Empirical studies have shown that the greater the anticipated reciprocal relationships are, the more favorable the attitude toward knowledge sharing will be.

Electronic knowledge repositories are electronic stores of content acquired about all subjects for which the organization has decided to maintain knowledge. Such repositories can comprise multiple knowledge bases, as well as the mechanisms for acquisition, control, and publication of the knowledge. The process of knowledge sharing through electronic knowledge repositories involves people contributing knowledge to populate repositories (e.g., customer and supplier knowledge, industry best practices, and product expertise) and people seeking knowledge from repositories for use (Kankanhalli, Tan, & Wei, 2005).

In Stage 3, firms apply the codification strategy in knowledge management. According to Hansen et al. (1999), the codification strategy centers on information technology: knowledge is carefully codified and stored in knowledge databases, and can be accessed and used by anyone. With a codification strategy, knowledge is extracted from the person who developed it, is made independent from the person, and stored in form of interview guides, work schedules, benchmark data, and so forth, and then searched and retrieved and used by many employees.

According to Grover and Davenport (2001), firms increasingly view attempts to transform raw data into usable knowledge as part of their knowledge management initiatives. These approaches typically involve isolating data in a separate warehouse for easier access, and the use of statistical analysis or data mining and visualization tools. Since their goal is to create data-derived knowledge, they are increasingly addressed as part of knowledge management in Stage 3.

Stage 3 can be labeled *what-they-know* or *people-to-docs,* as information technology provides knowledge workers with access to information that is typically stored in documents. Examples of documents are contracts and agreements, reports, manuals and handbooks, business forms, letters, memos, articles, drawings, blueprints, photographs, e-mail and voice mail messages, video clips, script and visuals from presentations, policy statements, computer printouts, and transcripts from meetings.

Sprague (1995) argues that concepts and ideas contained in documents are far more valuable and important to organizations than facts traditionally organized into data records. A document can be described as a unit of recorded information structured for human consumption. It is recorded and stored, so a speech or conversation for which no transcript is prepared is not a document. A document is a snapshot of some set of information that can incorporate many complex information types, exist in multiple places across a network, depend on other documents for information, change as subordinate documents are updated, and be accessed and modified by many people simultaneously.

4. **Information systems solving knowledge problems** are made available to knowledge workers and solution seekers. Artificial intelligence is applied in these systems. For example, neural networks are statistically oriented tools that excel at using data to classify cases into one category or another. Another example is expert systems that can enable the

knowledge of one or a few experts to be used by a much broader group of workers requiring the knowledge.

According to Alavi and Leidner (2001), an insurance company was faced with the commoditization of its market, and declining profits. The company found that applying the best decision-making expertise via a new underwriting process, supported by a knowledge management system based on best practices, enabled it to move into profitable niche markets and, hence, to increase income.

According to Grover and Davenport (2001), artificial intelligence is applied in rule-based systems, and more commonly, case-based systems are used to capture and provide access to resolutions of customer service problems, legal knowledge, new product development knowledge, and many other types of knowledge.

Biodiversity is a data-intense science, drawing as it does on data from a large number of disciplines in order to build up a coherent picture of the extent and trajectory of life on earth. Bowker (2000) argues that as sets of heterogeneous databases are made to converge, there is a layering of values into the emergent infrastructure. This layering process is relatively irreversible, and it operates simultaneously at a very concrete level (fields in a database) and at a very abstract one (the coding of the relationship between the disciplines and the production of a general ontology).

Knowledge is explicated and formalized during the knowledge codification phase that took place in Stage 3. Codification of tacit knowledge is facilitated by mechanisms that formalize and embed it in documents, software, and systems. However, the higher the tacit elements of the knowledge, the more difficult it is to codify. Codification of complex knowledge frequently relies on information technology. Expert systems, decision support systems, document management systems, search engines, and relational database tools represent some of the technological solutions developed to support this phase of knowledge management. Consequently, advanced codification of knowledge emerges in Stage 4, rather than in Stage 3, because expert systems and other artificial intelligence systems have to be applied to be successful.

Stage 4 can be labeled *how-they-think* or *people-to-systems,* where the system is intended to help solve a knowledge problem. The label how-they-think does not mean that the systems, as such, think. Rather, it means that the thinking of people has been implemented in the systems.

Stage 1 is a *technology-centric* stage, while Stage 2 is a *people-oriented* stage, Stage 3 is a *technology-driven* stage, while Stage 4 is a *process-centric* stage. A people- oriented perspective draws from the work of Nonaka et al. (Nonaka, Toyama, & Konno, 2000). Essential to this perspective of knowledge sharing and knowledge creation is that people create knowledge, and that new knowledge, or the increasing of the extant knowledge base, occurs as a result of human cognitive activities and the effecting of specific knowledge transformations (Wasko & Faraj, 2005). A technology-driven perspective to knowledge management at Stage 3 is often centered on the computerized technique of data mining, and the many mathematical and statistical methods available to transform data into information and then meaningful knowledge (e.g., Poston & Speier, 2005). A process-centric approach tries to combine the essentials of both the people-centric and the technology-centric and technology-driven perspectives in the earlier stages. It emphasizes the dynamic and ongoing nature of the process, where artificial intelligence might help people understand how to proceed in their tasks. Process-centered knowledge generation is concerned with extraction of critical and germane knowledge in a decision-making perspective (Bendoly, 2003).

The stages-of-growth model for knowledge management technology is mainly a sequential and accumulative model. However, in practice, the model can also be applied in a cyclical mode. For example, when a firm reaches 2020 in Figure 1, the firm might return to Stage 3 from Stage 4 to improve information sources and information access at Stage 3 that will improve the performance of systems applied at Stage 4. Therefore, in a short-term perspective, the stages model is sequential, while in a long-term perspective it consists of several cycles.

When companies want to use knowledge in real-time, mission-critical applications, they have to structure the information base for rapid, precise access. A Web search yielding hundreds of documents will not suffice when a customer is waiting on the phone for an answer. Representing and structuring knowledge is a requirement that has long been addressed by artificial intelligence researchers in the form of expert systems and other applications. Now their technologies are being applied within the context of knowledge management. Rule-based systems and case-based systems are used to capture and provide access to customer service problem resolution, legal knowledge, new product development knowledge, and many other types of knowledge. Although it can be difficult and labor-intensive to author a structured knowledge base, the effort can pay off in terms of faster responses to customers, lower cost per knowledge transaction, and lessened requirements for experienced, expert personnel (Grover & Davenport, 2001).

Expert systems are in Stage 4 in the proposed model. Stewart (1997) argues for Stage 2, stating that knowledge grows so fast that any attempt to codify all is ridiculous; but the identities of in-house experts change slowly. Corporate yellow pages should be easy to construct, but it's remarkable how few companies have actually done this. A simple system that connects inquirers to experts saves time, reduces error and guesswork, and prevents the reinvention of countless wheels.

What may be stored in Stage 3, according to Stewart (1997), are lessons learned and competitor intelligence. A key way to improve knowledge management is to bank lessons learned, in effect, prepare checklists of what went right and wrong, together with guidelines for others undertaking similar projects. In the area of competitor intelligence, companies need to organize knowledge about their suppliers, customers, and competitors.

Information technology can be applied at four different levels to support knowledge management in an organization, according to the proposed stages of growth. At the first level, end-user tools are made available to knowledge workers. At the second level, information on who knows what is made available electronically. At the third level, some information representing knowledge is stored and made available electronically. At the fourth level, information systems capable of simulating human thinking are applied in the organization. These four levels are illustrated in Figure 2, where they are combined with knowledge management tasks. The entries in the figure only serve as examples of current systems.

One reason for Stage 3 emerging after Stage 2 is the personalization strategy vs. the codification strategy. The individual barriers are significantly lower with the personalization strategy, because the individual professional maintains the control through the whole knowledge management cycle. According to Disterer (2001), the individual is recognized as an expert and is cared for.

Knowledge management strategies focusing on personalization could be called communication strategies, because the main objective is to foster personal communication between people. Core IT systems with this strategy are yellow pages (directories of experts, who-knows-what systems, people finder database) that show inquirers who they should talk to regarding a given topic or problem. The main disadvantages of personalization strategies are a lack of standards, the high dependence on communication skills, and the will of the

Figure 2. Examples of IS/IT in different knowledge management stages

STAGES TASKS	1 END USER TOOLS people-to-technology	2 WHO KNOWS WHAT people-to-people	3 WHAT THEY KNOW people-to-docs	4 WHAT THEY THINK people-to-systems
Distribute knowledge	Word Processing Desktop Publishing Web Publishing Electronic Calendars Presentations	Word Processing Desktop Publishing Web Publishing Electronic Calendars Presentations	Word Processing Desktop Publishing Web Publishing Electronic Calendars Presentations	Word Processing Desktop Publishing Web Publishing Electronic Calendars Presentations
Share knowledge		Groupware Intranets Networks E-mail	Groupware Intranets Networks E-mail	Groupware Intranets Networks E-mail
Capture knowledge			Databases Data Warehouses	Databases Data Warehouses
Apply knowledge				Expert Systems Neural Networks Intelligent Agents

professionals. Such disadvantages make firms want to advance to Stage 3. In Stage 3, independence, in time, among knowledge suppliers and knowledge users is achieved (Disterer, 2002).

When we look for available computer software for the different stages, we find a variety of offers from software vendors. At Stage 1, we find Microsoft software such as Word, Outlook, Excel, and Powerpoint. At Stage 2, we find knowledge software such as Knowledger from Knowledge Associates (http://www.knowledgeassociates.com). The Knowledger 4.0 helps companies collect and categorize internal and external information. It allows individuals to capture information, together with its context, into a knowledge repository.

At Stage 3, we find Novo Knowledge Base Enterprise (http://www.novosolutions.com), Confluence the Enterprise Wiki (http://www.atlassian.com), and Enterprise Edition X1 Technologies (http://www.x1.com). While Novo's KnowledgeBase provides Web support and documentation solutions, Atlassian's JIRA is tracking and managing the issues and bugs that emerge during a project.

Finally, at Stage 4, we find DecisionScript by Vanguard Software Corporation (http://www.vanguardsw.com) and CORVID Knowledge Automation Expert System Software by Xsys (http://www.exsys.com). Vanguard provides decision-support system software ranging from desktop tools for managing decision-making to server-based systems that help the entire organization work smarter. Vanguard's desktop software, DecisionPro, is designed for managers, consultants, and analysts who make business decisions based on uncertain estimates and imperfect information. Exsys argues that their software and services enable businesses, government, and organizations to distribute a company's most valuable asset-expert knowledge-to the people who need it, through powerful interactive Web-enabled systems.

Benchmark variables have been developed by Gottschalk (2005) for the stages-of-growth model. Benchmark variables indicate the theoretical characteristics in each stage of growth. Examples of benchmark variables include trigger of IT, management participation, critical success factor, and performance indicator.

References

Alavi, M., & Leidner, D. E. (2001). Knowledge management and knowledge management systems: Conceptual foundations and research issues. *MIS Quarterly*, *25*(1), 107-136.

Benbasat, I., Dexter, A. S., Drury, D. H., & Goldstein, R. C. (1984). A critique of the stage hypothesis: Theory and empirical evidence. *Communications of the ACM*, *27*(5), 476-485.

Bendoly, E. (2003). Theory and support for process frameworks of knowledge discovery and data mining from ERP systems. *Information & Management*, *40*, 639-647.

Bock, G. W., Zmud, R. W., & Kim, Y. G. (2005). Behavioral intention formation in knowledge sharing: Examining the roles of extrinsic motivators, social-psychological forces, and organizational climate. *MIS Quarterly*, *29*(1), 87-111.

Bowker, G. C. (2000). Biodiversity datadiversity. *Social Studies of Science*, *30*(5), 643-683.

Byers, C., & Byers, W. A. (1998, June). Sliding scale: A technique to optimize the assessment of knowledge level through ordering theory. *Annual Conference of the International Personnel Management Association Assessment Council*, Chicago. Retrieved from http://www.ipmaac.org/conf98/byers.pdf

Disterer, G. (2001). Individual and social barriers to knowledge transfer. In *Proceedings of the 34th Hawaii International Conference on Systems Sciences (HICSS-34)*. IEEE.

Disterer, G. (2002). *Veränderungen der Rechtsberufe durch neue Technologien. Beispiel: Wissensmanagement bei Anwälten.* Arbeidspapier 68/2002, Fachbereich Wirtschaft, Fachhochschule Hannover, Germany.

Earl, M. J. (2000). Evolving the e-business. *Business Strategy Review, 11*(2), 33-38.

Earl, M. J. (2001). Knowledge management strategies: Toward a taxonomy. *Journal of Management Information Systems, 18*(1), 215-233.

Fichman, R. G., & Kemerer, C. F. (1997). The assimilation of software process innovations: An organizational learning perspective. *Management Science, 43*(10), 1345-1363.

Frankfort-Nachmias, C., & Nachmias, D. (2002). *Research methods in the social sciences* (5th ed.). Arnold.

Garud, R., & Kumaraswamy, A. (2005). Vicious and virtuous circles in the management of knowledge: The case of Infosys Technologies. *MIS Quarterly, 29*(1), 9-33.

Gottschalk, P. (2005). *Strategic knowledge management technology.* Hershey, PA: Idea Group Publishing.

Grover, V., & Davenport, T. H. (2001). General perspectives on knowledge management: Fostering a research agenda. *Journal of Management Information Systems, 18*(1), 5-21.

Guttman, L. (1950). The basis for scalogram analysis. In S. A. Stouffer, L. Guttman, E. A. Suchman, P. F. Lazardsfeld, S. A. Star, & J. A. Clausen (Eds.), *Measurement and prediction, studies in social psychology in World War II, IV*, (pp. 60-90). Princeton University Press.

Hansen, M. T., Nohria, N., & Tierney, T. (1999, March-April). What's your strategy for managing knowledge? *Harvard Business Review*, 106-116.

Housel, T., & Bell, A. H. (2001). *Measuring and managing knowledge.* New York: McGraw-Hill Irwin.

Kankanhalli, A., Tan, B. C. Y., & Wei, K. K. (2005). Contributing knowledge to electronic knowledge repositories: An empirical investigation. *MIS Quarterly, 29*(1), 113-143.

Kazanjian, R. K. (1988). Relation of dominant problems to stages of growth in technology-based new ventures. *Academy of Management Journal, 31*(2), 257-279.

Kazanjian, R. K., & Drazin, R. (1989). An empirical test of a stage of growth progression model. *Management Science, 35*(12), 1489-1503.

King, W. R., & Teo, T. S. H. (1997). Integration between business planning and information systems planning: Validating a stage hypothesis. *Decision Sciences, 28*(2), 279-307.

Kline, P. (1998). *The new psychometrics: Science, psychology and measurement*. Routledge.

Ko, D. G., Kirsch, L. J., & King, W. R. (2005). Antecedents of knowledge transfer from consultants to clients in enterprise system implementations. *MIS Quarterly, 29*(1), 59-85.

Levina, N., & Vaast, E. (2005). The emergence of boundary spanning competence in practice: Implications for implementation and use of information systems. *MIS Quarterly, 29*(2), 335-363.

Lin, L., Geng, X., & Whinston, A. B. (2005). A sender-receiver framework for knowledge transfer. *MIS Quarterly, 29*(2), 197-219.

Malhotra, A., Gosain, S., & El Sawy, O. A. (2005). Absorptive capacity configurations in supply chains: Gearing for partner-enabled market knowledge creation. *MIS Quarterly, 29*(1), 145-187.

Nolan, R. L. (1979, March-April). Managing the crises in data processing. *Harvard Business Review*, 115-126.

Nonaka, I., Toyama, R., & Konno, N. (2000). SECI, ba and leadership: A unified model of dynamic knowledge creation. *Long Range Planning, 33*(1), 5-34

Poston, R. S., & Speier, C. (2005). Effective use of knowledge management systems: A process model of content ratings and credibility indicators. *MIS Quarterly, 29*(2), 221-244.

Ryu, C., Kim, Y. J., Chaudhury, A., & Rao, H. R. (2005). Knowledge acquisition via three learning processes in enterprise information portals: Learning-by-investment, learning-by-doing, and learning-from-others. *MIS Quarterly, 29*(2), 245-278.

Sprague, R. H. (1995, March). Electronic document management: Challenges and opportunities for information systems managers. *MIS Quarterly*, 29-49.

Stewart, T. A. (1997). *Intellectual capital: The new wealth of organizations.* Nicholas Brealy Publishing.

Trochim (2002). *Guttman scaling.* Retrieved from http://trochim. human.cornell.edu/kb/scalgutt.htm

Venkatesh, V. (2000). Determinants of perceived ease of use: Integrating control, intrinsic motivation, and emotion into the technology acceptance model. *Information Systems Research, 11*(4), 342-365.

Venkatesh, V., & Davis, F. D. (2000). A theoretical extension of the technology acceptance model: Four longitudinal field studies. *Management Science, 46*(2), 186-204.

Wasko, M. M., & Faraj, S. (2005). Why should I share? Examining social capital and knowledge contribution in electronic networks of practice. *MIS Quarterly, 29*(1), 35-57.

Zack, M. H. (1999). Developing a knowledge strategy. *California Management Review, 41*(3), 125-145.

Chapter V

Officer-to-Technology Systems

Knowledge management, as a field of study, is concerned with simplifying and improving the process of sharing, distributing, creating, capturing, and understanding knowledge. Hence, knowledge management has direct relevance to policing. So much so that Europol has a Knowledge Management Centre (KMC) at The Hague in The Netherlands. Europol regularly updates its databases at KMC to ensure it keeps abreast of new developments in technology, science, or other specialized fields in order to provide optimal law enforcement.

It is argued that knowledge is the most important resource in police investigations, and several police researchers make the case that successful investigation depends on knowledge availability (e.g., Chen, Schroeder, Hauck, Ridgeway, Atabakhsh, Gupta, Boarman, Rasmussen, & Clements, 2002). Furthermore, Chen et al. (2002) also point out that knowledge management in the knowledge-intensive and time-critical work of police investigations presents a real challenge to investigation managers.

Part of the reason for this challenge that knowledge management presents to police investigations has to do with the level of IT support required in organizations as knowledge management becomes more sophisticated. In this regard, Figure 1 depicts the KMT stage model that conceptualizes, on a continuum, the stages involved in the growth of knowledge management systems, and their relationship to the level of information technology support required.

Figure 1. Officer-to-technology systems at Stage 1 of the knowledge management technology stage model

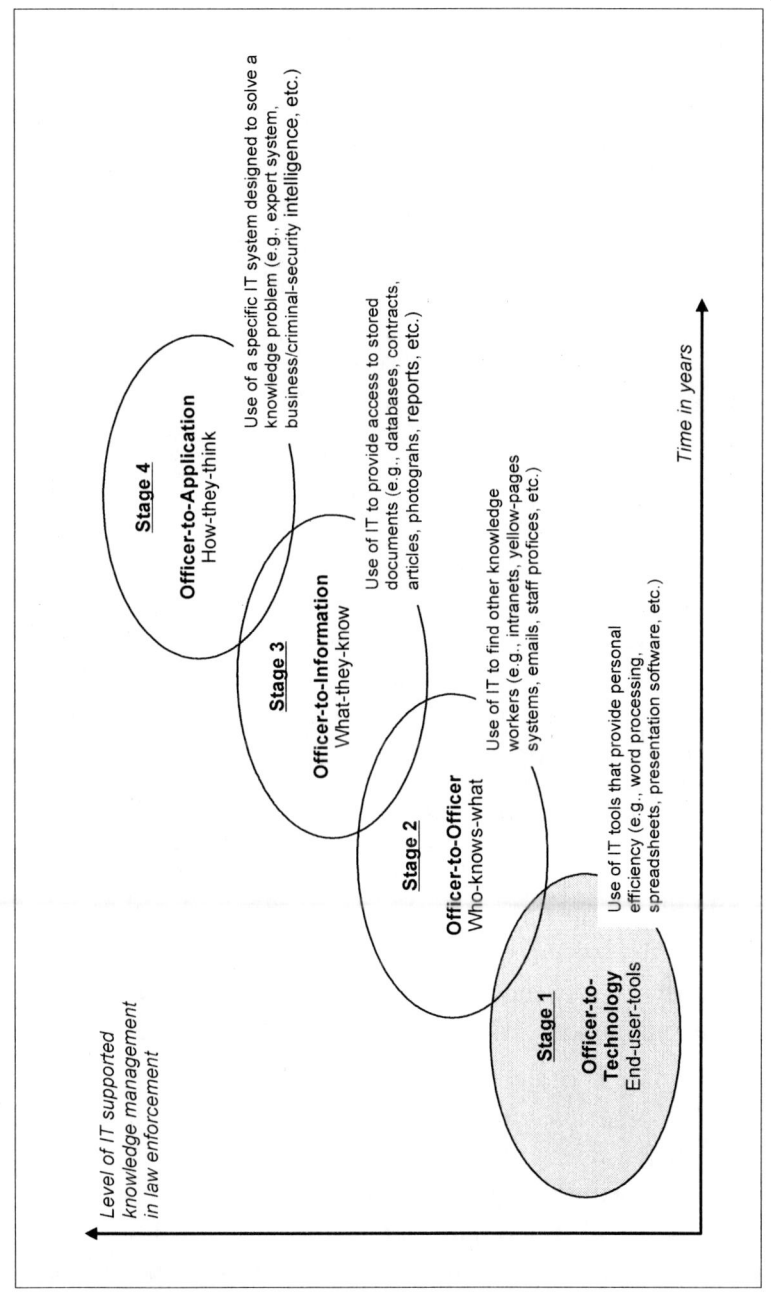

Related to the new changes in computer technology is the transformation that has occurred in report writing and record keeping. Every police activity or crime incident demands a report on some kind of form. The majority of police patrol reports written before 1975 were handwritten.

Today, officers can write reports on small notebook computers located in the front seat of the patrol unit; discs are handed in at the end of the shift for hard-copy needs. Cursor keys and spell-check functions in these report programs are useful timesaving features (Thibault, Lynch, & McBride, 1998).

An example of an officer-to-technology system is the Major Incident Policy Document in the UK (Home Office, 2005a). This document is maintained whenever a Major Incident Room using the HOLMES system is in operation. Decisions that should be recorded are those that affect the practical or administrative features of the enquiry, and each entry has clearly to show the reasoning for the decision. When the HOLMES system is used, the senior investigating officer (SIO) directs which policy decisions are recorded on the system.

The basic information entered into HOLMES is location of incident, data and time of incident, victim(s), senior investigating officer, and date enquiry commenced. During the enquiry, which has been run on the HOLMES system, a closing report is prepared and registered as another document linked to a category of Closing Report. The report will contain the following information: introduction, scene, the victim, and miscellaneous.

At Stage 1, we find mobile technology. Knowledge work, like many other types of work, is influenced by development of an increasingly mobile workforce. Due to changes in work processes and structures as well as the adoption of information and communication technology, workplaces become increasingly mobile. Here we find mobile devices, which are devices for information and communication that have been developed for mobile use. Thus, the category of mobile devices encompasses a wide spectrum of appliances.

Although the laptop is often included in the definition of mobile devices, Derballa and Pousttchi (2006) have reservations about including it here without precincts, due to its special characteristics: It can be moved easily, but it is usually not used during that process. They argue that mobile devices are characterized by voice functionality, capability to send and receive short messages, Internet-enabled, and capability of executing applications. Mobile phones, smartphones, and personal digital assistants (PDA) are typical examples of mobile devices.

Examples of Policing Systems

Four examples of information technology in police work will be presented in the following. These systems have functionality that typically covers more than one stage in the stages of knowledge management technology model. Therefore, these examples of policing systems suggest that the stages are overlapping. However, as we shall see at the functional and user level, stage perspectives might determine system perceptions.

Our first example is COPLINK, described by Chen et al. (2002; Chen, Zheng, Atabakhsh, Wyzga, & Schroeder, 2003), the second is geocomputation, described by Ashby and Longley (2005), the third is SPIKE, described by *Computer Weekly* (2002), and the fourth and final example is closed-circuit television, described by Surette (2005).

COPLINK Connect is an application for information and knowledge sharing in law enforcement. The system uses a three-tiered architecture. The user accesses the system through a Web browser. The middle tier connects the user interface and the backend databases, and implements the work logic.

COPLINK Detect is targeted for detectives and crime analysts. The system shares the same incident record information as the Connect module, and utilizes the database indexes it generates. However, the Detect system has a completely redesigned user interface, and employs a new set of intelligence analysis tools to meet its users' needs.

Much of crime analysis is concerned with creating associations or linkages among various aspects of a crime. COPLINK Detect uses a technique called concept space to automatically identify such associations from existing crime data. In general, a concept space is a network of terms and weighted associations within an underlying information space. COPLINK Detect uses statistical techniques such as co-occurrence analysis and clustering functions to weight relationships between all possible pairs of concepts.

In COPLINK Detect, detailed criminal case reports are the underlying information space, and concepts are meaningful terms occurring in each case. These case reports contain both structured (for example, database fields for incidents containing the case number, names of people involved, address, and date) and unstructured data (narratives written by officers commenting on an incident, for example, witness A said he saw suspect A run away in a white truck).

Several field user studies have been conducted to evaluate the COPLINK system. For example, a group of 52 law enforcement personnel from the Tucson Police Department, representing a number of different job classifications and backgrounds, were recruited to participate in a study to evaluate COPLINK Connect. Both interview-data and survey-data analyses support a conclusion that use of the application provided performance superior to using the legacy police records management system. In addition to the statistical data, these findings were supported by qualitative data collected from participant interviews (Chen et al., 2003).

The other application to be presented here is concerned with geocomputation for geodemographics. Geodemographic profiles of the characteristics of individuals and small areas potentially offer significant breakthroughs in clarifying local policing needs in the same way they have become an integral part of many commercial and marketing ventures. Geodemographic systems were one of the first emergent application areas of what is now known as geocomputation.

Ashby and Longley (2005) conducted a case study of the Devon and Cornwall Constabulary. They found that geodemographic analyses of local policing environments, crime profiles, and police performance provided a significantly increased level of community intelligence for police use. This was further enhanced by the use of penetration ranking reports, where neighborhood types were ranked by standardized crime rates, and cumulative percentage of the crime was compared with the corresponding population at risk.

SPIKE (Surrey Police Information and Knowledge Environment) is an information management system. Surrey Police recognized that it needed to transform itself into a virtual organization if it wanted to continue to deliver its unique community-based policing service under the pressure to become more efficient. Only a drastic improvement in productivity and reduced costs would allow their style of policing to survive. The solution was SPIKE, which enables real-time knowledge sharing, and has become a catalyst for a quantum change in the organization's structure and the method by which it delivers its services (*ComputerWeekly*, 2002).

To be a truly useful utility, Surrey Police had to decide what information had to go into it in the first place. Conceptual work was done to develop an information architecture. Staff had to be able to create and access information using a consistent method and interface. Moreover, the criteria for access-ensuring that only those personnel with a right to know can access what it is they are authorized to know, and no more-had to be both preset and nonintrusive. All the issues of security levels and clearance were worked out up front.

In the end, the system had to prove itself on the street. Like most people with real jobs to do, police officers tend to regard a heavy burden of administrative paperwork as an unnecessary evil. Since the information utility is only as valuable as the information it contains, convincing officers that taking the time to input that information in the first place can be a challenge. Only when they experience the fruits of that input, by way of receiving the output they need to ease and speed up their real jobs, will it be accepted. Key to the value to be gotten out of SPIKE is making it possible for officers to have mobile information and access. Increasingly, information is most useful when it is delivered on the beat (*ComputerWeekly*, 2002).

A final interesting example of information technology in police work is closed-circuit television (CCTV). The second generation of CCTV is called the thinking eye, since the main difference between first and second generation surveillance is the change from a dumb camera that needs a human eye to evaluate its images to a computer-linked camera system that evaluates its own video images.

Stages of Policing Technology

Information technology to support knowledge work of police investigators is improving. According to Chen et al. (2002), the problem is not necessarily that the information has not been captured: any officer who fills out up to seven forms per incident can attest to that. The problem is one of access. Typically, law-enforcement agencies have captured data only on paper, or have fed it into a database or crime information system. If the agency involved has more than one database (which are possibly incompatible), information retrieval can be difficult or time consuming.

The ambition level using knowledge management systems can be defined in terms of stages of knowledge management technology, as illustrated in Figure 1.

Police officers often need to document the manner in which they have drawn a conclusion. This document is used in legal proceedings to justify subsequent actions. According to Chen et al. (2002), an officer may have to fill out up to seven forms per incident. This is a typical example of technology use at Stage 1.

According to Chen et al. (2002), database technology plays an important role in the management of information for a police department. The use of relational database systems for crime-specific cases such as gang-related incidents, and serious crimes such as homicide, aggravated assault, and sexual crimes, has been proven highly effective. These systems are typical examples of information technology at Stage 3.

An example of such a police system at Stage 3 is COPLINK, which is used by the Tucson Police Department (Chen et al., 2003). The records management part of the system contains approximately 1.5 million incident records sets. The criminal information computer in the system tracks approximately 1,200 individuals the department considers responsible for a majority of major crimes.

According to Chen et al. (2002), we also find examples of information technology at Stage 4 in police investigation work. Use of expert systems includes an expert system for police investigators of economic crimes, and an artificial intelligence crime analysis and management system (AICAMS). These systems attempt to aid in information retrieval by drawing upon human heuristics, or rules and procedures, to investigate tasks. The AICAMS project is a collaboration between the Chinese University of Hong Kong and the Hong Kong Police Force.

Another interesting example of information technology in police investigations is geodemographics. According to Ashby and Longley (2005), the field of geodemographics is one of the most fertile application areas of geocomputation systems. Geodemographic profiles of the characteristics of individuals and small areas are becoming central to efficient and effective deployment of resources by public services. Geocomputation systems are an IT application that belongs to both Stage 1 as a tool and Stage 3 as an information source.

SPIKE is a knowledge management system at Stage 3. The system enables real-time knowledge sharing, and has become a catalyst for a quantum change in the organization's structure and the method by which it delivers its services (*ComputerWeekly*, 2002).

The first generation systems of CCTV are found at Stage 1, while second generation systems belong to Stage 2 of the stages-of-growth model for knowledge management technology. Second generation systems reduce the human factor in surveillance, and address some of the basic concerns associated with first generation surveillance systems such as swamping, boredom, voyeurism, and profiling (Surette, 2005).

Police Officers' Performance and Policing Systems

Holgersson (2005) wrote his doctoral dissertation on police performance in Sweden. His research indicates that there is a large variation in performance between different police officers. This becomes clear when an analysis is made of, for example, the number of issued reports, the way police officers treat people, and to what extent police officers work in a problem-oriented manner. It is not unusual that a small group of police officers is responsible for a large part of the production.

Holgersson (2005) found that the degree of experience has a large impact on the performance of police officers, among others, because of the effect it has on police officers' motivation to take their own initiatives. There was a significant correlation between the number of years of service and the production. Years of experience influence police officers in such a way that more years of service result in a decrease in the number of own interventions, not an increase.

Considering the number of people working with IT-related issues within the police organization, as well as the amount of investments in the development of IT systems through purchases, education, support and maintenance, it can be concluded that IT systems are seen as an important key to success by decision makers at high levels. But how important are IT systems really for the police officers? Are there more important factors that influence the performance of police officers?

Holgersson (2005) was interested in examining the factors that make the performance of different police officers vary to such a great extent, and which role IT systems play in this. In a large number of interviews that were carried out throughout Sweden, police officers pointed to factors that they experience being negative influences on their work performance. Based on these interviews, a list of factors was compiled and grouped into the following nine categories:

1.   Discontent of the present management, the way the organization is run and work practice follow-ups

2.   Legislation is perceived as unclear/insufficient in relation to the tasks of the police

3.   Discontent with the way in which the legal system functions

4.   Discontent with reorganizations

5.   Insufficient feedback

6.   Insufficient education program

7.   Insufficient possibilities for development

8.   Ineffective debriefing/IT systems that are difficult to use

9.   Negative impact of colleagues

The profession of police officer is surrounded by many actors who have different demands on the tasks that are to be executed by police officers. Different norms and standards within the work practice are often in conflict with each other, usually caused by varying apprehensions of different tasks. Formal standards, such as legislation and regulation, form one type of standard. Another type consists of presentation standards that regulate how the work practice should be presented to the society. The presented reality can then develop into standards being effective within the police work practice. The third type of standard that Holgersson (2005) found contains those that arise within the police collective. These often have a great impact on the way in which tasks are performed.

The basis, here consisting of the persons that a police officer meets, influences, to a great extent, the behavior of the police officer. Police officers often divide clients into different categories, which affect the way in which these persons are treated.

An insufficient feedback within the police increases the need for external judgments. Clients often articulate judgments about the work practice and, in particular, about its products, and that these clients form an important category of external judges. Because of reorganizations, there is a decreased possibility to establish a continuous contact with the public, which affects the possibility to receive feedback. Media (newspaper, radio, TV, etc.) form another type of external judges that can express judgments about a work practice. Employees often articulate frustration about the information that is given by media.

It is often argued that police work is a craft, and that it relies heavily upon experience and intuition. If knowledge shall have a function in reality, it must become a part of the abilities of the producer, and not only exist in external descriptions. Certain types of knowledge are difficult to obtain by written or other types of documented presentation. The elementary education of police officers has developed into a more theoretical direction, and an insufficient further education affects the abilities of the police officers in a negative way. Usually there is no organized possibility to pass along further knowledge that has been acquired over time.

The abilities to produce in a work practice are related to the aids (instruments) that are being used. Holgersson (2005) found that IT systems play an important role in different contexts of the work practice, but that the possibilities that modern information technology provides are not being exploited to the fullest.

In his research, Holgersson (2005) identified two factors for the performance of police officers: professional knowledge and motivation. In some cases, a certain measure is taken because the police officer lacks the required knowledge. Sometimes a police officer lacks both knowledge and motivation to be able to perform a measure.

Holgersson (2005) identified several factors in the police work practice that have a negative effect on the possibilities to introduce work practice-adapted IT systems. As mentioned, there are fundamental circumstances that have a negative impact on the performance of the staff. Some of these circumstances can also affect the possibility to develop the work practice in the way that was originally planned, among others in the development and application of information systems. He exemplified six fundamental factors within the police work practice that were found to have affected the prospect to exploit the possibilities of information technologies to the fullest:

- IT systems are designed to support a bureaucratic control system, rather than the police work practice
- Legal obstacles
- Territory guarding
- Striving for an adaptation on the surface
- Many activities in the work practice are knowledge intensive
- Standard to not express deviating opinions

As a consequence of territory guarding between different value areas and between operational organization structures, the expressed needs of police activities are not considered high priority. Territory guarding between different initiatives for organization development in combination with legal obstacles is also decreasing the possibility to develop work practice-adapted IT systems. Within the police, it is considered important that the organization is perceived as professional. As a result of this, there has been a focus on adaptations on the surface. Instead of implementing IT systems, Holgersson (2005) argues that development work has often resulted in visions on paper. Because of the factors listed here, there has been a weak, driving force to carry out changes that can meet the needs of policemen.

There are two perspectives in the work practice, knowledge and motivation, that are important to decision makers and IT designers to successfully plan and develop information systems for policing. It is crucial that those who are responsible for and participate in the development of IT systems, which are to be implemented for knowledge-intensive police activities, have a thorough understanding of the work practice that IT systems are supposed to support.

According to the sociotechnical tradition, system development should not only be focused on the technology, but also take into account organizational and human needs. It is important that systems development affects the work practice in such a way that they will contribute to the development of a more efficient and effective work practice. Information system and work practice must be looked at together.

A relevant notion here is actability, which addresses the usefulness of the systems within the work practice, and how they can contribute to reaching the goals of the work practice. Usefulness of systems can be measured in terms of both performance and outcome. In terms of performance, a scale applied by Ang and Slaughter (2001) is interesting, where one would expect to find an increase in the following statements if systems are actable: The overall performance effectiveness of my work is high, the quality of work completed by me is high, the quantity of work completed by me is high, I fulfill my responsibilities, and I meet quality standards in my work.

Decisions made by the police are often based on information about IT systems. Holgersson's (2005) research showed that important work practice knowledge is filtered out by IT systems. IT people usually have a great influence on the development of IT systems, which means that there often is much focus on technical issues. The technical demands, rather than the core activity, form the central issues. IT projects often address the legal demands too late in the development process, at the same time as some employees working with legal matters interpret the legislation in a too limited manner. As a result of this, it has not been possible to fully take advantage of the information technology in the police organization.

Those who appoint user representatives often have an insufficient insight into the work practice. This means that there is a risk that certain aspects of the work practice will not be looked into. Field tests are often being performed at a too late stage, causing new technology not to be as useful for the work practice as it could have been.

From action research and interviews, it became clear to Holgersson (2005) that conflicts easily arise between employees that have a "floor" perspective and those that have a "theoretical" perspective. Employees that have a floor perspective must dare to get into a conflict if they want user needs from the regular practice to become established. Employees experience that having a deviating opinion or speaking freely leads to a disadvantageous position in appointments for vacant positions. Therefore, work practice representatives will not be eager to put energy in trying to influence the outcome of development work. Instead, it will be more appealing to show a positive attitude towards expressed proposals for changes. As a consequence, there is a risk that certain questions and needs are discussed insufficiently.

There are other fundamental factors within the police organization that influence the development of IT systems into work practice-adapted support for the police officer. An example of such a factor is that the management within the organization does not take into account the freedom that comes with being a police officer. The situation in police organizations is often opposite to those in other bureaucratic organizations. Police officers in lower positions have a larger degree of freedom than their superiors. Holgersson (2005) believes that this is something that has not been taken into account when the forms of management in Swedish police were defined. The forms of management are based on control, where information from the IT systems plays a central role.

According to Holgersson (2005), the conditions described previously lead to a situation where IT systems contribute to a contraproductive work practice, as employees spend time accounting for certain conditions that do not exist in the organization. The quality of the information in the IT systems is, therefore, low. Since different decisions are often based on information in IT systems, a vicious cycle might arise.

Policing Technologies

A way of viewing the relationship between the police and technology is to review the progress made with respect to various existing types of technology. If the technology available to the police is clustered into ideal types, five types of technology with salient features are currently in use (Manning, 2003): mobility technology, training technology, transformative technology, analytic technology, and communicative technology. The presentation, in the following, of these five types of technology is based on Manning (2003):

- **Mobility technology.** The consistent leader in expenditure and maintenance costs for technology is means of mobility. These technologies increase rapid and flexible patrol. The focus is on the capacity to allocate officers to areas and poise them to respond. The role of material technology in this connection has changed little since the 1930s, except for increases in the speed, number, and types of available vehicles. This cluster of technological advances grew in popularity with the recent emphases on satisfying citizen demand, presence, and availability. As a result, the car and driver are the core material technology of modern policing: a mobile office, an insulated compartment, a retreat, and a work setting, a place in which patrol officers may spend from 8 to 12 hours, a focus of conditions of work and union contracts. The costs of random uniformed patrol are the fundamental and abiding costs of modern policing.

- **Training technology.** A second area of technology is training. These are systematic means to modify people, their attitudes and behavior (officers as well as the public). They vary but tend to be brief, and combine in-class lecture learning with field training by a field-training officer. Little is known systematically about the content of police training curricula, but the core remains physical and symbolic (shaming, harassing, conditioning, rapid response to orders) and to a lesser degree, academic learning about the law, diversity, and cultures, interpersonal relationships, and problem solving. Training modalities also include educating officers in crowd control procedures, hostage and antiterrorist activity, and training in noncoercive persuasive techniques such as mediation and hostage negotiation. Field training tends to be highly variable, and a function of skills and interests of senior and respected officers, and produces highly variable skills in young officers.

Transformative technology. A third area of technology consists of transformative devices to extend the human senses and present technical evidence in scientific form. This area of technology is one that has seen great advances in recent years as a result of general scientific progress. Most of the advances are processes for refining, enhancing, and reviewing criminal evidence. Police cars are often equipped with video cameras, allowing police to capture, in video and audio, their interactions with suspects. Forensic scientists, once restricted to fingerprint evidence and blood typing, are now able to identify individuals by their DNA, or place them at the scenes of crimes using a variety of trace evidence (e.g., hair, fiber). The FBI, as well as some states, is also creating a DNA bank of known felons convicted of certain crimes. These have enormous potential to extend police power, as well as to augment civil liberties of the accused and wrongly convicted.

The Boston Police Department has computerized its mug-shot database. Police are able to compare fingerprints via computer, taking mere minutes vs. the visual comparison of fingerprint cards that in the past could take weeks if not months. While the percentage of municipal police departments with their own automated fingerprint identification system (AFIS) is still small, the FBI is sponsoring the use of computerized fingerprint files for online checks of criminal records. Technological advances in this area are embraced by police as being consistent with the professional crime-fighter image, even while they continue to complain about failures in technological support, and often lack the skills to properly use computer software.

- **Analytic technology.** A fourth area of technological innovation in policing is the introduction of analytic devices: those designed to aggregate, model, and simulate police data to facilitate crime analysis, crime mapping, and activities in aid of crime prevention. Police have made advances in the last 30 years in their ability to acquire, store, and aggregate data. Some of these innovations are quite remarkable, such as the purchase by Charlotte-Mecklenburg police of 1,300 laptops (defined as personal equipment for use at home and work), and the handheld computers used by motorcycle officers in San Diego. Seventy-nine percent of municipal police forces staffed by 100 or more officers in 1996 used mobile computers or terminals in the field. The access to such data in the field has been shown in a few studies to increase productivity.

In 1998, the Charlotte-Mecklenburg Police Department began work on a custom-built offense reporting and records-management system. The system was part of a strategic technology plan called knowledge-based community-oriented policing systems. Later, the FBI's National Incident-Based Reporting System (NIBRS) was integrated into the management system (Sorban, 2005).

Collection, storage, and retrieval of data by police, however, do not mean that the data are used for analytic purposes. Perhaps the technology of greatest interest to the law enforcement community at this time is crime mapping, in large part due to its ability to facilitate problem solving and community policing via the identification of areas with repeat calls for service or other underlying problems. Depending on the software used and the skill of the data analysts, crime mapping can be used to identify the locations of crime incidents and repeat calls for service, make resource allocation decisions, evaluate interventions, and inform residents about criminal activity and changes in such. Despite the overwhelming interest in this technology, research indicates that few departments (13% of those surveyed) use any computerized crime mapping.

Where crime mapping is used (typically in larger urban police departments with greater resources), one of the most important innovations has been the crime-analysis meeting, first introduced in the NYPD, and adapted by departments in Hartford, Connecticut, Boston, and other venues. In such meetings, data on crimes, gunshots, traffic problems, calls for service, arrests, drug problems, and problems of disorder are displayed. In monthly meetings in Boston, for example, PowerPoint presentations are used to project maps, pictures, tables, graphs, and animated figures onto a screen while officers present a narrative to an audience of top command and others. A book is created and rehearsal used to polish the presentation. Questions are asked and officers are urged to use the problem-solving scanning, analysis, response, and assessment model, and present results. Districts rotate in their presentations, and sometimes a special presentation is made, such as a report on a recent successful drug raid and seizure. In these meetings, a management approach is combined with data and feedback and evaluation to integrate the technology-derived data with practice and accountability.

- **Communicative technology.** The fifth type of technology consists of communicative devices used to diffuse information to the public at large, rather than to gather in and analyze data. The external network of communications centered at the police department has been radically expanded and made more sensitive in the form of the Internet, the World Wide Web, and changes in the screening and allocation of calls to the police using 311 and 911. Technological advances in this realm have allowed, if not greater direct contact with the public, greater sharing of information with the public. For example, the Hartford (Connecticut) Police Department has provided 17 computers for community groups to access crime reports and other data. Distribution of banal information that had previously been done through newsletters, handouts, ads, or meetings can now be distributed via Web sites and citizen-accessible terminals (as in Hartford and Chicago). San Diego has the capacity to distribute warnings (of tornadoes and other disasters) to local areas via e-communication, faxes, and telephone, and alert officers via e-mail to their laptops.

In 2000, about 5% to 6% of criminal justice agencies maintained sites registered with search engines. One use of the Internet involves the posting of crime information for citizens. Police are able to use their departments' Web sites to show maps, diagrams, statistics, and pictures. The FBI, in June 1997, placed some 16,000 pages of case files on the Internet, and plans to post a total of 1.3 million pages. This is said to serve a public requesting information under the Freedom of Information Act. Other uses of the Internet include posting the names and offenses of sex offenders in several states, a Web site featuring people who are delinquent in their child support payments, and a search engine to find arrestees' home addresses in Philadelphia and San Antonio.

Some departments use the Internet, e-mail, and visuals for information and educational purposes. The San Diego and Chicago police have created elaborate videos, to be given out, to publicize their community policing programs. The Chicago police have a large media budget for advertising on radio and television, preparing and distributing their tapes to neighborhood associations and the media. Communication technology has also created newer, more efficient forms of communication among officers. E-mails are generally not favored within police departments, even when available, for direct orders or commands, because of the lagged or temporal feature of the communication. That is, messages may not be read, and another rule must be created and enforced requiring acknowledgement or response to e-mail. E-mail communication, as well as that afforded by cellular or digital phones, does have advantages, however. Chan's (2001) study in Australia showed that IT has facilitated information sharing among officers, accountability, and improved communication, resulting in a more cooperative and positive work atmosphere.

Technologies in Cyberspace Against Cybercrime

Law enforcement could use electronic sanctions to react to cybercrime. Electronic sanctions include hacking and denial-of-service attacks, along with disseminating viruses, worms, and other types of malware. Officers could use these techniques to shut down or destroy foreign Web sites used to commit crimes in their country.

However, Brenner (2004) finds that this is not an advisable strategy for improving law enforcement's ability to react to cybercrime because (1) it suffers from the problems outlined next and (2) it adds the official imprimatur of the state to what is conceded are illegal acts.

Cybercrime can be defined as using computer technology in the commission of unlawful activity. The activity can consist of traditional crimes (fraud, theft, extortion) or new types of criminal activity (denial-of-service attacks, malware). Cybercrime raises new and difficult challenges for a society's need to maintain internal order; the challenges arise not from the need to adopt new laws criminalizing the activity at issue, but from law enforcement's ability to react. Cybercrime does not share the characteristics of real-world crime that shaped the current model of law enforcement.

The most high-profile form of policing aimed at the Internet, to date, has been targeted at pornography, especially material that exploits children. Another target is hate crime, which is the promotion of racial hatred by connecting similarly minded people across the world and coalescing their belief system.

Such crimes pose significant challenges for the police service. An example is the case of Operation Ore, a police investigation targeting UK subscribers to child pornography sites. Ore was launched in the UK in May 2002 after the FBI passed details of 7,272 British subscribers who had accessed a Texas-based subscription Web site called Landslide, a gateway to pornography sites whose names (e.g., Cyber Lolita and Child Rape) indicate their content. The seizure of Landslide's database by police and the U.S. Postal Inspection Service yielded the names and credit card details of some 390,000 subscribers in 60 countries. Of the 7,272 British subscribers, only a fraction have been investigated, with police prioritizing individuals in positions of authority, and those who have access to children (Jewkes, 2003).

Online Crime Reporting

Law enforcement turns to the Internet for savings. One idea is using the Internet for online crime and incident reports. Online reporting systems permit citizens to file specified types of police reports themselves, over the Internet, 24/7, when on holidays. Law enforcement employees can later download the reports during normal working hours. The system has the added benefit of keeping patrol officers in service for proactive activities, instead of tying them up on routine reports.

According to Smith (2005), filing a crime or incident report online is a clear-cut process. The citizen who needs to file a report can access the form through the police department's Internet Web site. A set of instructions will precede the report form, explaining what types of reports can be filed and giving explicit warnings that the system is not for emergency incidents or in-progress crimes, but rather for "cold" crimes—those that are no longer in progress.

This form might include required fields for identifying such information as name, address, and date of birth. There may also be a warning that outlines the penalties for filing a false report. Once the report has been entered online, police personnel can later download the form and check to make sure that the report meets the department's criteria for the types of incidents to report. A case or file number can be assigned to the report, and then the form can be printed and filed in the records division of the agency.

In a perfect world, the form could be downloaded directly into the agency's records management system. Most departments using online reporting, however, have not been able to accomplish a direct download. To keep the time spent by employees on the report to a minimum, the complainant's name and date of birth, along with the assigned file number, can be entered by a record's employee, so that the printed form can later be tracked, if needed. Records staff can send the complainant the case number by e-mail (Smith, 2005).

Knowledge Acquisition: Thinking Styles

Dean (2000) conducted, in his doctoral dissertation, a study on how police detectives experience, understand, and think about the process of doing serious and complex criminal investigations. The following presentation of four investigative thinking styles is based on his doctoral dissertation. Each thinking style will have a need for situational knowledge management systems.

Investigative Thinking Styles

In police investigations, the experience of investigation begins for detectives when they are given a crime to solve. When handed a case, detectives apply methods they were trained in. Often, they follow a set of five basic procedural steps: collecting, checking, considering, connecting, and constructing.

As detectives conduct a series and/or complex investigation, they become driven by the intensity of the challenge, which motivates them to do the best job they can for the victim(s) by catching the criminal(s) and solving the crime through the application of their investigative method.

In meeting this investigative challenge, detectives require skill to relate and communicate effectively with a variety of people to obtain information so as to establish a workable investigative focus. Such skill also requires detectives to be flexible in the how they approach people and the case, while maintaining an appropriate level of emotional involvement towards victims, witnesses, informants, and suspects.

When exercising their investigative skill, detectives seek to maximize the possibilities of a good result by taking legally sanctioned and logically justifiable risks across a wide latitude of influence. Such justifiable risk-taking requires detectives to be proactive in applying creativity to how they seek to discover new information and, if necessary, how they develop such information into evidence.

Many detectives are only trained in one way of investigative thinking—the method style. This style of investigative thinking is all about following the basic police procedural steps when doing an investigation, which are the five Cs above. However, there are three other levels or preferred ways of thinking about the investigative process that experienced detectives use with serious and complex crimes. The three other levels are the challenge style, the skill style, and the risk style of investigative thinking.

The challenge level is all about what motivates detectives. At this level detectives think about the job, the victim, the crime, and the criminal. These four elements (job-victim-crime-criminal) are the key sources of intensity that drive detectives to do the best they can do in a particular investigation.

At the skill level of investigative thinking, detectives are concerned with how they relate to people. Detectives must think about how they are going to relate to the victim, witnesses, possible suspects, the local community, and the wider general public in order to get the information they need to make the case.

The risk style revolves around how detectives think through being proactively creative enough to discover new information and if necessary, develop it into evidence that will stand up to testing in a court of law.

Although experienced detectives and investigators intuitively use these four levels of thinking in an investigation, it is rare that any one detective will give equal weight to all four styles of investigative thinking in a particular case, because detectives, like everyone else, have a preference for maybe one or two particular styles or ways of thinking.

Dean (2005) calls this phenomenon the cognitive psychology of police investigators. It is about how police investigators (detectives) think when conducting a criminal investigation. The nature of the subject matter falls within the realm of the cognitive sciences, especially in relation to two branches of psychology. That is, cognitive psychology, with its focus on the mental processes and complex behaviors involved in problem solving and decision making, and the domain of investigative psychology as a more generic term that subsumes many of the more specific areas associated with police psychology and field of criminal or offender profiling.

Investigation is, essentially, a mind game. When it comes to solving a crime, a detective's ability to think as an investigator is everything. Four distinctively different ways of thinking are investigation as method, investigation as challenge, investigation as skill, and investigation as risk. All four ways of describing a criminal investigation can be seen as more or less partial understandings of the whole phenomenon of investigation.

The four distinctively different ways of thinking (styles) about the investigation process by detectives are illustrated in Figure 2.

As can be seen in Figure 2, there is a hierarchical structure to how investigators think. Not all cases will require the use of all four investigative thinking styles to

Figure 2. Ways of thinking about the investigation process

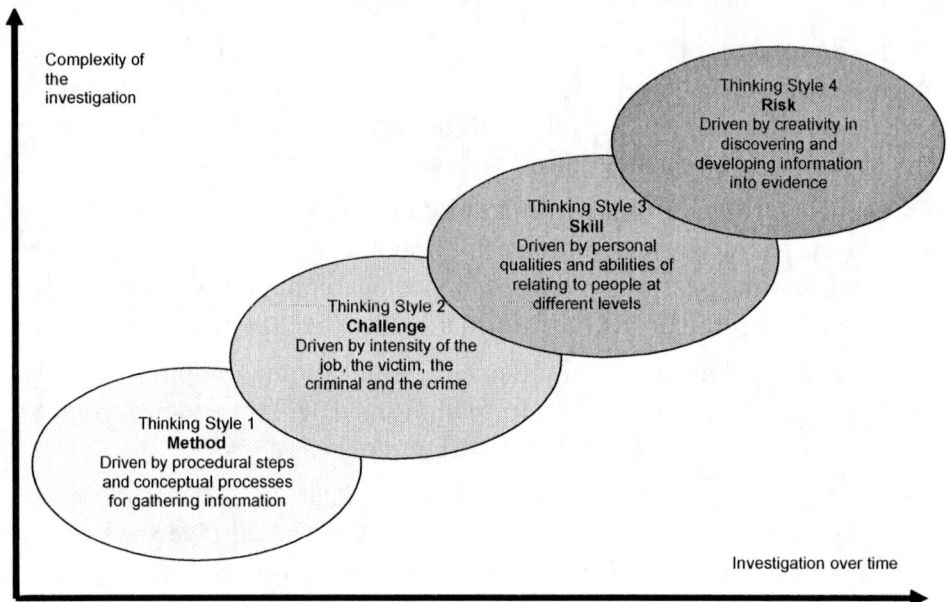

solve them. However, as time marches on in an investigation without a result, other styles of investigative thinking will need to come into play to increase the likelihood of a successful outcome. In essence, the more complex the crime, the higher the investigative thinking style required to solve it.

These four ways of thinking can be related to the codification vs. the personalization strategy for knowledge management systems suggested by Hansen et al. (Hansen, Nohria, & Tierney, 1999). Thinking styles 1 and 3 are based more on explicit knowledge, and are more suitable for codification than thinking styles 2 and 4. Hence, the focus of our second research proposition in relation to how the thinking styles of method and skill may be more important to apply knowledge management systems to than the thinking styles of challenge and risk.

Investigation as Method

In this conception, an investigation is seen as a procedurally driven method that detectives apply to every investigation. This investigative method is characterized as following a set of basic procedures for gathering the facts and building evidence for a case.

The basics of this procedurally driven method of investigation are described by detectives at two levels: a very specific level about the procedural steps to be followed in any investigation, and at a more general level to do with the overall processes that come into play when carrying out these steps.

At the specific level, there are five basic steps to this police procedural method, which are as follows: collecting and checking information to establish the facts of the case, considering the information that has and is being collected and checked, in order to reflect on and analyze its relevance and where it might lead, so that it becomes possible to connect suspects to the crime, and construct a brief of evidence to prove the case. These five interlocking steps of collecting-checking-considering-connecting-constructing have a cyclical nature and throughout the course of an investigation, generally reoccur numerous times.

At a more general level, detectives' descriptions of the basics of this investigative method emphasize particular conceptual processes that underlie the procedural nature of this investigative method. There are three such overall interrelated processes described by detectives. They are the processes of fact establishment, reflective analysis, and evidence building.

A key feature of the first process of fact establishment is that it represents the conceptual outcome of the synthesis between procedural steps, one and two: that is, the collecting and checking of information to establish facts. A central feature of the second process of reflective analysis is its wider focus on the meaning of the facts that have been established. Hence, this reflective-analysis process is not only inclusive of the third procedural step of considering, it also acts as a linking process between the other two processes of fact establishment and evidence building.

Finally, the main feature of the third process of evidence building is that it involves the conceptual ability to take the facts of a case and the information gathered, in such a way as to turn the facts and information into acceptable evidence in a court of law. Clearly, this evidence-building process incorporates procedural step four, connecting, and five, constructing.

A central feature of all three conceptual processes is the use of analogous reasoning (metaphors) by detectives to describe how they conceptually represent the nature and method of carrying out a criminal investigation.

This basic investigative method (i.e., steps and processes) for police practice does not exist in a vacuum. The method exists within a sociocultural framework of rules and protocols. There are legal rules for how the investigative method must be carried out according to the laws of a particular society. Such legal rules provide the formal or structural aspect of the investigative method in that these rules cannot be broken without calling into question the entire legal structure of the investigation. There are also police protocols for how the method of investigation should be done. These protocols reflect the customary way of doing an investigation within a particular police service, and are often contained in training manuals, operational orders, commissioner's circulars, and the like.

Such protocols provide the flexible or nonstructural aspect of the investigative method in that these protocols represent optional ways or approaches that police can take in an investigation. For example, detectives can vary their approach to how and when they decide to interview a suspect; or when they want to elementize offences; and also what focus they wish to adopt towards suspects in terms of trying to incriminate them or eliminate them from an investigation. Finally, this method of investigation remains essentially the same for all types of crimes, although how detectives approach the basic steps of this method and carry out the conceptual processes varies considerably in practice.

In this conception of investigation as method, police are trained at a very specific level, that of following the basic procedural steps involved in building a case about a crime. Detectives describe these basic steps as a sort of automatic response that has been developed in them through a combination of training and experience.

The first basic procedural step, that of *collecting* information, is described by detectives as a cycle that involves searching, gathering, and exploring for sources of information about a crime. Along with the processing of any forensic information obtained from the crime scene, detectives start this information collecting exercise with victims and/or witnesses to the crime. Detectives describe how this collection cycle is fundamental to policing and is always necessary, no matter what technological innovations may occur.

Some detectives describe the way investigators do their homework of collecting information as being methodological, while others prefer the phrase being thorough. Regardless of personal preferences, detectives use terms like methodological, thoroughness, and systematic to highlight the need to capture, in this collection cycle of an investigation, all the information they can about everything to do with the crime.

While all possible avenues of inquiry should be followed through on in this collection phase, that is also a resource issue. Clearly, high-profile crimes like homicides get the resources dedicated to them in the initial stages of an investigation, but the same does not apply to the more common crimes like property offences.

The second basic procedural step in this conception of investigation as method, that of *checking* information, is described by detectives as a cycle of verification in order to establish factual details concerning a crime and the person involved. The aim of an investigator is not only to collect all the information one can on a crime, but also to test, wherever possible, such information during the investigation. One of the ways that detectives use to test and verify details is through corroboration. The human mind can be very fragile when it comes to recalling accurately an incident. There can be as many versions as the number of people who witnessed it.

The same concern for thoroughness in the collecting cycle also exists with checking details. Again, detectives use terms like clinical and methodical to describe this need to be thorough in making sure that what information they have is factually based. This need to be as certain as one can about the correctness of details is reinforced in relation to making absolutely sure that any differences in witnesses' statements are tracked down and resolved, as far as possible, by microscopically examining everything.

The third procedural step of this basic investigative method, that of *considering* the information as it is being collected and checked, is described by detectives as a cycle of thinking about all the factors involved in the current investigation from every angle. As detectives describe it, this considered thinking is of the how-am-I-going-to-do-it type. How am I going to get this bit of information or that piece of evidence I need?

Moreover, in this considering cycle, detectives describe not only their procedural type of thinking, but also how they think about an investigation in terms of the metaphors they use to consider it.

The fourth basic procedural step in this conception of investigation as method, that of *connecting* information, is described by detectives as a cycle that involves linking and relating together information about a crime. The possibilities increase of connecting up bits of information when a major incident occurs like a murder.

In the procedural step, detectives describe the connecting style as having a sense of things coming together in a way that makes the investigation progress. Again, an apt metaphor for this sort of progressive connecting up is described as a jigsaw where the pieces are being put into place.

The fifth and final procedural step under this conception of investigative method is that of *constructing* information that will provide evidence. Anyone can gather information, but the real value of a detective's ability lies in the constructive application of such information to the investigation.

The most consistent term that detectives use to describe this constructing cycle is that of building up a case about the crime. In this sense, the cycle of construction represents the culmination of all the other steps in the investigative method, as this cycle, of necessity, must build on these steps in order to construct a case.

From this examination of the distinguishing characteristics of each of the five procedural steps that constitute what detectives refer to as the basics of their method of investigation, two general findings emerged. They are:

- Firstly, that analogous reasoning in the form of metaphors plays a significant part in detectives thinking throughout the investigation process, and

- Secondly, that detectives' understanding of the basics of the investigative method encompasses a wider set of conceptual processes than is conveyed by just the five procedural steps identified.

To summarize the method category, this conception views an investigation simply as applying the same procedurally driven method to every crime. This investigative method is characterized by a set of basic procedures to follow for gathering the facts and building the evidence for a case. The basics of this investigative method are understood by detectives as the specific level of the procedural steps involved, and a more general level of the conceptual processes that underpin the carrying out of these steps.

Investigation as Challenge

In this conception, the nature of investigative work is not so much understood by detectives on a cognitive level, as experienced at a gut level as a mentally and emotionally charged form of intensity that drives them to meet the challenge that the investigative process poses. The central characteristic in this conception is the multidimensional notion about the experience of investigation being a challenge.

This notion holds positive and negative aspects for detectives. They experience an investigation as both excitingly stimulating and frustratingly demanding. A successful outcome brings immense satisfaction and conversely, a less satisfactory result leaves detectives disappointingly frustrated.

The key feature of this conception's central characteristic about the challenge of an investigation is the intensity of such a challenge. This intensity represents an inner driving force within detectives that has obsessive-compulsive qualities.

The source of such intensity resides in four specific yet distinct processes. They are job-driven intensity, victim-driven intensity, criminal-driven intensity, and crime-driven intensity. The combined effect of these four processes captures the drive that detectives experience in terms of the interest and the worth of the job, empathy towards the victims and their families, the criminal's attempts to outwit them, and the mind-stimulating nature of the crime.

Metaphors featured prominently in this conception as a means that detectives use to describe how they think and reason with analogies about a crime and its investigation. The most commonly used analogies to which an investigation is likened are a "jigsaw," a "picture," and a "tree."

Dean (2000) found that detectives overwhelmingly describe the central characteristic of a criminal investigation as a challenge. The motivation to get a result is what detectives see as providing the challenge. However, the really challenging part of an investigation is trying to get the best result. At every turn throughout the investigation process, detectives are presented with a number of other challenges that they have to find a way of overcoming in order to achieve a good result by bringing the investigation to a successful conclusion.

A key feature of the obsessive-compulsive nature of the emotionally charged intensity is that it drives detectives in a number of ways. Detectives describe four processes of inner drive. The first process of job-driven intensity has two aspects to it in relation to how detectives described this source of drive.

The first aspect of *job-driven* intensity has to do with the nature of the particular type of investigative job. That is, detectives seek out jobs in which they can find personal interest and excitement. Detectives' descriptions emphasize the stimulating interest they find in building a picture of the crime, and the enjoyment of putting things together, as well as the exciting potential for out-of-the-ordinary experiences. Such features are the driving forces that keep them going to succeed with an investigation.

The second aspect of job-driven intensity has to do with the inherent worth of investigation, in general, as a job. Detectives, particularly those with some experience, have a strong sense that the job of investigation is an important one for society as a whole. They view their job as doing something good for the community. This sense of helping people in the community by doing a professional job of investigating a crime is seen as arising from or being reinforced by human tragedies that detectives at times experience in very personal ways.

The second process of *victim-driven* intensity overlaps to some extent with the worth aspect of the job-driven process outlined previously. Here the plight of victims and their families who suffer horrific crimes also intensifies the feeling of wanting to do some good for the community by catching the perpetrator of the crime. While the worthwhile nature of the job is always in the back of the mind of a detective, the actual victim before a detective's eyes emotionally drives this second process of intensity right into the front of their heads.

Detectives describe this sense of empathetic intensity for the victim and their family as giving them a greater drive to succeed at the one thing they can do for them, place the offender before a court. Also, detectives' descriptions emphasize the importance of their understanding of wanting to be of some assistance to victims, and how much personal satisfaction they get from serving the victim by apprehending the perpetrator and putting the offender before the court.

The third process of *criminal-driven* intensity is described by detectives as feeling that they are being challenged by the criminal to engage in a battle of wills to prove who is the smarter. This driving force to outwit the criminal is seen as a hallmark of an effective investigator. Such an adversarial contest is viewed by detectives as being a very personalized engagement type mode of operation towards the criminal. This term, "personalized engagement," is not used in the sense of a detective's personal issues intruding into an investigation in an inappropriate or unprofessional manner, but rather that the criminal is seen as a person who has the attributes of being a cunning opponent.

For example, detectives' descriptions clearly reflect the passion of their personal engagement contest with the criminal often over a long period of time. To be able to "pit your brain" against the criminal, whether in an interview situation or more generally throughout the investigation, and to "come out on top" is the basis for an immense degree of satisfaction for detectives.

The fourth process of *crime-driven* intensity is described by detectives as feeling that they are being challenged by the crime to come up with a logical and plausible account of how it occurred, and to prove beyond reasonable doubt who is responsible for the crime. The nature of being challenged by the crime is slightly different to being challenged by the criminal. As indicated previously, the adversarial contest with the criminal becomes a highly personalized type of engagement, whereas descriptions of the challenge offered by the crime have more of a mental involvement type mode about them.

Detectives' descriptions of the constancy of thinking about the crime and how to piece together the puzzle it presents to them clearly indicate the mental situation that drives them. Moreover, detectives describe how the investigation is in the back of their mind all the time not only to work out the puzzle, but also the awareness that everything they do in an investigation could be microscopically examined in court.

Detectives work long and hard to analyze the crime from every angle, and pick through every piece that could have the potential to solve the mystery of the crime. In so doing, detectives rely on analogous thinking, and represent their conceptual efforts in the form of metaphors. That is, detectives' perceptions of the type of thinking about the crime they engage in throughout the investigative process contain a range of metaphors.

Jigsaw puzzle, picture, and tree are among the most common analogies that detectives use to describe their experience of the investigative process. For example, investigative thinking is likened to putting together the pieces of a jigsaw puzzle and building up a picture of the crime, as well as being like a tree.

The tree metaphor represents how an investigation initially grows out in all directions from its root, which is the crime scene. The investigative process then becomes one of following each branch to its logical conclusion. Some of these branches are dead ends. But the live branches, that is, ones that are actively related to the tree root (crime scene), help the tree to grow.

A key feature of the conception of investigation being a challenge is the intensity that such a challenge brings. This notion of intensity captures the mentally and emotionally charged essence of the investigative challenge as an inner-motivated driving force with obsessive-compulsive qualities. Within this key feature of intensity, four specific yet distinct processes were explicated from detectives' descriptions of what drives the intensity to meet the investigative challenge: job-driven, victim-driven, criminal-driven, and crime-driven intensity.

Investigation as Skill

This conception emphasizes the human dimension in investigative work, particularly the personal qualities of detectives. Hence, the central characteristic in this conception is relatability. That is, a detective's ability to relate skillfully to a wide variety of people. This relational skill encompasses three levels.

The first level of relationship for detectives is the immediate investigation, and this involves relating well to victims, witnesses, and suspects, as well as working as part of a larger police team. The second level of relational involvement is the legal system comprising magistrates, judges, barristers, and solicitors. The third level of relationship is involvement with the public and general community.

Since the key feature in this conception is detectives' personal qualities, there is a core set of abilities described by detectives that characterize what the substance of such personal qualities are seen to involve. These core abilities are described as the ability to communicate effectively, the ability to adopt a flexible approach, the ability to maintain an investigative focus, and the ability to remain emotionally involved yet detached in an investigation. Each of these abilities has a number of dimensions or aspects to them.

In contrast to the other conceptions of investigation, this conception addresses the phenomenon of investigation from the perspective that you can "take a method out of a detective" but you cannot "take the detective out of the method." Detectives who hold this conception of investigation as fundamentally involving relational skill emphasize the importance of the human dimension in investigative work.

While an investigation clearly involves an evidence-gathering enterprise by human beings, this conception further emphasizes the quality of who is doing the gathering. Detectives see any investigation as going nowhere unless they are able to extract good quality information out of people, and their ability to do that depends on the quality of detectives' relational skill, particularly with regard to communicating well with people.

A further characteristic of this emphasis on the quality of the detective doing the investigation is the prime significance placed on the mix of innate abilities that an individual brings to the role of detective, and his/her exposure to life experiences. In regard to the innateness dimension, detectives use phrases like "born not made," or "having base talents," and "being a certain kind of person" to describe the significance they place on a range of innate abilities that they view as essential for the job of investigating. These abilities are seen primarily as revolving around a real liking or "love" of people and "people person."

Detectives use a range of terms to describe what they consider to be core abilities for an investigator. However, a detailed phenomenographic analysis of the meanings underlying the diversity of terms used for what detectives view as core abilities revealed that such terms clustered around four attributes in the set of personal qualities desired by detectives. These attributes are described as follows: the ability to communicate effectively, the ability to adopt a flexible approach, the ability to maintain an investigative focus, and the ability to remain emotionally detached in an investigation.

The first core ability, to *communicate effectively*, is seen as the fundamental ability in this set of personal qualities. That is, the ability to communicate effectively to a diversity of people is a central thrust of this conception's perspective on the personal qualities that make for a good detective. Given the strong focus on the relational aspects of this conception's view of investigation, it is not surprising to find that communication is seen as the main ability in this set of core abilities for relating well to people.

Moreover, communication is seen in this conception of investigation as the central ability on which all others are dependent. Other abilities in the core set are seen as reinforcing this foundational ability. The ability to communicate effectively is often described in terms of the verbal ability to talk to people (the relatability aspect), but it also involves written ability. That is, the ability to communicate on paper by being able to put a report or brief of evidence together in a clear and coherent manner.

The second core ability, that of *personal flexibility*, involves both behavioral and mental dimensions, and further underscores the emphasis on this conception's key feature of relatability. That is, personal flexibility is seen as the ability to adopt the appropriate communicative style for the persons you need to relate to throughout an investigation.

The behavioral aspect of this personal flexibility extends the description of this emphasis on communication by adding the notion of being flexible enough to go from role to role. That is, a detective could still conceivably be regarded as an effective communicator within a limited role of playing the "tough guy" or the "sensitive cop." However, what this behavioral notion of flexibility is descriptive of is the added ability to be able to change from one role to another depending on what is seen as required.

The mental or cognitive aspect of maintaining a personal flexibility towards an investigation is described by detectives in a number of ways. The most frequent term used by detectives to describe this mental flexibility aspect is open-mindedness. To be open-minded is described as the conceptual skill of remaining open to new ideas and ways of approaching the task of gathering evidence. This conceptual ability is seen as a necessary personal quality not only for generating ideas and approaches, but also for avoiding "tunnel vision" in an investigation. Tunnel vision occurs when detectives become derailed in an investigation by favoring their own assumptions. That is, detectives who focus too exclusively on one possibility or explanation tend to close off and narrow down their mind to other equally valid possibilities or explanations about some aspects of the investigation. Descriptions by detectives highlight this notion of being open-minded, and its associated meanings of tunnel vision and the need to watch one's assumptions in an investigation.

The third core ability, which is maintaining an *investigative focus*, represents a sort of midway point between being open-minded and close-minded. That is, detectives have to remain open in their minds to new ideas and approaches for collecting evidence and other possible interpretations for various events and the feedback gained in an investigation.

But detectives also have to know when to close down or narrow their mind in order to focus on what they consider the relevant and important aspects of an investigation. This focusing ability takes place at micro- and macro-levels of an investigation. That is, at the microlevel of tasks like interviewing witnesses, victims, and suspects, and the more macrolevel of keeping an overall directional focus throughout the entire investigation. The ability to focus is seen as necessary in order to be both efficient and effective in an investigation, and to avoid getting lost and buried in the mountain of details that a serious and complex criminal investigation presents to detectives.

This ability to focus an investigation is expressed by detectives in a range of ways that essentially reflect a similar meaning. For example, at the microlevel of an investigation, the ability to focus is described as remaining on track in an interview by focusing on the objective of what the information is that needs to be gotten from a particular interview. Also, having the ability to pay attention to detail in order to mentally "keep yourself sharp" and therefore focused, expresses similar meaning, as does the ability to "run with what's important" in an investigation by being able to "think on your feet."

At the macrolevel of investigation, the same need, to be able to focus on what has to be done to make the case, is seen as a demarcation line that separates average detectives from the best detectives. That is, the best detectives can look at a complicated crime and sort out where they need to go to build the case. Conversely, average detectives try and work too many angles in an investigation and hence, lose focus on what needs to be done. They will find it difficult to be successful.

The ability to have a clear and definite focus on where the investigation is going is seen by detectives as essential. This ability to focus by detectives is very different from detectives who are checklist investigators. That is, such detectives need a checklist of what to do in an investigation. They may have other skills that they are good at, but these checklist detectives lack the skill to quickly work out what is going on in a case, and how to focus the investigation to get to where they need to go.

The fourth core ability is to maintain an *emotional involvement* towards the crime and the criminal being investigated, while at the same time remaining sufficiently detached in order to maintain a more objective view. This is a difficult ability to master, as the very nature of being a detective requires personal involvement with a range of people. This is especially so in the light of this current conception, as it characterizes the importance of detectives' personal qualities, like the ability to relate and communicate effectively through demonstrating understanding and rapport in order to achieve success in an investigation.

Such relating to others in an investigation involves competing demands. That is, detectives need to detach themselves from the emotional trauma that a serious and complex criminal investigation presents to them, while at the same time trying to establish and maintain a productive working relationship of gathering evidence from both the victims and the offenders. The issue, therefore, of not becoming emotionally involved in an investigation is one of degree in this conception.

Detectives describe a range of strategies they use to distance themselves, emotionally, to the degree that allows them to not be overwhelmed by the tragedy of some of the circumstances they are required to investigate. These strategies attempt to minimize the emotional impact, not deny its existence. Such strategies involve learning to put aside feelings and not dwell on sad and unsuccessful cases. Detectives describe this ability to turn off, emotionally, from tragic situations as one of depersonalizing the situation or in similar way, to dehumanize the circumstances and just focus on what has to be done.

Other more active strategies that detectives describe involve redirecting the strong emotions that arise from a very serious crime into a greater desire to focus on the investigation and to work harder and longer at it. However, experienced detectives observe that the focus for the redirected energy needs to be on proving the crime, rather than getting a negative fixation on a suspect.

Communicate effectively, flexible approach, investigative focus, and emotionally detached in an investigation are core abilities in the conception of investigation as skill. This conception views the personal qualities of detectives as a key feature. It stresses the fundamental importance of the human dimension in investigative work, and the skill this necessarily entails.

Investigation as Risk

This category describes investigation as an actively creative process that inevitably involves taking risks. Moreover, any investigative risk must be able to be justified in terms of three considerations that are the legality of taking the risk, the logic behind the risk, and the latitude of the risk in relation to both economic and conceptual aspects.

The central feature of this conception of investigation as risk is its proactive nature. Such proactivity revolves around three key investigative processes: creativity, discovery, and development. The process of creativity involves coming up with and applying new and/or different ideas that help in the process of discovery of information and evidence, as well as in the process of development of such information and evidence.

The first process of *creativity* primarily involves the fostering of a creative mindset that detectives use to look at or approach an investigation, and how they apply the ideas from this creative mindset in a way that reduces the investigative risk of carrying out such ideas. The creative process can manifest itself in an investigation through constantly exploiting opportunities to develop the investigative picture by focusing all that is known and what is unknown.

This notion of pursuing the unknown throughout an investigation also highlights that creativity is primarily about perception, that is, how something is looked at or approached in a cognitive-perceptual sense. A similar view of the perceptual nature of creativity is described by some detectives as creativity only being limited by your own imagination; in that, there is no limit to the way a detective can go about getting information and evidence.

Furthermore, creativity can be viewed as a search for alternative ways of doing something, that is, having a mindset to try and think of something different on the belief that there is always another way of getting evidence. Descriptions of creativity are sometimes associated with flexibility in thinking, that is, the ability to be able to mentally change directions and to be adaptable and innovative in a lateral thinking sort of way.

Detectives use a range of terms and phrases to describe the sort of creative outlook that successful investigators must have like "only limited by your own imagination," "there is always another way," be "flexible," "adaptable," "innovative," and "lateral" in your thinking, and "make your own luck" through adapting a mindset of "pursuing the unknown."

The second process of *discovery* is characterized by determination and confidence. With regard to the first characteristic, that of determination, unless detectives are strongly determined to seek out the information and evidence needed to make a case, then they are less likely to be successful. The tenacity of this sort of "dogged determination" is seen as a personal quality that detectives must have if they want to be successful at investigation by exploring and exhausting all leads, and keeping on digging up every piece of possible evidence to make a case.

In relation to the second characteristic associated with this discovery process, that of confidence, detectives describe a "belief in your own ability" as a good indicator for knowing that any investigation you do will go as well as it can, given the things a detective does have control over. That is, particular circumstances can arise in the best of investigations that cannot be controlled, like witnesses changing their story or not wanting to testify now as the trial approaches.

By its nature, confidence is a personal assessment made by detectives about how good they are doing in an investigation. The descriptions offered by detectives highlight this personal aspect of being "confident of your own abilities" and "knowing" that you have done a good job.

The third process of *development* involves identification of quality information. This process is seen as essential by detectives for the whole point of taking justifiable risks in an investigation. It is to develop information and, where possible, hopefully into evidence. Such a development process is inherently proactive; to develop information and evidence is only possible by an actively seeking and thinking human being.

For example, the term "fine tuning" is sometimes used to describe the ability to progressively extract and build up "quality information" from witnesses. That is, to fine-tune information is to develop the initial information from a witness to such an extent that when it is played back to them, the witness is able to further play back quality information to the detective.

This process of development of information and evidence in one sense shares a similarity to the process of evidence building that was explicated from category three's conception of investigation as method. In this sense, these processes of evidence building and development help to construct information and evidence about a crime into a case.

However, there is also a sense in which the process of developing information and evidence as described by detectives is qualitatively different from the process of building up information and evidence as described under category three's conception. This difference is illustrated by a good investigator building up information and evidence using a logical and systematic piece-by-piece methodology, while a great investigator goes a step further to develop the information and evidence that has been built up to figure out the mental processes and thought patterns of the offender.

In summary, investigation as risk views an investigation as primarily a proactive process that inevitably involves taking risks. There are three key investigative processes that detectives see as essential in order to be proactive within this conception of investigation of risk. They are the processes of creativity, discovery, and development.

Thinking Styles and Knowledge Management

It is possible to talk about there being a style to how investigators think. The term style is used as a way of thinking, and something quite different from an ability. A style is a preferred way of using abilities one has. Furthermore, not only are there different thinking styles that investigators prefer to use when investigating crime, but also each style has its own anatomy or discernible conceptual structure with regard to the nature and quality of the thinking an investigator engages in during an investigation.

In our perspective of knowledge management systems along the stages-of-growth model for knowledge management technology, we can identify different systems for different thinking styles. Investigation as method will be heavily based on access to best practices and previous cases found at Stage 3. Investigation as challenge will mainly be based on communication between police officers at Stage 2. Investigation as skill will mainly be based on end-user tools at Stage 1. Investigation as risk will mainly be based on expert systems at Stage 4.

Technologies and Techniques

We conclude this chapter by discussing practical and workable technologies, tools, and techniques for knowledge management in law enforcement. While this section focuses on technologies and techniques at Stage 1, the last section in each of the following chapters will focus on technologies and techniques at Stages 2, 3, and 4, respectively.

End-user tools at Stage 1 enable police officers to enter, store, systematize, analyze, and present information. Furthermore, end-user tools enable police officers to work and handle electronic information independent of time and space because of communication media that support such tools. In police cars and police offices, a variety of devices are available to codify knowledge in terms of information, and to retrieve and apply the same information, as well as combine this information with information from other sources.

Of special interest is mobile technology. Knowledge work, like many other types of work, is influenced by development of an increasingly mobile workforce. Due to the characteristics of police work, workplaces are mobile. Here we find the usefulness of mobile devices that are characterized by voice functionality, capability to send and receive short messages, and capability of executing applications.

An interesting example is the HOLMES system in the UK, where the police officer can enter information on the location of incident, date and time of incident, victim(s), senior investigating officer, and date enquiry commenced (Home Office, 2005a). The police officer can use the system as an end-user tool at various phases of the investigation. At each phase, the officer uses the system to write a report on the status of the investigation. As an end-user tool, the HOLMES system provides support for entry of different information elements and work on electronic information.

Another interesting example is the COPLINK system in the U.S., where the user accesses the system through a Web browser (Chen et al., 2003). In addition to end-user tools for information entry and retrieval, statistical techniques such as co-occurrence analysis and clustering functions are available to weight relationships between all possible pairs of concept.

A final example is the Basic Solutions toolbox available to police officers in Norway. Basic Solutions includes not only word processing, spreadsheet, and presentation graphics, but also tools to work on a case, to produce standard documents, and to write individual reports with desired layouts.

References

Ang, S., & Slaugther, S. A. (2001). Work outcomes and job design for contract vs. permanent information systems professionals on software development teams. *MIS Quarterly, 25*(5), 321-350.

Ashby, D. I., & Longley, P. A. (2005). Geocomputation, geodemographics and resource allocation for local policing. *Transactions in GIS, 9*(1), 53-72.

Brenner, S. W. (2004). Distributed security: A new model of law enforcement. *Internet Law, 8*(5), 1-25.

Chan, J. B. L. (2001). The technological game: How information technology is transforming police practice. *Criminal Justice, 1*(2), 139-159.

Chen, H., Schroeder, J., Hauck, R. V., Ridgeway, L., Atabakhsh, H., Gupta, H., et al. (2002). COPLINK Connect: Information and knowledge management for law enforcement. *Decision Support Systems, 34*, 271-285.

Chen, H., Zheng, D., Atabakhsh, H., Wyzga, W., & Schroeder, J. (2003). COPLINK - Managing law enforcement data and knowledge. *Communications of the ACM, 46*(1), 28-34.

ComputerWeekly. (2002, February 28). Knowledge management: Surrey Police.

Dean, G. (2000). *The experience of investigation for detectives.* Unpublished PhD thesis, Queensland University of Technology, Brisbane, Australia.

Dean, G. (2005). *The cognitive psychology of police investigators.* Conference paper, School of Justice Studies, Faculty of Law, Queensland University of Technology, Brisbane, Australia.

Derballa, V., & Pousttchi, K. (2006). Mobile technology for knowledge management. In D. G. Schwartz (Ed.), *Encyclopedia of Knowledge Management*, Schwartz. Hershey, PA: Idea Group Publishing.

Hansen, M. T., Nohria, N., & Tierney, T. (1999, March-April). What's your strategy for managing knowledge? *Harvard Business Review*, 106-116.

Holgersson, S. (2005). *Yrke: POLIS—yrkeskunnskap, motivasjon, IT-system og andre forutsetninger for politiarbeide.* PhD doctoral dissertation, Institutionen för datavetenskap, Linköpings universitet, Sweden.

Home Office (2005a). *Guidance on statutory performance indicators for policing 2005/2006*. Police Standards Unit, Home Office of the UK Government. Retrieved from http://www.policereform.gov.uk

Jewkes, Y. (2003). Policing cybercrime. In T. Newburn (Ed.), *Handbook of policing*. Portland, OR: Willan Publishing.

Manning, P. K. (2003). *Policing contingencies*. Chicago: The University of Chicago Press.

Smith, E. (2005, July). Online crime reporting: Should law enforcement turn to the Internet for savings. *Public Management*, 26-30.

Sorban, V. L. (2005). Incorporating NIBRS into the custom development of an offense reporting and records management system in Charlotte-Mecklenburg. In D. Faggiani, B. Kubu, & R. Rantala (Eds.), *Facilitating the implementation of incident-based data systems* (pp. 29-32). Police Executive Research Forum, Connecticut Avenue, Washington, DC, 20036.

Surette, R. (2005). The thinking eye—pros and cons of second generation CCTV surveillance systems. *Policing—an International Journal of Police Strategies & Management, 28*(1), 152-173.

Thibault, E. A., Lynch, L. M., & McBride, R. B. (1998). *Proactive police management* (4th ed.). Upper Saddle River, NJ: Prentice Hall.

Chapter VI

Officer-to-Officer Systems

Officer-to-officer systems are found at Stage 2 of the stages-of-growth model for knowledge management technology. Information about who knows what is made available to all police officers, and to selected, outside partners. At Stage 2, organizations apply the personalization strategy, which implies that knowledge is tied to the person who developed it, and is shared mainly through person-to-person contact.

As in the previous chapter, we will focus on police investigations. While Chapter V presented individual thinking styles, this chapter discusses the tasks involved in police investigations in general, and in interviewing in particular.

People can meet electronically, even though they are hundreds or thousands of miles apart, by using teleconferencing, data conferencing, or videoconferencing. Teleconferencing allows a group of people to confer simultaneously via telephone or via e-mail group communication software. Teleconferencing that includes the ability of two or more people at distant locations to work on the same document or data simultaneously is called data conferencing. With data conferencing, users at distant locations can edit and modify data files. Teleconferencing, in which participants see each other over video screens, is termed video conferencing (Laudon & Laudon, 2005). These forms of electronic conferencing, found at Stage 2, are growing in popularity because they save travel time and cost.

Figure 1. Officer-to-officer systems at Stage 2 of the knowledge management technology stage model

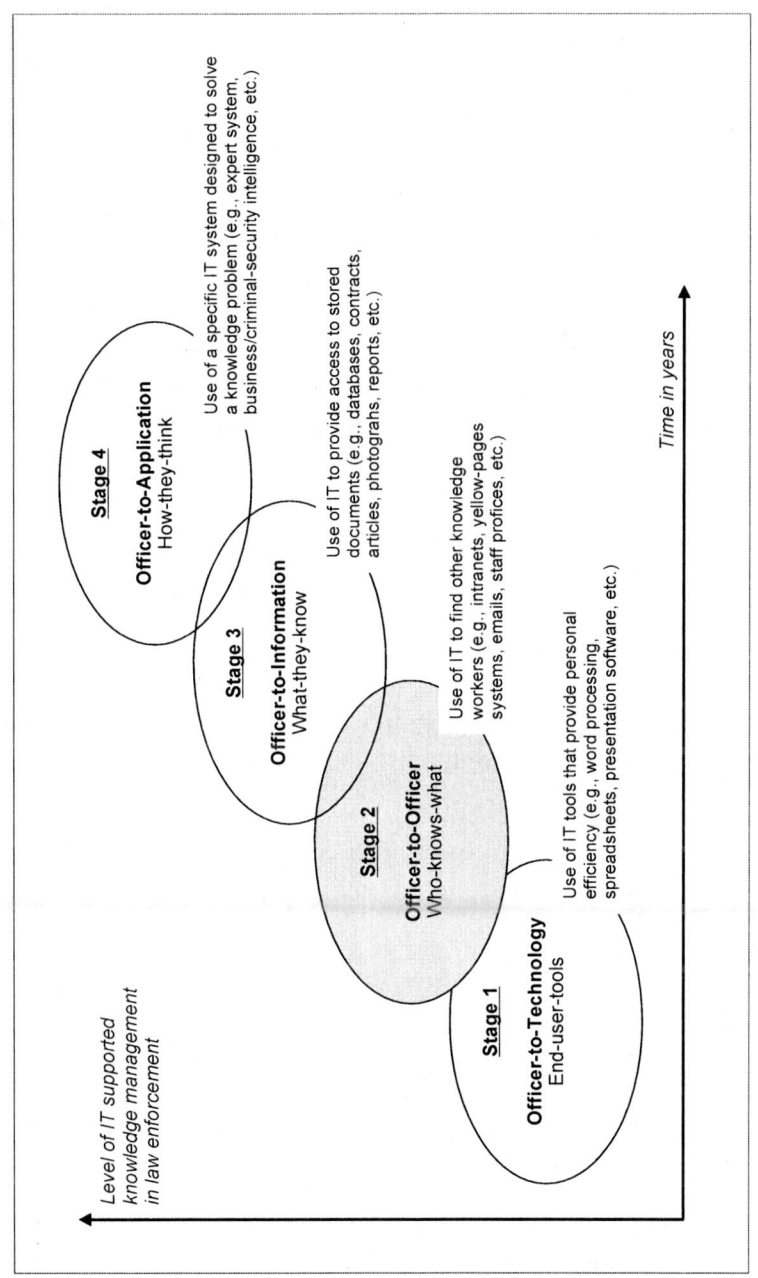

The typical system at Stage 2 of knowledge management technology is the intranet. Intranets provide a rich set of tools for creating collaborative environments in which members of an organization can exchange ideas, share information, and work together on common projects and assignments, regardless of their physical location. Information from many different sources and media including text, graphics, video, audio, and even digital slides can be displayed, shared, and accessed across an enterprise through a simple, common interface (Laudon & Laudon, 2005).

One of the most visible information systems and information technology trends of the last decade has been the rapid proliferation of intranet applications in organizations both in the public and private sector. Because of the crucial role of communications in information and knowledge sharing, the capabilities of intranets in supporting these processes are critical. Compared with Internets and extranets, the intranet provides a closed communications infrastructure, access to which is exclusive to the members of the organization. Intranet technologies are capable of providing a communications infrastructure for information and knowledge sharing.

In an empirical study of intranet applications, Breu et al. (Breu, Ward, & Murray, 2000) identified three critical success factors for intranets:

- The **sociocultural factors** such as user training, the negotiation of guidelines for use, and the anchoring of knowledge sharing in the organizational value system.

- The **organizational and management factors** such as the adequate structuring, archiving, and continuous updating of the published information and knowledge resources; the determination of ownership; the specification of roles and responsibilities; and the adaptation of traditional reward systems to encourage knowledge sharing.

- The **technological factors** such as the provision of appropriate design, bandwidth, and platform specifications; user-friendly information access tools; and continual technical support of the user community.

If these sociocultural, organizational, management, and technological factors were addressed in a detailed organization case prior to the adoption, organizations could significantly reduce the risk of benefits realization failure that largely results from technology-driven investment decisions. Without the prior demonstration of the technology's contribution to the organizational performance, and the determination of the stakeholder roles and responsibilities in realizing the investment objectives, there is a high risk of failure in achieving benefits as a result of the implementation of the technology.

A study in the UK found that the force Internet site was identified as a primary communication medium both for disseminating knowledge and capturing the opinions of the general public (Collier, Edwards, & Shaw, 2004). The intranet was identified as the primary communication channel for internal communications.

Police Investigations

Investigation is the police activity concerned with (1) the apprehension of criminals by the gathering of evidence leading to their arrest and (2) the collection and presentation of evidence and testimony for the purpose of obtaining convictions. Investigation is normally divided into two major areas of activity: (1) the preliminary investigation normally carried out by officers in the uniform patrol division and (2) the follow-up investigation normally carried out by officers formally trained in investigative techniques, often part of a detective bureau (Thibault, Lynch, & McBride, 1998).

Knowledge work in police investigations is based on a variety of information sources, such as incident reports, crime scene investigator reports, witness statements, suspect statements, tip lines, crime scene photographs and drawings, fingerprints, DNA, physical evidence (ballistics, tool marks, blood spatters), informants, and property tracking (Fraser, 2004).

In larger departments, a division or bureau is responsible for follow-up investigations; special investigations are assigned by the chief of police. Additionally, this function also covers the recovery of stolen property, the gathering of criminal intelligence, and the preparation of cases for trial. Organizationally, this division may be titled Detective, Central Investigation, or Criminal Investigation.

The role of the investigator is probably the most glamorous one in the police department. This modern Sherlock Holmes is portrayed in movies, television, and novels as a meticulous and tireless gatherer of evidence that miraculously leads to the arrest and conviction of criminals. As shown on several television series, this super police officer is a bit unorthodox, normally at odds with his superiors, and normally willing to bend the rules, especially if this involves a deliberate violation of departmental directives. Embedded in a web of unsavory informers, the heroic investigator maintains integrity in his unrelenting pursuit of crime and the master criminal.

The public, and to some extent the patrol officer, maintains this glorified notion of what an investigator is all about. Reality, as usual, is a mixture of fact and fiction. In some cases, detective work is all that the media says it is, but in most investigative jobs, it is a series of monotonous tasks that may or may not lead to a break in a case. Long, hard hours are put in interviewing neighbors after a major crime has taken place. One of the best examples of the everyday work of the detective is found in the portrayal of Al Seedman, chief of the New York City detectives (Thibault et al. 1998, p. 164):

Throughout his career Seedman often obtained his solution by using his intelligence on the mundane, seemingly unrelated information that a record-oriented society can provide if only one knew how to find it.

For example, police in a small town found a male skeleton and asked Seedman for advice on how to find out who it was. Seedman asked if there were signs of dental work and the answer was no, even though the teeth were in poor repair. Normally, dental work is the easiest way of identifying a body, even though the investigator has to interview dentist after dentist until the correct records are found.

Seedman then reasoned that if the person had money, his teeth would have been repaired; also, the teeth would have been repaired if the man had worked in a union job or was on welfare. The skeleton didn't match any missing person report. Seedman told the local police to wait until the end of the year and then go to the Internal Revenue Service and get a printout of all single males making less than $10,000 a year, but more than the welfare ceiling, who paid tax in the first three quarters, but not on the fourth. Chances are the name of the skeleton will be on the printout.

This is the way many investigations are solved: step by laborious step. Unlike the outcomes on television and in the movies, clearance on crimes investigated against property is less than 20% in the U.S. This means that over 80% of these types of crimes investigated are never solved.

Preliminary Investigations

Cases would not be solved and offenders would not be arrested unless patrol officers were willing and able to use some preliminary investigation skills. The patrol officer's tasks in crime incidents normally entail both investigative and noninvestigative action.

One of the most important duties of the police officer responding to a crime call is to secure the crime scene. Cases are often lost because reporters, higher administrative officials, and various other personnel are allowed to indiscriminately contaminate a scene by handling evidence or walking through the area. There have even been cases of patrol officers taking weapons from a crime scene and turning them in two or three days later.

To win a case, there must be continuity of the evidence from the scene of the crime, to the vaults of the police laboratory or property room, to the hands of the prosecuting district attorney. Documentation must be made of any person who handled any piece of evidence, and the circumstances under which these pieces of evidence were handled. Otherwise, alert defense lawyers can point to the discrepancies and win cases on technicalities.

Follow-Up Investigations

This is a continuation of the preliminary investigation through the arrest stage and, it is hoped, conviction. It starts with a thorough review of all reports relative to the offence, a possible reinterview of all persons with information relating to the offence, an attempt to relate the physical evidence to the crime, a continuing search for persons with information relating to the crime, and a refinement of the pickup broadcasts on suspects and the distribution of pickups to the appropriate law enforcement agencies.

This phase continues by application of the modus operandi files to the particular offence in an attempt to identify the perpetrator, identification of the perpetrator by fingerprints, physical evidence, or eyewitnesses. Then, there is the filing of appropriate criminal charges against the perpetrator, the arrest of the perpetrator, and recovery of additional evidence associated with the crime. Hopefully, the recovery of property stolen in the offence can take place.

This phase ends by the preparation of reports upon which the prosecution of the case is based. The provision of sufficient relevant testimony to prove all necessary elements of the offence takes place, as well as the presentation, in court, of testimony relating to the follow-up investigation.

As long as the U.S. has its present court system, these talks will have to be fulfilled. In the future, however, the intermediate stage of follow-up investigations will become increasingly complex as computers are used as a tool by investigative units. At the present, it is possible to do a computer search by alias, modus operandi, and thousands of other set sorts. Currently, systems are being interlocked so that a search can take in a local area, country, state, and in some instances, the nation. However, no matter how good the tools, cases will ultimately be solved by a well-trained investigator with an instinct for human folly.

Traditional Structure

Historically, the investigations divisions of large urban police departments have been removed from the mainstream of police operations in the station houses. In general, a person enters a detective or investigative squad room by invitation only.

In the early days of policing in the United States, it was the prime task of the police investigator to cultivate informers. This was relatively easy at the time as both the criminals and the police most often grew up in the same neighborhoods. Related to the cultivation of informers was another task, the regulation of vice activity. The combination of these two tasks, with few records being made of payoffs for information and the considerable amount of unrecorded money surrounding vice activity, led to the problem in police corruption, a problem that has persisted to the present.

However, as any competent detective will continue to tell you, his informers are his stock in trade, and he could not stay in business without them. In one crucial area, drug investigation, it has been well documented that these investigators could not operate without informants. Without a network of informers—usually civilians, sometimes police—narcotic police can hardly operate. The use of flipped and paid informants sometimes gives narcotic agents their best opportunity to enforce drug laws that are, by and large, unenforceable.

Managing Criminal Investigations

Management is concerned with investigative performance by increasing the number of arrests and convictions. The four key management elements are as follows (Thibault et al., 1998):

- **Enhancing the investigative role of police officers.** In many departments, the patrol officer is merely a reporter of crimes that come to the attention of the police; the important follow-up work is conducted by investigators. In many cases, when the investigation division is called to the crime scene, the same questions are asked over and over again to witnesses and victims. For minor felony property crimes, there is often a time lag of hours and perhaps days before the investigator actually arrives at the scene to ask questions, process the crime scene for fingerprints and photographs, and do neighborhood canvassing. As a result, many departments have expanded the tasks of patrol officers to include investigative work.

- **Case screening.** How does one decide to continue further investigation of an incident? Typically, there is no set answer. By rule of thumb, a seasoned officer working a case can predict whether the incident has any chance of being solved, based on the variety and amount of information gathered within a given period of time. One might ask what types of information, what variety, and how much time? Experience might be the only answer. In an effort to quantify this process, a screening instrument has been developed to predict the chance for future success of any given criminal investigation. An important aspect of case screening, and overall investigative processes, is the advisement of witnesses and crime victims on case progress. Too often, the victim is kept in the dark as to what efforts were made to solve the case. With case screening, the person making the complaint is advised when the case is suspended, based on lack of leads or variables related to the case.

- **Managing criminal investigation.** This important step of the investigative process involves assigning the case to a single investigator or a group of investigators to solve the crime. Traditionally, the follow-up portion of the investigative process has been characterized by the absence of a management system for assigning, coordinating, directing, and monitoring the continuing investigative effort. To solve this problem, managerial control over the continuing investigation process is required. An administrator must be able to deploy resources, organize workloads, and determine economical and effective assignment policies for the investigative unit. The application of such administrative control will typically include a centralized filing of all investigative folders, allocation of review dates by a supervisor, and use of investigative checklists.

• **Improving police/prosecutor relations.** The police investigator, and the person who will ultimately prosecute the case, the district attorney or the public prosecutor, often act in isolation with regard to the tasks that each performs. Seasoned investigators often look upon prosecutors as people who do not understand the reality of the case, which results in plea-bargaining or an inept presentation of the case in the courtroom. The prosecutor, on the other hand, often has to deal with a staggering caseload. Except in sensational cases, the prosecutor does not have the opportunity or the time to analyze every aspect of a criminal investigation. Moreover, the first thing that the prosecutor may observe when presented with the investigation case folder is poor grammar, spelling errors, and the lack of concise information needed to plug legal and criminal procedural gaps related to the case. Therefore, it is recommended that prosecutors and investigators start communicating on a more frequent basis before the disposition of the case. This communication can be formal or informal.

Visual thinking is sometimes applied in police investigations. In thinking, there are many responses given automatically, or almost so, because they are readily available, or because the needed operations are so simple as to be almost instantaneous. Therefore, imagery may do its work below the level of consciousness. What are mental images like? According to the most elementary view, mental images are faithful replicas of the physical objects they replace.

Police investigators take both written and visual notes. Visual notes are simply the graphic equivalent of written notes. Taking visual notes refers to recording information that is primarily visual and, therefore, could not be recorded effectively with words. Keeping notes has always been an effective hedge against an imperfect memory. Moreover, the act of taking notes, selecting and sifting through them, is an important tool for creativity (Crowe & Laseau, 1984). Finally, notes are important as documentation of work in investigations.

In the picture of inference that emerges from traditional logic, the vast majority of valid pieces of reasoning, perhaps all, take place in language, and this sort of reasoning is thought to be well understood. Barwise and Etchemendy (1996a) think this picture is wrong on both counts. First, it is wrong in regard to the frequency with which nonlinguistic forms of information are used in reasoning. There are good reasons to suppose that much, if not most reasoning makes use of some form of visual representation. Second, it is wrong in regard to the extent to which even linguistic reasoning is accounted for by our current theories of inference. Human languages are infinitely richer and subtler than the formal languages for which we have anything like a complete account of inference.

Barwise and Etchemendy (1996a) argue further that when one takes seriously the variety of ways in which information can be presented and manipulated, the task of giving a general account of valid reasoning is, to say the least, daunting. Nevertheless, we think it is important for logicians to broaden their outlook beyond linguistically presented information. As the computer gives us even richer tools for representing information, we must begin to study the logical aspects of reasoning that uses nonlinguistic forms of representation.

Inference can be taken to concern relationships among structured representations in some sort of conventional representation system. A broader notion of inference would include nonconventional inference. For example, it could be said that one infers the sentence "There is someone at the door" from certain knocking sounds heard at certain places. While it is of interest to develop mathematical models of inference thus broadly construed, we are not inclined to think of them as logical systems, so we restrict attention to the narrower class (Barwise & Hammer, 1996).

A logical system is a mathematical model of some pretheoretic notion of consequence and an existing (or possible) inferential practice that honors it. A model of first-order inference must at least capture its most coarse-grained features: it must provide a characterization of logical consequence that is faithful to the information practice being modeled (Barwise & Hammer, 1996).

Barwise and Etchemendy (1996b) approach inference from an informational perspective. Wherever there is structure, there is information. But in order for agents (animals, people, or computers) to traffic in information, the information must, in some way or other, be presented to or represented by an agent. Typically, a given representation or family of representations will represent certain information explicitly, while other information will be implicit in the information explicitly represented. Inference is the task of extracting information implicit in some explicitly presented information.

In carrying out a reasoning task, part of the solution lies in figuring out how to represent the problem. In problem solving, well begun really is half done. Figuring out how to represent the information at hand is often the most important part of the solution (Barwise & Etchemendy, 1996b).

Diagrammatic (or pictorial) representations are sometimes applied in police investigations. They are used in problem solving and reasoning. Glasgow and Papadias (1995) studied representations of diagrams and mental images, and the functions played by them in problem solving. Mathematical reasoning is another approach, applying analogies, metaphors, and images (English, 1997). Reasoning by analogy is generally defined as the transfer of structural information from one system, the base, to another system, the target. This transfer of knowledge is achieved through matching or mapping processes that entail finding the relational correspondences between the two systems.

Criminal profiling is concerned with the process of inferring distinctive personality characteristics of individuals responsible for committing criminal acts (Turvey, 1999). This process has also been referred to, among other less-common terms, as behavioral profiling, crime-scene profiling, criminal-personality profiling, offender profiling, and psychological profiling.

The extrapolation of characteristics of criminals from information about their crimes, as an aid to police investigation, is the essence of profiling. Canter and Heritage (1990) proposed that for such extrapolations to be more than educated guesses, they must be based upon knowledge of (1) coherent consistencies in criminal behavior and (2) the relationship those behavioral consistencies have to aspects of an offender available to the police in an investigation. Coherent consistencies are concerned with the behavior of offenders during a crime having some comprehensible coherence to them.

Criminal profiling is a subcategory of criminal investigative analysis; a term that accounts for several of the services that may be performed by forensic behavioral specialists. These services are said to include indirect personality assessment, equivocal death analysis, trial strategy, and criminal profiling. The profiling community is made up of professionals and nonprofessionals from a variety of related and unrelated backgrounds (Turvey, 1999).

Information from witnesses is typically assigned great importance in criminal investigations. The important role of witness reports has spurred a great deal of research investigating witnesses' memories for criminal events. As an example, the aim of the research conducted by Fahsing et al. (Fahsing, Ask, & Granhag, 2004) was to provide reliable documentation on the nature of offender descriptions provided by witnesses to actual crimes, and to conduct indirect tests of some of the established notions within witness psychology.

In doing so, some complexities underlying witnesses' psychological processes were revealed. An archival study was conducted using 250 offender descriptions by witnesses of armed bank robberies. The accuracy of the descriptions was gauged against authentic video documentation of the witnessed crimes. In general, witnesses provided accurate descriptions of the offenders, but reported few identifying details. Multiple regression analyses revealed that the witnesses' role (bank tellers vs. customers), the type of weapon used, and the number of perpetrators involved were moderately predictive of the quality of offender descriptions. However, several of the observed relationships were conditional on whether descriptions of basic attributes (e.g., height, age, build) or more detailed features were considered. Hence, the authors concluded that verifying all aspects of witness descriptions is crucial when studying memories for actual crimes.

The investigation of economic crime is an intriguing subject. The complexity of the crime challenges the investigators, the richness of the investigation process challenges the researcher. Economic criminality efficiently exploits the loopholes of the legislation and the new opportunities provided by the changes in the operational environment. Economic crime is an increasingly planned, professional activity, the form of which constantly changes (Puonti, 2004a).

Computers as a Medium for Communication

In Denmark, there is a department of the Danish National Police called the Flying Squad. The Flying Squad numbers around 100 detectives divided into five sections (homicide, fraud, theft, drugs, and environment). It works all over the country in cases that require more expertise than exists within the local police force. Christiansen (1996) studied human-computer interaction within three police investigation teams from various sections (homicide, theft, fraud).

A way to understand police investigation is to study the social organization of electronic paperwork, to see how documents as social constructs are part of the working division of labor and the ongoing structure of the work. In police investigation, the paperwork is organized by cases.

A case begins with a notice, information about a situation that somebody suspects to be illegal. Based on the notice information, a case is framed in terms of category of potential crime, the form of investigation to be applied, and the amount and quality of skills required and available. Next, an investigation team is formed. The investigation team shares information, and computers are used as a medium for communication between team members.

An example of an officer-to-officer system is the automatic vehicle locator that enables an officer to locate another officer. Real policing for patrol officers is construed as actions taken in the here and now, and the core of real police work is thought to be revealed by the rapid resolution of an ongoing problem, often employing threats and force, if seen as necessary. Information is personalized, often retained in memory rather than written, and embedded in the preference for secrecy characteristic of policing (Manning, 2001). In such action-oriented situations, an automatic vehicle locator can find another officer without calling him or her on the cellular phone.

Knowledge Acquisition: Interviewing

Investigative interviewing is maybe the most important fact-finding and knowledge acquisition tool for police investigation purposes. Investigative interviewing has been found to represent as much as 70-80% of a police investigator's daily activity. However, prior to the last two decades, no substantial guidance existed on how to conduct appropriate investigative interviews. Fahsing (2005) has worked on investigative interviewing for many years. He is an experienced detective superintendent in Norway. The following presentation is based on his work.

Empirical studies on the functioning of human memory gave rise to methods like the cognitive interview. This method has led to a significant increase in the knowledge obtained from cooperative witnesses. Similarly, extensive research on children's testimony has strengthened their position in the court system as knowledge sources, and improved interview procedures have arisen.

In addition, research on interview practice has revealed how the police, in their desire to solve cases, may act in overzealous manners and jeopardize the rights of suspects. These findings have led to improved legislation, and the traditional, and not very effective, methods of questioning suspects have been forced to give way to interviewing methods that are informed by psychological knowledge. However, research has shown that further training is needed before the desired standards are met (Clarke & Milne, 2001).

Despite the apparent importance of reliable eyewitness knowledge in criminal investigation, police officers have received little instruction on how to conduct an effective and reliable witness interview. As a reflection of the lack of formal training, police often display a rather superficial understanding of the basic aspects in this core activity in police investigations.

The human ability to remember and to recollect stored knowledge is a crucial component in any investigative interview. Hence, the psychological knowledge of memory has formed an essential part in the development of enhanced interviewing methods.

Memory can be divided into three phases: encoding, storage, and retrieval. In the encoding phase, an event is perceived and registered in the mind, then, a mental record of the event is stored for later use. The recorded knowledge remains stored until it someday gets activated again in the retrieval phase, where the mental record is activated and brings about the conscious phenomenon of recollection.

The human memory has some resemblance to the information processing systems found in computers since both systems code incoming information in order to make it accessible in the future. However, the human memory is significantly more complex, and able to turn information into knowledge. Hence, another vital difference from the computer is the fact that human memories do not necessarily store an identical picture of the incoming information. The memory can be described as a complicated network of interactions between the observed event and a number of other, more or less, unpredictable factors like the observer's mood and thoughts, the surrounding context, general knowledge of related experiences, and so forth. The human memory turns information into knowledge by understanding.

After the event has been encoded, the stored mental image may be altered as it comes into contact with other stored knowledge, or if the observer receives postevent information. Further, the memory will deteriorate over time, although most rapidly soon after the encoding process. Lofthus and Doyle (1997) found that the chance of interference is at its greatest when postevent information is introduced long after the encoding of the original event, and only shortly before it is to be retrieved. The effect of deterioration, or forgetting, may also make the observer less confident in the retrieval process, and less able to separate new information from details of the original event.

Failure to recall often is due to problems in the retrieval stage. Research has uncovered that witnesses may become distorted by the way an interviewer formulates the questions. Furthermore, since both the encoding and storage phases largely take place at a subconscious level, little can be done to enhance these mental processes. On the other hand, the retrieval process is, for the most part, under conscious control; hence, is the easiest phase both to alter, and to improve.

A number of studies on the process of retrieval have suggested that forgotten memories are not, in general, lost memories; it is rather a matter of not finding the right cues in order get access to the stored information. Experiments have shown that events, which were not recognized initially, could later be recalled correctly, if an appropriate retrieval cue was provided. For example, external factors, like physical or mental context reinstatement, have been identified as important retrieval cues. Equally, reconstruction of internal factors, such as emotions or internal state, may enhance the retrieval process.

Consequently, the psychological research on the functioning of the memory system is crucial for investigative interviewers as they, through interviewing procedures, indirectly may control the observers or the eyewitness' retrieval plan. Therefore, in order to improve the interviewer's operational approach and generate more accurate and complete knowledge, Fisher and Geiselman (1992) developed the cognitive interview.

The Cognitive Interview

The cognitive interview (CI) consists of four main mnemonic principles derived from the scientific literature on information retrieval. The principles are believed to increase the amount of correct information obtained without an increase in incorrect details (Milne & Bull, 1999). The four principles are (Fisher & Geiselman, 1992):

1. **Reinstatement of context.** This can be done either physically by visiting the scene, or mentally by instructing the witnesses to form an image of the scene of the incident. Because we store information from all senses, witnesses should be instructed to imagine and describe thoughts, feelings, sounds, smells, and physical conditions present at the time of the event.

2.   **Report everything.** No matter how trivial it may seem. Witnesses will often consider relevant information to be not relevant and, therefore, withhold it.

3.   **Change the temporal order of the event.** By instructing witnesses to report the incident in reverse order or from the middle.

4.   **Recount the event from different perspectives.** Recall the incident from another physical viewpoint. This strategy is based on the assumption that a mental change of observation perspective may activate additional retrieval cues in memory.

During the interview, additional memory aids should be used in conjunction with the four CI techniques described above. Questions such as: "Does the person remind you of someone you know?" have been found to facilitate the description of a specific person, or object-related details. When using such techniques, it is strongly recommended to follow up with the question: "Why," in order to bring forward the exact characteristic that made the witness do the actual comparison (Milne & Bull, 1999).

The CI has been tested against alternative interview methods, like hypnosis or the standard interview (SI). On average, the CI was found to yield between 25% to 35% more information than the SI, without an increase in incorrect information. Furthermore, the CI has been found to significantly reduce the impact of potential misleading questions. All four main strategies in CI have been found to effectively aid recollection. Context reinstatement turned out to be the most effective strategy when studied in isolation (Fahsing, 2005).

In studies of real-life CI interviews conducted by American police officers, it was found that a police officer's lack of interpersonal communication skills lessened the effect of the technique (Milne & Bull, 1999). Common findings were insufficient rapport building, constant interruptions, extensive use of short-answer questions, and inappropriate sequencing of questions. This led to a revision of the CI into a version called the enhanced cognitive interview (ECI). The new and improved version was constructed by elements from both cognitive psychology and the psychology of interpersonal communication.

The ECI starts with a rapport building section where the interviewer transfers control to the witness. The witness is requested to report everything. The context reinstatement section is similar to the CI strategy, and this is followed by a probing phase with the use of focused memory guidelines and open-ended questions. Then, there is an extensive and varied use of retrieval cues, such as change of temporal order and change of perspective, focusing on all of the witnesses' senses. The interviewer will motivate and assist the witnesses' recall, for example by the use of active listening techniques and appropriate use of pauses. Finally, the interviewer should summarize the interviewee's account, and end up with a closure of the interview in the purpose of leaving the witness with a positive frame of mind (Fisher & Geiselman, 1992).

In a laboratory test, the ECI was compared with the original CI. The study showed that the ECI elicited between 45-50% more correct information than the original version. Field studies done with U.S. police officers produced about the same results (Fisher & Geiselman, 1992).

Although some studies have shown a slight increase of incorrect information, a number of research studies from a range of different countries have confirmed the positive effect of the CI/ECI. The increase in correct recollection has been found in studies of diverse categories of interviewees like adults, children, elderly, and adults with learning disabilities (Milne & Bull, 1999).

Extensive research on children's testimonies has shown that children, if given appropriate instructions, are able to give an accurate free recall, yet young children are less capable to give a complete free recall. As a result, young children need more external cues, and also need to be questioned more in order to gain more details. This may lead to an increase in incorrect information being recalled if questions are asked in an improper way or in the wrong order. Children exposed to the CI strategies often find it difficult to answer; thus, a modification in order to make the children understand the strategies better seems required. Nevertheless, several studies have established evidence for the CI's effectiveness in order to enhance the free recall of children over eight years old. On the other hand, it is clear that the completeness and accuracy of children's recall is dependent on the interviewing skills of the adult (Fahsing, 2005).

Inappropriate Interviewing Practices

As in any other police interview, the purpose of an interview with a suspect is to obtain accurate and reliable information about a crime that has been committed. However, the methods considered by the police as adequate to obtain information have been widely divergent. The techniques used when interviewing suspects have traditionally been called "interrogation," and a number of the techniques used seem to be based on an assumption that most suspects are guilty and uncooperative (Vrij, 1998).

The third edition of the book *Criminal interrogation and confessions* by Inbau et al. (Inbau, Reid, & Buckley, 1986) exemplifies this police attitude. It provides the reader with a "step by step" method on how to manipulate an assumed guilty person to confess. Accordingly, the training book states:

The vast majority of criminal offenders are reluctant to confess and must be psychological persuaded to do so, and unavoidably, these interrogation procedures involve elements of trickery and deceit. The legality of such procedures is well established.

After an observational field study of more than 500 hours in three U.S. police departments, it was argued that contemporary U.S. police interrogation "can be best understood as a confidence game based on manipulation and betrayal of trust" (Fahsing, 2005).

Research studies have shown that this approach is widespread also outside of the U.S. In a study of the interviews of suspects at Brighton Police Station, commissioned by the Royal Commission of Criminal Procedure, it was found that the main purpose with the interrogation was to obtain a confession. In the same study, he found that in two-thirds of the cases, the police used persuasive or manipulative interrogation tactics in order to get information or admissions. These tactics included (Milne & Bull, 1999):

- Pointing out the futility of denial
- Pretending that the police were in possession of more evidence than they actually were
- Minimizing the seriousness of the offence
- Manipulating the suspect's self-esteem
- Advising interviewees that it was in their best interests to confess

Several other research studies have reported similar findings. Also in Norway, recent research indicates that the police have been influenced by this approach. Fahsing (2005) writes that the obvious first consideration to this culture is that it is highly unethical to treat a possible innocent person as if he/she was guilty. Vrij (1998) holds that such techniques are aimed to impress the suspect, and to break down the interviewee's resistance. Furthermore, considering that all such methods have an implicit assumption of the suspect's guilt, Vrij (1998) states that these methods cannot be seen as a part of an information gathering system. Researchers emphasize police officer's assumption of guilt, combined with use of pressure, trickery, and deceit, as a main cause to why suspects ultimately may give false confessions.

In an effort to provide safeguards relating to the police interviewing of suspects, the Police and Criminal Evidence Act 1984 (PACE) was introduced in 1986. PACE included new legislation governing the way in which suspects were arrested, detained, and interviewed by police officers. For example, a special code ensured that suspects were not subjected to undue police tricks and pressure. Moreover, PACE prescribed that all police interviews with suspects should be audio taped (Vrij, 1998).

After the introduction of PACE, a decline in the use of persuasive and manipulative tactics was observed. In spite of this, however, the overall proportion of interviews that ended in a confession did not decrease (Milne & Bull, 1999).

Furthermore, Baldwin (1992) examined 600 taped police interviews of suspects in England, and found that most interviewees were cooperative and answered fully to questions asked by the police officer. Another interesting finding was that in only 20 of the 600 interviews did suspects change their story during the interview. Hence, the vast majority of suspects, whether admitting or denying, stuck to their original account, regardless of how the interview was conducted.

Similarly, other studies have found that only very rarely, interviewees changed from denying to admitting during an interview, or from one interview to the next. Therefore, some have concluded that police interview techniques seem to have a minimal effect on whether admissions occur. The only variable found to significantly influence the suspect's confession rate were the amount of evidence (Milne & Bull, 1999).

Baldwin's (1992) research revealed comprehensive limitations in the officer's approach to interviewing. The main shortcomings identified included general ineptitude, lack of preparation, poor technique, and assumption of guilt. Baldwin (1992) argued that his findings could be a result of PACE, successfully outlawing oppressive techniques, and nothing having been brought in to replace it. Accordingly, Baldwin (1992) recommended the compilation of a national handbook and a practical training program. He supported a less offensive approach to the interviewing of suspects based on thorough planning, empathy, social, and communication skills.

In the light of this research and of juridical criticism of police interviewing in several high profile cases, a national review of investigative interviewing was initiated. This review led to the development of the investigative interviewing ethos and the PEACE training approach (Milne & Bull, 1999).

The PEACE Training Approach

In an attempt to deal with the "confession-culture" and instead maintain a neutral inquisitorial interviewing style, the Home Office and the Association of Chief Police Officers approved seven principles considered to be relevant to all investigative interviewing. According to the new ethos, the primary role of the police officer was to open-mindedly, gather "evidence and obtain information" in order to "discover the truth about matter under police investigation." Furthermore, the officers were instructed to act fairly, and to take particular consideration of vulnerable people (Milne & Bull, 1999).

Additionally, all police officers in England and Wales were issued with two handbooks that recommended a five-step model of investigative interviewing. Under the acronym PEACE, a suggested structure of an interview was put forward: Planning and Preparation, Engage and Explain, Account, Closure, and Evaluation. The new interview approach was heavily influenced by Baldwin's (1992) recommendations with regard to planning, communication skills and ethics. Also, modern interviewing techniques, like CI and conversation management (CM), were incorporated in the program.

In conjunction with the distribution of the handbooks, a five-day PEACE course was initiated, aiming to ensure that the officers developed basic interviewing skills necessary to apply the model. During the 1990s, the PEACE-training had been assigned to all operational police officers at a national level and in 1998, about 70% of the police officers in England and Wales had accomplished the training (Clarke & Milne, 2001).

The training-effect of four pilot courses was evaluated by assessing the interviewing skills of the participants up against untrained officers. The results demonstrated that both interviewing skills and knowledge increased after the training. It was also found that the increase was sustained 6 months later. The research report concluded that if the learning outcome was acted upon, it should ensure a safe execution of investigative interviews (Clarke & Milne, 2001).

However, despite the fact that information-gathering interviews actively have been promoted in England and Wales, a number of studies have indicated that such interview techniques are relatively rare. For example, a study of taped interviews with suspects fortified that police officers lacked basic communication skills. The interviewers demonstrated a lack of empathy or compassion, were inflexible, and used leading questions. In fact, one study concluded that differences between "skilled" and "not skilled" interviews could be attributed to the communication skills of the interviewer (Vrij, 1998).

Correspondingly, in a study of the workplace impact of the PEACE training, Clarke and Milne (2001) found that the interviewer's use of basic communication skills such as listening were insufficient. As the first study, this also included a sample of recorded interviews with victims and witnesses. However, the overall impression of the interviews was poor, with no evidence of the use of memory enhancing techniques, like the ECI. Nevertheless, they reported an overall improvement with regard to the interviewing of suspects. Moreover, when time was afforded to officers, like in murder investigations, the interviews were rated at a higher standard.

Previous research of the CI technique in the field has concluded that many police officers seemed to lack the sufficient time to conduct a full, enhanced cognitive interview. A possible disadvantage of the ECI technique is that it leads to an increased cognitive load on interviewers Therefore, in order to use the ECI effectively, police officers need further training to help increase their concentration, flexibility, and patience during interviews (Fahsing, 2005).

Since a number of previous studies of police interviews have pointed out a lack of such qualities, this might be adequate also to ensure an overall improvement of police officers interviewing skills. As mentioned above, an improvement of the police officer's basic social and communication skills was one of Baldwin's (1992) main recommendations, just as similar findings in the U.S. made Fisher and Geiselman (1992) develop the enhanced cognitive interview. It has been pointed out that Baldwin's (1992) approach to police interviews does not differ substantially from interviews in other contexts, such as interviews with patients or selection interviews. Vrij (1998) advocates this approach since in all interview situations, the outcome relies on the interviewer's ability to create an atmosphere in which the interviewee is willing to talk.

Fahsing (2005) finds that there is little doubt that research has facilitated the development of improved forensic interviewing methods. The cognitive interview technique, the PEACE training approach, the phased interview of children and vulnerable adults are all developed on the basis of extensive psychological research material. This development has provided a valuable platform for further improvement of investigative interviewing.

As we have illustrated, there is strong scientific evidence that CI, as an isolated approach, is superior to other known methods in the way it brings about significantly more reliable information, without an increase in fabrications. However, the approach has its limitations, such as its insufficiency with regard to uncooperative interviewees, and the aspect that many police officers find it demanding to employ.

On the other hand, the research that gave rise to the PEACE approach has had an invaluable significance in the way that it has highlighted the importance of ethics, empathy, and social and communication skills in any investigative interview.

As all interviews largely depend on these elements, it is scarcely possible to rate which of these contributions have had the most influence on the practical information gathering in forensic contexts.

Even though the desired investigative interview standards are far from accomplished in England and Wales, research findings, and the development of a scientific methodology in the field, have embarked on a major change in practice. As a result, it is clear that the American and British police interrogation techniques are now vastly different. Also, the mere fact that both basic and advanced interview courses now exist in England and Wales illustrates how committed the police service is to raising standards with regard to investigative interviewing.

Besides, recent psychological research has led to important understanding and awareness with regards to eyewitness accuracy and false confessions. Legislations such as the PACE insisting that all suspect's interviews are tape recorded, has contributed to the reduction of some of the more dubious police practices and, hopefully, reduced the chance of miscarriages of justice (Fahsing, 2005).

Technologies and Techniques

We conclude this chapter by discussing practical and workable technologies, tools, and techniques for knowledge management in law enforcement. While technologies and techniques at Stage 1 were concerned with end-user tools that can make each individual police officer more efficient and effective, technologies and techniques at Stage 2 are concerned with tools for cooperation between officers to make their cooperation more efficient and effective.

The typical system at Stage 2 is the police intranet. Since the police network in most countries is a closed network with secure access points, the police intranet might provide a rich set of tools for creating collaborative environments in which members of the organization can exchange ideas, share information, and work together on common projects and assignments, regardless of their physical location. The closed electronic network for law enforcement enables detectives to get in touch with other detectives, laboratories, cars, and undercover units.

An interesting example is the Flying Squad in Denmark. The Flying Squad works all over the country on cases that require more expertise than exists within the local police force. Closed computer networks serve as medium for communication within the squad, as well as between the squad and local police (Christiansen, 1996).

Another interesting example is the automatic vehicle locator that enables an officer to locate another officer. In action-oriented policing situations, an automatic vehicle locator can find another officer without calling him or her on the cellular phone (Manning, 2001).

References

Baldwin, J. (1992). Videotaping police interviews with suspects: An evaluation. *Police Research Series. No 1.* London: Home Office.

Barwise, J., & Etchemendy, J. (1996a). Visual information and valid reasoning. In G. Allwein & J. Barwise (Eds.), *Logical reasoning with diagrams* (pp. 3-25). New York; Oxford: Oxford University Press.

Barwise, J., & Etchemendy, J. (1996b). Heterogeneous logic. In G. Allwein & J. Barwise (Eds.), *Logical reasoning with diagrams* (pp. 179-193). New York; Oxford: Oxford University Press.

Barwise, J., & Hammer, E. (1996). Diagrams and the concept of logical system. In G. Allwein & J. Barwise (Eds.), *Logical reasoning with diagrams* (pp. 49-78). New York; Oxford: Oxford University Press.

Breu, K., Ward, J., & Murray, P. (2000). Success factors in leveraging the corporate information and knowledge resource through intranets. In Y. Malhotra (Ed.), *Knowledge management and virtual organizations.* Hershey, PA: Idea Group Publishing.

Canter, D., & Heritage, R. (1990). A multivariate model of sexual offence behaviour: Developments in "offender profiling." *Journal of Forensic Psychiatry, 1*(2), 185-212.

Christiansen, E. (1996). Tamed by a rose: Computers as tools in human activity. In B. Nardi (Ed.), *Context and conciousness: Activity theory and human-computer interaction.* Boston: Massachusetts Institute of Technology.

Clarke, C., & Milne, R. (2001). *National evaluation of the PEACE investigative interview course.* Retrieved from http://www.hum.port.ac.uk/icjs/ support/PeaceEvalFula.pdf

Collier, P. M., Edwards, J. S., & Shaw, D. (2004). Communicating knowledge about police performance. *International Journal of Productivity and Performance Management, 53*(5), 458-467.

Crowe, N., & Laseau, P. (1984). *Visual notes for architects and designers.* New York: Van Nostrand Reinhold.

English, L. (1997). Analogies, metaphors, and images: Vehicles for mathematical reasoning. In L. English (Ed.), *Mathematical reasoning: Analogies, metaphors, and images.* NJ: Lawrence Erlbaum Associates.

Fahsing, I. (2005). *Investigative interviewing.* Research report, Norwegian Police University College, Oslo, Norway.

Fahsing, I., Ask, K., & Granhag, P.A. (2004). The man behind the mask: Accuracy and predictors of eyewitness offender descriptions. *Journal of Applied Psychology, 89*(4), 722-729.

Fisher, R. P., & Geiselman, R. E. (1992). *Memory enhancing techniques for investigative interviewing.* Springfield, IL: Charles C. Thomas.

Fraser, C. (2004). Strategic information systems for policing. *Police Executive Research Forum*, Washington, DC.

Fraser, C. (2005). Strategic information systems for policing. In D. Faggiani, B. Kubu, & R. Rantala (Eds.), *Facilitating the implementation of incident-based data systems* (pp. 1-12). Washington, DC: Police Executive Research Forum.

Glasgow, J., & Papadias, D. (1995). Computational imagery. In B. Chandrasekaran, J. Glasgow, & H. Hari Harayanan (Eds.), *Diagrammatic reasoning: Cognitive and computational perspectives* (pp. 453-480). Menlo Park, CA; Cambridge, MA: AAAI Press/MIT Press.

Inbau, F. E., Reid, J. E., & Buckley, J. P. (1986). *Criminal interrogations and confessions* (3rd ed.). Baltimore: Williams & Wilkins.

Laudon, K. C. & Laudon, J. P. (2005). *Essentials of management information systems: Managing the digital firm* (6th ed.). Upper Saddle River, NJ: Prentice Hall.

Lofthus, E. F., & Doyle, J. M. (1997). *Eyewitness testimony: Civil and criminal* (3rd ed.). Charlottesville, VA: Lexis Law Publishing.

Manning, P. K. (2001). Information technology in the police context - The 'sailor' phone. In Yeates & Van Maanen (Eds.), *Information technology and organizational transformation*. Thousand Oaks, CA: Sage Publications.

Milne, R., & Bull, R. (1999). *Investigative interviewing: Psychology and practice*. Chichester, UK: John Wiley and Sons Ltd.

Puonti, A. (2004a). *Learning to work together: Collaboration between authorities in economic-crime investigation*. Doctoral dissertation, University of Helsinki, Vantaa, Finland.

Thibault, E. A., Lynch, L. M., & McBride, R. B. (1998). *Proactive police management* (4th ed.). Upper Saddle River, NJ: Prentice Hall.

Turvey, B. (1999). *Criminal profiling: An introduction to behavioral evidence analysis*. CA: Academic Press.

Vrij, A. (1998). Interviewing suspects. In A. Memon, A. Vrij, & R. Bull (Eds.), *Psychology and law: Truthfulness, accuracy and credibility* (pp. 124-146). London: McGraw-Hill.

Chapter VII

Officer-to-Information Systems

Information from knowledge workers is stored and made available to everyone in the police force who is in need of, and eligible for this information. Data-mining techniques can be applied here by law enforcement personnel to find relevant information, and combine information in data warehouses. Search engines and Web browsers enable police officers to quickly search and find information in criminal cases.

At this stage of knowledge management technology, information is stored and made accessible as a resource. The resource perspective is important, and we start this chapter by describing the resource-based theory of the firm. As an example of police work using stored information at Stage 3, we discuss eyewitness reports stored in databases. Again, we are more interested in understanding the difficulties of trusting eyewitness reports in police investigations, rather than the database technology.

Strategy has traditionally focused on products and services to gain competitive advantage. Recent work in the area of strategic management and economic theory has begun to focus on the internal side of the equation, the organization's resources and capabilities. This new perspective is referred to as the resource-based theory of the firm.

The resource-based theory has been adopted in police organizations because of rising costs, limited resources, and growing service demands. Murphy (2004) documents the police adoption of neoliberal business models and values in order to facilitate rationalization of police governance, organization, manage-

Figure 1. Officer-to-information systems at Stage 3 of the knowledge management technology stage model

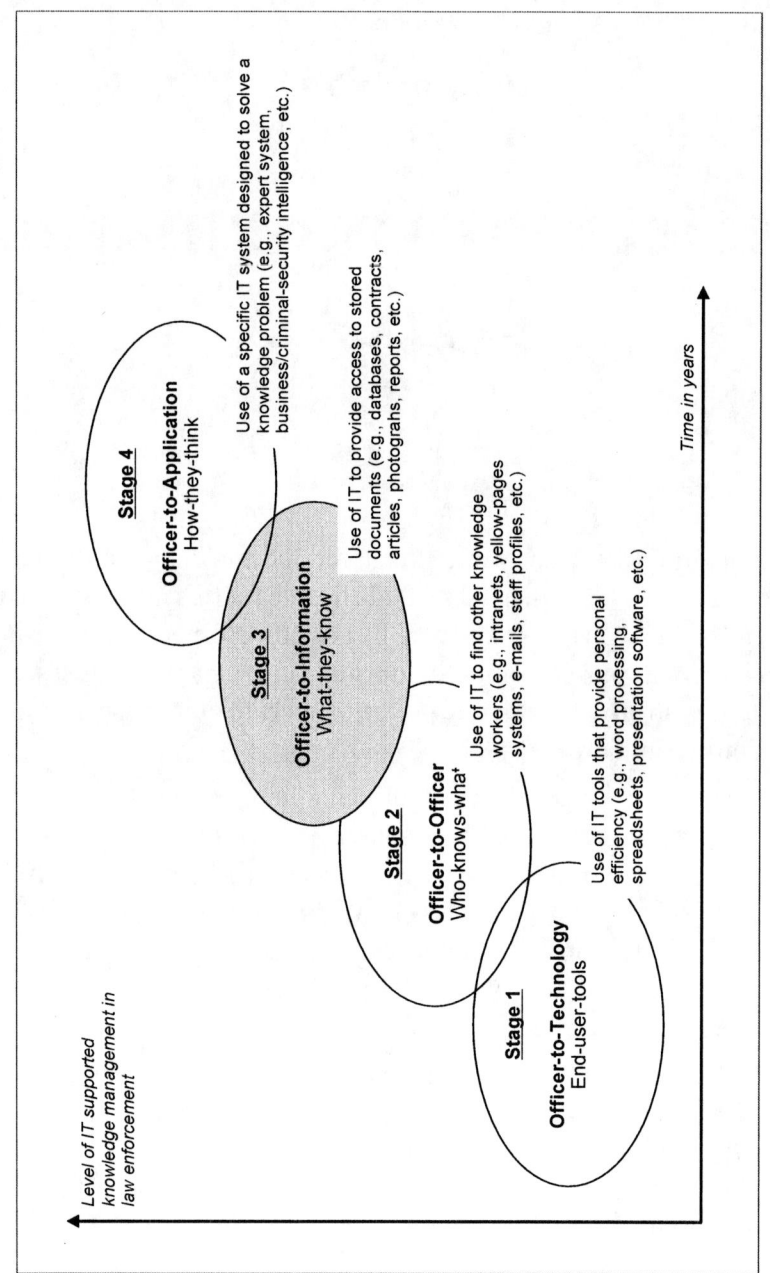

ment, and services. His analysis concludes that limited, rationalized, modern police services require a new strategic formulation of the police role to address public interest and the rapidly expanding policing and security demands of late-modern Canadian society. He argues that without institutional capacity for generation, accumulation, communication, and implementation of knowledge resources, a skeptical and challenging market-society may well be unsympathetic to the expensive and expansive needs of public policing.

Widespread use of computers and networks in both business and personal life has created new forms of documentary evidence used in courts of law. Much of the evidence today for stock frauds, embezzlements, theft of company trade secrets, computer crimes, and many civil cases is in digital form. In the past, documentary evidence used to prove crimes was on paper. In addition to information from printed or typewritten pages, legal cases today will increasingly rely on evidence represented as computer data stored on computer disks, as well as e-mail, instant messages, and e-commerce over the Internet.

A new field called computer forensics has sprung up to deal specifically with computer-based evidence. Computer-forensics is the scientific collection, examination, authentication, preservation, and analysis of data held on or retrieved from computer storage media in such a way that the information can be used as evidence in a court of law. It deals with the following problems (Laudon & Laudon, 2005):

- Recovering data from computers while preserving evidential integrity
- Securely storing and handling recovered electronic data
- Finding significant information in a large volume of electronic data
- Presenting the information to a court of law

Computer evidence can reside on computer storage media in the form of computer files, and as ambient data that are not visible to the average user. Data that a computer user may have deleted on computer storage media may be recoverable through various techniques. Computer forensics experts try to recover such "hidden" data for presentation as evidence.

At Stage 3 of the knowledge management technology model, we find both structured and semistructured systems. A structured system has the content of explicit, codified knowledge that exists in formal documents. Here we find online corporate libraries based on organization documents. Semistructured information is all the digital information in an organization that does not exist in a formal document or a formal report that was written by a designated author. It has been estimated that at least 80% of an organization's work content is unstructured: information in folders, messages, memos, proposals, e-mails, graphics, electronic slide presentations, and even videos created in different formats and stored in many locations.

Two examples of knowledge management systems at Stage 3 in law enforcement are COPLINK and geodemographics. COPLINK has a relational database system for crime-specific cases such as gang-related incidents, and serious crimes such as homicide, aggravated assault, and sexual crimes. Deliberately targeting these criminal areas allows a manageable amount of information to be entered into a database (Chen et al., 2002). Geodemographic profiles of the characteristics of individuals and small areas are central to efficient and effective deployment of law enforcement resources. Geocomputation is based on geographical information systems (Ashby & Longley, 2005).

Resource-Based Theory of the Organization

In this book, we apply the knowledge-based view of the firm that has established itself as an important perspective in strategic management. This perspective builds on the resource-based theory of the firm. According to the resource-based theory of the firm, performance differences across organizations can be attributed to the variance in the organizations' resources and capabilities. Resources that are valuable, unique, and difficult to imitate can provide the basis for organizations' competitive advantages. In turn, these competitive advantages produce positive returns. According to Hitt et al. (Hitt, Bierman, Shumizu, & Kochhar, 2001), most of the few empirical tests of the resource-based theory that have been conducted have supported positive, direct effects of resources.

The essence of the resource-based theory of the firm lies in its emphasis on the internal resources available to the organization, rather than on the external opportunities and threats dictated by industry conditions. Organizations are considered to be highly heterogeneous, and the bundles of resources available to each organization are different. This is both because organizations have different initial resource endowments, and because managerial decisions affect resource accumulation and the direction of firm growth as well as resource utilization.

The resource-based theory of the firm holds that, in order to generate sustainable competitive advantage, a resource must provide economic value, and must be presently scarce, difficult to imitate, nonsubstitutable, and not readily obtainable in factor markets. This theory rests on two key points. First, that resources are the determinants of firm performance and second, that resources must be rare, valuable, difficult to imitate and nonsubstitutable by other rare resources. When the latter occurs, a competitive advantage has been created (Priem & Butler, 2001).

Resources can simultaneously be characterized as valuable, rare, nonsubstitutable, and inimitable. To the extent that an organization's physical assets, infrastructure, and workforce satisfy these criteria, they qualify as resources. A firm's performance depends fundamentally on its ability to have a distinctive, sustainable competitive advantage that derives from the possession of organization-specific resources (Priem & Butler, 2001).

The resource-based theory is a useful perspective in strategic management. Research on the competitive implications of such organizational resources as knowledge, learning, culture, teamwork, and human capital, was given a significant boost by resource-based theory: a theory that indicated it was these kinds of resources that were most likely to be sources of sustainable competitive advantage for organizations (Barney, 2001).

Organizations' resource endowments, particularly intangible resources, are difficult to change except over the long term. For example, although human resources may be mobile to some extent, capabilities may not be valuable for all organizations, or even for their competitors. Some capabilities are based on firm-specific knowledge, and others are valuable when integrated with additional individual capabilities and specific firm resources. Therefore, intangible resources are more likely than tangible resources to produce a competitive advantage. In particular, intangible firm-specific resources, such as knowledge, allow organizations to add value to incoming factors of production (Hitt et al., 2001).

Resource-based theory attributes advantage in an industry to a firm's control over bundles of unique material, human, organizational, and locational resources and skills that enable unique value-creating strategies. A firm's resources are said to be a source of competitive advantage to the degree that they are scarce, specialized, appropriable, valuable, rare, and difficult to imitate or substitute.

Capabilities and Resources

A fundamental idea in resource-based theory is that a firm must continually enhance its resources and capabilities to take advantage of changing conditions. Optimal growth involves a balance between the exploitation of existing resource positions and the development of new resource positions. Thus, a firm would be expected to develop new resources after its existing resource base has been fully utilized. Building new resource positions is important if the organization is to achieve sustained growth. When unused productive resources are coupled with changing managerial knowledge, unique opportunities for growth are created (Pettus, 2001).

The term resource is derived from Latin, resurgere, which means "to rise," and implies an aid or expedient for reaching an end. A resource implies a potential means to achieve an end, or as something that can be used to create value. The first strategy textbooks outlining a holistic perspective focused on how resources needed to be allocated or deployed to earn rents. The interest in the term was, for a long time, linked to the efficiency of resource allocation, but this focus has later been expanded to issues such as resource accumulation, resource stocks, and resource flows (Haanaes, 1997).

Organizations develop firm-specific resources, and then renew these to respond to shifts in the business environment. Organizations develop dynamic capabilities to adapt to changing environments. According to Pettus (2001), the term dynamic refers to the capacity to renew resource positions to achieve congruence with changing environmental conditions. A capability refers to the key role of strategic management in appropriately adapting, integrating, and reconfiguring internal and external organizational skills, resources, and functional capabilities to match the requirements of a changing environment.

If organizations are to develop dynamic capabilities, learning is crucial. Change is costly; therefore, the ability of organizations to make necessary adjustments depends upon their ability to scan the environment to evaluate markets and competitors, and to quickly accomplish reconfiguration and transformation ahead of competition. However, history matters. Thus, opportunities for growth will involve dynamic capabilities closely related to existing capabilities. As such, opportunities will be most effective when they are close to previous resource use (Pettus, 2001).

According to Johnson and Scholes (2002), successful strategies are dependent on the organization having the strategic capability to perform at the level that is required for success. So the first reason why an understanding of strategic capability is important is concerned with whether an organization's strategies continue to fit the environment in which the organization is operating, and the opportunities and threats that exist. Many of the issues of strategy development are concerned with changing strategic capability better to fit a changing environment. Understanding strategic capability is also important from another perspective. The organization's capability may be the leading edge of strategic developments in the sense that new opportunities may be created by stretching and exploiting the organization's capability, either in ways which competitors find difficult to match, or in genuinely new directions, or both. This requires organizations to be innovative in the way they develop and exploit their capability.

In this perspective, strategic capability is about providing products or services to customers that are valued, or might be valued in the future. An understanding of what customers value is the starting point. The discussion then moves to whether an organization has the resources to provide products and services that meet these customer requirements.

By a resource is meant anything that could be thought of as a strength or weakness of a given organization. More formally, a firm's resources at a given time can be defined as those (tangible and intangible) assets that are tied to the organization over a substantial period of time. Examples of resources are brand names, in-house knowledge of technology, employment of skilled personnel, trade contracts, machinery, efficient procedures, capital, and so forth. According to the economic school, resources include human capital, structural capital, relational capital, and financial capital.

Priem and Butler (2001) find it problematic that virtually anything associated with a firm can be a resource, because this notion suggests that prescriptions for dealing in certain ways with certain categories of resources might be operationally valid, whereas other categories of resources might be inherently difficult for practitioners to measure and manipulate. One example of a resource that might be difficult to measure and manipulate is tacit knowledge. Some have argued for tacit knowledge—that understanding gained from experience, but that sometimes cannot be expressed to another person, and is unknown to oneself—as a source of competitive advantage.

Another example is the CEO resource. Prescriptions have been made to top managers of poorly performing organizations that they are the cause of the problem and should think about voluntarily exiting the organization. This is a case where viewing a CEO as a resource would have more prescriptive implications for boards of directors than for the CEO (Priem and Butler, 2001).

Barney (2002) discusses how value, rarity, imitability, and organization can be brought together into a single framework to understand the return potential associated with exploiting any of a firm's resources and capabilities. The framework consists of the following five steps (Barney, 2002):

1. If a resource or capability controlled by a firm is *not valuable*, that resource will not enable a firm to choose or implement strategies that exploit environmental opportunities or neutralize environmental threats. Organizing to exploit this resource will increase a firm's costs or decrease its revenues. These types of resources are weaknesses. Organizations will either have to fix these weaknesses, or avoid using them when choosing and implementing strategies. If organizations do exploit these kinds of resources and capabilities, they can expect to put themselves at a competitive disadvantage compared to organizations that either do not possess these nonvaluable resources, or do not use them in conceiving and implementing strategies. Organizations at a competitive disadvantage are likely to earn below-normal economic profits.

2. If a resource or capability is *valuable but not rare*, exploiting this resource in conceiving and implementing strategies will generate competitive parity and normal economic performance. Exploiting these valuable-but-not-rare resources will generally not create above-normal economic performance for a firm, but failure to exploit them can put a firm at a competitive disadvantage. In this sense, valuable-but-not-rare resources can be thought of as organizational strengths.

3. If a resource or capability is *valuable and rare but not costly to imitate*, exploiting this resource will generate a temporary competitive advantage for a firm and above-normal economic profits. A firm that exploits this kind of resource is, in an important sense, gaining a first-mover advantage, because it is the first organization that is able to exploit a particular resource. However, once competing organizations observe this competitive advantage, they will be able to acquire or develop the resources needed to implement this strategy through direct duplication or substitution at no cost disadvantage compared to the first-moving organization. Over time, any competitive advantage that the first mover obtained would be competed away as other organizations imitate the resources needed to compete. However, between the time a firm gains a competitive advantage by exploiting a valuable and rare but imitable resource or capability, and the time that competitive advantage is competed away through

imitation, the first-moving organization can earn above-normal economic performance. Consequently, this type of resource or capability can be thought of as an organizational strength and distinctive competence.

4.   If a resource is *valuable, rare, and costly to imitate*, exploiting this resource will generate a sustained competitive advantage and above-normal economic profits. In this case, competing organizations face a significant cost disadvantage in imitating a successful organization's resources and capabilities and thus, cannot imitate this organization's strategies. This advantage may reflect the unique history of the successful organization, causal ambiguity about which resources to imitate, or the socially complex nature of these resources and capabilities. In any case, attempts to compete away the advantages of organizations that exploit these resources will not generate above-normal or even normal performance for imitating organizations. Even if these organizations are able to acquire or develop the resources and capabilities in question, the very high costs of doing so would put them at a competitive disadvantage compared to the organization that already possessed the valuable, rare, and costly to imitate resources. These kinds of resources and capabilities are organizational strengths and sustainable distinctive competencies.

5.   The question of organization operates as an adjustment factor in the framework. If a firm with a resource that is *valuable, rare, and costly to imitate, is disorganized*, some of its potential above-normal return could be lost. If the organization completely fails to organize itself to take advantage of this resource, it could actually lead the organization that has the potential for above-normal performance to earn normal or even below-normal performance.

Barney (2001) discusses how value and rarity of resources can be determined. *Value* is a question of conditions under which resources will and will not be valuable. Models of the competitive environment within which a firm competes can determine value. Such models fall into two large categories: (1) efforts to use structure-conduct-performance-based models to specify conditions under which different firm resources will be valuable and (2) efforts to determine the value of firm resources that apply other models derived from industrial organization models of perfect and imperfect competition.

As an example of resource value determination, Barney (2001) discusses the ability of cost leadership strategy to generate sustained competitive advantage. Several firm attributes may be associated with cost leadership, such as volume-

derived economies of scale, cumulative volume-derived learning curve economies, and policy choices. These firm attributes can be shown to generate
economic value in at least some market settings. The logic used to demonstrate
the value of these attributes is a market structure logic that is consistent with
traditional microeconomics. After identifying the conditions under which cost
leadership can generate economic value, it is possible to turn to the conditions
under which cost leadership can be a source of competitive advantage (i.e.,
rare) and sustained competitive advantage (i.e., rare and costly to imitate).

The resource-based theory postulates that some resources will have a higher
value for one firm than for other firms. The reasons why the value of resources
may be firm-specific are multiple and include (Haanaes, 1997): the experience
of working together as a team, the organization possessing superior knowledge
about its resources, the bundling of the resources, and the existence of
cospecialized or complementary assets.

The value of a given resource may change over time as the market conditions
change, for example, in terms of technology, customer preferences, or industry
structure. Thus, it is often argued that organizations need to maintain a dynamic,
as opposed to static, evaluation of the value of different resources.

Rarity is a question of how many competing organizations possess a particular
valuable resource. If only one competing organization possesses a particular
valuable resource, then that organization can gain a competitive advantage, that
is, it can improve its efficiency and effectiveness in ways that competing
organizations cannot. One example of this form of testable assertion is
mentioned by Barney (2001). The example is concerned with organizational
culture as a source of competitive advantage. If only one competing organization possesses a valuable organizational culture (where the value of that culture
is determined in ways that are exogenous to the organization), then that
organization can gain a competitive advantage, that is, it can improve its
efficiency and effectiveness in ways that competing organizations cannot. Both
these assertions are testable. If a firm uniquely possesses a valuable resource
and cannot improve its efficiency and effectiveness in ways that generate
competitive advantages, then these assertions are contradicted. One could test
these assertions by measuring the extent to which a firm uniquely possesses
valuable resources, for example, valuable organizational culture; measuring the
activities that different organizations engage in to improve their efficiency and
effectiveness, and then seeing if there are some activities a firm with the unique

culture engages in to improve its effectiveness and efficiency; activities not engaged in by other competing organizations.

In general, the rarity of a resource is present as long as the number of organizations that possess a particular valuable resource is less than the number of organizations needed to generate perfect competition dynamics. Of course, there is difficult measurement problems associated with testing assertions of this form. Barney (2001) points out that additional research work is needed to complete the parameterization of the concept of rarity.

Efficient organizations can sustain their competitive advantage only if their resources can neither be extended freely nor imitated by other organizations. Hence, in order for resources to have the potential to generate rents, they must be rare. Valuable, but common resources cannot, by themselves, represent sources of competitive advantage because competitors can access them. Nobody needs to pay extra for obtaining a resource that is not held in limited supply.

In addition to value and rarity, inimitability has to be determined. *Inimitability* can be determined through barriers to imitation and replication. The extent of barriers and impediments against direct and indirect imitation determine the extent of inimitability. One effective barrier to imitation is that competitors fail to understand the organization's sources of advantage. The lack of understanding can be caused by tacitness, complexity, and specificity, which form bases for competitive advantage (Haanaes, 1997).

Several authors have categorized resources. A common categorization is tangibles vs. intangibles. Tangibles are relatively clearly defined and easy to identify. Tangible resources include plants, technology, land, geographical location, access to raw materials, capital, equipment, and legal resources. Tangible resources tend to be property based and may also include databases, licenses, patents, registered designs and trademarks, as well as other property rights that are easily bought and sold.

Intangibles are more difficult to define and also to study empirically. Intangible resources encompass skills, knowledge, organizational capital, relationships, capabilities, and human capital, as well as brands, company and product reputation, networks, competences, perceptions of quality, and the ability to manage change. Intangible resources are generally less easy to transfer than tangible resources, as the value of an intangible resource is difficult to measure (Haanaes, 1997).

Knowledge Categories

The types of knowledge involved in the practice of law enforcement can be categorized as administrative, policing, legal, procedural, and analytical knowledge:

- **Administrative knowledge** is knowledge about the operations of the investigation, offices, services, locations, uniforms, budgets, and statistics.

- **Policing knowledge** is knowledge about actions, behavior, procedures, and rules.

- **Legal knowledge** is knowledge of the law and court rulings.

- **Procedural knowledge** is knowledge of evidence and rights of suspects.

- **Analytical knowledge** is knowledge of investigative behavior, including investigative thinking styles.

At a seminar with participants from investigation units in Norwegian law enforcement, the detectives were asked to list strategic knowledge resources in their units. They were asked to mark criteria that were relevant for each resource. The result is listed in Figure 2.

Figure 2 illustrates different levels of strategic value from knowledge resources. For example, the computer crime knowledge is valuable, unique, nonsubstitutable, exploitable, and combinable. But this knowledge is at the same time both imitable and transferable. Of more strategic value is Schengen cooperation police knowledge, which is a knowledge category satisfying all seven strategic criteria.

Centrex (2005) identified knowledge categories for police investigators. Knowledge assists investigators to make effective and accountable decisions during an investigation. It enables them to locate, gather, and use the maximum amount of material generated by the commission of an offence to identify and bring offenders to justice. There are four areas of investigative knowledge required to conduct an effective investigation: these are:

- **The legal framework.** All investigators must have a current and in-depth knowledge of criminal law and the legislation that regulates the process of investigation. It is essential that all investigators understand legal defini-

Figure 2. Knowledge categories in police investigations and their strategic value

	1 Valuable	2 Unique	3 Not imitable	4 Not subsitutable	5 Exploitable	6 Not transferable	7 Combinable
Analyzing handwriting	Yes	Yes	Maybe	Maybe	Yes	Yes	Yes
Analyzing pictures	Yes	Yes	Yes	Yes	Yes	Yes	Yes
Analyzing weapons	Yes	Yes	Yes	Maybe	Yes	Yes	Yes
Schengen cooperation	Yes	Yes	Yes	Yes	Yes	Yes	Yes
Analyzing documents	Yes	Yes	No	No	Yes	No	Yes
DNA identification	Yes	Yes	No	No	Yes	No	Yes
Police intelligence	Yes	Yes	Yes	Yes	Yes	Yes	Yes
Computer crime	Yes	Yes	No	Yes	Yes	No	Yes

tions of offences likely to be encountered, points that have to be proven, potential defenses available from statute and case law, powers that support and regulate the investigation process, and relevant rules of evidence.

- **Characteristics of crime.** Crime can be placed into three broad categories: property crime, crimes against the person, and crimes against society. An examination of the types of crime in each category shows that they vary widely in terms of the behaviors involved, the types of victims, the motives of offenders, methods used to commit the crime, and the degree of planning involved. The wide range of criminal behavior, the circumstances in which it can occur, and the numerous ways in which victims, witnesses, and offenders are likely to behave, means that investigators can be faced with numerous sources that may produce material. Making an appropriate decision in these circumstances requires knowledge of the factors involved.

- **National and local force policies.** The police service is a complex organization with a wide range of tasks. In order to manage the range of tasks it is required to perform, the police service develops policies at both a national and local level. The reasons for producing policy include ensuring compliance with the law, procedural good practice, improving customer service, resource management, and managing interagency cooperation. Many of these policies have a direct bearing on the conduct of investigations, and investigators should have knowledge of those that are relevant to the type of investigations they are involved in. Such knowledge enables investigators to comply with legislation, follow procedural good practice, and gain access to the most appropriate resources or level of interagency cooperation required to successfully conclude an investigation.

- **Investigative skills.** Investigations should be conducted with integrity, commonsense, and sound judgment. Actions taken during an investigation should be proportionate to the crime under investigation, and take account of local cultural and social sensitivities. The success of an investigation relies on the goodwill and cooperation of victims, witnesses, and the community. Creative thinking requires the investigator to look at the problem in another way, to question any assumptions that may have been made, and to query the validity of all information. Investigators must continually question whether there may be another possible explanation for the material gathered.

Although investigators can acquire knowledge from formal training courses and the literature that exists on criminal investigation, they also need practical experience of investigations to underpin this knowledge. However, investigators should never rely on experience alone. This is because experience is unique to the individual, people learn at different speeds, and each will learn something different from the process (Centrex, 2005).

In the following, different forms of professional knowledge that a police officer should possess are discussed. The length of each description and the order in which they appear shall not be seen as a valuation of which skills are most important. In certain situations, one type of knowledge may be important, while in other contexts, other types are needed. The following 30 knowledge categories were identified in doctoral research conducted by Holgersson (2005):

1. **Using the skills of other police officers.** The ability to use police officers' skills can be coupled to individuals, patrols, and groups. One type of knowledge that is coupled to the level of the individual is a police officer's ability to understand his own and his colleagues' stronger and weaker sides in case of an intervention. This means that he has an intuitive feeling for how the tasks shall be divided, when to step forward and take

the initiative, and when to step backwards and leave the initiative to a colleague, for example, when a patrol is involved in a discussion. The ability to distribute the tasks in an appropriate manner is important within a patrol as well as between patrols, when several patrols are involved in a certain situation. A commander's ability to form patrols and take advantage of a group in the best possible way is a part of this knowledge category. For a distribution of the working tasks in a way that fits the situation, it usually is of central importance that there is a dialogue between the police officers (Garud & Kumaraswamy, 2005).

2. **Showing empathy towards a victim.** Persons who have been the victim of a crime can have different reactions. Some may not need any support at all, while others react strongly over crimes that a police officer does not find so grave. The police officer must adjust his supporting measures depending on the subjective needs that a victim has. Even when a police officer thinks a police case is unimportant, he must be able to show empathy. Furthermore, he must be able to be indulgent towards persons who have been the victim of a crime and are angry, or come with malicious remarks, for example, when a crime victim sharply points out that the police surely can catch speeding offenders or beat demonstrators, but are not able to get hold of burglars that rage in an area. A police officer must have the ability to let the victim tell his story in a way that seems best to the victim, at the same time as he gets enough information to be able to make a judgment of what has happened (Kiely & Peek, 2002).

3. **Prioritizing cases and using available resources effectively.** A police officer must be able to make a well-thought-out judgment about how much time can be put in a certain case. Is there reason to put energy in the case, or should the aim be to finish it as fast as possible, as the police organization's resources for that case are minimized. There are many factors that can affect this decision. First of all, the police officer must take the victim into account. An 80-year old woman who has been the victim of a crime may be in bigger need of support than a 22-year old man who has had a burglary into his car. A second factor is the crime's gravity, and the police officer's analysis of the possibilities that the case will be taken to court (Dean, 2005).

4. **Distinguishing deviations and categorizing individuals, objects and events.** Police officers automatically notice people's way of walking, their clothes, their car, and so forth, to be able to distinguish deviations. These routine controls of the environment help make police work more efficient. One of the most important things in the working day of police

officers is how they examine the environment, and what they do on their own initiative. However, it is easy to believe that being active, for example stopping and carrying out a control, is the same as being efficient. Believing that being active and being efficient is the same thing is at best debatable, but can lead to over-control. That police officers sort the impressions they get, usually consisting of meager and superficial information, is a prerequisite for police work. A broken headlamp, an expired tax control sticker, the driver not using a safety belt, and the looks of the driver in combination with the state of the car are other factors that can be reasons for an intervention (Dean, 2005).

5.   **Forming a suspicion.** To be able to form a suspicion and from there get the possibilities to perform coercive measures, a police officer needs to possess different types of knowledge. He must be well up in the legislation that regulates police officers' possibilities to use coercive measures, as well as in the legislation that a certain individual has violated. A police officer must constantly draw conclusions from the things he sees and the conversations he has, and connect these conclusions to the current legislation. Are his pupils really normal? Doesn't he hold his plastic bag a bit too tightly? How is it possible that he says he just came from the gas station when in fact, we saw him coming from the other direction? Doesn't his pocket stick out? Doesn't he all the time put his hands in his pockets, as if he has something to hide? Doesn't he act nervous? Why is his right hand in a fist all the time? Why did he bend down behind the shrubbery when he saw us? Do these indications form enough circumstantial evidence to perform a personal search? Are there enough reasons to suspect him of the crime? The police officer must constantly be active in his observations, questions, and judgments. The ability to form a suspicion requires both theoretical as well as practical knowledge (Fielding, 1984).

6.   **Communicating with individuals and groups.** By observing the police in London, Waddington (1999) found that police officers show a large social competence, and an ability to deal with different types of meetings with different persons. Police officers are more involved in role-play than the average citizen, and they therefore are very skilled at it. Police officers often appear to be strict and determined when they rebuke someone, but this usually is acted. They often are not at all as harsh as they seem. The purpose of a conversation can vary (Puonti, 2004b). One purpose can be to control a suspicion and possibly build up a case (see previous section), another to search for information. The goal can also be to make certain

criminals aware of the fact that the police have observed them, the clothes they wear, and who they are together with. The dialogue can also be intended to create "social glue." A dialogue that takes place out on "the street" differs usually from the dialogues held in a meeting room.

7.   **Getting an informant and interacting with an informant.** There are different types of informants. Some are in the centre of a criminal group, while others are more in the outskirts. An informant can be a parent, a brother or sister, or a neighbor to the criminal person. The quality and usefulness of the information varies (Puonti, 2004b).

8.   **Using and understanding different social language variations.** In contact with the prosecutor and lawyers, or when writing different types of reports, the police officer uses a formal language filled with legal terms. Contact with professional criminals requires knowledge of the words that are used by them. When communicating with children, it is crucial to understand certain other terms. A central part of a police officer's work consists of communication with persons who are not working within the police, even though communication between police officers is important as well. As some parts of the police work is done under time pressure, knowledge of certain terms is important to enable effective communication (Kiely & Peek, 2002).

9.   **Dealing with mentally ill and instable persons.** For knowledge type 6, communicating with individuals and groups, the importance of a police officer's ability to communicate with others was described. This ability is also important when a police officer comes in contact with mentally ill persons. A police officer expressed it like this: "Rather talk in twenty minutes than fight in two." Knowledge concerning contact with mentally ill persons is treated separately because this type of communication and contact is special. If a police officer wants to be successful, he must be able to understand and deal with the difficulties that come along when communicating with a mentally ill person.

10.   **Saving lives and minimizing the proportions of injuries.** A police officer must be able to take care of injured persons, as well as handling the initial work at the scene of an accident.

11.   **Preparing mentally and communicating with colleagues.** Police officers get involved in different kinds of situations. These can range from a police officer himself being exposed to danger, to seeing severely injured and dead persons. It is not unusual that a police officer encounters strong emotions such as grief and aggression.

12. **Mediating peace and solving problems.** A central skill for a police officer is being able to solve problems. Sometimes it is not enough to write a report or to arrest someone, although in some cases this can be a solution.

13. **Performing in-house investigation and using information in, among others, computer systems.** A police officer must be able to use the information that can be found in the police computer system. Usually, the police officer wants to acquire more information about a certain registration plate, or wants to determine a person's identity in case the person does not have any identification.

14. **Acting preventive.** Even though measures that are discussed in this section can be part of a strategy for solving problems and should therefore belong in the section "To mediate a peace and solve problems," it was chosen to discuss these measures as a separate point. Preventive measures form a central part of police work, and are taken without a special action plan and without someone needing help with a specific problem.

15. **Showing authority and inspiring with respect.** In certain situations, it is important that a police officer shows authority, in order to reach his goal.

16. **Conveying a serious message.** A police officer must be able to convey a serious message. It is a difficult balance between being considerate and at the same time, explain clearly what has happened. It can be that a family member has died or been severely injured, or that a relative has disappeared from a home for old people. How someone will react is difficult to predict. The police officer will have to adjust his approach depending on the reaction.

17. **Acting in case of an attack.** A police officer must dare and be able to act when he is exposed to a criminal attack. In these cases, it is particularly important to act decisively and to be mentally prepared.

18. **Thinking safety.** Safety thinking can be expressed in various ways. It can concern the choice of protective equipment, car driving, and not exposing one's own self or others to unnecessary risks. Another skill is to make sure to have one or more patrols "behind you" to report the need of enforcement in an early stage when there is a risk for the situation to escalate, and to back up colleagues on their way to a certain address or certain types of assignments.

19. **Taking investigation measures at the crime scene.** It is important that a police officer is able to take extensive immediate measures. To finish as

much as possible at the scene will help the investigation. The initial measures are very important.

20. **Keeping feelings under control and supporting each other.** That a police officer must be able to control his feelings does not mean he unaffected by the things he sees and experiences. To be able to talk about these things is, therefore, important for being able to process feelings and experiences.

21. **Debriefing an event.** To be able to debrief an event, it is mainly theoretical knowledge that is required about different law sections, and those routines that are relevant for a certain type of crime or event. Practical knowledge is also needed, for example, about how to work with IT-systems, and how to express oneself in a comprehensible and exact manner.

22. **Planning measures based on a certain problem picture and existing legislation.** It is important to have planned what to focus on during a shift if nothing particular takes place. This is made easier by good knowledge about the district, specific problems and individuals in the area, and routines and applicable law sections.

23. **Showing consideration and humbleness.** A closely related ability is being able to admit a mistake.

24. **Using different communication aids.** A police officer must constantly be aware of the possibility that the things he says are listened in to. Sometimes he must avoid giving out certain information over the radio as, for example, his position when on his way to an alarm. When many cars are on their way to a certain address, it can be appropriate to not burden the radio traffic unless a patrol has something important to report.

25. **Conducting a technical investigation.** A police officer must be able to secure technical evidence at a crime scene. Even though some evidence, for example, shoe traces, will not lead to anyone being convicted for a crime, it can still be useful for future events as it can give the police an indication that the crime was committed by a certain individual.

26. **Giving advice and instructions.** A police officer must be able to give different types of advice. In case of a burglary, it is fitting to give advice about outer protection, that is, measures that aim at making a break-in less interesting and more difficult.

27. **Balancing between common sense, ethics and legislation.** Waddington (1999) illustrates police officers' approach to legislation by

using the following comparison: When the obstacles are too high, the horses will go around them. He believes that police officers do not follow "the book" (legislation) because the book simply is too extensive and incomplete. The size makes it difficult for police officers to be able to grasp and have access to all the parts of the law that can be relevant in a certain situation.

28. **Using imagination and adapting, among others, driving techniques to increase the chances of catching an offender.** A central skill is a police officer's knowledge about different ways in which to reach a crime scene.

29. **Finding an offender.** Police personnel must have an ability to find offenders. This involves partly trying to enter the offenders' perspective, but also seeing signs when someone went in a certain direction. Using help from the general public is important in this context. I have experienced cases in which the public formed telephone chains to be able to catch an offender who fled from the crime scene. In one of these cases, a robbery in a small village, this led to the arrest of the offender.

30. **Presenting a case to decision makers.** Police personnel must have an ability to present a case to decision makers. They have to be clear and pedagogical. It is an advantage if the decision maker, already from the start, has faith in the person who presents the case. Sometimes it can be good to present a case before carrying out a planned action. In that way, decision makers can be better informed about the case, and the police officers can also get an indication of whether it is worth carrying out the action at all. Working two days on finding a certain address and then not being allowed to carry out a house search can be meaningless, and has often a devastating effect on motivation. Police officers must have a clear vision of how they are going to present a case, and based on which grounds a decision maker might make his decisions.

Holgersson (2005) has pointed out that there are two perspectives in the work practice of the police. These two perspectives have a big influence on how people look at different phenomena in the organization, for example, the need of knowledge about laws and rules. The two perspectives are called street-level perspective vs. theoretical perspective.

The probability is quite large that the theoretical perspective represents the main influence on how information and knowledge will be organized, instead of having information and knowledge categorized from the view of the street-level perspective. Holgersson (2005) pointed out that one reason is the fact that people working with categorization and classification in an organization mostly belong to the theoretical perspective. When the theoretical perspective's point of view guides the way of categorizing the work practice, the structure seems to be good and well defined. However, from the view of the street-level, it may not be suitable. In the example about information of the law and other rules, the police officer needs information to solve a specific situation. In the specific situation, for example, to eventually act according to information from the public that a person has an aggressive dog, it is necessary to read information from different laws and rules. It is not easy for the police officer to use an IT system organized in the way of how the theoretical perspective is looking at the information need when he wants to find out what is the right thing to do in a specific situation.

Sometimes, for example, it can be a conflict between different laws and rules, or the police officer can find the text obscure. It is not possible, or at least very difficult, for the police officer to manage to make an analysis by himself when such a problem occurs. The limit of time to succeed with such an analysis is the most critical factor. It is a big risk that the officer will find his knowledge level too low to feel comfortable to act in a specific situation. It is therefore important to define the need for knowledge support from the view of the street-level. One way of doing that is to use the concept of a value shop, as discussed in the following section.

Knowledge Management Matrix

To identify knowledge management applications, we can combine knowledge levels with knowledge categories. Core knowledge, advanced knowledge, and innovative knowledge are combined with administrative knowledge, policing knowledge, legal knowledge, procedural knowledge, and analytical knowledge in Figure 3. We have created a knowledge management matrix with 12 cells for IS/IT applications.

The knowledge management matrix can first be used to identify the current IS/IT that support knowledge management in the firm, as illustrated in Figure 4.

Now the knowledge management matrix can be applied to identify future IS/IT, as illustrated in Figure 5. The systems do only serve as examples; they illustrate that it is possible to find systems than can support all combinations of knowledge categories and knowledge levels.

Knowledge Acquisition: Eyewitnesses

Police investigators have established that when we experience an important event, we do not simply record it in our memory as a videotape recorder would. The situation is much more complex. Most theoretical analyses of the process

Figure 3. Knowledge management matrix

Levels / Categories	Core Knowledge	Advanced Knowledge	Innovative Knowledge
Administrative Knowledge			
Policing Knowledge			
Legal Knowledge			
Procedural Knowledge			
Analytical Knowledge			

Figure 4. Knowledge management matrix for the current IS/IT situation

Levels / Categories	Core Knowledge	Advanced Knowledge	Innovative Knowledge
Administrative Knowledge	Text Spreadsheet	Internet Intranet	Mobile communications Geographical system
Policing Knowledge	Fingerprints Investigation manual	Documents Methods database	Work flows Imaging
Legal Knowledge	Law database Library system	International laws Evidence system	Search engine Case-based reasoning
Procedural Knowledge	Document standards Procedural standards	Public databases Experience datawarehouse	Video conferencing Case system
Analytical Knowledge	Legal summaries Case summaries	Groupeware Voice recognition	Expert register Expert system

Figure 5. Knowledge management matrix for desired IS/IT situation

Levels Categories	Core Knowledge	Advanced Knowledge	Innovative Knowledge
Administrative Knowledge	Text Spreadsheet *Electronic diary*	Internet Intranet *Quality system*	Mobile communications Geographical system *Executive information*
Policing Knowledge	Fingerprints Investigation manual *Document management*	Documents Methods database *Voice recognition*	Work flows Imaging *Best Practices*
Legal Knowledge	Law database Library system *Electronic law book*	International laws Evidence system *Extranet*	Search engine Case-based reasoning *Artificial intelligence*
Procedural Knowledge	Document standards Procedural standards *Planning system*	Public databases Experience datawarehouse *Document generation*	Video conferencing Case system *Intelligent search*
Analytical Knowledge	Legal summaries Case summaries *Case interpretations*	Groupeware Voice recognition *Crime monitoring*	Expert register Expert system *Research reports*

divide it into three major stages. First, the event is perceived by a witness and knowledge is entered into the memory system. This is called the acquisition stage. Next, some time passes before a witness tries to remember the event, and this is called the retention stage. Finally, the witness tries to recall the stored knowledge, and this is called the retrieval stage. This three-stage analysis is central to the concept of human memory. Psychologists who conduct research in this area try to identify and study the important factors that play a role in each of the three stages (Lofthus & Doyle, 1997).

The duration, lighting, and violence of an event are factors that influence knowledge from eyewitnesses. These are factors inherent in the event itself. In addition, there are other factors inherent in the witness. For example, the amount of stress or fear that a witness experienced during the acquisition stage will influence the quality of knowledge that is stored in memory. Drugs, such as alcohol and marijuana, have distinct effects on memory. Furthermore, witnesses often make mistaken identifications as a result of being exposed to new knowledge subsequent to the time of their initial description of the perpetrator (Lofthus & Doyle, 1997).

Research into the credibility of witness testimony is important, as witness testimonies often are the main source of information and knowledge in police investigations. Fahsing (2002) conducted an archival study of 250 eyewitness statements. The following presentation and discussion of knowledge from eyewitness statements is based on his work.

Research into the credibility of witness testimony has the longest history of psychological research, stretching back to the end of the 19th century. Although, noticeable work was done even then, the interest increased in the 1970s, and has persisted to the present day. In fact, eyewitness testimony has become one of the most researched fields within applied psychology. This expanding field of research has mainly been based on laboratory studies, and a wide range of issues and topics have been brought to light.

Hence, witnesses often play an important part in criminal investigations and prosecutions. In a survey, Kebbell and Milne (1998) asked 159 police officers in the UK, how often eyewitnesses' information constituted major leads for an investigation. Thirty-six percent of the officers said "always" or "almost always," while 51% said "usually." In addition to providing leads in investigations, eyewitness evidence given in court may lead to a conviction. Another study found that witnesses' descriptions of offenders were used as a source of evidence in 43% of "primary detected" burglary cases in the UK.

Experienced detectives know that they must treat descriptions made by witnesses with caution. If misleading descriptions are not discovered, then an investigation can waste precious time and resources following wrong leads, and the actual perpetrators are ignored because they do not fit the description or, even worse, innocent people can get convicted of crimes they did not commit. Several studies have suggested that the single leading cause of false convictions in the U.S. is mistaken eyewitness identifications. Correspondingly, many forensic psychologists have concentrated their research efforts on the limitations and errors of eyewitness memory. One survey showed a consensus amongst a number of "eyewitness-experts" on several important issues; nevertheless, there seems to be conflicting findings in laboratory and field studies of eyewitness testimony. This has resulted in a serious disagreement amongst researchers regarding the external validity of the laboratory findings.

A wide range of variables relevant to eyewitness research has been identified. The variables have been categorized in numerous ways, for example Loftus and Doyle (1997) separated event and witness factors. Others make a distinction between variables that, in real life, can be controlled by the justice system (system variables) and those variables impossible to control (estimator variables), and some identified interrogational factors, as an additional category. While the distinctions suggested are of great importance when considering policy implications of research findings, it should be emphasized that in real life, there will inevitably be a close interaction between a multitude of factors, and theoretical distinctions do not always apply. Below follows an outline of findings considered most relevant to the study by Fahsing (2002).

Event Factors

As crimes take place almost everywhere and around the clock, there will naturally be shifting lighting and observation conditions. These factors will inevitably influence eyewitnesses' ability to accurately encode and report knowledge. Some crimes might only take a few seconds while others may last for several minutes or longer. In general, psychological research supports the belief that the longer a witness has to study an incident and the better the opportunity to observe, the more details will be encoded and reported. However, most witnesses seem to overestimate the duration of the event (Loftus & Doyle, 1997).

Intuitively, most people may believe that the more dramatic or unexpected an event is, the better memory performance. However, research in the field indicates that this belief is too simplistic. Inherent in the incident itself are a number of factors that can affect a witness's ability to report accurately. Several studies have indicated that there is an interaction between violence and the complexity of a crime. Not surprisingly, witnesses tend to give less complete descriptions when several perpetrators are involved in the incident. Furthermore, witnesses' ability to report accurate knowledge from a complex crime scene might decline significantly if the scene also included violent actions.

In cases where violence and weapons are present, arousal is likely to increase. It has been predicted from the so-called Easterbrook-hypothesis that high arousal causes a narrowing of the range of factors to which the witness attends. However, a possible linear relationship between arousal and memory performance has been challenged. In a review of the literature on arousal and eyewitness memory, it was found that 11 studies suggested that higher arousal levels decrease eyewitness accuracy, and 10 studies suggested the reverse. However, some speak for a more intricate explanation of the phenomenon, and argue for an interaction between factors such as type of event, type of information, time-delay, and retrieval conditions.

In a study of 22 bank robberies, levels of arousal between threatened bank tellers (victims) and bystanders were compared. They found no evidence of a higher arousal level amongst the bank tellers. Furthermore, there was no significant discrepancy between the two groups' ability to recall details from the events. Laboratory studies have found that when a weapon is used, those threatened tend to pay greater attention to the weapon than to other events and people at the scene. One metaanalysis reports that the effects of "weapon focus" seem to be consistent across a number of studies. Consequently, the presence of a weapon may impair the witness's memory for details other than these pertaining to the weapon.

Witness Factors

In line with that different events will be remembered with different accuracy, some witnesses will certainly give more complete and accurate information than others. Surely, it would be of great value if one could isolate certain personal characteristics or conditions that could predict who will be a good witness and who will not. A number of studies have focused on gender as an influencing factor in eyewitness identification. "Gender differences" have been known in criminology for a long time, but the phenomenon is not as tangible in eyewitness research. A series of studies on the impact of gender have yielded inconsistent findings (Loftus & Doyle, 1997). Yet, some interesting differences have been detected. Sporer (1996) reported that female witnesses tended to give less wordy descriptions of other people, but their accounts included just as many important details. Another point to bear in mind is that men, as a group, are more likely to suffer from hearing loss and color deficiency (Ainsworth, 1998). Furthermore, females might be more accurate in their memory recall than males for "female-oriented" details, and vice versa. Other studies have indicated that gender differences are more a matter of interest than of gender (Loftus & Doyle, 1997). One reason why research produces contradictory findings seems to be that the witness tasks are often different over the studies conducted.

Not surprisingly, age appears to be an important predictor of memory performance. In fact, it has been indicated that age is the most important individual variable of all to affect memory performance. Both the very young and the very old generally perform less well than young or middle-aged adults. The ability of children, and probably also older people, to give accurate accounts, however, depends on how they are interviewed.

Therefore, whilst both children and older people, in general, seem to offer less information than adults when first asked, there is no empirical evidence for considering these groups incompetent as witnesses by virtue of their age.

Whether or not the witness, while viewing the crime, expects to have to make a subsequent identification, appears to have little impact on accuracy. However, the way in which a witness processes a perpetrator's facial characteristics does seem to matter. Those who make a deep and individual encoding of the perpetrator, like "he reminds me of my neighbor," seem to perform better on identification tests. In addition, people's use of stereotypes and schemas seem to distort their perception of reality. In situations where our memory of what actually happened is incomplete, we tend to unconsciously fill the memory gaps with information from schemas, or expectations, based on previously experienced incidents (Loftus & Doyle, 1997).

Further, the general belief that training improves performance has not been supported by research on facial identification. Some professionals, such as police officers, bank tellers, and security personnel, undergo "witness training." However, the available evidence indicates that it is very difficult to train adults to improve their ability to recognize faces. On the other hand, the study of bank tellers indicates that the bank tellers have learned how to better function under stressing situations (e.g., a robbery). Consequently, a number of relevant factors have been identified and even though far from all are dealt with, it still seems premature to make conclusive predictions as to whether a given witness will or will not produce an accurate testimony of a particular incident.

Interrogational Factors

Being unable to retrieve and report information stored in our memory is perhaps the most common cause of forgetting. The way in which witnesses are interviewed, and their responses interpreted, decides the quantity and the quality of the information retrieved. A vast amount of experimental studies has demonstrated that memory can be altered also during the retrieval stage. Although there are disagreements amongst psychologists about how to explain the "misinformation-effect," there is consensus among researchers that subjects exposed to misleading postevent information are likely to report such information in a later interview (Loftus & Doyle, 1997).

The so-called "questioner expertise" might influence the error rates of subjects who were asked misleading vs. unbiased questions. Research results indicate that misleading questions decrease witness accuracy when the questioner is assumed to be knowledgeable about the crime, but have no effect on accuracy when the questioner is assumed to be naïve. Consequently, police and court procedures used to elicit eyewitness testimony can introduce inaccuracy into potential evidence.

Studies of the occurrence of the "misinformation effect" indicate greater risk of postevent contamination when the misleading information is retrieved after a long retention interval. Furthermore, it has been reported that postevent information interferes more easily with peripheral memory information than central. However, it should be noted that even though these effects intuitively seem plausible, their persistence in real-life settings have not been investigated.

One of the most common sources of contamination of eyewitnesses' testimony is a leading question. For example, interviewers using the definite article ("the"), rather than the indefinite ("a"), give rise to different expectations about an object. Thus, use of "the," such as "did you see *the* car?" significantly increased the percentage of subjects who reported seeing a nonexisting car in a previously shown film.

Accordingly, the influence of leading questions can be understood in terms of the demands of the different questions. For specific, closed questions, the task might change to one of providing the interviewer with what he, or she, wants the witness to remember. The result of such a questioning style might be that witnesses provide less accurate answers because they replace gaps in memory with incorrect information. In other words, they may become suggestible to the demands of the interviewer.

In contrast, use of more open questions generally provides more accurate and complete answers; moreover, even eyewitnesses who typically show poorer memories than the general population (e.g., children or older adults) can show high accuracy rates when asked open-ended questions. Studies summarized by Fisher and Geiselman (1992) suggest that the kind of questions generating the most accurate answers are open-ended, uninterrupted, free recall questions, such as "Concentrate, and tell me everything you saw." Nevertheless, closed questions may often have to be used as a last remedy to elicit information about details the witness may have omitted.

Similarly, the sequence of the questions is an important factor. It is unlikely that all the witnesses have had the very same view of the incident. Hence, it is recommended that the questioning is adapted in order to best correspond with each unique witness's memory (Fisher & Geiselman, 1992). Studies of actual police interviews indicate that police officers tend to use fixed series of questions.

Most police forces around the world have developed special routines for recording facial and other descriptions (Sporer, 1996). As an example, the Norwegian Police College teaches police officers to use a joint template for descriptions of people and objects in police interviews. The model was probably developed to ensure that investigative interviewers should obtain the presumed most vital components in a description. It is, however, Fahsing's (2002) experience, after more than 10 years as a detective in the Norwegian Police Service, that such a model may lead the interviewer to fire off a series of closed questions in relation to the appearance of the offender.

Perpetrator Factors

A fundamental, yet somewhat neglected issue in eyewitness research is whether there are any observable and distinct features of offenders that forensic witnesses seem to recall more correctly. Evidence drawn from research on facial identification implies that not all faces are equally easy to memorize. For example, faces judged as highly attractive, or highly unattractive, are sometimes better recognized than less distinct ones.

Similarly, male witnesses seem to remember more details about a woman's clothing if she had been wearing makeup, than without. Research on the relative saliency of facial characteristics has shown a general preference for upper, as opposed to lower, facial features in descriptions.

It is also possible to disguise and transform one's appearance with the intention of concealing distinct personal characteristics, and thereby lower the chance of a later recognition. At the most obvious level, full face masks and stockings pulled over the face are effective in obscuring the facial features for later identification. However, even seemingly moderate covering might come out as effective. For example, the chance of witnesses identifying a robber wearing a hat can significantly deteriorate.

A large body of research has shown that cross-racial identification seems to be more difficult than same-race identification. Witnesses also tend to be less accurate when describing a person of a different race. For example, Caucasian and Asian witnesses recalled an Asian perpetrator as being shorter than a Caucasian one, despite the fact that both perpetrators were of the exact same height. According to the findings from theses studies, it appears that perpetrators from different ethnic groups are likely to be remembered by witnesses as being more consistent with their normative ethnic height than their actual height. On the other hand, and perhaps not surprising, it has been demonstrated that people need very little information in order to make accurate decisions about the gender of the target.

True Witness

"It is more important that innocence be protected than it is that guilt be punished," John Adams said, arguing in defense of the British officers charged with the murder of colonial demonstrators in the Boston Massacre trial. When an eyewitness goes to a lineup and picks Number Three as the robber, but Number Three turns out to be a patrolman from the traffic unit who is standing in as a "filler" in the lineup, no one is placed in jeopardy. It is only when the eyewitness wrongly identifies the man whom the police have chosen as an actual suspect that we have a problem (Doyle, 2005).

The police reflex, once a suspect is uncovered through the interviewing and investigation process, is to show the eyewitness a photo array or a lineup. Modern research psychologists claim that they have developed an improvement in the way crimes are investigated; that they have derived from the scientific study of human memory a protocol for handling eyewitness identification cases twice as reliable as the traditional methods currently in use. The psychological researchers claim they have developed an improved method for preventing eyewitness mistakes before they happen. The prime beneficiaries of their efforts are innocent citizens who will never be wrongly identified, citizens, in other words, who will never need to hire a lawyer in the first place. However, as a defense lawyer, Doyle (2005) is skeptical.

Technologies and Techniques

We conclude this chapter by discussing practical and workable technologies, tools, and techniques for knowledge management in law enforcement. Building on Stages 1 and 2, Stage 3 enables police officers to access information that is needed as raw material in their knowledge work. While Stage 1 made it possible for police officers to enter information by means of end-user tools, Stage 2 made it possible to communicate with colleagues to solve cases.

At this stage of knowledge management technology, information is stored and made accessible as a resource. Again, we can look at Holmes in the UK (Home Office, 2005a) and COPLINK in the U.S. (Chen, Zheng, Atabakhsh, Wyzga, & Schroeder, 2003) as examples of systems. However, at this stage, we focus on the information sharing technologies and techniques rather than the information gathering and communication aspects of such systems.

In COPLINK Detect, detailed criminal case reports are the underlying information space, and concepts are meaningful terms occurring in each case. These case reports contain both structured (for example, database fields for incidents containing the case number, names of people involved, address, and date) and unstructured data (narratives written by officers commenting on an incident, for example, witness A said he saw suspect A run away in a white truck).

During the enquiry, which is run on the HOLMES system, detectives have access to information that affects the practical and administrative features of the enquiry. Basic information is found concerning location of incident, data and time of incident, victim(s), senior investigating officer, and date enquiry commenced.

In addition to such dedicated investigative systems, police officers have access to a wide variety of information sources. They use information technology to access previous cases, previous suspects, jailed persons, missing persons, missing vehicles, and missing money. In their search, they apply techniques such as free-text search, keyword search, and intelligent agents.

An interesting system at the officer-to-information stage is the National Incident-Based Reporting System (NIBRS) in the U.S. The following story of how NIBRS was implemented in Kansas is based on Howerton (2005). It started a long time ago, in 1982, when the Kansas Bureau of Investigation began studying the utility of establishing an incident-based reporting system. As a result, in 1986, the first Kansas Incident-based Reporting System was implemented to collect relevant information on the occurrence and composition of crime in Kansas.

In 1997, the state of Kansas implemented the Kansas Criminal Justice Information System Improvement Project. The project focus was to create an integrated criminal justice system involving state and local agencies. Since the Kansas Bureau of Investigation is the central repository for criminal history records, the initial focus of the project was to improve the core systems at the bureau. In 1998, the state awarded contracts to Paradigm4 for the development of a data entry program.

In 2000, Kansas Bureau of Investigation started testing with FBI's NIBRS program. Sixteen test submissions were made, with an ending error rate for both arrests and incidents of less than 0.4%. Kansas was certified NIBRS compliant on February 16, 2001. Paradigm4, the vendor responsible for the Kansas database and Kansas' conversion to NIBRS, went out of business in March, 2001. This set Kansas back several months, and a new cycle of testing was not started until January 2002.

NIBRS significantly altered the way law enforcement agencies reported crime to the FBI. NIBRS allows agencies to collect data in which the criminal incident, rather than a single offense within the incident, is the basic unit of measurement. Within each incident, a variety of facts on victims, offenders, arrestees, offenses, and properties are collected, allowing for the possibility of true policy-relevant analysis.

Specifically, the NIBRS system provides incident-level details on 22 different categories of crimes covering 46 different offenses. A total of 53 different data elements are included in an NIBRS report including basic incident details such as arrest date, time, and type of arrest, along with many other incident-level factors. NIBRS also provides details specific to all individual offenses reported within an incident, demographics on all victims, offenders, and persons arrested, as well as details on property involved.

References

Ainsworth, P. (1998). *Psychology, law and eyewitness testimony.* Chichester, UK: Wiley.

Ashby, D. I., & Longley, P. A. (2005). Geocomputation, geodemographics and resource allocation for local oolicing. *Transactions in GIS, 9*(1), 53-72.

Barney, J. B. (2001). Is the resource-based "view" a useful perspective for strategic management research? Yes. *Academy of Management Review, 26*(1), 41-56.

Barney, J. B. (2002). *Gaining and sustaining competitive advantage.* Upper Saddle River, NJ: Prentice Hall.

Centrex (2005). *Practice advice on core investigative doctrine.* National Centre for Policing Excellence. UK: Cambourne.

Chen, H., Schroeder, J., Hauck, R. V., Ridgeway, L., Atabakhsh, H., Gupta, H., et al. (2002). COPLINK Connect: Information and knowledge management for law enforcement. *Decision Support Systems, 34*, 271-285.

Chen, H., Zheng, D., Atabakhsh, H., Wyzga, W., & Schroeder, J. (2003). COPLINK—managing law enforcement data and knowledge. *Communications of the ACM, 46*(1), 28-34.

Dean, G. (2005). *The cognitive psychology of police investigators.* Conference paper, Queensland University of Technology, Brisbane, Australia.

Doyle, J. M. (2005). *True witness: Cops, courts, science, and the battle against misidentification.* New York: Palgrave Macmillan.

Fahey, L., & Prusak, L. (1998). The eleven deadliest sins of knowledge management. *California Management Review, 40*(3), 265-276.

Fahsing, I. (2002). *The man behind the mask: An archival study of 250 eyewitness statements in 48 cases of armed robbery.* Master of Science thesis, University of Leicester, UK.

Fielding, N. (1984). Police socialization and police competence. *The British Journal of Sociology, 35*(4), 568-590.

Fisher, R. P., & Geiselman, R. E. (1992). *Memory enhancing techniques for investigative interviewing.* Springfield, IL: Charles C. Thomas.

Garud, R., & Kumaraswamy, A. (2005). Vicious and virtuous circles in the management of knowledge: The case of Infosys Technologies. *MIS Quarterly, 29*(1), 9-33.

Haanaes, K. B. (1997). *Managing resource mobilization: Case studies of Dynal, Fiat Auto Poland and Alcatel Tecom Norway.* PhD series 9.97, Copenhagen Business School, Copenhagen, Denmark.

Hitt, M. A., Bierman, L., Shumizu, K., & Kochhar, R. (2001). Direct and moderating effects of human capital on strategy and performance in professional service firms: A resource-based perspective. *Academy of Management Journal, 44*(1), 13-28.

Holgersson, S. (2005). *Yrke: POLIS—yrkeskunnskap, motivasjon, IT-system og andre forutsetninger for politiarbeide.* PhD doctoral dissertation, Institutionen för datavetenskap, Linköpings universitet, Sweden.

Home Office. (2005a). *Guidance on statutory performance indicators for policing 2005/2006.* Police Standards Unit, Home Office of the UK Government. Retrieved from http://www.policereform.gov.uk

Howerton, M. A. (2005). Implementing NIBRS in Kansas. In D. Faggiani, B. Kubu, & R. Rantala (Eds.), *Facilitating the implementation of incident-based data systems* (pp. 15-18). Washington, DC: Police Executive Research Forum.

Johnson, G., & Scholes, K. (2002). *Exploring corporate strategy.* Harlow, Essex, UK: Pearson Education, Prentice Hall.

Kebbell, M. R., & Milne, R. (1998). Police officers' perception of eyewitness in forensic investigations: A survey. *The Journal of Social Psychology*, *138*, 323-30.

Kiely, J. A., & Peek, G. S. (2002). The culture of the British police: Views of police officers. *The Service Industries Journal*, *22*(1), 167-183.

Laudon, K. C., & Laudon, J. P. (2005). *Essentials of management information systems: Managing the digital firm* (6th ed.). Upper Saddle River, NJ: Prentice Hall.

Lofthus, E.F., & Doyle, J.M. (1997). *Eyewitness testimony: Civil and criminal* (3rd ed.). Charlottesville, VA: Lexis Law Publishing.

Murphy, C. (2004). The rationalization of Canadian public policing: A study of the impact and implications of resource limits and market strategies. *The Canadian Review of Policing Research*.

Pettus, M. L. (2001). The resource-based view as a development growth process: Evidence from the deregulated trucking industry. *Academy of Management Journal, 44*(4), 878-896.

Priem, R. L., & Butler, J. E. (2001). Is the resourced-based view a useful perspective for strategic management research? *Academy of Management Review, 26*(1), 22-40.

Puonti, A. (2004b). Tools for collaboration: Using and designing tools in inter-organizational economic-crime investigation. *Mind, Culture, and Activity, 11*(2), 133-152.

Sporer, S. L. (1996). Psychological aspects of person descriptions. In S. L. Sporer, R. S. Malpass, & G. Köhnken (Eds.), *Psychological issues in eyewitness identification* (pp. 55-87). NJ: Lawrence Erlbaum Associates.

Waddington, P. A. J. (1999). *Policing citizens.* London: UCL Press.

Chapter VIII

Officer-to-Application Systems

Information systems solving knowledge problems are made available to knowledge workers and knowledge seekers. Artificial intelligence is applied in these systems. Expert systems, decision support systems, document management systems, intelligent search engines, and relational database tools represent some of the technologies and techniques developed to support Stage 4.

Officer-to-application systems will only be successful if they are built on a thorough understanding of law enforcement. Therefore, this chapter concentrates on presenting two important knowledge application tasks in police investigations: profiling and "cross+check." Offender profiling and cross+check in police investigations are examples of law enforcement work that can benefit from technologies such as artificial intelligence, knowledge-based systems, and case-based reasoning systems (Becerra-Fernandez, Gonzalez, & Sabherwal, 2004).

Artificial intelligence (AI) is an area of computer science that endeavors to build machines exhibiting humanlike cognitive capabilities. Most modern AI systems are founded on the realization that intelligence is tightly intertwined with knowledge. Knowledge is associated with the symbols we manipulate.

Knowledge-based systems deal with solving problems by exercising knowledge. The most important parts of these systems are the knowledge base and the inference engine. The former holds the domain-specific knowledge, whereas the latter contains the functions to exercise the knowledge in the knowledge

Figure 1. Officer-to-application systems at Stage 4 of the knowledge management technology stage model

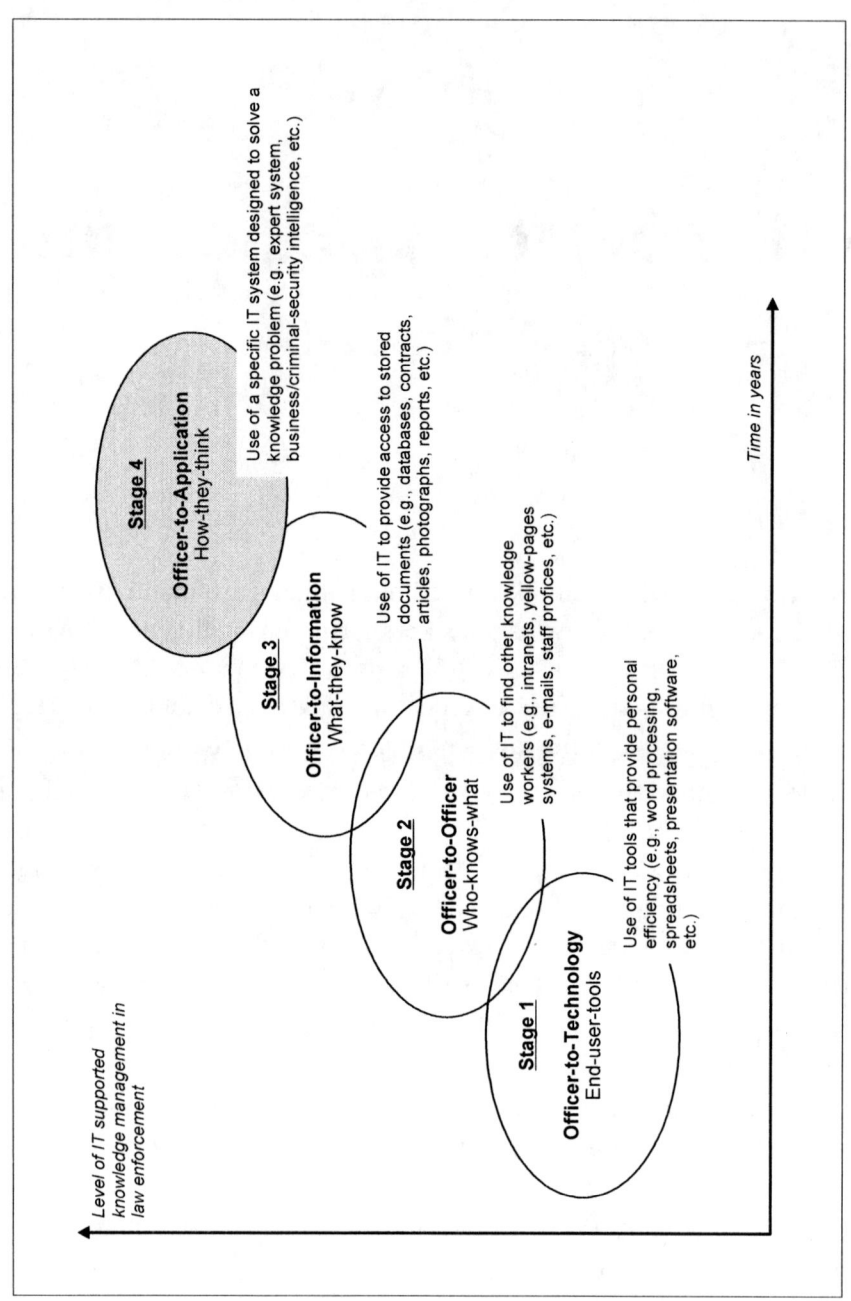

base. Knowledge can be represented as either rules or frames. Rules are a natural choice for representing conditional knowledge that is in the form of if-when statements. Inference engines supply the motive power to the knowledge. There are several ways to exercise knowledge, depending on the nature of the knowledge. For example, backward-chaining systems work backward from the conclusions to the inputs. These systems attempt to validate the conclusions by finding evidence to support them. In law enforcement, this is an important system feature, as evidence determines whether a person is charged or not charged for a crime.

Case-based reasoning systems are a different way to represent knowledge through explicit historical cases. This approach differs from the rule-based approach because the knowledge is not complied and interpreted by an expert. Instead, the experiences that possibly shaped the expert's knowledge are directly used to make decisions. Learning is an important issue in case-based reasoning, because with the mere addition of new cases to the library, the system learns. In law enforcement, police officers are looking for similar cases to learn how they were handled in the past, making case-based reasoning systems an attractive application in policing.

Use of expert systems in law enforcement includes systems that attempt to aid in information retrieval by drawing upon human heuristics, or rules and procedures to investigate tasks. The AICAMS project is a knowledge-based system for identifying suspects. AICAMS also includes a component to fulfill the needs for a simple but effective facial identification procedure based on a library of facial components. The system provides a capability for assembling an infinite number of possible facial composites by varying the position and size of the components. AICAMS also provides a geomapping component by incorporating a map-based user interface (Chen et al., 2002).

Knowledge Application: Offender Profiling

This first knowledge application description engages in an analysis of the use of offender profiling as developed in a criminal context, and asks what relevance does such a paradigm have when applied in a terrorism context? More specifically, does offender profiling have potential to assist in developing a more comprehensive understanding of terrorism? The following sections are based on research work by Dean (1995, 2000, 2005).

The criminal investigation literature is littered with terms that are currently used, or have been used, to try and capture the meaning behind the concept of profiling. For example, the history of profiling reveals terms like psychological profiling, criminal profiling, criminal personality profiling, criminal investigative analysis, and behavioral evidence analysis have all been used, and some are still used almost interchangeably to describe a similar process of coming up with a profile of a likely perpetrator of a crime. The FBI used to use the term psychological profiling, but now call what they do in the profiling arena criminal investigative analysis.

As well as these terminological differences, there are also definitional differences in regard to what exactly does the term profiling mean. A selection of definitions of profiling by several writers is offered . The definitions are presented in chronological order, along with the label used by various writers at the time to depict the concept of profiling.

- A **psychological profile** is an educated attempt to provide investigative agencies with specific information as to the type of individual who committed a certain crime (Geberth, 1981).

- A **profile analysis** is the identification of the major personality and behavioral characteristics of an individual based upon an analysis of the crimes he or she has committed (Douglas, Ressier, Burgess, & Hartman, 1986).

- **Criminal personality profiling** is the process of analyzing various aspects of violent crime to derive a set of hypotheses about the characteristics of an unknown assailant (McCann, 1992).

- **Offender profiling** is an approach to police investigations whereby an attempt is made to deduce a description of an unknown offender based on evaluating minute details of the crime scene, the victim, and other available evidence (Copson, 1995).

- An **offender profile** is based on the premise that the proper identification of crime scene evidence can indicate the personality type of the individuals who committed the offense (Jackson & Bekerian, 1997).

- **Offender profiling** is commonly associated with inferring characteristics of an offender from the actions at a crime scene (Canter & Alison, 1999).

The profiling field contains about as many approaches to profiling as there are definitions. However, the task of sorting out approaches becomes a little easier if viewed from the perspective of the nature of the framework or orientation that underpins a particular approach. In broad terms, the profiling field can be divided into two quite distinct orientations based on whether or not a particular approach is based on a more clinical or statistical methodological framework. A brief review of the types of approaches that fit under each of these frameworks or orientations is presented next.

Clinical Orientation to Profiling

This methodological framework includes profiling approaches that are deemed to be based on a clinical perspective in the construction of a profile. However, this does not mean that each approach has to be practiced by clinicians in the sense of a medical practitioner or similarly allied professional, like a therapist or mental health worker. Rather, the emphasis is that the approach is clinically based in terms of the perspective drawn upon involving a psychological and/or psychiatric knowledge base.

Approaches that rely on a clinical orientation can be subdivided into two distinct groups of profilers. Those that are more investigative driven and those that are therapy driven as indicated

- **Investigative-driven approaches.** This subgroup of profilers, which can be grouped as having a general clinical orientation, is more experientially focused, and tends to rely on their investigative intuition and experience to reconstruct an offender profile from a detailed analysis of the crime scene(s). Typically, such profilers are detectives and police investigators like FBI special agents. More recently, the method called behavioral evidence analysis fits comfortably within this orientation. BEA does not so much present a new approach, but rather is a more sophisticated process of much of the FBI's work, without being tied to and therefore hamstrung by the original and simplistic organized/disorganized crime scene typology in the earlier work of the FBI.

- **Therapy-driven approaches.** This subgroup, because of their professional training, takes a more therapeutic insight-oriented approach to profiling. Such profilers are typically forensic psychologists and psychiatrists.

Statistical Orientation to Profiling

This type of methodological framework is statistically based and hence, includes profiling approaches that are deemed to be based on this type of perspective in the construction of a profile. Again, this does not mean that each approach has to be practiced by statisticians or only practitioners who are well versed in the rigors of statistical analysis like psychologists or forensic scientists.

The framework emphasizes that an approach is statistically based if it uses various statistical techniques to test hypotheses, model theories, and/or develop databases based on offender populations to augment its knowledge base. For example, the *investigative psychology* approach fits within this statistically based framework. The IP approach uses police records and other data sources to build an empirical database from which to develop theories and test hypotheses.

Approaches that rely on a statistical orientation can be subdivided into two distinct groups of profilers. Those that are more "database driven" and those that are "theory driven" as indicated in the following:

- **Database-driven approaches.** One group of researchers use descriptive statistics from police records, interviews, victim and witness statements, and so forth, to develop crime-specific *databases* of likely offender characteristics. The work on geographic profiling can be related to this group since, like databases, it is an information management strategy that relies on collecting geographical data on a crime series.
- **Theory-driven approaches.** The other group of researchers is more guided by theories and hence, makes specific use of inferential statistics to *analyze* a crime(s).

Offender Profiling in a Terrorism Context

The Ministry of Home Affairs in Singapore released a white paper on terrorism in 2003. In that publication, they identified Jemaah Islamiyah (JI) as the most significant terrorist network currently operating in the Asia Pacific region. The Council on Foreign Relations regards Jemaah Islamiyah as a militant Islamic group with strong links to Al Qaeda that seeks to establish a pan-Islamic state across much of Southeast Asia, according to Gunaratna (2003).

However, Gunaratna (2003) also makes the point that, in so far as this Southeast Asian terrorism network is concerned, the security and intelligence services, accustomed to collecting intelligence by technical methods, have limited high-quality information about this group.

The historical background of JI is that it was formed by a group of radical militants, formally known as the "Darul Islam" or House of Islam, who have been trying to establish an Islamic state in Indonesia through armed and violent struggles after Indonesia gained their independence in 1949. During the Suharto regime, the "Darul Islam" was suppressed by the Indonesian government, and members were forced to flee to Malaysia to avoid arrest. They settled in Malaysia, and later regrouped and formed the JI in 1985.

The JI membership expanded during this period through recruitments in Malaysia and Singapore. After the fall of the Suharto regime in 1988, some of the JI leaders returned to Indonesia, and they continue to pursue their vision of establishing a "Daulah Islamiyah" or Islamic state in the region through the use of violence.

This Daulah Islamiyah vision is to include under its Islamic umbrella the countries of Indonesia, Malaysia, south Philippines, and, inevitably Singapore and Brunei. This vision was spelt in a JI manual known as Pedoman Umum Perjuangan Jemaah Islamiyah (General Guidelines of the Struggle of Jemaah Islamiyah).

In 2001, the JI terrorist network was planning its most ambition undertaking so far in the region to match actions with the Guidelines. It could be speculated that the seemingly stunning success of the Al Qaeda attack on the twin towers in New York in September of 2001 may well have inspired the JI network to up the stakes of the struggle in the Asia Pacific region.

Thankfully, the JI plans for several attacks to take place in Singapore did not eventuate. A total of 36 members of the Jemaah Islamiyah (JI) network were arrested by the Internal Security Department (ISD) of the Singapore Police Force (SPF) for terrorism-related activities in Singapore in two separate operations between December 2001 and August 2002.

In the first operation, 15 JI members were arrested by the ISD. All of these persons were served with a Detention Order that remains in place for two years under Section 8.1(a) of the Internal Security Act of the Singapore Government. All of these persons were Muslims and residents of Singapore.

The picture that emerged in terms of profiling was that such "terrorists" are in the main married, middle class, home owning, early middle-aged, employed men with technical qualifications and a devout desire for a deeper religious experience, as evidenced by their attendance at religious schools and willingness to undergo terrorist training.

Such a profile is entirely consistent with the bulk of the research literature on terrorism that, by and large, "terrorists" are very "normal" people, especially in relation to those who identify with the "religious" or fourth wave of terrorism the world is currently experiencing.

To underscore the point, these "terrorists," from a profiling and behavioral analysis perspective, do not stand out and in fact, will appear as the average person on the street, with the only discernable thing that sets them apart from the crowd being that they take their religion, in this case Islam, very seriously. This is the "indset" of a devout follower, not a fanatic. Although it could be argued that some "devout" followers may become "fanatical" in seeking to apply their beliefs. But this type of "fanaticism" would be more appropriately termed an obsessive-compulsive drive infused with religious significance, rather than a classic psychiatric type "insane" or personality disorder. Unfortunately, offender profiling of any type is not good at reading peoples' minds.

When this JI terrorist profile is considered alongside the terrorism process, then some interesting findings emerge. Firstly, the aggregated profile of a JI terrorist is one of individuals who are predominately married, middle class, middle-aged, employed, home owning, technically qualified, religiously devout men who attended religious schools and underwent terrorist training.

Therefore, one should look at the JI terrorist profile as being a product of context-constraining and context-shaping factors that individuals have over

Figure 2. A model of systemic terrorism development

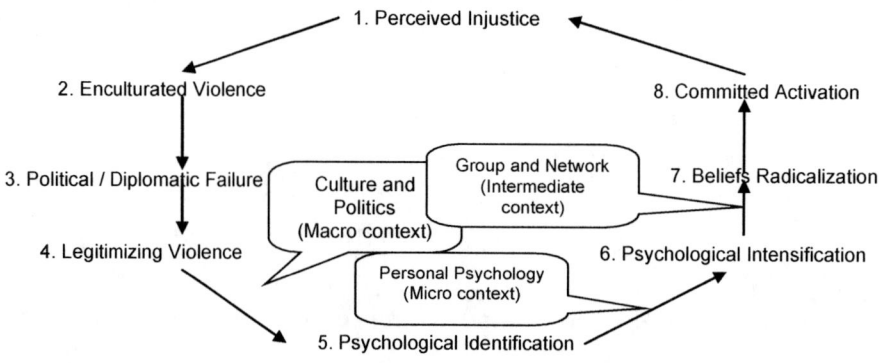

time incorporated as sense-making and meaning-creating responses to their lived experience. In this light, such a context-constrained and context-shaped individual has available only a limited range of acceptable parameters or choices to make in each of these multileveled contexts. Thus, from this perspective, the relevance of profiling the "process" of terrorism rather than the terrorist makes for better logic on the basis of the existing research literature available on terrorism. The process perspective is illustrated in Figure 2.

These eight aspects in the model in Figure 2 are considered factors rather than stages or phases. The term factor is preferred, as it allows for a more flexible understanding of how an individual enters into the process of becoming a terrorist. For example, it means that on the model, it would be misleading to suggest that all eight factors must be present for someone to become a terrorist.

Factors at the macro level set in motion a delegitimization process of the sociocultural and political context that conditions individuals to consider the use of violence as an acceptable response to perceived and/or actual injustices that the authorities have failed to remedy. Factors at the micro level are concerned with psychological intensification. Individuals who commit terrorist acts have already psychologically identified with certain causes; hence, they are not changing their convictions as a brainwashing process implies. The intermediate context of group and network allows the dynamic nature of group-organizational-networks to support the directional nature of the already brain-hardened beliefs, and further reinforces self-appointed leaders of secular or religious ideologies.

Here we close our presentation of offender profiling. It has provided valuable insights into knowledge application work that is carried out by detectives and other investigation officers.

At Stage 4 of the knowledge management technology model, we find officer-to-application systems. Several systems can emerge from this discussion of offender profiling. We can think of statistical tools, visualization media, and databases. In particular, case-based reasoning and system dynamics simulation are artificial intelligence techniques that can be applied to offender profiling. A case-based reasoning system can be used to store, retrieve, and compare criminal profiles. A system dynamics model can be used to simulate the process of systemic terrorism. In system dynamics terminology, the circle in Figure 2 is a positive feedback loop causing exponential growth in behavior over time.

Knowledge Application: Cross+Check

Dean (1995, 2000, 2005) developed the cross+check system, which is an integrating profiling approach for police and security investigations. His work is presented in this section.

The core of the C+C system is its ability to bring together and focus on the interrelationships between four qualitatively different levels of information. The goal of the C+C system is to generate and then prioritize the investigative leads that logically flow out of systematically cross+checking informational interrelationships in order to not only plan and manage an overall investigative strategy, but also to develop leads into evidence (Dean & Schroder, 2003).

The innovative aspect of the C+C system is that it is based on visual thinking and reasoning. The advantages of thinking visually over other forms of thinking are well documented across a range of quite diverse disciplines. For example, within the disciples of mathematics, the use of visual imagery has long been recognized, and is currently having something of a renaissance.

In information technology at Stage 4 of knowledge management technology, the field of cognitive psychology, artificial intelligence, and computer sciences are leaping ahead in great strides on the springboard of diagrammatic reasoning, Diagrammatic reasoning is this diverse field's preferred term for our form of visual thinking that involves mental images and externally drawn diagrams (Chandrasekaran, Glasgow, & Harayanan, 1995).

In relation to the cross+check system, there are five main properties involved in visual thinking and reasoning with images and diagrams that have specific value for the C+C model. Each property represents a cluster of traits identified by various researchers that can be associated with the main feature of each property. A label has been attached to each of the five clustered properties to highlight the focal aspect involved in a specific property. These five clustered properties are itemized here:

- **Locality property.** Efficiency of visually relating elements in the data structure via locality of searching, recognizing, and retrieving related information (Fischer, 1997).

- **Spatiality property.** Explicitness of spatial relations via compactness, consistency, and maximality of spatially related information (Barwise & Hammer, 1996).

- **Modifiability property.** Ease of dynamically modifying spatial relationships via visual inspection and manipulation of spatially related information (Barwise & Etchemendy, 1996a).

- **Extractability property.** Ease of extraction of spatial information via making visual connections, interpretations, and perceptual inferences (Fischer, 1997).

- **Qualitativeness property.** Enhancement of qualitative understandings via comparisons, analysis checks, analogical reasoning, and predictions (Iwasaki, 1995).

Each of these properties and their clustered traits are embedded in the way the cross+check system works. Hence, the C+C system adds these five advantages of thinking visually, that is, locality, spatiality, modifiability, extractability, and qualitativeness to the systematic and logically deductive reasoning process of deriving inferences from the visual cross-referencing analysis of the four informational quadrants that comprise the C+C system.

The cross+check system consists of four qualitatively different sources of information, that of *police/security* information, *descriptive* information, *diagnostic* information, and *research* information. Figure 3 presents a graphical representation of the interrelated nature of these four informational sources arranged as levels of analysis in a diamond-shaped pattern that forms the operational basis of the C+C system.

The C+C system utilizes these four types of qualitatively different information to develop inferences, and then test the veracity of such inferences by checking

Figure 3. Operational framework of cross+check model as a knowledge management system (based on Dean, 2005)

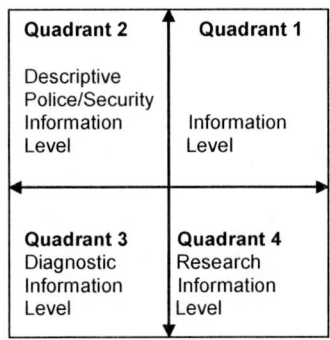

them against each of these four levels of information in the system. This systematic process of analysis also allows an investigator to place a relative weighting on developed inferences and hence, to prioritize investigative leads.

- **Quadrant 1—Police/security information level.** This quadrant contains what can be considered factually based information derived primarily from a crime scene, in the case of a reactive crime, or from various operational sources in relation to a proactive crime, or security operation or threat. With regard to the type of information required at this police/security level, the range of variables would cover items like type of crime/security investigation, crime/security elements, and victim elements. Chapter VI's Figure 2 illustrates how these types of informational sources, as a component part, relate to the overall C+C analysis as a knowledge management system.

- **Quadrant 2—Descriptive information level.** Police/security databases contain a wealth of descriptive information that can be used to not only perform routine police/security work like computer checks on car and license details and matching of crime/security characteristics, but also to generate statistically based profiles of various crimes, offender types, and/or security threat suspects. The type of information required at this descriptive level would cover variables such as the following: witness statements, members of the public, informant/anonymous calls, victim statements, forensic/pathology reports, interviews of victim's family and friends, surveillance/intelligence reports, and suspect characteristics.

- **Quadrant 3—Diagnostic information level.** This quadrant contains any type of information that can be considered as diagnostic of the crime and/or security situation. Hence, it draws on clinical insights by criminal and forensic psychiatrists and psychologists as well as sociocultural and political scientists, especially in the case of security-terrorist threats or actions. The type of information required at this diagnostic level would cover variables such as behavioral elements, psychological elements, sociocultural/political elements, and specific crime/security elements.

- **Quadrant 4—Research information level.** This quadrant contains research-derived information that allows for some level of generalizability to the current crime/security situation to be productively undertaken. The type of information required at this research level would cover specific variables for both crime and security situations. In relation to crime, the type of research findings that would be useful to generalize from would cover items like the following: criminal history, residential location, crime location, offender population, motivational themes, narrative themes, and specific crime/security findings.

In relation to the policing/security field, the implications of the distinction between information that can be stored in a computer and knowledge that is the outcome of human thinking is that police/security database systems can be crammed full of information, but not knowledge. That is, databases only contain information; it is up to people to take the stored information and make it into knowledge.

As cross+check is currently only a conceptual framework, there are no empirical studies of its use. However, we can think of ways of using information technology to support C+C knowledge work. A knowledge management system integrating and comparing-crossing and checking-will certainly have potential for real knowledge management cases.

Senior Investigating Officer Development Program

The performance of the police in the area of investigation is continually under scrutiny by the government, the criminal justice system, and the media. There is widespread recognition within the police service that there is a need to improve the professionalism of the investigative response. In the UK, the professionalizing investigation program was introduced in 2005. The purpose is to significantly improve the personal, functional, and organizational ability of the service to investigate crime of any category. In performance terms, the aim of the program is to deliver (Home Office, 2005b):

- Improved rates of crime detection
- Improvement in the quality of case files
- A reduction in the number of failed trails
- Improved levels of judicial disposal
- Increased public confidence in the police service

Figure 4. Characteristics of investigative levels

Investigative Level	Example of Role	Description of Typical Investigative Activity
Level 1	Patrol Constable/Police Staff/Supervisors	Investigation of volume crime
Level 2	Dedicated Investigator (e.g., CID officer)	Substantive investigation into more serious and problem offences including road traffic deaths
Specialist Investigative Roles	Child Protection, Family Liaison, Major Crime	Child Protection, Special Branch, Family Liaison, Force Intelligence Bureau
Level 3	Senior Investigating Officer	Lead investigator in cases of murder, stranger rape, kidnap or crimes of complexity Category, A, B-C

The long-term outcomes of the program shall deliver the professional development of staff against robust national occupational standards by developing police staff who are better qualified and thereby better skilled in investigation, more focused training for investigation, and minimal accreditation bureaucracy.

Levels of investigators have been identified based on investigative activities. Although there are four distinct levels, initially, development has been carried out on levels 1-3, as illustrated in Figure 4. The levels are identified within the investigative activities for the differing roles.

To achieve this, there will be a need to train investigators, and then assess individuals against the National Occupational Standards (NOS), leading to registration as an investigator within the four levels. The register for level 3 investigators will be held and maintained nationally.

In order to be effective, the investigator must develop the ability to make reliable and accountable decisions. This may often be under pressure or in difficult circumstances. There are many forces that affect an investigator's ability to make decisions. A number of measures, including the investigative mindset and investigative and evidential evaluation, are proposed within the program that will assist investigators in making accountable decisions, and minimize the chance of errors. At the end of the program, level 3 investigators will be able to:

- Apply a robust and universal investigative methodology to the management of major crime investigations
- Demonstrate the effective management of the initial response to major investigations

- Recognize the benefits of the involvement of individuals, families, and communities to major crime investigations

- Demonstrate cooperative working practices with other agencies, partnerships, and communities

- Demonstrate the effective management of family liaison

- Demonstrate effective and efficient resource management

- Coordinate the gathering of material (information, intelligence, and evidence) to support major crime investigations

- Coordinate the effective recording and retention of material for use in major crime investigations

- Demonstrate accountability by recording investigative decisions

- Use advances in forensic science to support major crime investigations

- Justify decisions and actions in proceedings

- Review decisions in light of emerging facts

- Demonstrate effective evaluation of the performance of self and of the investigation team

A framework for the training and assessment of senior investigative officers (SIOs) at level 3 has been developed. The framework consists of a number of phases: selection, distance learning and induction, three-week course, workplace assessment, one-week training, and registration and maintenance.

Decision Support Systems in Law Enforcement

Computers, and especially some artificial intelligence technologies, excel in supporting law enforcement agencies, according to Wright (2001). For example, using computer-mapping systems, police can track the location of 911 callers who use cell phones. Brown and Hagen (2002) provide an overview of decision support system methods used in law enforcement.

A decision support system (DSS) has the purpose of supporting and improving decision-making. A DSS is usually built to support the solution of a certain problem, or to evaluate an opportunity. As such, it is called a DSS application, belonging to the stage of officer-to-application systems. A DSS is an approach (or methodology) for supporting decision making. It uses an interactive, flexible, adaptable, computer-based information system especially developed for supporting the solution to a specific, nonstructured, management problem. It uses data, provides an easy user interface, and can incorporate the decision maker's own insights. In addition, a DSS usually uses models, and is built (often by end users) by an interactive and iterative process. It supports all phases of decision-making, and includes a knowledge component. A DSS is typically composed of the following subsystems (Turban, Aronson, & Liang, 2005):

- **Data-management subsystem.** The data management subsystem includes a database that contains relevant data for the situation, and is managed by software called the database management system. The data management subsystem can be interconnected with the organizational data warehouse, a repository of organizationally relevant decision-making data. Usually, the data are stored and accessed via a database Web server.

- **Model management subsystem.** This is a software package that includes financial, statistical, management science, and other quantitative models that provide the system's analytical capabilities and appropriate software management. Modeling languages for building custom models are also included. This software is often called a model-base management system. This component can be connected to corporate or external storage of models. Model solution methods and management systems are implemented in Web development systems (like Java) to run on application servers.

- **User interface subsystem.** The user communicates with and commands the DSS through this subsystem. The user is considered part of the system. Some of the unique contributions of DSS are derived from the intensive interaction between the computer and the decision maker. The Web browser provides a familiar, consistent, graphical user-interface structure for most DSS.

- **Knowledge-based management subsystem.** This subsystem can support any of the other subsystems or act as an independent component. It provides intelligence to augment the decision-maker's own. It can be interconnected with the organization's knowledge repository (part of knowledge management system), which is sometimes called the organizational knowledge base. Knowledge may be provided via Web servers.

Many artificial intelligence methods have been implemented in Web development systems like Java, and are easy to integrate into the other DSS components.

By definition, a DSS must include the three major components of a database management system, model base management system, and use interface. The knowledge-based management subsystem is optional, but can provide many benefits by providing intelligence in and to the three major components. It is the fourth component of a knowledge-based management subsystem that qualifies a DSS for Stage 4 in knowledge-management technology.

An intelligent agent can also be part of a DSS. An intelligent agent (IA) is a computer program that helps a user with routine computer tasks. It performs a specific task based on predetermined rules and knowledge stored in its knowledge base. IAs are a powerful tool for overcoming the most critical limitations on the Internet, information overflow, and making electronic commerce a viable organizational tool. The term, agent, is derived from the concept of agency, referring to employing someone to act on your behalf. A human agent represents a person, and interacts with others to accomplish a predefined task.

Intelligence is a key feature related to defining intelligent agents because it differentiates them from ordinary agents. Intelligence, in this sense, possesses the following features (Turban et al., 2005):

- **Reactivity.** Intelligent agents are able to perceive their environment and respond in a timely fashion to changes that occur in it, in order to satisfy their design objectives.
- **Proactiveness.** Intelligent agents are able to exhibit goal-directed behavior by taking the initiatives in order to satisfy their design objectives.
- **Social ability.** Intelligent agents are capable of interacting with other agents (and possibly humans) in order to satisfy their design objectives.

Of the various characteristics of agents, three are of special importance: agency, intelligence, and mobility (Turban et al., 2005):

- **Agency** is the degree of autonomy vested in the agent, and can be measured, at least qualitatively, by the nature of the interaction between the agent and other entities in the system.

- **Intelligence** is the degree of reasoning and learned behavior, the agent's ability to accept the user's statement of goals and carry out the tasks delegated to it.

- **Mobility** is the degree to which the agents themselves travel through the network.

Over the last two decades, researchers have developed a number of automated tools to support law enforcement activities. These tools assist in a wide variety of tasks, from identifying potential suspects to assisting in hostage negotiations. Examples are decision support systems, including intelligent agents, as described previously.

For crime analysis, Brown and Hagen (2002) present examples by organizing them into three categories: expert systems, investigative support systems, and nonautomated crime analysis methods. Specifically, they studied data-association methods with applications to law enforcement. Data association enables crime analysts to associate incidents possibly resulting from the same individual or group of individuals.

Expert systems provide the most common approach to the data association problem for law enforcement. For example, the Armed Robbery Eidetic Suspect Typing (AREST) system helps simplify and enhance the investigative process and perform data association. The system searches for similar information contained in multiple reports and attempts to associate the reports. AREST uses an expert-system approach to accomplish its tasks. Working with the Comanche County Sheriff's Department, Brown and Hagen (2002) assembled a list of suspect traits that could be identified by a witness. Each of these traits was assigned a confidence level that indicates "the level of certainty that a given suspect is probable for a crime for which his observed traits match a suspect file." The experts from the police department then established a set of rules based on these traits. Using this knowledge base, the expert system classifies people in a suspect file as probable suspects, possible suspects, or not a suspect.

Investigative support systems support law enforcement investigations, for example by performing link analysis. Link analysis looks for links between suspect attributes. For example, a suspect report could indicate that the suspect has an acquaintance with a first name of Ken who drives a red truck. The system then searches for other records of suspects with the first name of Ken who drive a red truck. If it finds one or more records, then these are linked to the first record. This system looks for exact matches of attributes that link different people (or objects) together, but does not associate incidents possibly committed by the same person through inexact or partial matches.

Nonautomated crime analysis applies statistical models to analyze crime behavior. An example is the fireman in Norway who always happened to have visited a place where a forest fire broke out. From a statistical point of view, it was determined that it was close to certain that the fireman must have been the criminal who started all the fires. It was close to statistically impossible that he had nothing to do with the fires, having been to all these places all those times when forest fires started.

Every crime has a crime scene that can be scoured for clues. But sometimes the evidence being analyzed is not a bloodstain, a footprint, or a carpet fiber. It is the bits and bytes of data hidden inside a computer. In those cases, criminal investigators need to know how to coax secrets from the silicon chips (Wright, 2001).

Much like their physical crime-scene counterparts, computer forensics investigators follow several basic steps. In the case of a crime that has already been committed, they must preserve evidence and then analyze what is collected. In the case of an investigation into an ongoing crime, they may be required to conduct surveillance of a suspect or a locale. In either type of situation, they will ultimately have to prepare a detailed report of their findings (Wright, 2001).

Technologies and Techniques

We conclude this chapter by discussing practical and workable technologies, tools, and techniques for knowledge management in law enforcement. At this final stage of the stages-of-growth model for knowledge management technology, we build on the previous stages where the organization has end-user tools, collaboration systems, and information storage farms at Stages 1, 2, and 3, respectively.

A case-based reasoning system is an important application at this stage. By learning how similar cases were handled in the past, detectives are supported in their investigative steps in the new case. Furthermore, previous cases might contain elements that can be included in the current case.

Another interesting example is the AICAMS project, which draws upon human heuristics or rules and procedures to investigate tasks. The AICAMS project is a knowledge-based system for identifying suspects. Furthermore, AICAMS includes a component to fulfill the needs for facial identification procedures based on a library of facial components. The system provides a capability for assembling an infinite number of possible facial composites by varying the position and size of the components (Chen et al., 2002).

Generally, systems at Stage 4 represent technologies and techniques that represent knowledge applications. For such systems to be successful, knowledge has to be codified and represented as information in the system. There are two kinds of information needed. First, there is the raw material representing information about cases. Second, there is the thinking style representing how cases should be analyzed.

As discussed in this chapter, offender profiling is an important application area. Offender profiling is an approach to police investigations whereby an attempt is made to deduce a description of an unknown offender based on evaluating minute details of the crime scene, the victim, and other available evidence.

Generally, as discussed in the next chapter, technologies and techniques used at Stage 4 will support police investigations in terms of primary activities of the value shop. When assessing incoming information, when selecting appropriate lines of enquiry, and in case development, expert systems are expected to play an important role in law enforcement in the future.

However, both the speed of technology development and the speed of organizational innovation will be such that we are talking about years rather than months, maybe even decades. In the area of knowledge applications in expert systems, we find, so far, more failures than successes. Medical diagnostics where patients communicate with an electronic doctor, and legal diagnostics where a client communicates with an electronic lawyer, have so far not at all met expectations (Gottschalk, 2005). Therefore, technologies and techniques at Stage 4 of knowledge management technology will probably emerge at a slow pace in law enforcement.

References

Barwise, J., & Etchemendy, J. (1996a). Visual information and valid reasoning. In G. Allwein, & J. Barwise (Eds.), *Logical reasoning with diagrams* (pp. 3-25). New York; Oxford: Oxford University Press.

Barwise, J., & Hammer, E. (1996). Diagrams and the concept of logical system. In G. Allwein, & J. Barwise (Eds.), *Logical reasoning with diagrams* (pp. 49-78). New York; Oxford: Oxford University Press.

Becerra-Fernandez, I., Gonzalez, A., & Sabherwal, R. (2004). *Knowledge management: Challenges, solutions, and technologies*. Upper Saddle River, NJ: Prentice Hall.

Brown, D. E., & Hagen, S. (2002). Data association methods with applications to law enforcement. *Decision Support Systems, 34*, 369-378

Canter, D., & Alison, L. (Eds.). (1999). *Profiling in policy and practice.* Aldershot: Ashgate/Dartmouth.

Chandrasekaran, B., Glasgow, J., & Harayanan, H. (Eds.). (1995). *Diagrammatic reasoning: Cognitive and computational perspectives* (p. xxii). Menlo Park, CA; Cambridge, MA: AAAI Press / MIT Press.

Chen, H., Schroeder, J., Hauck, R. V., Ridgeway, L., Atabakhsh, H., Gupta, H., et al. (2002). COPLINK Connect: Information and knowledge management for law enforcement. *Decision Support Systems, 34*, 271-285.

Copson, G. (1995). *Coals to Newcastle? Part 1: A study of offender profiling.* (Paper 7). London: Police Research Group Special Interest Series, Home Office.

Dean, G. (1995). Police reform: Rethinking operational policing. *American Journal of Criminal Justice, 23*(4), 337-347.

Dean, G. (2000). *The experience of investigation for detectives.* Unpublished PhD thesis, Queensland University of Technology, Brisbane, Australia.

Dean, G. (2005). *The cognitive psychology of police investigators.* Conference paper, School of Justice Studies, Faculty of Law, Queensland University of Technology, Brisbane, Australia.

Dean, G., & Schroder, D. (2003). Cross+Check als alternatives Modell Für die Analyse von Kriminalfällen. In *Polizei-Heute, 2*, 32. Jahrgang.

Douglas, J., Ressier, R. K., Burgess, A. W., & Hartman, C. R. (1986). Criminal profiling from crime scene analysis. *Behavioral Sciences and the Law, 4*, 401-421.

Fischer, M. (1997). *Qualitative computing: Using software for qualitative data analysis.* Aldershot, UK: Ashgate Publishing Ltd.

Geberth, V. J. (1981). Psychological profiling. *Law and Order*, 46-52.

Gottschalk, P. (2005). *Strategic knowledge management technology.* Hershey, PA: Idea Group Publishing.

Gunaratna, R. (2003). Al Qaeda's origins, threat and its likely future. In R. Gunaratna (Ed.), *Terrorism in the Asia-Pacific: Threat and response* (pp. 135-160). Singapore: Times Media Private Limited.

Home Office. (2005b). *Senior Investigating Officer Development Programme*. Police Standards Unit, Home Office of the UK Government. Retrieved from http://www.policereform.gov.uk

Iwasaki, Y. (1995). Problem solving with diagrams. In Bl Chandrasekaran, J. Glasgow, & H. Hari Harayanan (Eds.) *Diagrammatic reasoning: Cognitive and computational perspectives* (pp. 657-667). Menlo Park, CA; Cambridge, MA: AAAI Press/MIT Press.

Jackson, J., & Bekerian, D. (1997). Does offender profiling have a role to play? In J. Jackson & D. Bekerian (Eds.), *Offender profiling: Theory, research and practice* (pp. 3-7). Chichester, UK: John Wiley & Sons.

McCann, J. T. (1992). Criminal personality profiling in the investigation of violent crime: Recent advances and future directions. *Behavioral Sciences and the Law, 10*, 475-481.

Turban, E., Aronson, J. E., & Liang, T. P. (2005). *Decision support systems and intelligent systems* (7th ed.). Upper Saddle River, NJ: Prentice-Hall.

Wright, J. (2001, July). High-tech Holmes. *Security Management, 44-52*.

Chapter IX

Police Work in Value Shops

To comprehend the value that information technology provides to organizations, we must first understand the way a particular organization conducts business, and how information systems affect the performance of various component activities within the organization. Understanding how firms differ is a central challenge for both theory and practice of management. For a long time, Porter's (1985) value chain was the only value configuration known to managers. Stabell and Fjeldstad (1998) have identified two alternative value configurations. A value shop schedules activities and applies resources in a fashion that is dimensioned and appropriate to the needs of the client's problem, while a value chain performs a fixed set of activities that enables it to produce a standard product in large numbers. Examples of value shops are professional service firms, as found in medicine, law, architecture, and engineering. A value network links clients or customers who are, or wish to be interdependent. Examples of value networks are telephone companies, retail banks, and insurance companies.

A value configuration describes how value is created in a company for its customers. A value configuration shows how the most important business processes function to create value for customers. A value configuration represents the way a particular organization conducts business.

Infrastructure: Use of corporate intranet for internal communications				
Human resources: Use of corporate intranet for competence building				
Technology: Computer Aided Design (CAD)				
Procurement: Use of electronic marketplaces				
Inbound logistics: Electronic Data Interchange (EDI)	**Production**: Computer Integrated Manufacturing (CIM)	**Outbound logistics**: Web-based order-tracking system	**Marketing and sales**: Customer Relationship Management (CRM)	**Service**: System for local troubleshooting

The Organization as Value Chain

The best-known value configuration is the value chain. In the value chain, value is created through efficient production of goods and services based on a variety of resources. The company is perceived as a series or chain of activities. Primary activities in the value chain include inbound logistics, production, outbound logistics, marketing and sales, and service. Support activities include infrastructure, human resources, technology development, and procurement. Attention is on performing these activities in the chain in efficient and effective ways. In Figure 1, examples of IS/IT are assigned to primary and support activities. This figure can be used to describe the current IS/IT situation in the organization, as it illustrates the extent of coverage of IS/IT for each activity.

The knowledge intensity of systems in the different activities can be illustrated by different shading, where dark shading indicates high-knowledge intensity. In this example, it is assumed that the most knowledge intensive activities are computer-aided design and customer relationship management.

The Organization as Value Shop

Value cannot only be created in value chains. Value can also be created in two alternative value configurations: value shop and value network (Stabell &

Fjeldstad, 1998). In the value shop, activities are scheduled and resources are applied in a fashion that is dimensioned and appropriate to the needs of the client's problem, while a value chain performs a fixed set of activities that enables it to produce a standard product in large numbers. The value shop is a company that creates value by solving unique problems for customers and clients. Knowledge is the most important resource, and reputation is critical to firm success.

While typical examples of value chains are manufacturing industries such as paper and car production, typical examples of value shops are law firms and medical hospitals. Often, such companies are called professional service firms or knowledge-intensive service firms. Like the medical hospital as a way to practice medicine, the law firm provides a standard format for delivering complex legal services. Many features of its style—specialization, teamwork, continuous monitoring on behalf of clients (patients), and representation in many forums—have been emulated in other vehicles for delivering professional services (Galanter & Palay, 1991).

Knowledge-intensive service firms are typical value shops. Sheehan (2002) defines knowledge-intensive service firms as entities that sell problem-solving services, where the solution chosen by the expert is based on real-time feedback from the client. Clients retain knowledge intensive service firms to reduce their uncertainty. Clients hire knowledge-intensive service firms precisely because the client believes the firm knows something that the client does not, and believes it is necessary to solve their problems.

While expertise plays a role in all firms, its role is distinctive in knowledge-intensive service firms. Expert, often professional, knowledge is at the core of the service provided by the type of firm.

Knowledge-intensive service firms not only sell a problem-solving service, but equally a problem-finding, problem-defining, solution-execution, and monitoring service. Problem finding is often a key for acquiring new clients. Once the client is acquired and their problem is defined, not all problems will be solved by the firm. Rather, the firm may only clarify that there is no problem (i.e. the patient does not have a heart condition), or that the problem should be referred to another specialist (i.e., the patient needs a heart specialist). If a problem is treated within the firm, then the firm needs to follow up the implementation to assure that the problem, in fact, has been solved (i.e., is the patient's heart now working properly?). This follows from the fact that there is often uncertainty in both problem diagnosis and problem resolution.

Sheehan (2002) has created a typology of knowledge-intensive service firms consisting of the following three types. First, knowledge-intensive search firms search for opportunities. The amount of value they create depends on the size of the finding or discovery, where size is measured by quality rather than quantity. Examples of search firms include petroleum and mineral exploration, drug discovery in the pharmaceutical industry, and research in the biotechnology industry. Second, knowledge-intensive diagnosis firms create value by clarifying problems. Once the problem has been identified, the suggested remedy usually follows directly. Examples of diagnosis firms include doctors, surgeons, psychotherapists, veterinarians, lawyers, auditors and tax accountants, and software support. Finally, knowledge-intensive design firms create value by conceiving new ways of constructing material or immaterial artifacts. Examples of design firms include architecture, advertising, research and development, engineering design, and strategy consulting.

Knowledge-intensive service firms create value through problem acquisition and definition, alternative generation and selection, implementation of an alternative, and follow up to see if the solution selected resolves the problem. To reflect this process, Stabell and Fjeldstad (1998) have outlined the value configuration of a value shop.

A value shop is characterized by five primary activities: problem finding and acquisition, problem solving, choice, execution, and control and evaluation, as illustrated in Figure 2. Problem finding and acquisition involves working with the customer to determine the exact nature of the problem or need. It involves deciding on the overall plan of approaching the problem. Problem solving is the actual generation of ideas and action (or treatment) plans.

Choice represents the decision of choosing between alternatives. While the least important primary activity of the value shop in terms of time and effort, it is also the most important in terms of customer value. Execution represents communicating, organizing, and implementing the decision, or performing the treatment. Control and evaluation activities involve monitoring and measurement of how well the solution solved the original problem or met the original need.

This may feed back into the first activity, problem finding and acquisition, for two reasons. First, if the proposed solution is inadequate or did not work, it feeds back into learning why it was inadequate, and begins the problem-solving phase anew. Second, if the problem solution was successful, the firm might enlarge the scope of the problem-solving process to solve a bigger problem related to or dependent upon the first problem being solved.

Figure 2. Examples of IS/IT in the value shop

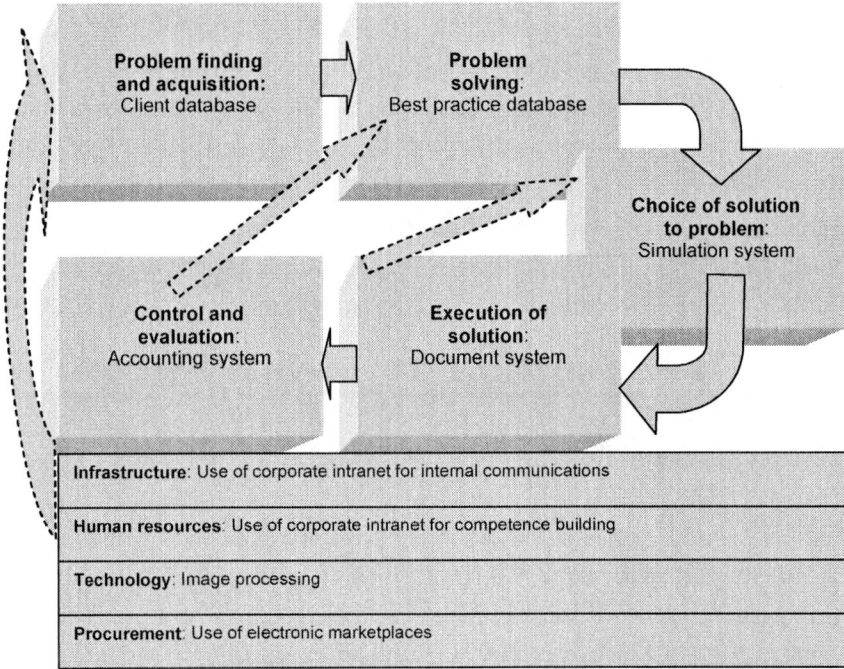

Knowledge-intensive service firms are typical value shops, and such firms depend on reputation for success, as reputation is a key driver of firm value creation. Reputation is a relational concept in the sense that firms are judged by their stakeholders relative to their competitors. Reputation is what is generally said or believed about an entity by someone: it is the net perception of a firm held by stakeholders judged relative to other firms. According to Sheehan (2002), there are four conditions that must be present for reputation to work. Firstly, rents earned from maintaining a good reputation must be greater than not. Secondly, there must be a minimum of contact among stakeholders to allow for the changes in reputation to be communicated. Thirdly, there needs to be a possibility of repeat business. And lastly, there must be some uncertainty regarding the firm's type and/or behavior.

Reputation is related to the asymmetry of information, which is a typical feature of knowledge intensive service firms. Asymmetry is present when clients believe the firm knows something that the clients do not, and believe it is necessary to know to solve their problems.

Reputation can be classified as a strategic resource in knowledge-intensive firms. To be a strategic resource, it has to be valuable, rare, costly to imitate, and possible to organize. Reputation is valuable as it increases the value received by the client. Reputation is rare as by definition, only a few firms can be considered best in the industry. Reputation is costly to imitate, as it is difficult to build a reputation in the short run. Reputation is possible to organize in the general sense of controllability, which implies that a firm can be organized to take advantage of reputation as a resource.

The Organization as Value Network

The third and final value configuration is the value network. A value network is a company that creates value by connecting clients and customers that are, or want to be, dependent on each other. These companies distribute information, money, products, and services. While activities in both value chains and value shops are done sequentially, activities in value networks occur in parallel. The number and combination of customers and access points in the network are important value drivers in the value network. More customers and more connections create higher value to customers.

Stabell and Fjeldstad (1998) suggest that managing a value network can be compared to managing a club. The mediating firm admits members that complement each other, and in some cases exclude those that do not. The firm establishes, monitors, and terminates direct or indirect relationships among members. Supplier-customer relationships may exist between the members of the club, but to the mediating firm they are all customers.

Examples of value networks include telecommunication companies, financial institutions such as banks and insurance companies, and stockbrokers. Value networks perform three activities (see Figure 3):

- Development of customer network through marketing and recruiting of new customers, to enable increased value for both existing customers and new customers
- Development of new services and improvement in existing services
- Development of infrastructure so that customer services can be provided more efficiently and effectively

Figure 3. Examples of IS/IT in the value network

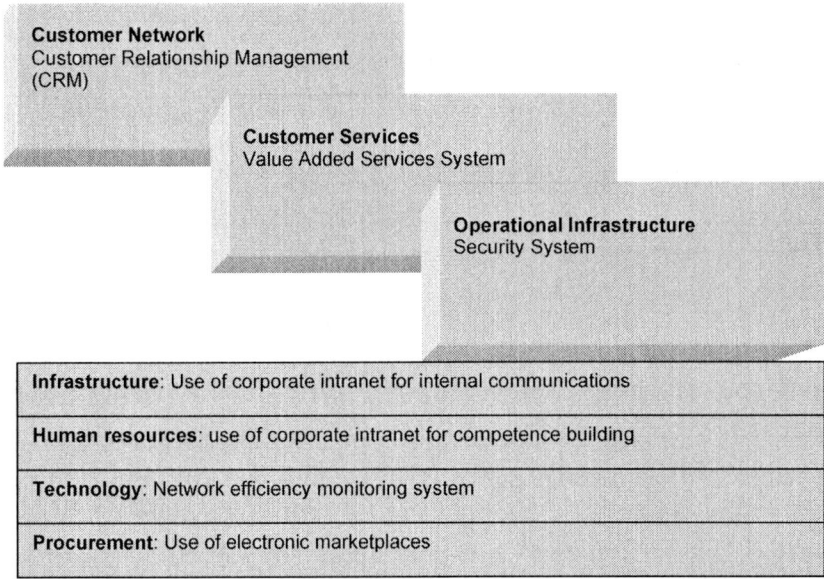

The current IS/IT situation in a value network will mainly be described through the infrastructure that typically will consist of information technology. In addition, many of the new services may be information systems that will be used by customers in their communication and business transactions with other customers. The knowledge component will mainly be found in the services of a value network, as information systems are made available to customers to exchange relevant information.

Comparison of Value Configurations

Value chain, value shop, and value network are alternative value configurations that impact the use of information technology in the company, as illustrated in Figure 4. While the role of IT is to make production more efficient in a value chain, IT creates added value in the value shop, while IT in the form of infrastructure is the main value in the value network. Some companies have

Figure 4. Characteristics of value configurations

Characteristics	Value Chain	Value Shop	Value Network
Value creation	Transformation of input to output	Solving clients and customers problems	Connecting clients and customers to each other
Work form	Sequential production	Integrated and cyclical problem solving	Monitored and simultaneous connections
Information systems	Making production more efficient	Adding value to the knowledge work	Main value by use of IT infrastructure
Example	Paper factory	Law firm	Telecom company

more than one value configuration, but most companies have one dominating configuration.

In the long term, business organizations can choose to change their value configurations. A bank, for example, can be a value shop when it focuses on converting inputs to outputs. The value resides in the output and once you have the output, you can remove the production organization. This removal does not impact on the value of the output. The value shop is a solution provider. It is somebody that solves problems. The input is a problem. The output is a solution to the problem. A bank that does this would view itself as a financial service operator, a financial advisor that also has the ability to provide the money. But what it would do is identify client problems, it would address those problems, it would select a solution together with the client, and help to implement it. It would have stringent quality controls. As part of its offering, it would probably supply the client with some cash as a loan, or accept some of the clients cash for investment (Chatzkel, 2002).

Or, the bank can be a value network, which is basically the logic of the marketplace. The bank would define its role as a conduit between people that do not have money and those people that do have money. What the bank does is to arrange the flow of cash between them. The bank will attract people with money to make deposits and investments. The bank will also attract people without money to make loans. As a value network, the bank will connect people with opposite financial needs. The network consists of people with different financial needs. Over time, persons in the network may change status from money needer to money provider, and vice versa (Chatzkel, 2002).

Both as a value shop and as a value network, the business organization can be identified as a bank. But it would have completely different consequences for what it will focus on doing well, what it will focus on doing itself, vs. what it would not want to do itself. This provides a kind of strategic systems logic. It asks, "Which strategic system in terms of value configuration are we going to operate in?" Choosing an appropriate value configuration is a long-term decision with long-term consequences.

Police Investigation as Value Shop

Criminal investigation can be defined as a method for reconstructing the past (Osterburg & Ward, 1992). In a knowledge management context, it brings insight to divide the principal methods of inquiry into two broad, distinct categories: those that reconstruct the past, and those that discover or create new knowledge. The first is the method of the historian, archeologist, epidemiologist, journalist, and criminal investigator; the second, that of the scientist in general. Although usefully stated as a dichotomy for the sake of conceptual distinction, these methods finally fuse in the minds of the better thinkers and practitioners, for the reconstruction of the past often makes use of the scientific method, while science builds on and digresses from the past.

The scientific method is a way of observing, thinking about, and solving problems objectively and systematically. Examples are induction (the process of reasoning based on a set of experiences or observations), deduction (the process of reasoning that commences with generalization), classification (the systematic arrangement of objects into categories), synthesis (the combining of separate parts), analysis (the separation of the whole), hypothesis (the conjecture accounting for a set of facts), theory (the development of a scheme of thought), a priori (the reasoning to empirical facts), and posteriori (the reasoning from empirical facts).

The use of the scientific method in criminal investigation is illustrated by the following situation, based on an actual case (Osterburg & Ward, 1992, p. 15):

A detective, called to the scene where a young woman had been murdered in her apartment, found the table set for two. There were melted-down candles, wine, supper still warm on the serving cart, and a radio softly playing. Finding no evidence of forced entry or struggle, the detective hypothesized that the woman admitted the killer into her home, probably as her dinner guest. In subsequent questioning of the victim's family, friends, and business associates, one name, that of her former lover, continually surfaced; indeed, several people indicated that his earlier behavior during a quarrel had been forgiven, and that this was to have been a reconciliation dinner.

The hypothesis that the killer was an invited guest is somewhat verified by the facts obtained through interviews. Needing additional information, however, the investigator must consider the following possibilities: Can the friend be located at his place of business, home, or other unusual haunts? Is flight indicated? If so, is any clothing or other item such as a prized trophy or razor missing? Did the suspect cash a large check or withdraw money from his bank the day of or on the morning following the homicide? If affirmative answers are obtained and applied inductively, the weight of evidence in support of the hypothesis is even greater. The former lover may now be considered the prime suspect (the generalization). An inductive result, however, is not necessarily a certainty: flight may be evidence of guilt, but it is not proof. The suspect could have innocently gone on a vacation at what would, in retrospect, have been an inappropriate time. Assuming that information from relatives and friends has failed to trace him, the homicide investigator must now discover his whereabouts.

The next logical step in the investigative process is deduction. The characterization of the lover as the prime suspect (the generalization) leads to the question: "Where would he be likely to flee?" (Answers to which are the particulars). Possible locations are suggested by such considerations as: Where was the suspect born? Had he lived for a time in some other area? Has he a favorite vacation spot? With additional facts or details elicited, investigative activities will seek answers (again, particulars) to other questions, such as: What else might he do to earn a living? Who might he write or telephone? Will he try to collect his last paycheck either by mail or other means? Will he continue to pay union dues? Will he change his driver's license? A sufficient amount of acquired and utilized facts (particulars) should allow the investigator to come to a generalization through the process of inductive reasoning. The generalization about the likely whereabouts or location of the subject permits the investigator to deduce the particulars (such as addresses) needed to apprehend the suspect. Again, reasonable premises (e.g., that suspects will turn up at their usual haunts) may prove to be invalid because of the illogical, often perverse aspects of human behavior.

Figure 5. Police investigation unit as value shop with activity examples

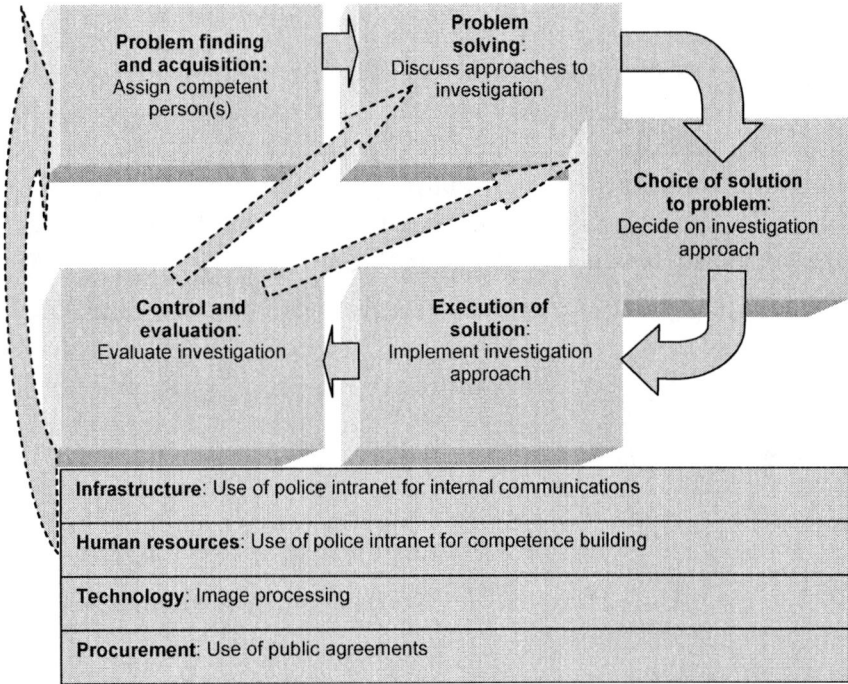

In summary, the cyclical process of scientific reasoning-moving from induction to deduction, and vice versa-is applicable to criminal investigation as a means of reconstructing past events.

We argue that police investigation units have the value configuration of a value shop, similar to law firms (Gottschalk, 2005). The value shop is an organization that creates value by solving unique problems. Knowledge is the most important resource. A value shop is characterized by five primary activities: problem finding and acquisition, problem solving, choice, execution, and control and evaluation, as illustrated in Figure 5.

Interrogation is a work task that typically is carried out during execution. Leo (1996) posed the following question: Why do some suspects confess while others manage to resist police pressures to incriminate themselves? What social and legal circumstances make the probability of a successful interrogation more or less likely?

Younger suspects were much more likely to confess than older ones, and suspects without a prior criminal record were slightly more likely to confess than suspects with a prior record. Suspects accused of property crimes were more likely to confess than suspects accused of crimes against persons. What really explained the differential confession rate was the evidence against a suspect prior to interrogation. Furthermore, the number of tactics employed by detectives, and the length of interrogation were significantly related to the likelihood of confession. The more interrogation tactics detectives use, the more likely they are to find something that works (Leo, 1996).

Efficient and effective deployment of resources is becoming central in police work. For example, UK Central Government has become increasingly focused upon the setting of targets in efforts to improve the efficacy of public services, and demonstrate value for money from increased expenditure (Ashby & Longley, 2005).

We define police investigation success in terms of the effectiveness of these five primary activities of police work organizations as value shops. Success is achieved if the unit is successful in understanding problems, finding investigation approaches, choosing an optimal investigation approach, implementing the optimal investigation approach, and solving the problem.

In terms of measurement of the construct success, we will apply two alternatives. First, success is only the final primary activity of solving the problem. Second, success is a combined result from all five primary activities.

Gottschalk (2005) developed a five-factor model of value shop activities. In the model, each factor is measured on a multiple item scale. The reliability of each scale was acceptable in terms of Cronbach's alpha, making them applicable for our current study.

The idea that police necessarily follow a decision-making logic, as suggested by the value shop, does not square with numerous instances of police action known to observers of police behavior, according to Fielding (1984). Because the police conceive of themselves as people of action, and because action assuages the tension of long periods of waiting for something to happen, the police often act impatiently and impulsively. Chance taking brings excitement, and the prospect of a return without deep investment.

There are five generally recognized stages in crime analysis: collection, collation, analysis, dissemination, and feedback. First, the analyst must collect data. Many sources of data and information are available to analysts, although the most obvious is probably the most important: police reports. Police reports include crime incident reports, investigative follow-up reports, calls-for-service records, and arrest reports.

Collation involves organizing the information through categorization and, often, subcategorization. If the analyst is dealing with a stack of paper reports, field interview reports, or outside agency crime bulletins, the analyst's job is to sort them out. During the collation process, the analyst may have to "clean" the data: look for errors and correct them, or format the data to be compatible with the tools one uses for analysis. For example, if an analyst is going to computer-map locations, it is important and efficient to make sure the address fields are in a format compatible to automating the geocoding (locating address to point on map) process in the available software.

The analysis stage is the heart of it all: analyzing the data collected and turning it into timely, useful, and accurate information for dissemination. The objective of analysis is to turn data into actionable information on crime series, patterns, and trends. Analysis is used to assist in identifying suspects and for matching cases. Analysis is further used in forecasting.

The fourth stage of dissemination is concerned with providing information to patrol officers, investigators, and command staff. In some police agencies, crime analysis information is available to the media, citizens, other city/government employees, and other law enforcement agencies. Departmental police will determine who gets the information crime analysis produces. One of the first and most prominent ways of disseminating the information is through various types of crime bulletins: this includes tactical, strategic, and administrative bulletins and reports.

According to Osborne and Wernicke (2003), the final stage of feedback and evaluation is probably the most neglected. One of the most important aspects of being a good crime analyst is having the knowledge that the customers are using the products, reports, and information created. An efficient way of receiving feedback is to attach a short evaluation form to the final product. Obviously, if the information were being disseminated over e-mail, the form would have to be automated.

In his doctoral dissertation on the police profession, Holgersson (2005) identified types of knowledge. He identified a total of 30 types of police officers' professional knowledge. These knowledge types are classified into the primary activities of the value shop, as illustrated in Figure 6.

Thirty types of knowledge were identified by Holgersson (2005), as illustrated in Figure 6. These knowledge types might be critical, important, or useful in the

Figure 6. Police officers' professional knowledge

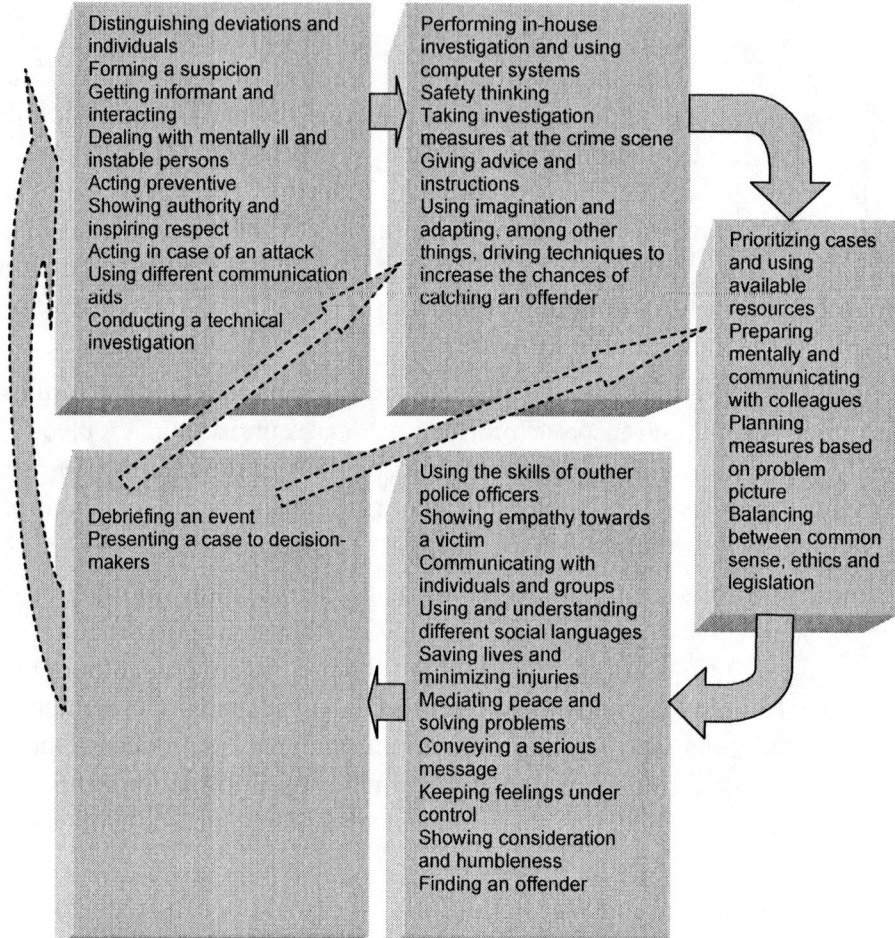

five primary activities of a value shop. We define a scale from very important (critical), important, and not important (useful) in this research, to be able to classify knowledge types. We apply critical, important, and useful to each knowledge type, as listed in Figure 7.

Not surprisingly, we find that most types of knowledge are applied in case development. By this stage of the investigative process, information has been integrated into the investigation and interpreted accordingly. Options for gathering additional information have been reviewed. If sufficient information has been gathered, it may be possible to move to the postcharge element of the

Figure 7. Importance of knowledge types in value shop activities (C - Critical, I - Important, U - Useful)

	1 Initial Crime Scene Assessment	2 Assessing Incoming Information	3 Selecting Appropriate Lines of Enquiry	4 Case Development	5 Post-Charge Case Development
I Using the Skills of Other Police Officers			C	I	U
II Showing Empathy Towards a Victim	I	U		C	
III Prioritizing Cases and Using Resources	I		C	U	
IV Distinguishing Deviations and Categorizing	I		C		U
V Forming a Suspicion	I	C		U	
VI Communicating with Individuals and Groups	I	U		C	
VII Getting an Informant and Interacting		I	U	C	
VIII Using and Understanding Variations	I	U		C	
IX Dealing with Mentally Ill and Instable Persons	I	U		C	
X Saving Lives and Minimizing Injuries	U		C	I	
XI Preparing Mentally and Communicating	I			C	U
XII Mediating Peace and Solving Problems		C	I	U	
XIII Performing In-House Investigation	C	I	U		
XIV Acting Preventive		C	U	I	
XV Showing Authority	I		U	C	
XVI Conveying a Serious Message	I	U		C	
XVII Acting in Case of an Attack		U	I	C	
XVIII Thinking Safety	C		U	I	
XIX Taking Measures at the Crime Scene	C	I		U	
XX Keeping Feelings under Control	I	U		C	
XXI Debriefing an Event			U	I	C
XXII Planning Measures Based on Legislation		I	U	C	
XXIII Showing Consideration and Humbleness		U		C	I
XXIV Using Different Communication Aids	U		I	C	
XXV Conducting a Technical Investigation	U	C		I	
XXVI Giving Advice and Instructions		C	U	I	
XXVII Balancing Common Sense and Ethics	I		C	U	
XXVIII Using Imagination and Adapting	U		C	I	
XXIX Finding an Offender	C		I	U	
XXX Presenting a Case to Decision-Makers			U	C	I

investigative process. Where additional information is required, the investigative cycle continues to iterate. If more information is required, it is important to consider where this information is likely to reside.

It is important to define the need of knowledge support from the view of the street-level. One way of doing that is to use a theoretical model as a value shop, but before you use the value shop or other theoretical model, it is important to define different professional knowledge from the views of the street-level. It is otherwise a risk that theoretical models will be in focus, not the street-level perspective. It is anyway prolific to use a theoretical model because it will hopefully lead to more distinct definitions. The use of the value shop regarding a police officer's professional knowledge shows that most types of knowledge are applied in the case development activity.

Organizational Knowledge

Earlier in this book, individual knowledge, possessed by people and police officers, was discussed. Now, when we define police work in terms of value configurations, the more relevant focus is organizational knowledge.

Organizational knowledge can be defined as the aggregate intellectual assets of an organization. Here we find both explicit and tacit knowledge that may or may not be explicitly documented. Organizational knowledge is specifically referenced, and crucial to the operation, efficiency, and effectiveness of an organization. Here, knowledge management is concerned with developing applications that stimulate knowledge reuse and development, and that prevent the loss of corporate memory (Becerra-Fernandez, Gonzalez, & Sabherwal, 2004).

Organizational knowledge is created through cycles of combination, internalization, socialization, and externalization that transform knowledge between tacit and explicit modes. The strategic management of organizational knowledge is a key factor that can help organizations to sustain effectiveness in volatile environments.

At the organizational level of police work, we can apply the knowledge management processes of knowledge creation, knowledge storage and retrieval, knowledge transfer, and knowledge application (Alavi & Leidner, 2001). In the first process of knowledge creation, the SECI cycle is a useful framework to identify knowledge management technology for police organizations. For example, in combination, end-user tools as well as expert systems can help knowledge creation in the organization. These technologies are found at Stage 1 and 4 in the knowledge management technology stage model.

In the second process of knowledge storage and retrieval, advanced computer storage technology and sophisticated retrieval techniques, such as query languages, multimedia databases, and database management systems, can be effective tools in enhancing organizational memory. These tools increase the speed at which organizational memory can be accessed. Such tools are found at Stage 3 in the knowledge management technology stage model.

In the third process of knowledge transfer, IT can increase knowledge transfer by extending the reach beyond the formal communication lines. The search for knowledge sources is usually limited to immediate coworkers in regular and routine contact with each other. Expanding the network to more extended connections is central to the knowledge diffusion process because such networks expose individuals to more new ideas. These technologies are found at Stage 3 in the knowledge management technology stage model.

Finally, the fourth process of knowledge application is supported by Stage 4 in the knowledge management technology stage model. For example, information technology can support knowledge application that is embedded knowledge in organizational routines. Procedures that are culture bound can be embedded into IT so that the systems themselves become examples of organizational norms.

Organizational Culture

Organizational culture is found to influence organizational performance. There is no consensus about its definition, but most authors will probably agree on the following characteristics of the organizational culture construct: it is (1) holistic, (2) historically determined, (3) related to anthropological concepts, (4) socially constructed, (5) soft, and (6) difficult to change (Hofstede, Neuijen, Ohayv, & Sanders, 1990).

The concept of culture has a long and distinguished history and, like most sociological concepts, is subject to wide variations in definition and application. An occupational culture is a reduced, selective, and task-based version of culture that is shaped by the socially relevant worlds of the occupation. Embedded in traditions and a history, occupational cultures contain accepted practices, rules, and principles of conduct that are situationally applied, along with generalized rationales and beliefs. Such cultures highlight, selectively, the contours of an environment, granting meaning to some facts and not others, and linking modes of seeing, doing, and believing (Bailey, 1995).

To some extent, occupational culture contains what is taken for granted by members, invisible yet powerful constraints, and thus it connects cognition and action, environment and organization, in an entangling and interwoven tapestry. They act as socially validated sources, one for the other (Bailey, 1995).

The principal works of the police vary in method, in conceptual focus, in depth of analysis, and in the degree to which they are comparative. In a comparative study of Scottish and American police roles, peacekeeping and law enforcement were identified as two different police roles. Another comparative study of rural and urban English forces found higher dependency on other officers in the urban force where the public was seen as unsupportive. There, the radio and the police vehicle became primary tools. Rural force was found less dependent on other officers (and more on the public), and less concerned with action, risk, excitement, and crime fighting.

Occupational culture arises from a set of tasks that are repeated and routinized in various degrees, and a technology that is various and indirect in its effects (it is mediated by the organizational structure), producing a set of attitudes and an explanatory structure of belief (ideology). The tasks of policing are uncertain; they are various, unusual, and unpredictable in appearance, duration, content, and consequence. They are fraught with disorderly potential. The police officer is dependent on other officers for assistance, advice, training, working knowledge, protection in the case of threats from internal or external sources, and insulation against the public and periodic danger. The occupation emphasizes autonomy, both with respect to individual decision-making, or what lawyers term "discretion"; the public it serves and controls (officers routinely experience adversarial relations with the public); and the rigid authority symbolized by the paramilitary structure of the organization. Finally, the occupational culture makes salient displaying, creating, and maintaining authority. The sources of the authority theme are multiple insofar as they draw on the state's authority, the public morality of the dominant classes, and the law (Bailey, 1995).

Police culture is a kind of occupational culture. According to Christensen and Crank (2001), an occupational culture is a reduced, selective, and task-based culture that is shaped by and shapes the socially relevant worlds of the occupation. Embedded in traditions and history, occupational cultures contain accepted practices, rules, and principles of conduct that are situationally applied, along with generalized rationales and beliefs. Police culture can be described as a confluence of themes. Themes are areas of activity and sentiments associated with these activities, linked to each other by a dynamic affirmation. By dynamic affirmation is the idea that activities and dispositions are not easily separable ideas, but reciprocally causal: activities confirm predispositions, and predispositions lead to the selection of activities. Themes are developed around particular contours of the day-to-day working environment of the police.

An examination by Christensen and Crank (2001) on the police revealed several cultural themes. Police culture emphasized secrecy, self-protection, violence, and maintenance of respect. For many observers of the police, force has been the defining characteristic of the occupation of police. Danger and fear of violence are thought to be heightened among the police. Fear is associated with other characteristics of the police such as camaraderie and solidarity. Uncertainty seems to be a characteristic feature of police work that uniquely characterizes police culture.

In analyzing the culture of a particular group or organization, Schein (1990) finds it desirable to distinguish three fundamental levels at which culture manifests itself: (1) observable artifacts, (2) values, and (3) basic underlying assumptions. When one enters an organization, one observes and feels its artifacts. This category includes everything from the physical layout, the dress code, the manner in which people address each other, the smell and feel of the place, its emotional intensity, and other phenomena, to the more permanent archival manifestations such as company records, products, statements of philosophy, and annual reports.

Values, as the second level, can be studies through interviews and question-naires in terms of norms, ideologies, charters, and philosophies. Basic under-lying assumptions at the third and final level are concerned with perceptions, thought processes, feelings, and behavior. Once one understands some of these assumptions, it becomes easier to decipher the meanings implicit in the various behavioral and artifactual phenomena one observes (Schein, 1990).

Hofstede et al. (1990) found in their research that shared perceptions of daily practices are the core of an organization's culture, not shared values. The research measurements of employee values differed more according to the demographic criteria of nationality, age, and education than according to membership in the organization, per se.

What Hofstede et al. (1990) called practices can be labeled conventions, customs, habits, mores, traditions, or usages. Culture is then that complex whole that includes knowledge, beliefs, art, morals, law, customs, and any other capabilities and habits acquired by man as a member of an organization.

Perceptions of daily practices can be measured in terms of shared practices. Practice differences can be found in terms of process oriented vs. results oriented, employee oriented vs. job oriented, parochial vs. professional, open system vs. closed system, loose control vs. tight control, and normative vs. pragmatic.

We choose the label professional investigation culture with the following characteristics: results oriented, job oriented, professional, open system, loose control, and pragmatic. We suggest that a more professional culture will improve investigation success, that is, that police investigation success is positively related to professional organizational culture.

This is in line with research conducted by Brehm and Gates (1993), who found that by far, the most substantively significant variable in police compliance is the role of professionalism. Professional norms constitute a significant aspect of police culture and mechanism for regulating the behavior of police officers. Professionalism, while a component of policy, is found to be contingent upon the extent of cooperative cultural norms in the police force.

Kiely and Peek (2002) studied the culture of the British police. The purpose of the study was to explore police culture and the perceived meanings of "quality" and "quality of service" in the police context. At the Police Staff College, the definition of culture suggested by police academic staff is that offered by Kiely and Peek (2002, p. 170):

A pattern of basic assumptions invented, discovered or developed by a given group as it learns to cope with its problem of external adaptation and internal integration—that has worked well enough to be considered valid and, therefore, to be taught to new members in the correct way to perceive, think and feel in relation to those problems.

In this definition, they used the shared-values perspective, rather than the shared-practices perspective. They found several organizational values. For example, police inspectors viewed values such as honesty, morality and integrity, providing a good service, value for money, and a desire to help as important. Others included commitment, self-discipline and restraint, courtesy, empathy and sympathy, fairness and impartiality: loyalty, consistency, trust, and sense of humor also featured.

The degree to which police inspectors and sergeants espoused values that were felt to match those of the organization was explored by Kiely and Peek (2002). Some considered their values matched those, stated in some form or other, by Chief Officers. Others argued their values were reflected in published annual objectives.

Interviewed inspectors and sergeants felt that most members of the organization shared the values of the police service. The view was expressed that what could differ was the degree of emphasis on particular values, or differences in priorities. The realities of police work were highlighted as "tarnishing" values, particularly those of young recruits. The greatest perceived influence was the "canteen culture." They learn their values 8 hours a day, spending long periods of time sitting in cars watching how other policemen do their job, eating with them, socializing with them. Dangers of "canteen cultures," with youngsters being influenced by "old cynics" and picking up outdated values, were repeatedly alluded to.

To those interviewed, quality of service signified "serving the community," "value for money," "just doing the best you can with the resources available," and "the public getting the service they fund us to supply." Half of those interviewed perceived quality of service to include internal quality, for example, service to the people within the police force, in other words, the way they treat each other.

In a different study, Brehm and Gates (1993) found that organizational culture determines police subordinates' levels of compliance, based on an examination of factors accounting for compliance by police officers. They examined and compared formal models of supervision through an empirical analysis of the behavior of police officers with respect to their supervisor's orders.

Brehm and Gates (1993) defined two archetypical settings for the police officer as the donut shop and the speed trap. In the former, we might view the officer as avoiding his or her ordinary duties; in the latter, we might view the officer as enforcing his or her orders with unusual diligence. The amount of time a police officer spends working or shirking-laying an archetypal speed trap or eating an archetypal donut-provides us with an unambiguous measure of the degree of compliance of subordinates, and an opportunity to evaluate these different models of supervision.

Models of organizational culture argue that defection varies by the attitudes of the subordinates toward policy. Such attitudes are largely considered to be products of organizational culture. The frequency of working and shirking can be proportional to subordinates' adherence to different cultural norms; in this manner, subordinates' efforts are proportional to their collective predisposition toward their jobs and what they produce. In the context of a police agency, attitudes toward particular policies may influence how officers carry out their duties.

The importance of organizational culture in determining subordinates' levels of compliance points to management actions in the police force. According to Brehm and Gates (1993), many police agencies, perhaps most, are staffed by policy bureaucrats with strong policy interests. Many subordinates put in long hours, yet may receive few direct rewards for extensive service. Perhaps the resolution to the discrepancy between wide latitude for subordinate bureaucrats and productive agencies washes out when both agent and principal share the same preferences.

Reuss-Ianni (1993) discussed two cultures of policing. She found that the emergence of two competing, and sometimes conflicting cultures within police departments demonstrate how competition between street cops and "bosses" is at the heart of the organizational dilemma of modern urban policing. The conflict of these two cultures is, in one respect, almost a classical case of what organizational theory describes as the opposition of bureaucratic and organic forms of organization.

The two cultures were labeled street cops and management cops. Street cop culture is determined by the day-to-day job of policing. Being a policeman is something special; a cop puts his life on the line and people appreciate and respect the willingness to do so. As a result, policemen were allowed to do their jobs without too many questions or too much interference from outside the department. Not only the street cops, but everyone in the department was socialized to this ethos.

Management cop culture is concerned with accountability and productivity. It is about management process and products that can be quantified and measured in a cost-effect equation. The loyalties of police bosses are not to the men, but to the social and political networks that embody management cop culture (Reuss-Ianni, 1993).

Organizational culture represents an imperfectly shared system of interrelated understandings shaped by its members' shared history and expectations. It defines the "shoulds" and "oughts" of organizational life (Veiga, Lubatkin, Calori, & Very, 2000).

Zamanou and Glaser (1994) studied a communication intervention program designed to change the culture of a governmental organization from hierarchical and authoritarian to participative and involved. This shift was measured through a triangulation approach. Specifically, questionnaires, interview data, and direct observation were combined to study the areas of cultural change. Subjects completed the organizational change scale (OCS) before the intervention, and a representative sample was interviewed. Then, the entire organization participated in an organizational development program. Two years later, subjects again completed the OCS and were interviewed. The postintervention results were statistically analyzed and compared to the preintervention data. Results suggest that the organization changed significantly in the following dimensions: information flow, involvement, morale, and meetings.

Using involvement as an example of significant change, ratings on the questionnaire were significantly higher after 2 years. Interview data revealed that prior to the intervention, employees expressed resentment and anger toward what they perceived to be a hierarchical, authoritarian organization that shut out their ideas. Employees reported that their opinions were not valued by management, that they had little say in decisions that affected their work, and that even though they had suggestions for improving work processes, their opinions were not welcome. Following the intervention, involvement and participation were viewed very differently. Most employees agreed that they were much more involved in decision making and that they were given more authority and responsibility (Zamanou & Glaser, 1994).

Closely related to the term organizational culture is the term organizational climate. The term has been used to denote many different concepts, both historically and currently. Organizational climate is something like an organization's personality, consisting of hopes, attitudes, and biases. It can be a measure of whether people's expectations are being met about what it should be like to work in an organization. Organizational climate can be an amalgamation of feeling tones, or a transient organizational mood. As such, organizational climate is not an element of organizational culture. It is a related, but separate phenomenon.

Organizational culture represents basic assumptions that are beliefs, values, ethical and moral codes, and ideologies that have become so ingrained that they tend to have dropped out of consciousness. These assumptions are unquestioned perceptions of truth, reality, ways of thinking and thinking about, and feeling that develop through repeated successes in solving problems over extended periods of time. Important basic assumptions are passed on to new members, often unconsciously.

Beliefs and values are consciously held cognitive and affective patterns. They provide explicit directions and justifications for patterns of organizational behavior, as well as the energy to enact them. Beliefs and values are also the birthplaces of basic assumptions.

Barton (2004) studied a case of cultural reformation within the police service. The English and Welsh police epitomize organizations that are steeped in tradition. As a result, instituting any meaningful and lasting reform has always been a major challenge. Over the past 2 decades, attempts at reform have arisen in response to Government and public concerns over perceived inadequacies of particular police practices and procedures that, in turn, have resulted in new legislation. Running in parallel, there have been greater levels of external scrutiny, with issues of value for money and performance measurement being central to the reform process. Such has been the scale of these changes that it has increased the resolve of many officers to resist further attempts at reform. Police occupational culture and its perpetuation are identified as key barriers that have substantially impeded the success of the reform agenda. It is argued that in order to mediate the influence of this strong occupational culture, there is a need for intervention in the form of independent mentoring and training at different stages during a police officers' career. Finally, it is argued that it is the failure of both Government and senior police managers to pay sufficient attention to these areas that has resulted in the apparent failure of the many initiatives at police reform.

The Effective Detective

The challenge of improving the quality of major investigations is one that faces all police forces. Therefore, Smith and Flanagan (2000), in the Policing and Reducing Crime Unit in the UK, wrote a report on identifying the skills of an effective detective.

The senior investigative officer (SIO) lays a pivotal role within all serious crime investigations. Concerns have been expressed, however, that there is a shortage of investigators with the appropriate qualities to perform this role effectively. The consequences of such a shortage could be severe. Not only might it threaten the effective workings of the judicial process, it can also waste resources, undermine integrity, and reduce public confidence in the police service. The principal aim of the research conducted by Smith and Flanagan (2000) was to establish what skills, abilities, and personal characteristics an SIO ought to possess to be effective in the investigation of low-volume serious crimes (stranger rape, murder, and abduction).

Interviews were conducted with 40 officers from 10 forces in the UK. These were selected to reflect a range of roles and experience with Criminal Investigation Departments (CID). Ten of these officers were nominated by their peers as examples of particularly effective SIOs.

Although the debate around SIO competencies has often polarized into arguments for and against specialist or generalist skills, the research highlighted the fact that the role of an SIO is extremely complex, and the skills required wide ranging. By applying a variety of analytical techniques, a total of 22 core skills were identified for an SIO to perform effectively in the role. The 22 skills were organized into three clusters:

- **Investigative ability.** This includes the skills associated with the assimilation and assessment of incoming information into an enquiry, and the process by which lines of enquiry are generated and prioritized.
- **Knowledge levels.** This relates to the different types of underpinning knowledge an SIO should possess.
- **Management skills.** These encompass a broad range of skill types that were further subdivided between people management, general management, and investigative management.

The research revealed that the effective SIO is dependent upon a combination of management skill, investigative ability, and relevant knowledge across the entire investigative process, from initial crime-scene assessment through to postcharge case management.

Ideally, an SIO should possess a high level of competency across each of the three clusters. In reality this is not always possible and, when this happens, there is an increased risk that the investigation will be inefficient or, in the worst case, will fail.

For example, an SIO from a predominantly non-CID background will have little experience within an investigative context. Hence, there is an increased risk that an investigation will fail due to suboptimal investigative decisions being made. Similarly, an SIO from a predominantly CID background may have less general management experience. Hence, there may be an increased risk of failure from suboptimal management decisions.

The research suggested that some, but not all, deficiencies in an SIO's skill portfolio can be compensated for by drawing on the skills and abilities of more junior officers within his/her investigative team. However, it was recognized that this was still a high-risk and short-term strategy.

Acknowledging the breadth and complexity of an effective SIO's skills has important implications for the future training and selection of investigators. A number of potential avenues exist for SIOs to acquire the necessary skills. These were identified as follows:

- **Selecting the right individuals to become SIOs at the correct point in their career.** The early identification of individuals with the potential to perform well as SIOs would allow more structured and considered approach to the career development of effective SIOs.

- **The nurturing of future SIOs.** Many interviewees highlighted the importance of nurturing potential investigators of the future. This could be accomplished through a formal system of mentoring and shadowing.

- **Ensuring a correct balance between training and appropriate experience.** There is a range of evidence that emphasizes the need for training and on-the-job investigative experience to go hand-in-hand: training on its own is not enough.

- **Encouraging the self-development of investigators.** SIOs have a professional responsibility to ensure that they remain up-to-date with current developments in the field.

- **Debriefing programs.** Debriefing was identified as a useful mechanism for transferring expertise, and should occur both formally and informally. For a debriefing to be effective, however, it needs to be conducted in an open and constructive environment where officers are encouraged to discuss their mistakes.

Developing effective SIOs for the future will also partly depend upon anticipating changes within the context in which investigators work. Interviewees identified a range of issues that are likely to affect the skill base of future SIOs, including the impact of tenure, the changing nature of crime types, and increased accountability.

We have established that an effective SIO relies on a combination of skill types. It is important, however, to clarify what skills are applied during the investigative process as a whole. Is it the case, for instance, that an integrated skill base is a feature of all elements of the investigative process? Alternatively, do particular skill types dominate within particular elements? This has important consequences for SIO development, training, and the active involvement of an SIO in serious crime enquiry. We need to identify the different skills and abilities associated with the different elements of the investigative process.

Figure 8. The investigative process for detectives

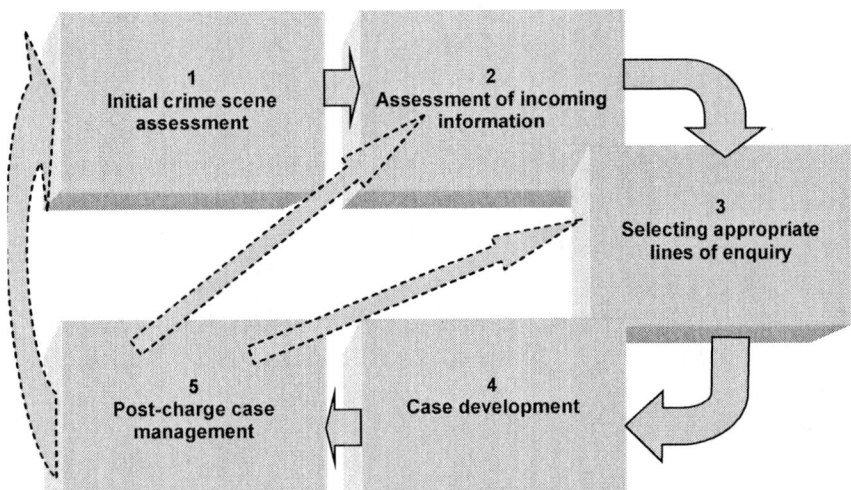

For the purpose of such analysis, it is helpful to divide the investigative process into a series of separate elements, although in practice, these principal components are interrelated, and the investigation has to be considered in a dynamic process. Figure 8 visually represents the elements contained within the investigative process, as suggested by Smith and Flanagan (2000). We see that it is identical to our general value-shop configuration.

The process begins with an initial crime-scene assessment, where sources of potential evidence are identified. The information derived from the process then has to be evaluated in order to gauge its relevance to the investigation. During the next stage, the information is interpreted to develop inferences and initial hypotheses. This material can then be developed by the SIO into appropriate and feasible lines of enquiry. The SIO will then have to prioritize actions, and to identify any additional information that may be required to test that scenario. As more information is collected, this is then fed back into the process until the objectives of the investigation are achieved. Providing a suspect is identified and charged, the investigation then enters the postcharge stage, where case papers are compiled for the prosecution. Subsequently, the court process will begin. Specifically, the primary activities of the value shop can be defined in this context as follows:

1.   **Initial crime scene assessment.** This element of the investigative process begins with the initial notification of a potential serious crime to the SIO, and ends when she/he decides to release the scene. It involves assessing whether a serious crime has actually been committed and, if so, the immediate gathering of relevant information.

   A number of investigative abilities underpin initial crime-scene assessment. First, the ability to assimilate information from the scene is important. SIOs need to be able to take a step back from all that is going on around them and adopt a considered approach. It is necessary to create slow time. This involves trying to establish what has happened, while at the same time preserving and managing the scene, and ensuring that the correct people have been alerted. The SIO has to consolidate the information at the scene within the appropriate investigative and legal boundaries. By correctly assimilating relevant information at this stage, the SIO can begin to build a picture of what is now known about both the offence and the offender(s), and start to formulate appropriate lines of enquiry. Secondly, at this initial stage, the SIO has to begin to interpret the material available at the crime scene, recognizing which information may act as a source of potential evidence, or identify suspect sets. Here the SIO's investigative knowledge and experience of specific crime types comes to fore. Finally, and perhaps most vital to this stage, the SIO needs to start managing the investigation. This involves planning and shaping the parameters of the investigation with all the parties involved. In order to identify salient information from the crime scene, close collaboration with relevant personnel is essential.

2.   **Assessing incoming information.** This involves the further application of the investigative knowledge held by the SIO. This knowledge will help provide the basis for interpreting the behaviors exhibited at the crime scene and, coupled with investigative experience and ability, should enable the SIO to make appropriate inferences from the crime scene. The SIO needs to assess incoming information to establish its likely value to the investigation, and establish what the investigation now knows about the offence. This includes assessing the quality and relevance of experts' interpretation of information. The SIO has to readily assess the information, produce a cogent response, and establish the substance of the information and whether it links with something already known to the investigative team.

A number of investigative abilities underpin assessing incoming information. First, the ability to assess the reliability and validity of a piece of information has to be accomplished in a short space of time. Second, appropriate delegation is critical. Because of the need to partially delegate the assessment of incoming information, particular emphasis is placed on the relevance of communication skills at this stage of enquiry. Full consultation with the investigative team is important. An effective SIO is one who can create an atmosphere where team members have the confidence to contribute ideas and theories on the case, so that the SIO uses them as sounding board. This consultation process ensures that the information coming into the enquiry is thereby evaluated by the whole team, and brings together their experience and expertise.

3.   **Selecting appropriate lines of enquiry.** This is closely linked to the previous stage. Having assessed and evaluated information, the SIO may be in a better position to begin to formulate hypotheses about the offence and the offender. In turn, this will enable the SIO to select appropriate lines of enquiry that might yield useful information to the investigation. Although ultimately responsible for the decisions adopted, the SIO accomplishes this with the aid of the investigative team.

Resource management is considered a key skill during this stage of the process. Although there are often guidelines in place that provide the SIO with a breakdown of staffing levels and resources available for a serious crime investigation, in reality, the acquisition of resources provides a challenge for many SIOs. Hence, an SIO needs to possess a realistic awareness of what resources are available and how to obtain them: negotiation skills are vital in this respect. An effective SIO should be able to appreciate the fluctuations within the investigative process, and know both where and when to concentrate the available resources.

4.   **Case development.** By this stage of the investigative process, information has been integrated into the investigation and interpreted accordingly. Options for gathering additional information have been reviewed. If sufficient information has been gathered, it may be possible to move to the postcharge element of the investigative process. Where additional information is required, the investigative cycle continues to iterate. If more information is required, it is important for the SIO to consider where this information is likely to reside. The SIO needs to establish what options exist to gather the required information, and which are the most appropriate to pursue.

At this stage, it is imperative that the SIO not become too focused on a particular line of enquiry at the expense of others, but is mindful of other avenues that can be pursued. The ability of the SIO to think laterally is important, going beyond the traditional methods of investigation. Effective SIOs are those who not only keep up-to-date with changes in legislation, forensics, and technology, but will actively incorporate new developments into the enquiry. Furthermore, constant reviewing of the situation through regular briefings and debriefings is also required: a single piece of evidence may result in the investigation changing direction. The SIO should also continue to balance the lines of enquiry against the available costs. An effective SIO needs to remain detached, open-minded, analytical, and ensuring that professional continuity is being maintained throughout the investigative process. An important skill at this stage of the investigation is attending to the welfare needs of the team. This is particularly important in long-running investigations. The SIO has to employ a variety of techniques to motivate staff in order to maximize their contribution. This requires an understanding of what motivates the different individuals in the team, and an awareness of when motivation is required.

5. **Postcharge case management.** Effective SIOs are typically those officers who have been anticipating the postcharge case management from the start; consequently, the investigative process has been documented as it occurred. A detailed and concise summary of the investigation, together with an audit trail documenting the decision-making process must be created. Policy books are seen as an integral part of this process. While the direct involvement of the SIO diminishes at this stage, the SIO still maintains overall responsibility for the investigation. Consequently, it is felt that an effective SIO should adopt a clear supervisory role regarding the preparation of the case file. This task should have been delegated to an officer from the start of the investigation, together with the responsibilities for disclosure and exhibits.

Many SIOs feel that it is beneficial to attend court hearings. This enables them to observe the judicial process and learn the protocol involved (e.g., the rules for presenting evidence and how such evidence can be tackled and interpreted by barristers). Therefore, knowledge of the legal process is perceived a key skill during this stage. It is also important that the SIO is able to communicate effectively with those involved in the legal process.

The postcharge phase of an investigation does not necessarily signal the end of the investigative process. Staffing levels and resources have to be maintained at an appropriate level. Additional information may still be required to strengthen the case. It is important that this is acknowledged by the SIO.

This stage of the investigative process is an opportunity for development. Effective SIOs are those who ensure that both they and their staff learn lessons from the particular investigation.

While the balance of skills and abilities varies throughout the course of an investigation, the most striking finding by Smith and Flanagan (2000) was the extent to which each element relies on the combination of skill types. Overall, the interviews they conducted revealed that to be effective, an SIO is dependent upon a combination of skills and knowledge across all elements of the investigative process. A major crime investigation is very much a synthesis of the three skill clusters: management skills, investigative ability, and knowledge levels.

Forensic science invariably plays a pivotal role in the investigation of murder and other serious crimes. Forensic science can be defined as the interpretation of scientific results in the context of the individual circumstances of a particular investigation. It is not purely the results of scientific tests. Forensic science connects scientific methodology to the principle that every contact leaves a trace, and every interpretation provides information. Forensic science can also be taken to mean all of those activities in the forensic process, that is to say, from recovery of material from scenes to the presentation of findings at court, which involve the scientific examination of items or material in connection with an investigation (Humphreys, 1999).

Figure 9. Examples of knowledge management systems in the value shop

Primary Activities	Policing Tasks	Information Systems
Problem understanding	Initial crime scene assessment	Registering crime information
Problem solutions	Assessing incoming information	Searching crime databases
Choice of solution	Selecting appropriate lines of inquiry	Applying case-based reasoning
Execution and implementation	Case development	Document management system
Control and evaluation	Post-charge case management	Quality assurance

Knowledge Management Systems

When law enforcement is defined as a value-shop activity, knowledge management systems should support the primary and secondary activities in the value shop. Some examples of knowledge management systems for primary activities are listed in Figure 9.

Project Planning

In police investigations, tools like project planning are used. A project plan includes information on the general background of the case, the goals, schedules, methods, division of labor, resources, and risk analysis. It includes several horizontal properties such as defining the exchange of information between participants, and a feedback section, the purpose of which is defined as trying to learn collectively by reflecting on the experience when the case is finished. This document acts as an electronic checklist, as it is an electronic template that can be edited, updated, and revised when necessary.

In Finland, the creation of a project-planning tool took place as part of the normal work process. The developers came from the tactical-investigation and criminal-intelligence sections in the National Bureau of Investigation (Puonti, 2004b). The electronic form of the document, and its distribution to all investigators facilitate its further modification. It was locally constructed, but it was taken as a standard for the particular unit. It thereby represents an attempt to resolve the tension between standardization and local construction by creating a local standard that is open to modification.

Finland is interesting because economic-crime investigation in Finland is in transition from hierarchically organized, sequential collaboration between authorities toward parallel, interorganizational collaboration. Puonti (2004b) described the tools used and developed for managing the new collaborative economic-crime-investigation process. The challenge is to find interorganizational investigative tools that are flexible enough to shift between vertical use within, and horizontal use across organizations. One such tool is project planning. Local construction is often needed in collaborative networks. Otherwise, the tool never meets the needs of the divergent users. A good tool is sensitive enough to adept to local settings, and robust enough to be transferable to other contexts.

The obscurity and complexity of economic crime in Finland has forced the authorities, including the police, the tax authorities, enforcement offices, and prosecutors, to seek new collaborative means of fighting economic crime more efficiently. Two new challenges have emerged in this interorganizational investigation: how to master the collaborative, multiorganizational investigation process, and how to represent and share vast amounts of information gathered about the suspected crime. Investigation work involves a variety of private-thought aids, as well as shared tools.

Economic-crime cases are typically large projects that involve several authorities. They proceed from the suspicion of a crime through initial information gathering that is coordinated by the police and culminates in a surprise house search conducted together by the authorities. It is the high point of the investigation and normally results in large amounts of data, both in electronic and paper forms. The house search provides material for further analysis, and leads to intensive interrogations of the suspects.

Economic-crime investigation is an increasingly important activity that generates complex webs of relationships between those who participate in it. In the traditional, hierarchical mode of collaboration between the authorities, each authority takes care of its sequential part of the process, and uses its standard, hierarchical tools. Crime investigation largely involves information acquisition concerning the suspected crime and its circumstances. However, there are other processes going on at the same time: actions have to be planned, and the influx of information has to be managed. These are continuous, parallel processes that cannot be totally separated from each other. From the collaborative viewpoint, planning the shared actions and sharing the information is critical.

However, these processes are much more hidden than the process of information gathering. According to Puonti's (2004b) observations in the cases she followed, the tools used for information acquisition were fairly advanced, but much less emphasis was put on those used in planning and managing the information.

Economic-crime investigation produces vast numbers of documents and different kinds of information. When there are participants from several agencies, the information should be in a sharable and transferable form. The shift from sequential toward parallel collaboration simultaneously with an ongoing crime includes a shift from mere passing of documents and information toward shared knowledge creation, finding out together what the suspected crime is about. Synchronization of the actions of various participants is another necessity.

Project planning enables this. However, locally constructed tools, such as the project plan, are often flexible and open for revision, but they tend to remain local despite their apparent usability. How can they be made available to other users as well? There is often no time to develop them in the course of normal work, and when they have initially been created in a preliminary form, they remain unfinished. The stabilized phase is never reached to facilitate the transfer to other working communities. The critical point is to manage the shift from a local and vertical tool to a standard and horizontal tool. How can a locally constructed tool be standardized and yet remain flexible? How can a horizontal, interorganizational tool be usable in single organizations as well?

According to Puonti (2004b), the crucial question is how to create a working culture that sustains the development and reflection of tools. The significance of tangible tools in carrying and distributing codified knowledge has not yet been fully recognized in the economic-crime investigation context. The infrastructure should support the tool development process more efficiently. Tools may help to articulate the obscure object, as well as to clarify the guidelines for collaboration in the process in which interorganizational coordination is a necessity. Shared, carefully designed, and systematically used project planning may also facilitate the shift from a sequential investigation model toward a parallel one, as indicated by standardized, horizontal tools.

The case of economic crime investigation in Finland is also interesting because there is no separate police unit for this kind of crime. It was probably not recognized early enough in history that economic crime investigation needs any special attention in the field of crime investigation, and the structures remained. At the NBI (National Bureau of Investigation in Finland - Keskusrikospoliisi), they had an economic crime department until mid-1990s but its status has been lowered, and now it is a section of a crime investigation department that investigates different kinds of crime. So the trend here seems to be quite the opposite of Norway and Sweden. There has been discussion about a separate economic-crime authority, but the objections towards it have been strong:- the horror scenario seems to be police units competing about crimes, who can investigate what, who gets the best cases. They have a cooperation unit on economic crime that analyses information, but it does not investigate crimes.

Reconstructing the Past: Sources of Information

The information needed to reconstruct the past is available through three sources: people, physical evidence, and records. Criminal investigators often put all three sources to use (Osterburg & Ward, 1992):

- **People.** As long as general, specific, or intimate knowledge concerning an individual endures, those who know how can acquire it. People are social beings, and information on them can usually be found in the possession of family and relatives, work or business associates, and others who share their recreational interests. It can also be picked up accidentally through those who were witness to, or the victim of, a crime. The careful investigator identifies and exploits all potential sources.

- **Physical evidence.** Any object of a material nature is potential physical evidence. The scientific specialties that undertake most examinations of physical evidence are forensic medicine and criminalistics. Their purpose being the acquisition of facts, the following questions arise: What is this material? If found at a crime scene, can it be linked to, or help exonerate, a suspect? Can it be used to reconstruct what happened (especially when witnesses give conflicting accounts)?

- **Records.** They are stored in computers, on tape, on film, and on paper. Examples of records are memoirs, letters, official documents, manuscripts, books, and paintings.

Rather than merely an exercise in objective, systematic thinking, criminal investigation is believed, by experienced detectives and some scholars of the investigative procedure, to involve an element of luck. As care-analysis suggests, it is not good fortune alone. The unknown factor of chance, and the way experienced investigators can interpret and deliberately exploit it, thereby opening up new knowledge and discovery, are exemplified in many criminal cases (Osterburg & Ward, 1992).

Economic Crime Investigation

According to Puonti (2004a), economic crime, in general, has only slowly and unevenly become a recognized subject of scholarly study. It is largely an underresearched area of criminality. The fact that the perpetrators are often claimed to be in the same social class as the decision makers may have an impact on this level of interest.

Economic crime can be defined as a criminalized act or neglect that is committed in the framework of, or using a corporation or other organization. The act is committed with the aim of attaining unlawful direct or indirect benefit. A criminalized, systematic act that is analogous to entrepreneurship and has the aim of considerable benefit is also defined as economic crime (Puonti, 2004a).

Puonti (2004a) asks the following questions: What makes economic crime different when compared with conventional crime, the type of crime the police are primarily trained to investigate? Contrasting the two is a common way of highlighting the special features of economic crime. With traditional crimes such as theft or assault, it is often evident that a crime has been committed, but the offender is unknown. The purpose of investigation is thus to find the offender. Economic crime investigation has a different setting: the offender can often be detected by following the flow of money, but the purpose of the investigation is to find out whether a crime has been committed or not.

The investigation of economic crimes may differ from the investigation of traditional crimes in how easy it is to distinguish a clear physical chain of events and a commonly accepted zone of criminality. Both are normally easy to distinguish in traditional crimes, whereas both vary in economic crimes. The tools used in committing economic and conventional crime are often totally different. Street criminals use knives and guns, whereas economic criminals rely on paper instruments and computers for their offences. Additionally, traditional crimes such as robbery and theft normally take place at a particular place and at a particular time, and there are identifiable victims and offenders. Economic crime, in turn, might involve massive amounts of money, time, and geography. It is often a problem in classifying the date and location of these offenses. Conceptions of time and space constitute significant differences between economic crime and conventional crime; they are both much less clear in connection with economic crime. It is difficult to decide where the crime was committed, which leads to unclear situations regarding who should investigate and who should prosecute.

According to Puonti (2004a), the legislation concerning economic crime has been left very open in order to guarantee that the law is able to include various criminal actions in various settings, and allow case-by-case consideration. This has led to a situation in which the legislation is very prone to interpretation, and at worst, each authority has its own conception of what is criminal and what is not.

The real-life events that constitute economic crime are externally often nothing different from normal business transactions. The criminal purpose may only be seen in connection with other transactions, or when viewed from a certain perspective. Instead of merely looking at separate actions, detectives have to analyze the interconnected nature of these actions.

The purpose of crime investigation is to solve the crime and to establish the circumstances in which it was committed, who the parties concerned are, and other relevant matters in consideration of the charges. Puonti (2004a) argues that collaboration between authorities is a necessity in economic crime investigation, because the necessary information and knowledge are distributed among them. Her study focused on how the authorities learn to collaborate in practice, in actual crime cases, given the pressure of changes. The changes can be studied at three levels. First, economic crime has become more complex and laborious to solve as the perpetrators have improved their "expertise." Second, the investigative strategies have shifted from action-centered toward actor-centered, as well as from reactive to real time and proactive. Third, this change in strategies has affected the quality of collaboration between authorities: the collaboration is moving away from sequential actions performed by individuals in various offices toward parallel collaboration involving surprise house searches as a central and visible investigative means.

References

Alavi, M., & Leidner, D. E. (2001). Knowledge management and knowledge management systems: Conceptual foundations and research issues. *MIS Quarterly, 25*(1), 107-136.

Ashby, D. I., & Longley, P. A. (2005). Geocomputation, geodemographics and resource allocation for local policing. *Transactions in GIS, 9*(1), 53-72.

Bailey, W. G. (Ed.). (1995). *The encyclopedia of police science* (2nd ed.). New York: Garland Publishing.

Barton, H. (2004). Cultural reformation: A case for intervention within the police service. *International Journal of Human Resources Development and Management* (IJHRDM), *4*(2), 191-199.

Becerra-Fernandez, I., Gonzalez, A., & Sabherwal, R. (2004). *Knowledge management: Challenges, solutions, and technologies.* Upper Saddle River, NJ: Prentice Hall.

Brehm, J., & Gates, S. (1993). Donut shops and speed traps: Evaluating models of supervision on police behavior. *American Journal of Political Science, 37*(2), 555-581.

Chatzkel, J. (2002). A conversation with Göran Roos. *Journal of Intellectual Capital, 3*(2), 96-117.

Christensen, W., & Crank, J. P. (2001). Police work and culture in a nonurban setting: An ethnographic analysis. *Police Quarterly, 4*(1), 69-98.

Fielding, N. (1984). Police socialization and police competence. *The British Journal of Sociology, 35*(4), 568-590.

Galanter, M., & Palay, T. (1991). *Tournament of lawyers, the transformation of the big law firms.* Chicago: The University of Chicago Press.

Gottschalk, P. (2005). *Strategic knowledge management technology.* Hershey, PA: Idea Group Publishing.

Hofstede, G., Neuijen, B., Ohayv, D. D., & Sanders, G. (1990). Measuring organizational cultures: A qualitative and quantitative study across twenty Cases. *Administrative Science Quarterly, 35*(2), 286-316.

Holgersson, S. (2005). *Yrke: POLIS—yrkeskunnskap, motivasjon, IT-system og andre forutsetninger for politiarbeide.* PhD doctoral dissertation, Institutionen för datavetenskap, Linköpings Universitet, Sweden.

Humphreys, I. (Ed.). (1999). *Murder investigation manual.* London: ACPO Crime Committee, Home Office.

Kiely, J. A., & Peek, G. S. (2002). The culture of the British police: Views of police officers. *The Service Industries Journal, 22*(1), 167-183.

Leo, R. A. (1996). Inside the interrogation room. *The Journal of Criminal Law & Criminology, 86*(2), 266-303.

Osborne, D., & Wernicke, S. (2003). *Introduction to crime analysis: Basic resources for criminal justice practice.* Binghamton, NY: Haworth Press.

Osterburg, J. W., & Ward, R. H. (1992). *Criminal investigation: A method for reconstructing the past.* Cincinatti, OH: Anderson Publishing.

Porter, M. E. (1985). *Competitive strategy*. New York: The Free Press.

Puonti, A. (2004a). *Learning to work together: Collaboration between authorities in economic-crime investigation*. Doctoral dissertation, University of Helsinki, Faculty of Behavioural Sciences, Center for Activity Theory and Developmental Work Research, and National Bureau of Investigation, Vantaa, Finland.

Puonti, A. (2004b). Tools for collaboration: Using and designing tools in inter-organizational economic-crime investigation. *Mind, Culture, and Activity, 11*(2), 133-152.

Reuss-Ianni, E. (1993). *Two cultures of policing: Street cops and management cops*. New Brunswick, NJ: Transaction Publishers.

Schein, E. H. (1990). Organizational culture. *American Psychologist, 45*(2), 109-119.

Sheehan, N. T. (2002). *Reputation as a driver in knowledge-intensive service firms*. Series of Dissertations 4/2002, Norwegian School of Management, Sandvika, Norway.

Smith, N., & Flanagan, C. (2000). *The effective detective: Identifying the skills of an effective SIO* (Police Research Series Paper 122). London: Policing and Reducing Crime Unit.

Stabell, C. B., & Fjeldstad, Ø. D. (1998). Configuring value for competitive advantage: On chains, shops, and networks. *Strategic Management Journal, 19*, 413-437.

Veiga, J., Lubatkin, M., Calori, R., & Very, P. (2000). Measuring organizational culture clashes: A two-nation post-hoc analysis of a cultural compatibility index. *Human Relations, 53*(4), 539-557.

Zamanou, S., & Glaser, S. R. (1994). Moving toward participation and involvement. *Group & Organization Management, 19*(4), 475-502.

Chapter X

Knowledge Management in Law Firms

Law enforcement is of concern to law firms. A law firm can be understood as a social community specializing in the speed and efficiency in the creation and transfer of legal knowledge (Nahapiet & Ghoshal, 1998). Many law firms represent large corporate enterprises, organizations, or entrepreneurs with a need for continuous and specialized legal services that can only be supplied by a team of lawyers. The client is a customer of the firm, rather than a particular lawyer. According to Galanter and Palay (1991, p. 5), relationships with clients tend to be enduring:

Firms represent large corporate enterprises, organizations, or entrepreneurs with a need for continuous (or recurrent) and specialized legal services that could be supplied only by a team of lawyers. The client 'belongs to' the firm, not to a particular lawyer. Relations with clients tend to be enduring. Such repeat clients are able to reap benefits from the continuity and economies of scale and scope enjoyed by the firm.

Law firm knowledge management is the behaviors and processes by which a group of lawyers increases and maintains their personal and collective actionable knowledge to compete, to increase performance, and to decrease risk. By extension, a knowledge strategy is the intended action, the plan, or the road map, for those behaviors and processes (Parsons, 2004).

Lawyers as Knowledge Workers

Lawyers can be defined as knowledge workers. They are professionals who have gained knowledge through formal education (explicit) and through learning on the job (tacit). Often, there is some variation in the quality of their education and learning. The value of professionals' education tends to hold throughout their careers. For example, lawyers in Norway are asked whether they got the good grade of "laud" even 30 years after graduation. Professionals' prestige (which is based partly on the institutions from which they obtained their education) is a valuable organizational resource because of the elite social networks that provide access to valuable external resources for the firm (Hitt, Bierman, Shumizu, & Kochhar, 2001).

After completing their advanced educational requirements, most professionals enter their careers as associates in law. In this role, they continue to learn and thus, they gain significant tacit knowledge through "learning by doing." Therefore, they largely bring explicit knowledge derived from formal education into their firms, and build tacit knowledge through experience.

Most professional service firms use a partnership form of organization. In such a framework, those who are highly effective in using and applying knowledge are eventually rewarded with partner status and thus, own stakes in a firm. On their road to partnership, these professionals acquire considerable knowledge, much of which is tacit. Thus, by the time professionals achieve partnership, they have built human capital in the form of individual skills (Hitt et al., 2001).

Because law is precedent driven, its practitioners are heavily invested in knowing how things have been done before. Jones (2000) found that many attorneys, therefore, are already oriented toward the basic premises of knowledge management, though they have been practicing it on a more individualized basis, and without the help of technology and virtual collaboration. As such, a knowledge management initiative could find the areas where lawyers are already sharing information, and then introduce modern technology to support this information sharing to make it for effective.

Lawyers work in law firms, and law firms belong to the legal industry. According to Becker et al. (Becker, Herman, Samuelson, & Webb, 2001), the legal industry will change rapidly because of three important trends. First, global companies increasingly seek out law firms that can provide consistent support at all business locations, and integrated cross-border assistance for significant mergers and acquisitions as well as capital-market transactions. Second, client loyalty is decreasing as companies increasingly base purchases of legal services on a more objective assessment of their value, defined as benefits net of price. Finally, new competitors such as accounting firms and internet-based legal services firms have entered the market.

In this book, the notion "lawyer" is used most of the time. Other notions such as "attorney" and "solicitor" are sometimes used as synonyms in this book. In reality, these words can have different meanings, together with notions such as "barrister," "counselor," and "advocate." In Norwegian, a distinction is made between a lawyer ("jurist") and a solicitor ("advokat"). There is no need to make such distinctions in this book.

Lawyers are knowledge workers. To understand the organizational form of lawyers as knowledge workers employed in companies such as law firms, there is a need to recognize the dual dependent relationship between knowledge workers and the organization. On the one hand, for the purpose of channeling the motivation and effort of employees to serve the interests of the firm, management will seek to exploit knowledge workers' need to rely on the organization for resources (for example, advanced computer software and hardware that are available at a high cost) to accomplish their work tasks. On the other hand, management depends on knowledge workers for their esoteric and advanced knowledge, and their ability to synthesize theoretical and contextual knowledge. Management, therefore, need to meet these employees' aspirations and expectations. As for knowledge workers, they need to depend on the organization as the locale to develop contextual knowledge and to create new knowledge. However, their ability to apply theoretical knowledge in other contexts, that is, in other organizations, means that to a certain extent, they are also able to pursue a limited form of marketization. This enables them to reap market-level rewards for their expertise (May, Korczynski, & Frenkel, 2002).

Knowledge Categories

To get started on this job, legal industry knowledge has to be understood. Edwards and Mahling (1997) have suggested that law firms have four categories of knowledge: administrative, declarative, procedural, and analytical knowledge, as defined earlier in this book. These knowledge categories are all important to the law firm. While any law firm needs to maintain efficient administrative records, there does not appear to be any significant possibility for gaining strategic advantage in the firm's core competency of providing sound legal advice to its clients by using these records. The detailed administrative knowledge they contain is essential to the operation of the law firm, but does not contribute to the substantive content. Declarative, procedural, and analytical knowledge offer greater possibilities for creating strategic value to the firm.

Edwards and Mahling (1997) present a case drawn from the case collection of one of the authors to illustrate the differences in strategic value among procedural, declarative, and analytical knowledge. In the early 1990s, one of the authors, at the time engaged in the practice of law, represented a corporate client as seller in several sales of corporate businesses and real estate. At the time, buyers of businesses and real estate had become concerned about their possible liability for pollution existing on property when they purchased it. The U.S. federal laws governing the legal responsibility of landowners for environmental contamination on their property had been adopted a few years earlier, and their full impact on sale of businesses was just beginning to be understood.

The relevant declarative knowledge was an understanding of several related state and federal laws and agency regulations governing liability for environmental contamination. The relevant procedural knowledge, in part, was to know how to transfer the environmental licenses and permits used by a given business to a new owner, and how to transfer the real estate as an asset. The relevant analytical knowledge was to understand what risks the buyer of a contaminated property faced (legal and financial), and what contractual protections the seller could reasonably give to the buyer.

Law firms are interesting in themselves from both a knowledge and a management perspective. From a management perspective, law firm partners own a typical law firm. Among themselves, the partners appoint a board and a managing partner. In addition, they hire a chief executive officer (CEO) to run all support functions in the firm such as financial management (CFO), knowledge management (CKO), and information technology management (CIO).

Jones (2000) found that top-down directives are complicated in the legal industry. In large U.S. and UK law firms, the power can be spread among as many as 150 partners, most of who have different specialty areas, different work and management styles, and vastly different groups under their control. Earning a consensus is not an easy proposition, especially when the funding for new initiatives such as knowledge management initiatives is coming directly out of the partners' yearly income. At the same time, partners are the ones who have the most to gain if their firm is able to manage knowledge effectively to keep lucrative clients on board, and draw new ones through new services.

The human capital embodied in the partners is a professional service firm's most important resource. Their experience, particularly as partners, builds valuable industry-specific and firm-specific knowledge that is often tacit. Such knowledge is the least imitable form of knowledge. An important responsibility of partners is obtaining and maintaining clients. Partners build relationships with current and potential clients and, over time, develop social capital through their client networks. Therefore, the experience a professional gains as a partner contributes to competitive advantage (Hitt et al., 2001).

Partners with education from the best institutions, and with the most experience as partners in particular legal areas represent substantial human capital to the firm. As partners, they continue to acquire knowledge, largely tacit and firm specific, and build social capital. This human capital should produce the highest-quality services to clients and thereby, contribute significantly to firm performance. The job of partner differs from that of associate, and new skills must be developed. Partners must build the skills needed to develop and maintain effective relationships with clients. Importantly, partners in law firms serve as project and team leaders on specific cases and thus, must develop managerial skills.

Partners own the most human capital in a firm, and have the largest stakes using the firm's resources to the greatest advantage. One of the responsibilities of partners is to help develop the knowledge of other employees of the firm, particularly its associates. Associates at law firms need to learn internal routines, the situation of important clients, and nuances in the application of law (Hitt et al., 2001).

Information technology support for knowledge management in law firms has to consider the very special knowledge situation in each law firm. Edwards and Mahling (1997) argue that knowledge is dispersed among many different members of the firm, and others outside the firm may contribute to knowledge. Law firm knowledge has a wide variety of sources, both inside and outside the firm. Much administrative knowledge is generated by the members of the firm as billing records for their services. The firm's administrative staff creates other administrative information. Attorneys are the major source of analytical, declarative, and procedural knowledge. Legal assistants have some declarative knowledge based on their experience. Declarative knowledge can also be found in publicly available sources intended for research purposes, primarily books, online subscription research sources, and CD-ROM resources. The quantity of publicly available research material for any given topic depends significantly on the size of the market for the information. The more specialized the legal area, the smaller the potential market for material, and the less that is usually widely available. Experienced legal assistants are usually an invaluable source of procedural knowledge, since much procedural work is delegated to them. Legal assistants are common in countries such as the U.S. and UK, but they are seldom found in law firms in countries such as Norway and Sweden.

Experienced legal secretaries may have a significant amount of procedural knowledge for transactions they handle often. Law firms in Norway employ many secretaries. It is common to find more than one secretary for every three lawyers in a law firm.

The role of others, outside the law firm, in generating analytical and procedural knowledge needs to be noted. While much of the useful procedural and analytical knowledge resides in firm employees, it is likely that there are sources outside the firm as well. One belief frequently expressed in the knowledge management literature is the view that learning is social: people learn in groups. These groups are known in the literature as communities of practice.

Communities of practice have been defined as groups of people who are informally bound to one another by exposure to a common class of problem. It is quite likely that the communities of practice for the lawyers in the firm include other members of professional associations such as bar associations. These groups usually have a number of committees devoted to practice areas, such as environmental law. In Norway, Den Norske Advokatforening (Norwegian Lawyers Association) has such committees.

Generally, the idea of communities of practice developed in the organizational learning movement. The idea posits that knowledge flows best through networks of people who may not be in the same part of the organization, or in the same organization, but have the same work interests. Some firms have attempted to formalize these communities, even though theorists argue that they should emerge in self-organizing fashion without any relationship to formal organizational structures (Grover & Davenport, 2001).

A few more technologically advanced lawyers may use the Internet, or such subscription services as Counsel Connect in the U.S. on the World Wide Web, as a sounding board for analytical and procedural issues in a community of legal practice. These external sources can provide knowledge in the form of informal conversations, written newsletters and updates, briefs filed in relevant litigation, and other forms.

An obvious problem in law firms is that knowledge is not consistently documented. Much administrative information is captured in electronic form as part of the firm's billing records. Other administrative data resides in the firm's payroll and benefits records and file and records management systems. Much of the firm's declarative knowledge resides in the memories of the firm's attorneys, and in their work product. At the same time, the firm has access to publicly available declarative knowledge in the form of published reference works.

Much procedural knowledge is documented throughout the firm's files in the form of completed records of transactions that provide guidance about what legal documents were necessary to complete a certain type of transaction. The knowledge of procedure reflected in these documents is often implicit rather than explicit. Explicit procedural knowledge is contained in a collection of written practice guides for popular areas like real estate transactions. These guides include standard checklists of items necessary to complete a particular transaction for the kinds of transactions that occur frequently.

Analytical knowledge resides primarily in attorneys' heads. Analytical knowledge is occasionally documented in client files through the notes of an attorney's thought processes. More often, it is reflected in the completed contract documents or other transaction documents by the inclusion of specific clauses dealing with a particular topic. The analytical knowledge reflected in completed documents is very often not explicit, in the sense that it is often not clear from the face of the document what analytical issues are dealt with in the document.

Another law firm problem is that knowledge is often shared on an informal basis. Certain methods of sharing knowledge, at least within the firm, have traditionally been part of large law firm culture. One of the most important ways of sharing knowledge has been through the process of partners training associates to perform tasks. In larger firms, the practice of hiring young, bright law-school graduates who were trained, supervised, and rewarded by a partner has been followed throughout most of this century. The method focuses on transmitting knowledge from more experienced attorneys to less experienced attorneys, as distinguished from transmitting it to other partners in the firm, or to legal assistants and other support staff.

This attorney training customarily has relied on informal methods of transmitting knowledge, such as rotating young attorneys through a series of practice groups within the firm. Much of this informal training takes place via collaborative work on documents such as contracts and pleadings. Some of it occurs through informal consultation between a senior attorney and a junior attorney about the best way to handle a specific task. These consultations may be carried out by face-to-face discussions, e-mail, or telephone conversations. No attempt is usually made to capture the substance of the training through these informal methods, even where a form of communication such as e-mail may often be used that could produce documentation. It is important to note that this training often takes place under intense time pressure. Further, in an hourly billing system, there is often little or no financial incentive to produce documentation that cannot be billed directly to a client.

In addition to problems of knowledge dispersion, inconsistent documentation, and informal knowledge sharing, Edwards and Mahling (1997) argue that if knowledge has been documented, it is contained in a mixture of paper and electronic formats, and located in dispersed physical locations. Administrative information typically exists in a combination of print and electronic formats. A large firm would customarily maintain computerized databases for key matters such as tracking lawyers' hourly billings, for its client contact data, and for staff assignments to projects, but would usually generate paper invoices to clients. The data physically resides in the firm's computer network and in paper files.

Declarative, procedural, and analytical knowledge is often documented in attorney work product such as briefs, memoranda, and actual legal documents such as contracts, wills, and instruments of transfer. Work product documents typically are created in electronic form, but are customarily stored in print-format client files. The electronic-format materials are stored in standalone personal computers or on the network. Paper materials are located throughout the firm's offices.

Where knowledge has been documented in a law firm, often only a few simple tools exist to facilitate the retrieval of knowledge by topic. Attorney work files are usually indexed by client name and matter name, but their contents are seldom indexed for subject matter in more than the most general way. An attorney creating a particular item of work product may place it in a firm's standards database, maintained in electronic format. These standard documents can then be used by other lawyers as examples or models. In a typical installation, the standard forms library is stored on the network, and is physically available to those who have network access. The standard forms library allows access to individual documents by name, but subject matter classification is often limited to what can be included in a descriptive DOS-format file name. Retrieving material from the forms library, thus, usually requires tedious sequential search and review of the contents of the library.

Access to the procedural and analytical knowledge embodied in client files is difficult, at best, for those not familiar with the files. The client files are often not indexed by subject matter, making it difficult to locate procedural or analytical knowledge on a particular topic if the contents of the file are not already familiar. Document management systems do support network-wide searches for documents in electronic form by selected attributes such as document author name, or keywords appearing in the document. In the absence of a consistent system of classifying the document's contents by subject or topic, however, keyword searches by topic produce incomplete retrieval of all relevant documents.

Even if knowledge is documented by work product such as a memorandum to file, access to the implicit procedural and analytical knowledge embodied in the firm's files is often difficult, at best. Client files that are indexed according to a subject-based system may offer some help in searching for analytical knowledge. A large transaction, however, may include dozens of analytical issues, and it is unlikely that all of them would be indexed. Procedural knowledge is unlikely to be indexed at all. This means that the user must often rely on the ability to search by keywords for relevant fact patterns to retrieve relevant procedural or analytical knowledge.

Some knowledge in a law firm raises issues of security and confidentiality. There are few confidentiality concerns with declarative knowledge. This type of knowledge is meant to be public and readily accessible to all. Analytical and procedural knowledge within the firm can, however, raise issues of security and client confidentiality. Attorneys in the firm have professional ethical obligations to their clients to maintain the confidentiality of information furnished by the client. While these ethical obligations are customarily interpreted to permit sharing the information among the firm's members and staff, appropriate precautions still must be taken to avoid disclosures outside the firm.

Figure 1. Knowledge management matrix

Levels Categories	Core Knowledge	Advanced Knowledge	Innovative Knowledge
Administrative Knowledge			
Declarative Knowledge			
Procedural Knowledge			
Analytical Knowledge			

Figure 2. Knowledge management matrix for the current IS/IT situation

Levels Categories	Core Knowledge	Advanced Knowledge	Innovative Knowledge
Administrative Knowledge	Accounting system Hours billing Clients database E-mail Word processing Spreadsheet Salary system	Competence database Client firm information Internet	
Declarative Knowledge	Library system Electronic law-book Electronic legal sources	Law database	
Procedural Knowledge	Case collection Document standards Procedural standards Document examples	Internal databases Intranet Public databases	
Analytical Knowledge	Law interpretations	Groupware	

Knowledge Management Matrix

To identify knowledge management applications, we can combine knowledge levels with knowledge categories. Core knowledge, advanced knowledge, and innovative knowledge is combined with administrative knowledge, declarative knowledge, procedural knowledge, and analytical knowledge in Figure 1. We have created a knowledge management matrix with 12 cells for IS/IT applications.

Figure 3. Knowledge management matrix for desired IS/IT situation

Levels Categories	Core Knowledge	Advanced Knowledge	Innovative Knowledge
Administrative Knowledge	Accounting system Hours billing Clients database E-mail Word processing Spreadsheet Salary system *Electronic diary* *Electronic reception* *Office automation* *Message system*	Competence database Client firm information Internet *Videophone* *Video conference* *Quality system* *Financial services* *Intranet* *Net agent* *Electronic meetings*	*Client statistics* *Lawyer statistics* *Recruiting system* *Scanning* *Quality assurance* *Benchmarking* *Customer* *relationships* *Net-based services* *Electronic diary* *Mobile office* *Executive information*
Declarative Knowledge	Library system Electronic law-book Electronic legal sources *Document* *management* *Legal databases* *Commercial* *databases*	Law database *Electronic library* *Electronic law-book* *Extranet* *International legal* *sources*	*Law change base* *Precedence base* *Conference system* *Intelligent agents* *Artificial intelligence* *Portals* *Work flow systems*
Procedural Knowledge	Case collection Document standards Procedural standards Document examples *Planning system* *Standards archive* *Publishing system*	Internal databases Intranet Public databases *Experience database* *Image processing* *Document generation* *International law base* *Public Web access*	*Video registration* *Case system* *Online services*
Analytical Knowledge	Law interpretations *Voice recognition* *Case* *interpretations*	Groupware *Intelligent agents* *Client monitoring* *Extranet* *Discussion groups* *Video conference*	*Expert register* *Expert system* *Research reports* *Subject database* *Data warehouse*

The knowledge management matrix can first be used to identify the current IS/ IT that support knowledge management in the firm, as illustrated in Figure 2.

Now the knowledge management matrix can be applied to identify future IS/ IT as illustrated in Figure 3. The systems do only serve as examples, they illustrate that it is possible to find systems than can support all combinations of knowledge categories and knowledge levels.

Software and systems suitable for knowledge management in a law firm can now be identified using the knowledge management matrix. In Figure 4, examples of software to support systems in Figure 3 are listed.

Figure 4. Knowledge management matrix for software supporting desired IS/IT situation

Levels Categories	Core Knowledge	Advanced Knowledge	Innovative Knowledge
Administrative Knowledge	Microsoft Word Microsoft Excel Microsoft Outlook SuperOffice Timex Concorde XAL DBMS SuperOffice Microsoft Office Oracle Agresso Powermarkt Uni økonomi Datalex Justice Data Systems GroupWise Alta Law Office ESI Law	Microsoft Access Lotus Approach Corel Paradox Infotorg IFS Rubicon Concorde K-link Akelius dokument Windows NT Explorer CheckPoint Firewall RealMedia Advisor klient Completo Advokat Visma Business Advokat	Intranet Internet Extranet WAP PDA/Palm KnowledgeShare IFS Business performance Mikromarc 2 statistic IFS Front Office Psion Nomade Netscape Netcaster
Declarative Knowledge	NorLex CarNov RightOn Lovdata NORSOK	Lovdata Celex BibJure Shyster Finder Prjus BookWhere	Hieros Gamos Eudor Abacus Law Lawgic Netmeeting Lov chat LegalSeeker KG Agent Lotus K-station Domino Workflow
Procedural Knowledge	Jasper Karnov Mikas Aladdin ePaper Action Request System DocuShare CyberWorks Training Learning Space	Lotus Domino Domino.Doc DOCS Open HotDocs Adobe photoshop EUR-Lex ODIN eCabinet	Justice Autonomy LegalSeeker Expert Legal Systems Hieros Gamos Real Media Amicus Attorney
Analytical Knowledge	PDA/Palm Lotus LearningSpace Lotus Quickplace Lotus Sametime IBM Content Manager IBM Enterprise Portal Voice Express Collaborative Virtual Work Search Sugar Vchip	Lotus Notes iNotes Lotus K-Station Jasper Novell GroupWise Microsoft Exchange Netscape Communicator JSF Litigator's Notebook Empolis K42 Legal Files	Summation Knowledger Lotus Raven Shyster XpertRule Miner Expert Choice Dragon Dictate

Let us look at one example in Figure 4. *Knowledger* is listed as potential software in the innovative-analytical knowledge location. This is an ambitious location of a software product that has yet to demonstrate its real capabilities in knowledge firms. According to the vendor, Knowledge Associates (http://www.knowledgeassociates.com), Knowledger 3.0 is complete knowledge management software that can be integrated with other systems in the firm. Knowledger is Web based, and supports the firm in categorizing internal and external knowledge, as well as helps with linking incoming knowledge to existing knowledge.

Let us look at one more application in the most demanding location of innovative-analytical knowledge. There we find something called Summation. *Summation* is a system for document handling for use in large court cases (http://www.summation.com). In the large court case of Balder in Norway, law firm Thommessen Krefting Greve Lund (TKGL) used Summation in 2001. The Balder case is a dispute between Exxon and Smedvig about the rebuilding of an offshore vessel costing 3 billion Norwegian crones. TKGL had more than 2,500 binders when the court case started in the city of Stavanger. All these documents were scanned into a database for use by Summation. When lawyers from TKGL present material in court, they submit it from their laptops. When new information emerges in court, then it is registered in Summation. When TKGL lawyers are to trace technical and financial developments for Balder, they make a search in the Summation database.

Another law firm is also using Summation. The law firm Bugge Arentz-Hansen Rasmussen (BA-HR) has the task of finding money after the late shipowner, Jahre. The money is expected to be found in banks in countries where there are no taxes. The hunt for Jahre funds has been going on for almost a decade, and BA-HR has developed a large Summation database enabling BA-HR lawyers to present important information in the court in the city of Drammen.

A third example of Summation use can be found in the U.S. The Justice Department used Summation in its legal struggle with Microsoft. It has been argued that Summation helped the Justice's lead prosecutor, David Boies, piece together the most damaging information for Microsoft. In presenting its defense, which ended on February 26 in 2001, Microsoft relied more than Justice did on a low-tech overhead projector.

According to Susskind (2000, p. 163), six kinds of expert systems can play an important role in law firms in the future:

- **Diagnostic systems.** Those systems offer specific solutions to problems presented to them. From the facts of any particular case, as elicited by such a system, it will analyze the details and draw conclusions, usually after some kind of interactive consultation. These systems are analogous to the medical diagnostic systems that make diagnoses on the basis of symptoms presented to them. An example of a diagnostic system in law would be a taxation system that could pinpoint the extent to which, and why a person is liable to pay tax, doing so on the basis of a mass of details provided to it.

- **Planning systems.** In a sense, planning systems reason in reverse, for these systems are instructed as to a desired solution or outcome, and their purpose is to identify scenarios involving both factual and legal premises that justify the preferred conclusion. In tax law, a planning system could recommend how best a taxpayer should arrange his affairs so as to minimize his exposure to liability. The knowledge held within planning systems can be very similar to that held within diagnostic systems; what is quite different is the way that knowledge is applied.

- **Procedural guides.** Many complex tasks facing legal professionals require extensive expertise and knowledge that is, in fact, procedural in nature. Expert systems as procedural guides take their users through such complex and extended procedures, ensuring that all matters are attended to and done within any prescribed time periods. An example of such a system would be one that managed the flow of a complex tax evasion case, providing detailed guidance and support from inception through to final disposal.

- **The intelligent checklist.** This category of system has most often been used to assist in auditing or reviewing compliance with legal regulations. Compliance reviews must be undertaken with relentless attention to detail, and extensive reference to large bodies of regulations. Intelligent checklists provide a technique for performing such reviews. They formalize the process. In taxation, an intelligent checklist approach could be used to assist in the review of a company's compliance with corporation tax.

- **Document modeling systems.** These systems, also referred to as document assembly systems, store templates set up by legal experts. These templates contain fixed portions of text, together with precise indications as to the conditions under which given extracts should be used. In operation, such a system will elicit from its user all the details relevant to a proposed document. This is done by the user answering questions, responding to prompts, and providing information. On the basis of the user's input, the system will automatically generate a customized and polished document on the basis of its knowledge of how its text should be used.

- **Arguments generation systems.** It is envisaged that these systems are able to generate sets of competing legal arguments in situations when legal resources do not provide definitive guidance. Rather than seeking to provide legal solutions (as diagnostic systems strive to do), argument generation systems will present sound lines of reasoning, backed both by legal authority and by propositions of principle and policy. These lines of reasoning will lead to a range of legal conclusions. Such systems would help users identify promising lines of reasoning in support of desired outcomes while, at the same time, advancing other arguments that may need to be refuted.

Research Model for Knowledge Sharing

The objective of this section is to deepen our understanding of the factors that increase or lessen employees' tendencies to engage in knowledge-sharing

Figure 5. Research model for determinants of knowledge sharing intentions

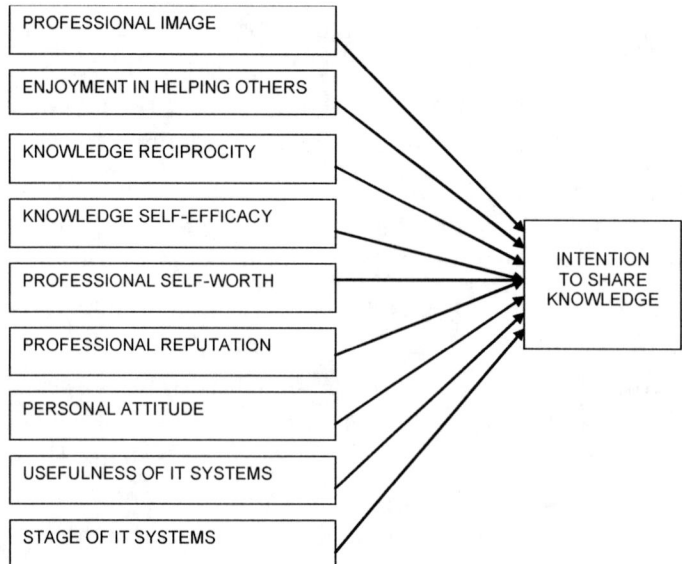

behaviors. Figure 5 depicts our research model. Intention to share knowledge is the dependent variable in the model.

Professional Image

In most organizations today, the importance of image is increasing as traditional contracts between organizations and employees based on length of service erode. In such working environments, knowledge contributors can benefit from showing others that they possess valuable expertise. This earns them respect and a better image. Therefore, knowledge sharers can benefit from improved self-concept when they share their knowledge. According to Kankanhalli et al. (Kankanhalli, Tan, & Wei, 2005), employees have been found to share their best practice due to a desire to be recognized by their peers as experts. People who provided high-quality knowledge have been found to enjoy better prestige in the workplace. Hence, this discussion suggests a positive relationship between image and intention to share knowledge.

Hypothesis 1: The more a lawyer's image is improved by knowledge sharing, the greater the intention to share knowledge will be.

Enjoyment in Helping Others

This benefit is derived from the concept of altruism. Altruism exists when people derive intrinsic enjoyment from helping others, without expecting anything in return. According to Davenport and Prusak (1998), altruism implies that a knowledge seller may be so passionate about his or her knowledge that he or she is happy to share it whenever he/she gets a chance. This seems to be the case with many university professors. Many knowledge sharers are motivated in part by a love of their subject and to some degree, by altruism, whether for the good of the organization or based on a natural impulse to help others.

Altruism exists when people derive intrinsic enjoyment from helping others, without expecting anything in return. Although there may be very few instances of absolute altruism (involving absolute lack of self-concern in the motivation for an act), relative altruism (where self-concern plays a minor role in motivating an act) is more prevalent. Knowledge sharers may be motivated by relative altruism based on their desire to help others. According to Kanhanhalli et al. (2005), prior research shows that knowledge contributors gain satisfaction by demonstrating their altruistic behavior. Such satisfaction stems from their intrinsic enjoyment in helping others. Knowledge sharers who derive enjoyment in helping others may be more inclined to share knowledge.

Hypothesis 2: The greater enjoyment a lawyer finds in helping others, the greater the intention to share knowledge will be.

Knowledge Reciprocity

Reciprocity has been highlighted as a benefit for individuals to engage in social exchange. According to Davenport and Prusak (1998), reciprocity implies payment in terms of knowledge. A knowledge seller will spend the time and effort needed to share knowledge effectively, if the person expects the buyer to be a willing seller when he or she is in the market for knowledge. Reciprocity may be achieved less directly than by getting knowledge back from the same person. In firms structured as partnerships, such as law firms, knowledge sharing that improves profitability will return a benefit to the sharer, now and in the future. Whether or not a knowledge seller expects to be paid with equally valuable knowledge from the buyer, the knowledge seller may believe that being known for sharing knowledge readily will make others in the company more willing to share with him or her. That is a rational assumption, since his or her reputation as a seller of valuable knowledge will make others confident of his/her willingness to reciprocate when he/she is the buyer and they have knowledge to sell: The knowledge seller's knowledge credit is good.

Reciprocity has been highlighted as a benefit for individuals to engage in social exchange. It can serve as a motivational mechanism for people to contribute to discretionary databases. Reciprocity can act as a benefit for knowledge contributors because they expect future help from others in lieu of their contributions. According to Kankanhalli et al. (2005), prior research suggests that people who share knowledge in online communities believe in reciprocity. Further, researchers have observed that people who regularly helped others in virtual communities seemed to receive help more quickly when they asked for it.

Furthermore, Kankanhalli et al. (2005) found a significant, positive relationship between reciprocity and usage of electronic knowledge repositories by knowledge contributors. These arguments suggest a positive relationship between reciprocity and intention to share knowledge.

Hypothesis 3: The more a lawyer expects knowledge reciprocity, the greater the intention to share knowledge will be.

Knowledge Self-Efficacy

Self-efficacy relates to the perception of people about what they can do with the skills they possess. When people share expertise useful in the organization, they gain confidence in terms of what they can do, and this brings the benefit of increased self-efficacy. This belief can serve as a self-motivational force for knowledge contributors to share knowledge. Knowledge self-efficacy is typically manifested in the form of people believing that their knowledge can help solve job-related problems, improve work efficiency, or make a difference to their organization.

Conversely, if people feel that they lack knowledge that is useful to the organization, they may decline from sharing knowledge because they believe that their contribution cannot make a positive impact for the organization.

These arguments suggest a positive relationship between knowledge self-efficacy and sharing by knowledge contributors that was found to be significant in the study by Kanhanhalli et al. (2005).

Hypothesis 4: The higher knowledge self-efficacy perceived by a lawyer, the greater the intention to share knowledge will be.

Professional Self-Worth

In an ongoing interaction setting such as knowledge sharing in an organization, appropriate feedback is very critical. When others respond in the way that we have anticipated, we conclude that our line of thinking and behavior are correct; at the same time, role taking improves as the exchange continues according to role theory, which is the cornerstone of the symbolic interactionist perspective on self-concept formation. According to Bock et al. (Bock, Zmud, & Kim, 2005), this process of reflected appraisal contributes to the formation of self-worth that is strongly affected by sense of competence, and closely tied to effective performance.

Therefore, Bock et al. (2005) found that employees who are able to get feedback on past instances of knowledge sharing are more likely to understand how such actions have contributed to the work of others, and/or to improvements in organizational performance. The understanding would allow them to increase their sense of self-worth accordingly. That, in turn, would render these employees more likely to develop favorable attitudes toward knowledge sharing than employees who are unable to see such linkages. Defining this cognition as an individual's sense of self-worth from their knowledge-sharing behavior leads to the fifth hypothesis.

Hypothesis 5: The greater the sense of self-worth through knowledge sharing behavior is, the greater the intention to share knowledge will be.

Professional Reputation

In order to share knowledge, individuals must think that their contribution to others will be worth the effort, and that some new value will be created, with expectations of receiving some of that value for themselves. These personal benefits or private rewards are more likely to accrue to individuals who actively participate and help others. Thus, the expectation of personal benefits can motivate individuals to contribute knowledge to others in the absence of personal acquaintance, similarity, or the likelihood of direct reciprocity (Wasko & Faraj, 2005).

According to Wasko and Faraj (2005), social exchange theory posits that individuals engage in social interaction based on an expectation that it will lead, in some way, to social rewards such as approval, status, and respect. This suggests that one potential way an individual can benefit from active participation is the perception that participation enhances his or her personal reputation in the firm. Reputation is an important asset that an individual can leverage to achieve and maintain status within a collective. Results from prior research on electronic networks of practice are consistent with social exchange theory, and provide evidence that building reputation is a strong motivator for active participation. Wasko and Faraj (2005) came to the same conclusion in their empirical study of knowledge contributions in electronic networks of practice.

Hypothesis 6: The more a lawyer can improve his or her reputation by sharing knowledge, the greater the intention to share knowledge will be.

Personal Attitude

Intention to engage in a behavior is determined by an individual's attitude toward that behavior. Here, attitude toward knowledge sharing is defined as the degree of one's positive feelings about sharing one's knowledge (Bock et al., 2005). This leads to the seventh hypothesis.

Hypothesis 7: The more favorable a lawyer's attitude toward knowledge sharing is, the greater the intention to share knowledge will be.

Usefulness of IT Systems

Information technology can play an important role in successful knowledge management initiatives (Kankanhalli et al., 2005; Wasko & Faraj, 2005). However, the concept of coding and transmitting knowledge is not new: training and employee development programs, organizational policies, routines, procedures, reports, and manuals have served this function for many years. What is new and exciting in the knowledge management area is the potential for using modern information technology (e.g., extranets, intelligent agents, expert systems) to support knowledge creation, sharing, and exchange in an organization and between organizations. Modern information technology can collect, systematize, structure, store, combine, distribute, and present information of value to knowledge workers.

The value of information presented to knowledge workers can be studied in terms of the organization's value configuration. A law firm has the value configuration of a value shop (Gottschalk, 2006). In the value shop, lawyers need information to access client problems, find alternative solutions to problems, select an optimal solution, implement the solution, and evaluate the implementation. In this value creation, IT systems can help gain access to new cases, help find relevant court rulings, retrieve relevant documents, collect views from opposing sides, and support quality assurance of the work.

A law firm as a value shop is an organization that creates value by solving unique problems. Knowledge is the most important resource. A value shop is characterized by five primary activities: problem finding and acquisition, problem solving, choice, execution, and control and evaluation, as illustrated in Figure 6.

Figure 6. Law firm as value shop with activity examples

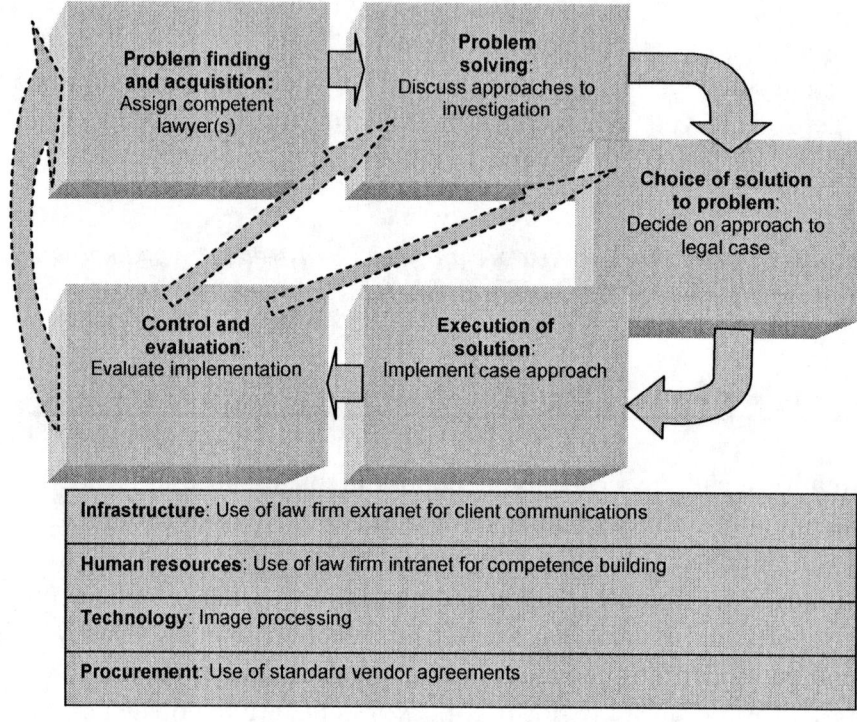

Hypothesis 8: The more a lawyer finds useful information in IT systems, the greater the intention to share knowledge will be.

Stage of IT Systems

The ambition level using knowledge management systems can be defined in terms of stages of knowledge management technology, as illustrated in Chapter I. When a firm reaches higher stages in the model, knowledge workers contribute information to the systems. At Stage 3, document systems and other information repositories are based on knowledge workers' contributions in electronic form. In our final hypothesis, we suggest that knowledge workers that are used to sharing information in IT systems will be more inclined to share their knowledge.

Hypothesis 9: The more higher-stage IT systems are available to a lawyer, the greater the intention to share knowledge will be.

The Case of Eurojuris

Eurojuris is a leading network of law firms in Europe, covering 610 different cities/locations in 17 countries: Austria, Belgium, Denmark, Finland, France, Germany, Ireland, Italy, Liechtenstein, Luxembourg, Netherlands, Norway, Portugal, Spain, Sweden, Switzerland, and UK. Eurojuris groups some 5,000 lawyers.

Each country has a national Eurojuris association that selects as members medium-sized independent law firms well established in their country, and who satisfy Eurojuris selection criteria. The objective is to provide to companies, corporations, public authorities, and private clients direct legal advice and local representation all over Europe.

When clients consult their nearest Eurojuris law firm, they have access to legal and commercial advice not only all over Europe, but also worldwide. The local Eurojuris lawyer will contact the appropriate lawyer abroad, or provide the client with details of the legal practitioners that the client needs to contact.

All Eurojuris law firms are well-established and reputable firms in their community. They are carefully selected, and abide by defined quality standards relating to fees, mandatory professional indemnity insurance, knowledge of foreign languages, promptness, and confidentiality. All firms maintain their professional independence (Eurojuris, 2005).

In 1994, Eurojuris pioneered the quality policy for legal services with a system of quality standards to be applied to Eurojuris firms. It was the so-called 10 commandments that every firm has to respect. This was the first step towards quality that enabled the network to harmonize its cooperation in Europe, a great benefit to its clients. Largely inspired by the Eurojuris UK/LawNet quality standards, the rules evolved towards the ISO standards that have the advantage of being internationally recognized and controlled by an objective external body (Cyberfax, 2005).

Eurojuris firms became certified from 1996 onwards. Hereafter, some national organizations made the certification mandatory for their membership, which is the case for the UK, France, and Norway. Firms in Germany, Italy, and Belgium also received their ISO certificate.

In 2000, a member of the Board was appointed to be specifically in charge of the quality policy. In 2001, the General Assembly voted for a set of quality rules for the Eurojuris national associations. In 2003, Interjuris/Group Eurojuris was the first association to be rewarded with the ISO certification. In 2005, Eurojuris International was awarded the ISO 9001 certification. It is still not over, since it was hoped that in Berlin during the 2005 congress of the network, it could be announced that more than 50% of the network is involved with the ISO certification (Cyberfax, 2005).

Knowledge management has been at the top of the agenda of Eurojuris for a long time. Substantial investments in information technology and knowledge management systems are made to support lawyers as knowledge workers.

Europe does not have a single legal system. The method of conducting business varies from one country to another. Using local expertise from qualified lawyers, who are based on the spot where the client's problem arises, can be an effective way to serve the client or the correspondent lawyer. The local lawyer can draw on his knowledge of local authorities and procedures, speaks the language, and is able to act effectively and promptly in his own environment. Using a relevant and local law firm also avoids the extra costs of traveling expense. It may sometimes be inappropriate to use a large firm from the state capital when immediate advice may be more usefully and cost-efficiently obtained at a decentralized location anywhere in Europe.

Empirical studies of Eurojuris Norway were conducted some years ago (Gottschalk, 2005). Information was collected on software and systems used to support interorganizational knowledge management among law firms. Eurojuris law firms used Lotus Notes very extensively in their cooperation. Lotus Notes is an application covering both level II (person-to-person) and level III (person-to-information) in the stages-of-growth model for knowledge management technology. This result implies that Eurojuris law firms in Norway had already advanced to levels II and III. This result was confirmed by e-mail being ranked second after Lotus Notes, while end-user tools, such as word processing, had dropped to third place in a ranking of most important IT tools. The conclusion from these studies indicated that Eurojuris law firms are advanced both in terms of knowledge management and in terms of knowledge management systems.

Research Methodology

To test the proposed research model, we adopted the survey method for data collection, and examined our hypotheses by applying multiple regression analysis to the collected data. Our unit of analysis was the individual.

We developed the items in the questionnaire by adapting measures that have been validated by other researchers. Our dependent variable-intention to share knowledge was adapted from Bock et al. (2005). One part of the scale is measuring intention to share explicit knowledge, and the other part of the scale is measuring intention to share implicit knowledge.

Items are listed in Figure 7. Reliability in terms of Cronbach's alpha was .92 and .93 for the two scale parts, respectively, in the research conducted by Bock et al. (2005).

The first independent variable, professional image, was measured on a scale adapted from Kankanhalli et al. (2005). Similarly, enjoyment in helping others was adopted from the same authors. Both Kankanhalli et al. (2005), and Wasko and Faraj (2005) have measured knowledge reciprocity, but in different ways, so both scales are included in the instrument. Knowledge self-efficacy is from Kankanhalli et al. (2005), while professional self-worth is from Bock et al. (2005), and professional reputation is from Wasko and Faraj (2005).

Usefulness of IT systems was measured in terms of systems providing useful access, help, and information in the five primary activities of a law firm as a value shop. Questionnaire items are listed in Figure 8. All items were derived from previous empirical studies, by Gottschalk (2005), of Eurojuris Norway.

Stage of IT systems was measured both by the current stage and the stage 5-years ago. Questionnaire items are listed in Figure 9. These items were derived from research conducted by Gottschalk (2005). They found that most law firms in Australia and Norway develop according to the four-stage model for the evolution of information technology support for knowledge management.

Figure 7. Questionnaire items on intention and perceptions provided to survey respondents

Construct	Items in the survey instrument	Reliability
Intention to share knowledge Bock et al. (2005)	*Intention to share explicit knowledge* I will share my documents in the firm more frequently in the future I will provide my methods to firm members more frequently in the future (new) I will contribute work reports to firm members more frequently in the future (new) I always provide my models for members of my firm *Intention to share implicit knowledge* I intend to share my experience in the firm more frequently I will always provide know-where and know-whom at colleagues' request I will try to share my expertise in the firm more frequently	.92 .93
Professional image Kankanhalli et al. (2005)	Sharing my knowledge improves my image within the firm Sharing my knowledge improves others recognition of me When I share my knowledge, the people I work with respect me People in the firm who share their knowledge have more prestige	.89
Enjoyment in helping others Kankanhalli et al. (2005)	I enjoy sharing my knowledge with others in the firm I enjoy helping others by sharing my knowledge It feels good to help someone else by sharing my knowledge Sharing my knowledge with others gives me pleasure	.96
Knowledge Reciprocity Kankanhalli et al. (2005) Wasko and Faraj (2005)	Reciprocity by Khankanhalli et al. When I share my knowledge, I expect somebody to respond when I'm in need When I contribute knowledge, I expect to get back knowledge when I need it I believe that my queries for knowledge will be answered in the future Reciprocity by Wasko and Faraj I know that others in the firm will help me, so it's only fair to help others I trust someone would help me if I were in a similar situation	.85 .95
Knowledge self-efficacy Kankanhalli et al. (2005)	I have the expertise needed to provide valuable knowledge in the firm It makes a difference to the firm whether I add to the knowledge others have Few other lawyers in the firm can provide more valuable knowledge than I can I have confidence in my ability to provide valuable knowledge to others	.96
Professional Self-Worth Bock et al. (2005)	My knowledge sharing helps other members in the firm solve problems My knowledge sharing creates new business opportunities for the firm My knowledge sharing improves work processes in the firm My knowledge sharing increases productivity in the firm My knowledge sharing helps the firm achieve its performance objectives	.91
Professional reputation Wasko and Faraj (2005)	I earn respect from others by sharing my knowledge I feel that participation improves my status in the profession I participate to improve my reputation in the profession	.90
Personal attitude Bock et al. (2005)	My knowledge sharing with others in the firm works fine My knowledge sharing with others in the firm is enjoyable My knowledge sharing with others in the firm is valuable to me My knowledge sharing with others in the firm is a wise move My knowledge sharing with others in the firm is harmful to me (reversed)	.92

Figure 8. Questionnaire items on value shop activities provided to survey respondents

Use of IT systems for:	My use of IT systems in lawyer collaboration in the firm provides me:	Reliability
Problem access	Access to new assignments Access to new clients Access to new cases Access to new projects Access to profitable cases Access to challenging cases	.98
Problem solutions	Help to solve difficult cases Help to find relevant laws Help to find relevant court rulings Help to analyze documents Help to draft documents Help to find experts in the field	.92
Solution choice	Information from relevant laws Information from relevant court rulings Information from relevant documents Information from relevant conclusions Information from relevant client advice Information about important views	.94
Solution execution	Solutions to client problems Clarification on opposing side Views from participating lawyers Views from clients Views from opposing side Information resolving issues with client	.95
Execution evaluation	Quality assurance of closed cases Evaluation of work quality Learning from own closed cases Learning from other's closed cases Ideas on how to better solve client cases Ideas on how to make a case more profitable	.95

New Technologies for Legal Work

Mountain (2001) has posed the question: Could new technologies cause great law firms to fail? In her article, she addresses the question why law firms ought to invest in online legal services when studies to date show that there is no correlation between law firm technology capabilities and profitability. She divides online legal services into two types: digital delivery and legal Web advisors. The framework set out by Clayton Christensen in his book, *The Innovator's Dilemma*, is used to explain how legal Web advisors is a disruptive technology that law firm competitors (i.e., accounting firms, dot-coms, and corporate clients) are beginning to harness to erode law-firm

Figure 9. Questionnaire items on technology stages provided to survey respondents

---

Please indicate with one check mark the description that most closely fits your firm's projects for information technology to support knowledge management in the firm in 2005:

➢ ( ) *End-user tools* will be made available to lawyers. This means a capable networked PC on every desk or in every briefcase, with standardized personal productivity tools (word processing, presentation software) so that documents can be exchanged easily throughout the firm. A widespread dissemination and use of end-user tools among lawyers in the firm is to take place.

➢ ( ) *Information about who knows what* will be made available to lawyers. It aims to record and disclose who in the organization knows what by building knowledge directories. Often called 'yellow pages', the principal idea is to make sure knowledgeable people in the firm are accessible to others for advice, consultation, or knowledge exchange. Knowledge-oriented directories are not so much repositories of knowledge-based information as gateways to knowledge.

➢ ( ) *Information from lawyers* are repositories of knowledge-based information that will be stored and made available to colleagues. Here data mining techniques can be applied to find relevant information and combine information in data warehouses. One approach is to store project reports, notes, recommendations, letters, and other documents from each lawyer in the firm. Over time, this material will grow fast, making it necessary for a librarian or knowledge manager to organize it.

➢ ( ) *Information systems solving knowledge problems* will be made available to lawyers. Artificial intelligence will be applied in these systems. For example, neural networks are statistically oriented tools that excel at using data to classify cases into categories. Another example is expert systems that can enable the knowledge of one or a few experts to be used by a much broader group of lawyers who need the knowledge. A third example is case-based reasoning where the system finds a similar case and comes up with a recommended solution for the current case.

Please indicate with one check mark the description that most closely fits your firm's projects for information technology to support knowledge management in the firm in 2000:

➢ ( ) *End-user tools* were made available to lawyers. This means a capable networked PC on every desk or in every briefcase, with standardized personal productivity tools (word processing, presentation software) so that documents can be exchanged easily throughout the firm. A widespread dissemination and use of end-user tools among lawyers in the firm took place.

➢ ( ) *Information about who knows what* was made available to lawyers. It aimed to record and disclose who in the organization knows what by building knowledge directories. Often called 'yellow pages', the principal idea is to make sure knowledgeable people in the firm are accessible to others for advice, consultation, or knowledge exchange. Knowledge-oriented directories are not so much repositories of knowledge-based information as gateways to knowledge.

➢ ( ) *Information from lawyers* are repositories of knowledge-based information that was stored and made available to colleagues. Here data mining techniques can be applied to find relevant information and combine information in data warehouses. One approach is to store project reports, notes, recommendations, letters, and other documents from each lawyer in the firm. Over time, this material grows fast, making it necessary for a librarian or knowledge manager to organize it.

➢ ( ) *Information systems solving knowledge problems* was made available to lawyers. Artificial intelligence is applied in these systems. For example, neural networks are statistically oriented tools that excel at using data to classify cases into categories. Another example is expert systems that can enable the knowledge of one or a few experts to be used by a much broader group of lawyers who need the knowledge. A third example is case-based reasoning where the system finds a similar case and comes up with a recommended solution for the current case.

---

margins. Unless law firms reinvent themselves as technology organizations, they could find themselves increasingly marginalized. Large law firms need to develop legal Web advisors, and should consider spinning off technology subsidiaries to do so. Small law firms need to link up with online advisory services on an application service provider basis.

Mountain (2001) finds that 15 years ago, artificial intelligence (AI) was set to radically change the face of the legal profession as we know it. As it turned out, neither expert systems nor any other kinds of AI lived up to their potential at that time. They required huge investments and provided marginal perceived payoffs. Eventually, both fell under the weight of their own start-up requirements. Today, AI has been reincarnated in the form of legal Web advisors. Legal Web advisors offer interactive legal advice delivered via extranets without human intervention, using questions to collect facts, and then using decision-tree analysis to produce answers. Some of the world's largest law firms in London, England are pushing ahead with developing legal Web advisors, despite the absence of a link between law firm profitability and use of technology. Why would the London firms, who bill out their services at the highest hourly rates in the world, involve themselves in such risky, low margin endeavors? The answers lie in the disruptive power of these new technologies.

According to Mountain (2001), legal Web advisors were pioneered in London in 1994 when the law firm, Linklaters, introduced a browser-based product called Blue Flag. Blue Flag is now a suite of products covering regulatory compliance, derivatives documentation, employee share plans, funds, share disclosure, and transaction management. Within months, another London law firm, Clifford Chance, followed with NextLaw, a Web-accessible online service that helps assess the legal and regulatory risks of e-commerce, and reportedly required an investment of more than 1 million pounds sterling. Today, there are approximately a dozen online legal services in the UK and Australia, and the pace of their introduction is accelerating. The revenue model, to date, has been to charge these services out by subscription, and then to have lawyers leverage from these online services to attract value added legal work.

Blue Flag is an interesting example. Blue Flag is a legal risk-management service designed to provide packaged legal advice on European financial and banking regulatory issues (hence the name Blue Flag). This service is designed to appeal to those concerned with legal compliance working in fund management, securities houses, investment, and commercial banks, and provides step-by-step legal advice on tap to subscribers for a fixed annual fee. Not surprisingly, having established the service, Linklaters have now extended it to cover other (non-European) jurisdictions where they have expertise. The benefits to clients of this Blue Flag type of system are clear. Consider the following fictional scenario (Terrett, 2000, p. 123):

An in-house lawyer works in a large corporate organization. The company is considering a purchase of a major overseas rival. The lawyer in question has been asked to present a paper to the board on the legal implications of this move. In-house lawyers, being generalists rather than specialists, might be tempted to instruct a firm of respected lawyers to be certain that they have all of the pertinent issues covered. However, they are also likely to be concerned about the resultant bill. Thus, they turn to Blue Flag. Here they can search for relevant information in the knowledge that it has been produced by a highly reputable firm of solicitors, they can print it out and present it to the Board and file it as though it were any other piece of legal advice. The task is completed more quickly and at no additional cost to the company. It is hardly surprising that the service is proving so successful. How have Linklaters achieved this in such a small space of time? They were very fortunate to have already produced much of the content that makes up the site and have it readily available in electronic form. All that was required was a degree of innovative thinking about how the information could be delivered to clients (i.e., via the Web rather than CD-ROM or paper).

Online legal services can be placed in two different categories: digital delivery services and legal Web advisors. Digital delivery services deliver human legal product by digital means: the simplest example is the use of e-mail to distribute legal documents. Both law firms and application service providers (ASPs) offer digital delivery. ASPs are companies that deliver software across the Internet by subscription instead of a packaged product. Many large London firms have opted for in-house capability instead, and host their own transactions through branded extranets (Web sites that provide a private body of information to a limited number of external organizations). Examples are Clifford Chance's Fruit Net, Allen & Overy's Newchange Dealroom, and Andersen Legal's Dealsight. Like e-mail, extranets will eventually become an invisible part of the technology infrastructure, and will not form a basis of competitive advantage.

Legal Web advisors, on the other hand, offer interactive legal advice delivered via extranets using artificial intelligence. Legal Web advisors use AI in a more cost-effective and pragmatic fashion than did the systems of 15 years ago. For example, they do not attempt to work independently of lawyer input. Lawyers and knowledge engineers work together to describe the order in which information is obtained and used to determine a solution. The software leads the client from one question to another using a decision tree system. This type of system uses a sequence of decisions based on user input to classify the problem before moving through nodes and subnodes to the problem solution. Once the client has completed the path and has answered all the relevant questions, the software produces output. This output is not in the form of a legal opinion; instead, it is in the form of "You need to do A, B, C, D, and E." It is more similar to the advice a lawyer gives to a friend at a party than it is to traditional legal advice. It provides 90% of the answer in situations where the client does not care about the other 10% and is not willing to pay for it. The distinction between digital delivery and legal Web advisors may blur in the future as online legal services become increasingly sophisticated.

In our perspective of knowledge management ambition, legal Web advisors represent knowledge management level IV. Expert systems are applied to give clients direct access to an information system that can develop and recommend a solution to the client's problem. The system is based on a thorough process, where lawyers and knowledge engineers worked together to describe the order in which information is obtained and used to determine a solution.

References

Becker, W. M., Herman, M. F., Samuelson, P. A., & Webb, A. P. (2001). Lawyers get down to business. *The McKinsey Quarterly*, (2), 45-55.

Bock, G. W., Zmud, R. W., & Kim, Y. G. (2005). Behavioral intention formation in knowledge sharing: Examining the roles of extrinsic motivators, social-psychological forces, and organizational climate. *MIS Quarterly*, *29*(1), 87-111.

Cyberfax. (2005). Eurojuris International becomes the first international legal network ISO Certified. *The Eurojuris Newsletter*, *15*(2).

Davenport, T. H., & Prusak, L. (1998). *Working knowledge*. Boston: Harvard Business School Press.

Edwards, D. L., & Mahling, D. E. (1997). Toward knowledge management systems in the legal domain. In *Proceedings of the International ACM SIGGROUP Conference on Supporting Group Work Group* (pp. 158-166). The Association of Computing Machinery ACM.

Eurojuris. (2005). Retrieved from http://www.eurojuris.net

Galanter, M., & Palay, T. (1991). *Tournament of lawyers, the transformation of the big law firms*. Chicago: The University of Chicago Press.

Gottschalk, P. (2005). *Strategic knowledge management technology.* Hershey, PA: Idea Group Publishing.

Gottschalk, P. (2006). *E-business strategy, sourcing and governance.* Hershey, PA: Idea Group Publishing.

Grover, V., & Davenport, T. H. (2001). General perspectives on knowledge management: Fostering a research agenda. *Journal of Management Information Systems, 18*(1), 5-21.

Hitt, M. A., Bierman, L., Shumizu, K., & Kochhar, R. (2001). Direct and moderating effects of human capital on strategy and performance in professional service firms: A resourced-based perspective. *Academy of Management Journal, 44*(1), 13-28.

Jones, E. (2000). Remaking the firm: How KM is changing legal practice. *Knowledge Management Magazine*. Retrieved from http://www.kmmag.com

Kankanhalli, A., Tan, B. C. Y., & Wei, K. K. (2005). Contributing knowledge to electronic knowledge repositories: An empirical investigation. *MIS Quarterly, 29*(1), 113-143.

May, T. Y., Korczynski, M., & Frenkel, S. J. (2002). Organizational and occupational commitment: Knowledge workers in large corporations. *Journal of Management Studies, 39*(6), 775-801.

Mountain, D. (2001). Could new technologies cause great law firms to fail? *Journal of Information, Law and Technology*, (1). Retrieved from http://elj.warwick.ac.uk/jilt/

Nahapiet, J., & Ghoshal, S. (1998). Social capital, intellectual capital, and the organizational advantage. *Academy of Management Review, 23*(2), 242-266.

Parsons, M. (2004). *Effective knowledge management for law firms*. UK: Oxford University Press.

Susskind, R. (2000). *Transforming the law*. UK: Oxford University Press.

Terrett, A. (2000). *The Internet—business strategies for law firms*. Law Society Publishing.

Wasko, M. M., & Faraj, S. (2005). Why should I share? Examining social capital and knowledge contribution in electronic networks of practice. *MIS Quarterly, 29*(1), 35-57.

Chapter XI

Policing
Research Studies

Results from a variety of empirical studies are presented in this chapter. All studies are concerned with knowledge management in law enforcement.

Police Officers' Professional Knowledge

Holgersson (2005) identified and described, in his doctoral dissertation, different types of knowledge that are part of police officers' practice. This case description is based on his work.

Even though an intervention usually forces a police officer to apply several different skills, Holgersson (2005) has chosen to discuss different forms of professional knowledge separately, in order to make things easier to comprehend for the reader. In general, a large part of police officers' professional knowledge, as well as professional knowledge in many other contexts, is complex and difficult to describe and explain in words. The police profession is distinguished by the broad range of skills that are required, and by the time pressure under which actions often must be taken.

Earlier in this book, Holgersson's (2005) total of 30 knowledge types in policing were presented. Six of the most important types are presented in the following. The six selected knowledge types are the first five types and the final thirtieth type presented earlier. These are different forms of professional knowledge that a police officer should possess.

Using the Skills of Other Police Officers

Fourteen-year old Sarah never came to school that day. She was lying with her face buried in her pillow and her eyes were bloodshot from crying. Patrol 7337 consisting of police inspector Fredrik Påhlsson and senior police officer Anna Ekeroth had the task to register a report. When they rang the doorbell to the apartment at Advokatbacken and were let inside by the girl's mother, they did not know much more of the case than that a pupil at Albyskolan had been attacked on her way to school. The mother told them briefly that a man in his forties had molested her daughter. He had pulled up her t-shirt from behind and held her in his grip, while he started to stroke her breasts. Since Fredrik Påhlsson and Anna Ekeroth had worked together so much, they did not need more than eye contact, some small movements with their eyebrows and a small nod to agree over how they would divide their tasks.

The ability to use police officers' skills can be coupled to individuals, patrols, and groups. One type of knowledge that is coupled to the level of the individual is a police officer's ability to understand his own and his colleagues' stronger and weaker sides in case of an intervention. This means that he has an intuitive feeling for how the tasks shall be divided, when to step forward and take the initiative, and when to step backwards and leave the initiative to a colleague; for example, when a patrol is involved in a discussion. The ability to distribute the tasks in an appropriate manner is important within a patrol as well as between patrols, when several patrols are involved in a certain situation. A commander's ability to form patrols and take advantage of a group in the best possible way is a part of this knowledge category.

To be able to distribute the working tasks in an appropriate manner, a police officer needs to know which measures and routines usually come up in a certain situation. Besides knowing the area well, it is important to have knowledge about reoccurring crimes, specific problems, and individuals within the area. For a distribution of the working tasks in a way that fits the situation, it usually is of central importance that there is a dialogue between the police officers.

Another form of knowledge is a type of collective knowledge related to a certain patrol or group. This knowledge form becomes visible when a group/patrol is involved in a case, and different roles and working tasks are distributed, more or less automatically, within the patrol/group. Even though the individuals within the group/patrol possess this ability, the knowledge is collective and maintained by the members of the patrol/group. This collective knowledge makes the individuals in the patrol/group experience a certain "flow" when they are working.

Showing Empathy Towards a Victim

Fredrik Påhlsson nodded understanding as he sat in the kitchen speaking with Sarah's mother, who was upset over what had happened. In Sarah's room Anna Ekeroth had just sat down on the side of the bed. She did not say anything. Sarah was sobbing and was still lying on her stomach, without looking at the police officer who had been in her room for several minutes at that point. Anna Ekeroth laid her hand on Sarah and said: "How are you?" Sarah turned around with a deep sigh and their eyes met. "Not so good" Sarah answered. "My name is Anna; I understand that this is difficult!" Anna Ekeroth continued. Without the police officer having asked for it, Sarah started to tell about what had happened. Anna Ekeroth sat silent and made notes, at the same time as she every now and then confirmed that she was listening by saying "I understand" and other short comments that made the conversation with Sarah easier.

Persons who have been the victim of a crime can have different reactions. Some may not need any support at all, while others react strongly over crimes that a police officer does not find so grave. The police officer must adjust his supporting measures depending on the subjective needs that a victim has. Even when a police officer thinks a police case is unimportant, he must be able to show empathy. Furthermore, he must be able to be indulgent towards persons who have been the victim of a crime and are angry or come with malicious remarks; for example, when a crime victim sharply points out that the police surely can catch speeding offenders or beat demonstrators, but are not able to get hold of burglars that rage in an area.

To be able to show empathy, body language, in the form of body position and distance, becomes important. Holding somebody may be right in one situation, while not so fitting in another when the victim wants to keep a distance. Another important component is to listen actively, where the police officer shows that he is listening. A police officer must have the ability to let the victim tell his story in a way that seems best to the victim, at the same time as he gets enough information to be able to make a judgment of what has happened.

At the same time as the police officer shall show empathy, he usually also has other tasks to perform, in most cases some form of interrogation or other crime investigating measures. The police officer must have a feeling for when it is suitable to, for example, ask a victim to come along to a hospital for corpse identification. He must be able to decide when sensitive questions can be asked. Should he wait with an interrogation? Should the interrogation with a victim take place at a calmer place than where they are at that point? A police officer must feel how fast, for example, crime-investigating measures can be carried out. He or she must have the ability to adjust treatment depending on the situation and the crime victim.

In addition, a police officer must be able to assess what type of support the victim needs when the police have left the crime scene. Is it fitting to drive the victim to an acquaintance, a hospital, or a women's refuge? Does the victim want the police to call when the offender is released? In some cases, giving some advice is enough to make the victim feel safer. In other situations, the police may find it important that the victim is in contact with, and receives support from somebody in his or her surrounding. The support that is needed is highly individual, and the police officer must make a judgment about which measures are needed and possible to carry through.

Prioritizing Cases and Using Available Resources Effectively

Fredrik Påhlsson looked at his watch as he and Anna Ekeroth walked down the stairs and towards the police car. Writing the report at Sarah's house had not taken much time. Both Fredrik Påhlsson and Anna Ekeroth knew that at that moment there were problems with the selling of drugs in the centre of Alby, and they had promised to try to engage themselves in the matter. Anna Ekeroth sat down in the radio seat and Fredrik Påhlsson took place in the driver seat, while he was complaining about the hockey game of the day before that started to come back to him. "Oh, I forgot my hat and gloves in the apartment," Fredrik Påhlsson said. "Mr. Absentminded has struck once again," Anna Ekeroth said with a tone of mild resignation. "Yes, I know," Fredrik Påhlsson sighed while he got out of the car again.

A police officer must be able to make a well-thought-out judgment about how much time can be put in a certain case. Is there reason to put energy in the case, or should the aim be to finish it as fast as possible, as the police organization's resources for that case are minimized. There are many factors that can affect this decision. First of all, the police officer must take the victim into account. An 80 year old woman who has been the victim of a crime may be in bigger need of support than a 22-year-old man who has had a burglary into his car. A second factor is the crime's gravity and the police officer's analysis of the possibilities that the case will be taken to court.

Even when a police officer concludes that it will be difficult to take legal proceedings against a person, he may still decide to lay down energy on a case; for example, when it concerns a serious type of crime or a reoccurring problem in an area. When, for example, there has been a series of fires, a small fire that only will be classified as damage can be enough to send out a dog patrol or perform a door-to-door search to find the offenders. Perhaps it is possible to find out who was behind the series of fires, without solving the issue that the patrol at that moment is involved in. In the same way, a police officer can decide that there are good reasons to lay energy on having a person arrested in a case that normally would not be important enough for a patrol to be engaged in. This can be the case when the offender already is being watched by the police organization.

Thus, a police officer needs different forms of knowledge to be able to select those cases where there is cause to put energy in. It is, among other things, important to be informed about particular problems and individuals that are active in a certain area. Good insights in investigation work and technical research as well as legal knowledge are also important. A police officer must also be able to decide how much time can be put on one case. A patrol must feel whether the estimated effect makes the amount of time put in a case justifiable. The effect of the time one puts into a case can differ.

Distinguishing Deviations and Categorizing Individuals, Objects and Events

They had just left Advokatbacken and only driven a short bit over Tingsvägen when Fredrik Påhlsson shouted: "There we have something!" and made a fast U-turn. The old red Opel started to drive faster but had no chance against the police car's 250 hp engine. The driver did not even reach the cycle lane that he intended to drive into in order to avoid the police patrol. Instead, the driver stopped the car and jumped in between the two passengers on the backseat. Both Fredrik Påhlsson and Anna Ekeroth were quickly out of the police car and approached the Opel. They knew exactly who had been driving the car.

Police officers automatically notice people's way of walking, their clothes, their car, and so forth, to be able to distinguish deviations. These routine controls of the environment help making police work more efficient. One of the most important things in the working day of police officers is how they examine the environment, and what they do on their own initiative. However, it is easy to believe that being active, for example, stopping and carrying out a control, is the same as being efficient. Believing that being active and being efficient is the same thing is at best debatable, but can lead to overcontrol. That police officers sort the impressions they get, usually consisting of meager and superficial information, is a prerequisite for police work. Police officers often can recognize suspect persons from a long distance.

A police officer observes his surroundings and judges what he sees. Different behaviors, individuals, and objects make the police officer form suspicions of different degrees. Does somebody walk too fast? Does somebody walk too slowly? Does somebody look around too much? Does somebody look around too little? Does somebody seem to be nervous? Is this a person the police know from before? How does a person behave when he looks at a police officer, does he look too long, too short, or does he avoid looking at all? The environment and the persons that accompany somebody are also affecting the judgment. A broken headlamp, an expired tax control sticker, the driver not using a safety belt, and the looks of the driver in combination with the state of the car are other factors that can be reasons for an intervention.

The ability to distinguish the deviant and to find reasons to act against an individual or a vehicle is developed as an experience-based knowledge. This ability consists partly of being able to discover the deviant, as described previously, and partly of being able to consider different factors once something deviant has been discovered. When, for example, a police officer starts to suspect a case of drunken driving as the driver of a car makes a "pear" or "truck" turn, brakes without reason, drives too slow or too staggering, only one of these signs, if clear enough, may be enough to motivate stopping the car. It is probable that a drunk driver behaves in a certain way, but not at all certain.

Even when a police officer discovers something illegal, he must constantly make the decision if it is an errand that is suitable to be engaged in at that moment. Shall a patrol, for example, stop and make a report about someone for not using a bicycle lamp or for illegal billposting? The police officer asks himself two things: Is the degree of suspicion high enough to motivate an intervention, and does the gravity of the suspected crime justify an intervention? It is important that a police officer makes a balanced decision and finds a suitable level for when to investigate something further. In that way, he can avoid controlling too many vehicles or individuals.

Forming a Suspicion

"Aren't his eyes a little faint?" Anna Ekeroth wondered. "Have you taken something?" Fredrik Påhlsson asked. "What do you mean, taken something?" the Opel driver said. But there was something in his eyes that made both Anna Ekeroth and Fredrik Påhlsson suspicious. Since three more persons were in the car, the patrol did not have the possibility to keep an eye on them and get permission to carry out a bodily search and a house search. Therefore Fredrik Påhlsson made the decision to search the car and the persons inside the car. Anna Ekeroth had seen that one of the persons in the car had dropped something to his feet. One thing led to another and five minutes later the patrol had confiscated about 350 rohypnol pills, two knives and one mobile phone that they suspected was stolen. Three of the four persons that had been in the car were suspected of a crime. But still there was more that could be done and Fredrik Påhlsson called the prosecutor to try to get permission to search the house of the person who had the stolen mobile phone in his inside pocket and of the person who had the main part of the rohypnol pills hidden in the sleeve of his jacket.

To be able to form a suspicion and from there, get the possibilities to perform coercive measures, a police officer needs to possess different types of knowledge. He must be well up in the legislation that regulates police officers' possibilities to use coercive measures, as well as in the legislation that a certain individual has violated. A police officer must constantly draw conclusions from the things he sees and the conversations he has, and connect these conclusions to the current legislation. Are his pupils really normal? Doesn't he hold his plastic bag a bit too tightly? How is it possible that he says he just came from the gas station when in fact, we saw him coming from the other direction? Doesn't his pocket stick out? Doesn't he all the time put his hands in his pockets, as if he has something to hide? Doesn't he act nervous? Why is his right hand in a fist all the time? Why did he bend down behind the shrubbery when he saw us? Do these indications form enough circumstantial evidence to perform a personal search? Are there enough reasons to suspect him of the crime? The police officer must constantly be active in his observations, questions, and judgments.

The ability to form a suspicion requires both theoretical as well as practical knowledge. A large portion of knowledge that could be classified as familiarity knowledge is needed as well. A police officer must constantly search for possibilities to move on in a case. The way in which a case is built up can vary. When a person is discovered driving a car on which a ban of driving was imposed, it is important to find out whether it was a permitted ride. In a situation in which someone is suspected of having robbed a person, the police must try to obtain information that can form a ground for an arrest or a bodily search.

In certain cases, for example, when a person drives a car on which a ban of driving has been imposed, the legislation often provides gaps for those who want to lie. A police officer must, in these cases, fill these gaps by asking thought-through opening questions. The same is true for interrogations. There, one method can be to approach the central issues carefully, that is, one begins to ask questions in a sort of outer ring that slowly becomes more and more narrow.

Presenting a Case to Decision Makers

After some computer searches and contact with the county communication centre, the police officers had a suspect for the crime. Stefan Dahlberg called the station commander at the police station in Flemingsberg for permission to search the house of the suspected person. However, the station commander thought that a prosecutor should take that decision. Therefore Stefan Dahlberg called the prosecutor who was on duty for that day, but he did not want to take a decision about a house search, since the crime was so mild, sexual assault. As the police officers already had a suspect, they could instead take him in for questioning. There was no need to undertake any coercive measures at that point. Stefan emphasized that there had been a serious problem with sexual assaults in that area, but the prosecutor's decision was clear. Anna Ekeroth took the elevator up to Fredrik Påhlsson who was standing outside the suspect's door. "Shall we go in?" Fredrik Påhlsson asked when Anna Ekeroth opened the elevator door. "No, it didn't work out." Fredrik Påhlsson sighed and went into the elevator.

Police personnel must have an ability to present a case to decision makers. They have to be clear and pedagogical. It is an advantage if the decision maker, already from the start, has faith in the person who presents the case.

Sometimes it can be good to present a case before carrying out a planned action. In that way, decision makers can be better informed about the case, and the police officers can also get an indication of whether it is worth carrying out the action at all. Working two days on finding a certain address and then not being allowed to carry out a house search can be meaningless, and has often a devastating effect on motivation.

Police officers must have a clear vision on how they are going to present a case, and based on which grounds a decision maker might take his decisions.

Impact of Information Technology in Policing

Chan (2001) studied an Australian police force. There are nine police forces in Australia, eight covering each of the States and Territories, plus a federal force. The Eastern Police Service (EPS) has several thousand sworn officers, and provides service to several million people over a vast geographical area.

Information technology had become an integral part of police life in EPS by the late 1990s. Survey respondents reported spending an average of 3 hours and

37 minutes per 8 hour shift using computers for administrative tasks. The vast majority of the respondents thought that information technology had made a great difference to police work.

In spite of many complaints in the focus groups about various technical problems with the systems, EPS officers' assessment of the impact of information technology on their own work was generally positive. The majority of respondents indicated that IT has allowed them to work more effectively (79% agreed vs. 3% disagreed), made their work easier (66% vs. 7%), and helped them cope with the amount of information police needed to do their work properly (59% vs. 10%). The gain in efficiency as a result of information technology was especially salient to police who had experienced the old technology. For example, one participant in a focus group of specialist investigators (FG9) said that 5- to 6-years ago, to type a record of interview for a large investigation would take 5 to 6 hours; now it could be done in half an hour from a taped record of interview.

Survey respondents also rated positively the impact of information technology on workplace relations and communication. The majority agreed that IT has led to improved information sharing between workers (70%), and improved communication between workers (58%). Less than 10% of respondents disagreed with those statements. Similarly, respondents tended to agree that information technology has allowed people to work more cooperatively (47% agreed vs. 7% disagreed), and created a more positive work atmosphere (30% vs. 13%). Improvement in communication between workers was largely the result of the availability of electronic mail that facilitated teamwork, information gathering, and sharing.

With the widespread use of technology in the organization, technical expertise became a much-valued form of cultural capital. The majority of survey respondents agreed that information technology has led to increased computer literacy among police. The growth in funding and staffing of IT-related functions within the EPS was a source of much envy and some bitterness among some officers. The ascendancy of officers with IT expertise may also threaten the traditional power structure of an organization where previously, leaders were predominantly drawn from the criminal investigation branch.

A fairly substantial proportion of survey respondents thought that, as a result of information technology, they spent more time satisfying accountability requirements (41%); doing "paperwork" (36%); planning, organizing, or analyzing information (30%); and supervising or checking the work of staff (26%). In addition, a fair proportion indicated that they spent less time patrolling the streets (39%); interacting with members of the community in noncrime or nonemergency situations (30%); informing citizens on the progress of their case (25%); and responding to calls from citizens (20%).

A substantial proportion of survey respondents thought that information technology has required police to follow unnecessary steps to get things done. This feeling was particularly strong among detectives.

There was a general feeling that with the advent of information technology came additional reporting and accountability requirements. Two-thirds of the survey respondents agreed that information technology has required them to report on their activities more frequently, and made them more accountable for their actions.

Archival Study of Eyewitness Statements

Fahsing (2002) conducted empirical research in eyewitness statements. The following description is based on his research.

The case files of the Robbery Squad of the Oslo Police Department in Norway were used as data source. The case files included all material from the police investigations and written files from all witnesses and suspect interviews. The vast majority of case files (92.5%) also contained a videorecording of the robbery. All robberies against banks and post offices committed in Oslo between January 1999 and December 2001 were examined ($n = 58$).

All witnesses ($n = 250$) saw the robbery itself, and almost all witness interviews (89.5%) were conducted on the same day as the robbery took place. There were 59.2% female and 40.8% male witnesses. Furthermore, 53.6% of the witnesses were bank employees and 46.4% customers. Amongst the bank employees were 67.2% females and 32.8% were males, with an overall average age of 37.11 years.

All robbers wore some kind of facial disguise and, with the exception of one, all were armed. Furthermore, all the witnesses were present within the robbed premises. Consequently, all witnesses should perhaps be regarded as victims. However, the degree of threat experienced by each individual witness is not only decided by the observable behavior of the perpetrator, but also a function of a large selection of individual witness factors. Thus, since the present study does not include immediate in-depth interviews with the witnesses, it would be very speculative to attempt to divide the witnesses into victim and nonvictim categories.

However, the vast majority of robbers in this study approached the bank employees, and threatened them to present the money. Hence, this group is the closest we get to a victim group. According to their employers, all bank employees in the study, with only a few exceptions, have undergone so-called "robbery-training." Usually, such training consists of a briefing on the bank's security routines, a realistic armed robbery (staged by the local police department), followed by a subsequent debriefing session with all involved personnel.

Independent Variables

All independent variable information was either copied directly, or coded from the recorded information in the case files to cells in a cross-table. These included typical natural witness characteristics, that is, (1) age and (2) sex. Furthermore, the witnesses' relation to robbery target was categorized as (3) bank employee and (4) customer. Finally, the number of perpetrators involved was registered as (5) one perpetrator and (6) two perpetrators. The independent variables were registered in four separate columns in the cross-table. The witnesses' age at the time of the interview was copied directly into the table, while the witnesses gender was coded into "0" for female and "1" for male, the witnesses' relation to the robbed target was coded into "0" for customer and "1" for bank employee and, similarly, cases with only one perpetrator were coded with "1" and cases with two perpetrators with "2."

Dependent Variables

Frequency. The present study has, with some exceptions, utilized similar registration and scoring routines as described in previous comparable studies. The witness interviews were analyzed, and the content of the witnesses' verbatim offender descriptions were divided into categories. All details mentioned by the witnesses' were registered, and every descriptor category was given its own column in a cross-table. For example, the statement "He had a big knife and a green bag" would be categorized as three different descriptors: *gender* (he), *weapon* (big knife), and *bag* (green bag). The descriptors were then registered in the same row as the independent variables for each witness.

Unlike previous similar studies, the descriptors were not classified as either permanent or temporary. Previous researchers had to do this due to the lack of verifying information for the temporary descriptors. However, since the present study also possessed videorecordings from the crime scenes, all information could be assessed on an equal basis and consequently, there was no need for such a distinction.

In general, it was a relatively uncomplicated task to detect, categorize, and register descriptors. Objects with comparable observational and functional features were categorized into main groups. For example, it seemed logical to register a description of a coat in the same column as a description of a jacket. Thus, descriptions of the perpetrator's clothing were categorized into three main groups: *"clothing head"* (hats, balaclavas, caps), *"clothing jacket"* (coats, sweaters, jackets) and *"clothing trousers."* In the same way, the perpetrator's arms (knifes, revolvers, guns) were considered as *"weapons,"* and the perpetrator's carrier bags (plastic bags, suitcases, bags) were categorized *"bag."*

The vast majority of descriptors were relatively unambiguously described, such as "white gloves," and hence, principally all descriptors were copied verbatim from the files and into the table. However, for some of the descriptors, such as build, age, and height, it is unrealistic to expect witnesses to estimate these in exact numbers since such estimations can be difficult, even in more daily situations. As expected, the content analysis of the statements showed that witnesses used a variety of etiquettes when describing these variables.

As an example, many witnesses illustrated the offenders age as numerically bounded age ranges, such as "between 20 and 25" or "in his mid-30s." In real life, this is totally unproblematic, since it probably only reflects a certain degree of realism in the witnesses' descriptions. However, to obtain a degree of conformity in the data set, these less specific descriptions had to be transformed into specific numbers. This was done by using the midvalue in the given age range. Accordingly, the two previously mentioned age ranges would be registered as "22.5 years" and "35 years," respectively. In the same way, a witnesses' height description as "170 to 180 cm" would be registered in the table as "175 cm." As dealt with next, the need of a fairly balanced rating system for age and height accuracy necessitated this transformation of height and age measures. The frequency of occurrence of the different variables was measured by summarizing every column, and summarizing the variables in each row arrived of the number of variables mentioned by each witness.

Accuracy. For each of the 26 types of descriptors in the cross-table, two additional columns were added. First, a column was used for the verifying information from the videorecordings or the police description files; second, a column was for the accuracy of each descriptor coded into a 4-point scale. *Wrong* ("0") corresponded to a description that, based on the verifying material, was totally inaccurate; *correct* ("1") to a description that was completely accurate; *partially correct* ("2") to a description that was partially accurate; and *unverifiable* ("3") to descriptions that could not be verified.

The distinction between "wrong information" and "partially correct information" was not always clear-cut, especially when descriptions were incomplete, but still included some correct information. Consequently, an unambiguous definition had to be made. As an experienced detective, the author knows that misleading eyewitness information often causes more trouble than incomplete information. Thus, descriptions that included misleading information (confabulations) were rated as *wrong,* and descriptions that did not contain wrongful information, but were incomplete, were rated as *partially correct.* Accordingly, if the videorecordings from a crime scene showed that an offender carried a *black and blue* handbag, a description was scored wrong if it said the handbag to be *black and red,* partially correct if it said the bag was *black,* and correct if they described it as *black and blue.* Hence, the scoring system in the current study was, possibly, a slightly more rigorous assessment procedure than used in previous similar studies.

To resolve the dilemma of scoring age and height in terms of accuracy, a clearly defined registration and scoring procedure was needed. If not, less specific descriptions would have a much higher chance of not being scored as wrong. As an example, both the description "175-180 cm" and "170-180 cm" might be said to be a correct description of a person 177 cm tall, even though the first is more precise. Hence, with an intention of a fair scoring of both specific and less specific descriptions, it was decided to score height and age as *correct* if the registered estimation was within the range $^+/-2.5$ cm or years of the correct height or age, *partially correct* if the registered estimation was within the range $^+/-5$ cm or years, and *wrong* for registered estimations outside $^+/-5$ cm or years of the actual height or age. In view of that, if an offender was 177.5 cm tall according to the official police record, witnesses scored *correct* with the description "175-180 cm." Likewise, any witness with a description of height with a specific number between 175 and 180 would have been scored as *correct.* The total accuracy measures for each specific descriptor were calculated by averaging each witness accuracy score.

In order to determine the reliability of these ratings, accuracy scorings for a random 40 (16%) of the witness reports were performed by an additional independent coder. The interrater agreement for the details included in these reports was 98.2%. That is, for 380 of the 387 coded details, the scorings were identical between the two coders. Discrepancies regarding the remaining seven details were resolved by the coders in confidence.

Completeness. Assessment of completeness is an ambiguous matter in real-life studies, mainly because it is very difficult to estimate the amount of information that each witness was exposed to. Combining the fact that there was a large variation in terms of information in each scenario, with different observational conditions for witnesses *within* each scenario, makes "input-bound" measures of completeness fairly impractical. Therefore, for the present study, the completeness of the offender descriptions was measured in a so-called "output-bound" manner. That is, the amount of correct and partly correct details in each description was summarized. Furthermore, by relating the amount of correct and partly correct information to the total amount of information mentioned in each offender-description, the reliability of each statement was captured.

Research Results

Frequency. In total, the 250 witnesses mentioned 2,345 perpetrator characteristics. The number of details mentioned in a witness' description ranged from 2 to 16, with a median of 9 descriptors.

Seventeen of the characteristics were mentioned by more than 10% of the witnesses, whereas the five least commonly mentioned characteristics (birthmark, watch, teeth, socks, and communication devices) were only reported by 0.4% of the witnesses. Over one-third (36.6%) of all descriptive details referred to relatively permanent general physical characteristics such as sex, build, ethnicity, and accent. Another 49.8% of the descriptors were more temporary characteristics such as the perpetrator's clothes and effects (weapons, bags), while a mere 2.5% of the witnesses described details from the perpetrators face.

Accuracy. Of the 2,345 descriptors, 2,234 (95.3%) could be matched against videorecordings of the perpetrator(s) from the crime scenes, and the police description files. The accuracy of reporting each of the 26 verifiable descriptors varied considerably. For example, the percentage of descriptions in which a mentioned characteristic was completely accurate ranged from 20.0% (eye-brows) to 100% (birthmarks).

However, as dealt with in the previous section, the frequencies of the mentioned characteristics varied greatly, from 99.6% (sex) to 0.4% (birthmark). Hence, to properly evaluate the accuracy statistics, the number of descriptions on which each percentage is based has to be considered. Therefore, descriptors mentioned by less than 10% of the witnesses will not be dealt with in this section.

For the 17 descriptors mentioned by 10% or more, 65.0% of all information was completely accurate, and 22.4% partially correct, whereas 12.6% of the information was incorrect. For each descriptor, accuracy levels ranged from 34.0% (age) to 97.2% (sex). However, most of these percentages were quite high; for 14 of the 17 descriptors, the proportion of completely accurate information was more than 50%. All verifiable information about the perpetrator's sex was completely correct and contained no misleading information. Further-more, for 6 descriptors (weapon, hair, ethnicity, accent, clothing (head), and glasses), more than 90% of all reported information was correct or partially correct. Seven descriptors (build, bag, gloves, face shape, scarf, clothing (jacket and trousers)) were correct or partially correct in more than 80% of the cases. The 3 descriptors containing the highest amount of misleading informa-tion were height (21.5%), shoes (24.7%), and age (35.3%).

In addition, 72.6% of all descriptive details referring to permanent physical characteristics (sex, height, age, build, race, accent, hair, and face shape) were either wholly or partially correct, compared to 83.4% for the descriptors of temporary characteristics (clothing, weapon, bag, shoes, gloves, scarf, and glasses).

Completeness. Overall, the completeness of the descriptions was fairly good. The total number of correct and partially correct details mentioned in a description ranged from 2 to 13, with a median of 8.

On average, male and female witnesses reported about the same number of correct or partially correct details. Furthermore, older witnesses (over 60 years) reported a nonsignificantly lower number of correct and partially correct details than witnesses under 60 years. Interestingly, however, bank employees performed somewhat better than did customers.

The completeness of descriptions for cases with only one perpetrator was compared with cases where the witnesses were exposed to two perpetrators. This difference turned out to be highly significant. However, the difference in size of the two groups should be noted ($n = 211$ for one perpetrator; $n = 30$

for two perpetrators). For the 243 verifiable descriptions, the reliability of the information mentioned was high, with the median percentage accuracy for mentioned characteristics being 88.9%. In none of these perpetrator descriptions did the accuracy of the information fall below 50%, while in 32.5% of the cases, all of the information provided was completely accurate.

In total, 79 (32.5%) of the witnesses were completely accurate. A slightly higher proportion of the bank employees (36.4%) than of the customers (28.1%) reported completely accurate descriptions; however, the two proportions did not differ significantly. Furthermore, neither witnesses' gender nor witnesses' age were significantly related to the likelihood of reporting a completely accurate description. The mean number of mentioned details for the 79 witnesses was 8.99.

The present study of eyewitnesses' descriptions of armed perpetrators confirms results found in earlier real-life and laboratory studies, namely; (1) even for stressful events, witnesses' descriptions of the perpetrator may be both detailed and accurate; and (2) the majority of the descriptions of permanent physical features include mostly general characteristics of the perpetrator, such as gender, height, build, age, and race. Additionally, the present study indicates that real-life eyewitnesses also manage to include, with remarkably high accuracy, important elements of the perpetrators' clothing, outfit, and arms. Furthermore, and most importantly, the high-accuracy rates seem to hold even when the number of descriptors increases.

Conclusion

The present study failed to find any strong predictor of description accuracy from either witness factors or from measures of description completeness. However, as posted in the introduction, the two main objectives of the study were to assess the accuracy of the different details in an offender description, and the overall reliability of the witness statements. The results show that the majority of descriptions in the study are remarkably detailed and accurate. Although the majority of the descriptions include mostly general characteristics of the perpetrator, such as gender, height, build, age, and race, the present study indicates that witnesses also manage to include, with remarkable high accuracy, important elements from the perpetrators' clothing, outfit, and arms. Furthermore, and most importantly, the high accuracy rates seem to hold even when the number of descriptors mentioned increases. This particular finding stands apart from previous real-life studies, and should therefore be specifically addressed in future research.

However, the overall picture that seems to emerge from the present study and previous research focusing on real-life witnesses is that there is a considerable correspondence in forensic witnesses' ability to provide descriptions, at least in cases of robbery. The pattern of reporting particular attributes of an offender, the number of details mentioned, and the overall accuracy of information contained within descriptions seems to be rather consistent. These findings suggest that although there has been a legitimate concern about the credibility of forensic eyewitnesses, that witnesses to stressful events can be highly reliable. This fact cannot be ignored, and should be accounted for when evaluating past and future eyewitness research using different methodology. Consequently, to facilitate the application of eyewitness research to real-world situations, findings from laboratory studies should, perhaps to a larger extent, be attuned against findings from studies of real eyewitnesses.

Effectiveness in the Detection of Money Laundering

Money laundering can be defined as the depositing of cash in a legitimate account, most commonly a bank, any movements or transactions that complicate and disguise the origin of funds, and the conversion, through the layering process, into a form that the perpetrator can control. Money laundering is concerned with placement, layering, and integration. Money must be placed into the financial system, for example traveller's cheques, postal orders or banker's drafts, retail economy, or smuggled out of the country. Layering is the concealment of the source of ownership of the funds. Typically, layers are created by moving money in and out of the offshore bank accounts of shell companies through electronic funds transfers. Integration is the stage where the money is integrated into the legitimate economy and financial system (Stedje, 2004).

Stedje (2004) evaluated the effectiveness in the detection of money laundering in Norway. Her study of effectiveness in prevention and detection of money-laundering crime confirmed results in earlier archival studies that the majority of offenders are known criminals, particularly from drugs. Except for two cases, all studied criminal cases involved currency. Just about half of the suspects were employed or held business positions. The age was lower than for sophisticated white-collar crime, but higher than street crime, as the average age was 35 years. The majority were males who had a personal account relationship with the institution.

Stedje (2004) finds it surprising that most of the suspects were from Asian origin, and that all cases, except for two, were of recorded criminals. This suggests that the police do not fight higher-up criminals, the man in the suite, but the already known criminal, the man in the street. Additionally, with remarkably bad score, no persons were convicted of money-laundering crime by the suspicious-based report system in 2001 in the Oslo Police District.

Previous studies of effectiveness in money-laudering investigations mostly concur with the findings by Stedje (2004). The studies have in common that the police seem less capable of detecting, and the courts less capable of punishing sophisticated money laundering and nonphysical currency. The greater universe of criminal financial activity remains largely untouched by the fight against

Figure 1. Examples of knowledge management systems in money laundering detection

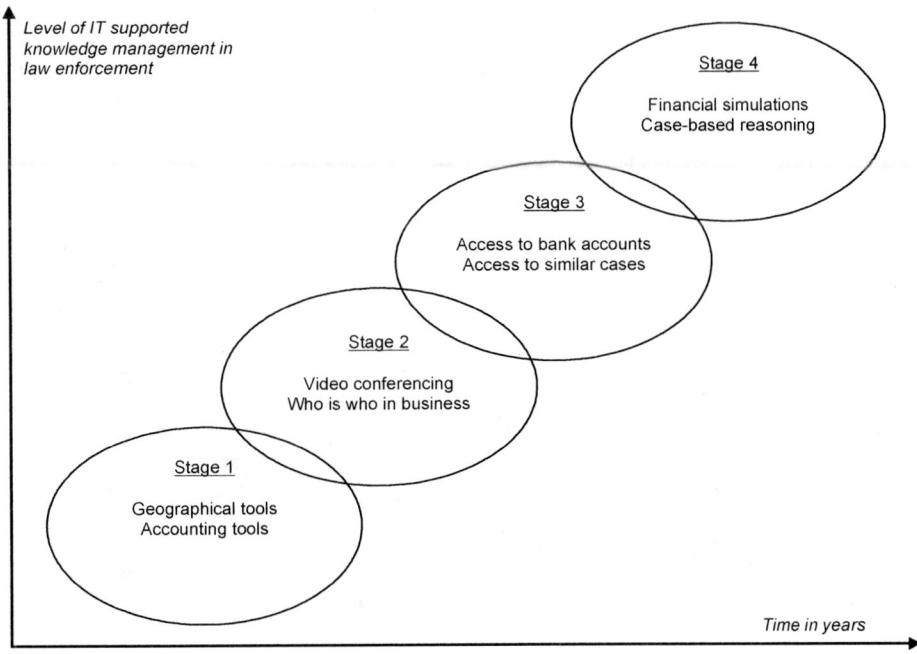

money laundering. None of the studies find that the practice meets the intentions and ambitions of money-laundering legislation, namely as a substantial method in order to fight organized crime and terror activity.

In a knowledge management technology perspective, several applications of information technology might improve the effectiveness in the detection of money laundering. In Figure 1, we apply the stages-of-growth model to illustrate potential applications.

Investigative Thinking Styles in Singapore

Dean (2005) conducted empirical research in the overlapping domains of cognitive/investigative psychology in relation to a specific focus on investigative thinking. An example of one of the cases from this research is presented to illustrate the process of investigative thinking, and the way in which various thinking styles come into play at critical points in the progress of this specific investigation in order to achieve a successful outcome.

The case involved a 73 year old man who was found bound with duct tape and murdered in his flat in a Northern district of Singapore on August 21, 2002. A selection of mobile phones, jewelry, watches, and cash were stolen from the safe in his house. The informant was a 56 year old female Chinese national who worked as a part-time cleaner for the deceased. There were no witnesses to the crime, and neighbors heard nothing unusual.

A state-action investigative chart was developed by Dean (2005) to assess the various states that a specific investigation goes through for a particular crime, and the actions that investigators take as a result. In this murder case in Singapore, the topics on the state-action chart included interview friends, forensic evidence, public pressure, investigator motivation, interview cleaner, locate cleaner's son, and so forth In this case, the state-action chart clearly represented how the method style of investigative thinking was carried out through the collection of forensic evidence at the scene, and gathered information from informal interviews with friends of the deceased indicated that the cleaner's son was most likely involved in some capacity. This speculation by the deceased's friends was, as indicated on the chart, based on the fact that the cleaner's son stayed over some nights in the deceased's house.

The investigation stalled when all leads appeared to reach a dead end. Even the stolen mobile phones had not been used to make calls, so the service provider was not able to pinpoint their exact location.

However, the determination of the investigator exemplified the challenge style of investigative thinking, as he was being driven by the intensity of the job, the crime, and the victim to such an extent that he engaged in some proactive creative thinking (an example of the risk style) that kicked off the investigation again in an eventual positive direction.

The investigator approached the service provider to check if any of the previous phone calls could reveal anything of use for the investigation. The service provider was able to give an estimated location of the missing mobile phones based on the signal picked up by their station. The investigator then made extensive enquiries at the local mobile phone shops in the estimated area, and eventually located the secondhand dealer's shop where the suspect sold the mobile for ready cash. Such an attempt was unprecedented in any other homicide cases in Singapore.

As the case example illustrates, a number of changes in thinking style took place throughout this investigation. The investigation started, as all investigations do, with the application of the "method" style of investigative thinking, then moved to investigation as "challenge," which helped spark off the next change from investigation as challenge to investigation as "skill" and finally, the use of the "risk" style of investigative thinking was applied to the analysis of phone-call details (Dean, 2005).

These four distinctively different ways of thinking (styles) about the investigation process by detectives were illustrated earlier in this book. As was shown, there is a hierarchical structure to how investigators think. Not all cases will require the use of all four investigative thinking styles to solve them. However, as time marches on in an investigation without a result, then other styles of investigative thinking will need to come into play to increase the likelihood of a successful outcome. In essence, the more complex the crime, the higher the investigative-thinking style required to solve it.

These four ways of thinking can be related to the codification vs. the personalization strategy for knowledge management systems suggested by Hansen et al. (Hansen, 1999). Thinking Style 1 and 3 are based more on explicit knowledge, and are more suitable for codification than thinking Style 2 and 4. In relation to the domain of knowledge management, the thinking styles of method and skill may be more important to apply knowledge management systems to than the thinking styles of challenge and risk.

Investigative Behavior in Norway

Based on the case from Singapore, a survey instrument was developed by Dean (2005). The survey instrument was applied in a study of police officers in Norway for profiling police investigative thinking. The only difference between the Singapore and Norway cases is that the Norwegian survey is concerned with behavior rather than preference in terms of thinking styles.

The survey instrument uses Likert scaling as the measurement tool, as each of the four investigative thinking styles are treated as one-dimensional in nature. Previous empirical research by Dean (2000) identified the four thinking styles as qualitatively distinct constructs that are arranged in a hierarchical order in terms of their cognitive complexity, as shown in Chapter VIII's Figure 1.

Furthermore, Likert scaling, as a one-dimensional scaling method, produces an ordinal level of measurement because the responses indicate a ranking only of the relative position of items, and does not measure the magnitude of difference. Hence, the advantage of using a Likert scale is that each item in the pool of item statements used to measure a particular investigative thinking style is of equal value, so that the direction of a respondent's total preference for a particular thinking style (either tending towards a strong or weak preference) is scored, rather than each individual item, per se.

Several pilot studies were conducted by Dean (1995, 2000, 2005) on small-scale samples drawn from Australian and Singaporean police to determine the validity and reliability of the item descriptors for each of the four investigative thinking styles (Method, Challenge, Skill, and Risk).

With regard to reliability, the pilot studies revealed consistent results in terms of respondents tending to rate and therefore, perceived themselves as performing higher on the risk style of investigative thinking than other measures used to assess elements of this particular style indicated. In this regard, Likert scaling has been found to improve reliability, as respondents who answer "agree" all the time will appear to answer inconsistently.

In relation to validity, the pilot tests of the "Investigative Thinking Styles" survey instrument were found to have very good content validation by respondents in that the item statements used to describe the attribute fitted well the particular investigative thinking style being measured. As for construct validity, this is always harder to determine in any test or measuring instrument, particularly in the domain of cognitive psychology, where attitudes only exit as hypothetical constructs. However, what makes the validity of the four constructs to be measured with this survey instrument more acceptable is that all four constructs, as described, belong to the specific domain knowledge of policing. Hence, as such on face value, police respondents can make a strong case for an acceptable level of construct validity as a group. The notion of investigative method, challenge, skill, and risk are well understood by police, and require no other special knowledge to comprehend these constructs.

As noted previously, a Likert scale format was adopted to measure the strength or weakness of the preference for each of the item statements used to describe a particular investigative thinking-style construct or variable. Each investigative thinking style has 8 item descriptors associated with it that assess the preferential strength of various elements that, collectively, constitute a particular way of thinking for an investigator. Hence, each one of the four investigative thinking styles yields an overall summative score of its preferential strength/weakness in the mind of the investigator.

A sample of the 8 questions that function as item descriptors for the first variable to do with "method" style of investigative thinking is shown:

1. **Method: Planning.** Before starting an investigation, I make a checklist of what needs to be done for a particular type of crime.

2. **Method: Structure.** I enjoy working on investigations that have a clearly defined goal and a set of protocols to follow.

3. **Method: Procedure.** I figure out how to solve a crime by following the basics of police procedure.

4. **Method: Collecting.** I gather as much information as I can in an investigation.

5. **Method: Checking.** I test the pieces of information I have picked up in an investigation.

6. **Method: Considering.** When I pick up pieces of information, I relate them to what I think is going on in the case, even if a piece does not seem all that relevant at the time.

7. **Method: Connecting.** When I have a suspect, I generate anything to link him or her to somebody or something else by doing computer searches on their name, or driving past their address, or driving past their associate's address and getting some number plates, and so on.

8. **Method: Constructing.** I get background information on a case so I can build it up step-by-step, and then think about how I can constructively apply what I have got.

The other three investigative thinking style variables (Challenge, Skill, and Risk) are set out using the same format with 8 questions each, thereby yielding a survey instrument of 32 questions in all. The item statements for each investigative thinking style variable are randomly distributed throughout the survey questionnaire instrument.

Professional Culture in the Antiterror Police in Norway

Norway has one police service that is based on the principle of coherence, meaning that all functions are in one organization. There are 27 local police districts, each under the command of a Chief of Police. The Chiefs of Police head all kinds of policing in their districts. Each police district has its own headquarters and several police stations. The districts are divided into rural police districts, under the command of a Police Chief Superintendent. All police officers are trained as generalists, able to fulfill every aspect of ordinary police work including criminal investigations, maintaining public order, and community policing (Glomseth, 2004).

The antiterror police in Norway are a group of specialists that are very well skilled and very well trained for extreme situations. The police officers are educated and trained to fight extremely serious and dangerous crime. The tasks are challenging and difficult. The officers are very carefully recruited. The level of competence is high, and the ability to execute demanding tasks is critical.

Through a survey, interviews, and observations, some important occupational values were identified. These values can help explain how the officers in the antiterror police think, plan, and act. The following values seem to be strongly shared among the officers:

- Orientation towards competence and development
- Orientation towards legality
- Orientation towards structure
- Orientation towards performance
- Orientation towards problems, cases, and tasks
- Orientation towards acting

- Orientation towards cooperation
- Orientation towards humility

In this section, we focus our attention on cooperative orientation in the antiterror police by identifying potential predictors of such an orientation.

Research Model

The dependent variable in the research model is cooperative orientation in terms of involvement, as illustrated in Figure 2. Cooperative orientation is concerned with the extent of task vs. relationship orientation, closed vs. open information sharing, competition vs. cooperation among police officers, and single work vs. balanced life orientation. The dependent variable measures the extent of participation and involvement (Zamanou & Glaser, 1994). Three potential predictors of cooperative orientation have been identified, as illustrated in the figure. The potential predictors are labeled time perspective, power structure, and leadership style.

First, we suggest that time perspective influences the extent of cooperative orientation (Fielding, 1984; Kiely & Peek, 2002). If the police officer perceives work to be short term, then the person will tend to be less cooperative oriented. If the police officer perceives work to be long term, then the person will tend to have a greater extent of cooperative orientation.

Figure 2. Research model to study predictors of cooperative orientation

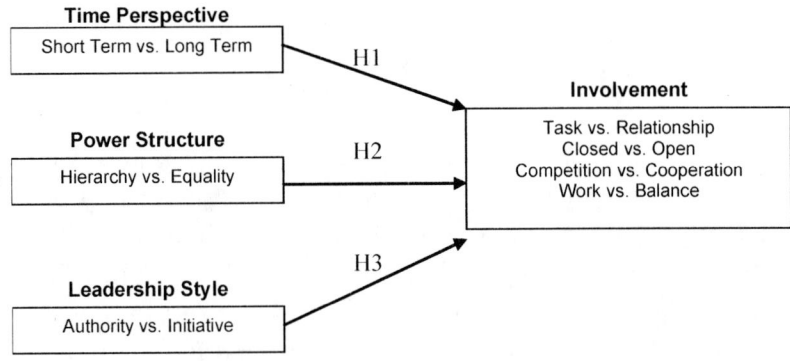

Hypothesis 1: A longer time perspective perceived by the police officer is positively related to the police officer's degree of cooperative orientation.

Next, we believe that hierarchy influences the extent of cooperative orientation. If the police officer perceives the organization to be hierarchical in terms of distance to the top of the antiterror organization, then the person will tend to be less cooperative oriented (Christensen & Crank, 2001). If the police officer perceives the organization to be nonhierarchical by having easy access to decision makers, then the person will tend to have a greater extent of cooperative orientation. Similarly, if the police officer perceives more equality in the organization, then the person will tend to be more cooperative oriented.

Hypothesis 2: More hierarchy and less equality perceived by the police officer are negatively related to the police officer's degree of cooperative orientation.

Finally, antiterror work needs cooperative initiative in critical situations. Therefore, an authoritarian leadership style might damage cooperative orientation (Brehm & Gates, 1993). On the other hand, a leadership style characterized by managed initiative and creativity might strengthen cooperative orientation (Ashby & Longley, 2005; Luen & Al-Hawamdeh, 2001). We suggest that if the police officer perceives an authoritarian leadership style, then the person will tend to be less cooperative oriented.

Hypothesis 3: Stronger authoritarian leadership style perceived by the police officer is negatively related to the police officer's degree of cooperative orientation.

Research Results

The dependent variable participation was measured using a multiple-item scale consisting of the four items: work vs. balance, task vs. relationship, closed vs. open, and competition vs. cooperation. This scale achieved an acceptable reliability in terms of Cronbach's alpha of .69. The scale implies that police officers in favor of balance would typically find relationship important, openness important, and cooperation important. At the other end of the scale, police officers in favor of single work focus would typically find tasks important, limited access important, and competition important.

Independent variables were measured using single-item scales consisting of a statement at each end of the scale. Each scale was a seven points Likert scale.

All police officers in the antiterror police responded to the questionnaire. The number of responses has to be kept confidential.

The research hypotheses were tested empirically using regression analysis. Regression analysis suggests that time perspective (short term vs. long term), power structure (hierarchy vs. equality), and leadership style (firm leader vs. individual) are all positively related to participation. This means that all three hypotheses are supported in this research.

The model summary shows an adjusted R square of .285, implying that our model explains 28.5% of the variation in participation. Anova shows that our model is significant. Finally, all coefficients for the independent variables are significant at the >.05 level. Statistical results are listed in Figure 3-5.

An occupational culture characterized by long time perspectives, flat power structure, and open leadership style is positively related to police officers' involvement in the antiterror police in Norway. This is in line with previous studies concerning occupational culture.

For example, Zamanou and Glaser (1994) found that involvement increased after team building interventions. Christensen and Crank (2001) found that the way police look at their work varies, and that equivalence stimulates involvement. Brehm and Gates (1993) emphasized their finding of the overwhelming importance of attributes of the organizational culture in determining the subordinates' levels of compliance in police behavior. Fielding (1984) stressed both police socialization and police competence in police work. Kiely and Peek (2002) discussed the need for cultural change in the British police.

The current study of Norwegian police documents that if cultural change is to occur in terms of involvement and cooperative orientation, then cultural intervention has to take place in at least three areas. First, a long-term perspective in terms of methods, approaches, and relationships has to be appreciated. Second, a short distance between top and bottom in the hierarchy should be established. Finally, freedom, trust, initiative, and creativity should be stimulated.

Our fourth and final proposition suggests that police investigation success is positively related to stages of knowledge management technology. However, there is a notion that organizations can be governed by texts. The notion is that

Figure 3. Explanatory power of the research model

Model Summary

Model	R	R Square	Adjusted R Square	Std. Error of the Estimate
1	,572[a]	,327	,285	,73024

a. Predictors: (Constant), VAR00009, VAR00018, VAR8A

Figure 4. Statistical significance of the research model

ANOVA[b]

Model		Sum of Squares	df	Mean Square	F	Sig.
1	Regression	12,456	3	4,152	7,786	,000[a]
	Residual	25,596	48	,533		
	Total	38,052	51			

a. Predictors: (Constant), VAR00009, VAR00018, VAR8A

b. Dependent Variable: AFFILIAT

Figure 5. Statistical significance of the predictors in the research model (var00009 is time perspective, var8A is power structure, var00018 is leadership style)

Coefficients[a]

Model		Unstandardized Coefficients		Standardized Coefficients	t	Sig.
		B	Std. Error	Beta		
1	(Constant)	1,592	,630		2,527	,015
	VAR8A	,245	,087	,337	2,827	,007
	VAR00018	,172	,077	,265	2,230	,030
	VAR00009	,200	,066	,362	3,030	,004

a. Dependent Variable: AFFILIAT

a few people, often managers, can formulate thoughts and intentions, write these down as texts, and then use the texts to govern the practice of other people. These texts are typically stored in databases at Stage 3.

The notion that organizations can be governed by texts has had a particularly large impact in the public sector. The police are a good example of an organization governed by texts, since police work is characterized by diversity and the task of dealing with society's monopoly on using violence.

The texts that should govern police work are, in a study by Ekman (1999), divided into police texts and neighborhood police texts. The police texts are first and foremost rules and regulations common to all police. Police texts are primarily taught at police training colleges. Neighborhood police texts are unique to a neighborhood police area. Neighborhood police texts are, in the main, broken down into goals and action plans.

Ekman (1999) investigated the relationship between texts and practice by first examining the practice and seeing what role the texts play. The norms found in the relationship between texts, superiors, and police were that police often have autonomy in their relationship to texts and superiors. In the relationship between citizens and police, norms about police needing to act, that police have authority, were found. The analysis concluded that police work is characterized by diversity. Police meet many citizens, in many different situations, and in many different circumstances.

The field of geodemographics is one of the most fertile applications areas of geocomputation systems and may, in fact, be more beneficial to police investigators than database containing texts. Geodemographic profiles of the characteristics of individuals and small areas are becoming central to efficient and effective deployment of resources by public services. Ashby and Longley (2005) considered the ways in which police forces might use geodemographics to better deploy resources at a variety of spatial scales. Interestingly, this is an application supporting both Stages 1 and 3, thereby making our fourth proposition even more problematic.

As mentioned in the introduction, the primary mission of any police force in the world is to protect life and property, preserve law and order, and prevent and detect crime. Knowledge is being generated every day within the police via various means. The responsibility to surface knowledge lies with everyone in the police force, as knowledge is generated in all phases of work. Such knowledge, when ascertained to have potential value to the organization, is to be channeled to the respective departments for analysis and selection for incorporation into exiting policies and procedures (Luen & Al-Hawamdeh, 2001). We try to capture important aspects of this line of reasoning in our research propositions.

In the case of knowledge sharing in the intelligence community, three major factors complicate efforts to produce high-quality intelligence products. First, other states, and increasingly nonstate actors such as international terrorist groups, actively seek to prevent the intelligence community (IC) from acquiring important pieces of data and information. Second, the explosion in access to open information, often described as the information revolution, provides a flood of information that makes it difficult for the IC to separate the wheat from the chaff. Although much of the information the IC needs is readily available, shifting through all potentially useful information, selecting relevant information, and accurately assessing its validity is a considerable challenge. Third, organizational realities impede the creation of high-quality knowledge. Although overlap exists, each agency of the IC performs specialized tasks that are largely its exclusive domain (Lahneman, 2004).

Intelligence communities are involved in several types of covert activities, even in friendly countries. An example is Mossad's attempt to obtain uranium in the 1950s. A principal reason for cooperation between intelligence communities is the maintaining of solidarity between them, even sometimes behind the backs of their governments (Kahana, 2001).

Information and knowledge management in a knowledge-intensive and time-critical environment presents a challenge to information technology professionals. In law enforcement, multiple data sources are used, each having different user interfaces. COPLINK addresses these problems by providing one easy-to-use interface that integrates different data easily (Chen et al., 2002). As part of nationwide, ongoing digital government initiatives in the U.S., COPLINK is an integrated information and knowledge management environment aimed at meeting some of these challenges (Chen, Zheng, Atabakhsh, Wyzga, & Schroeder, 2003). This example makes our fourth proposition relevant, despite the shortcomings addressed earlier.

In Norway, the police force was completely reorganized in 2000 (Stortingsmelding, 2000). An evaluation of the police reform was recently published (Norconsult, 2005). Based on such studies, the Norwegian police represent a feasible empirical setting for studying research propositions in this section.

Comparison of Antiterror
and Criminal Investigations

There seems to be no such thing as one single police culture. Depending on organization, structure, and task, culture in the police varies. In this research, antiterror police and criminal investigation police in Norway are compared. Although Norway has one police service that is based on the principle of coherence, meaning that all functions are in one organization, significant occupational differences were found. The most significant difference in occupational culture is found on the scale from time firm vs. time floats. Police officers in the antiterror police find that time schedules, deadlines, and speed are important in their job. On the other hand, police officers in the criminal investigation police find sufficient time and not being run by the watch are important in their job. The second most significant difference in occupational culture is found on the scale from legality vs. effective. Police officers in the antiterror police find it more important to follow laws and instructions.

There seems to be no such thing as one single police culture. Depending on organization, structure, and task, culture in the police varies. For example, Christensen and Crank (2001) found cultural differences between police officers in urban and nonurban areas, while Reuss-Ianni (1993) made a distinction between street cops and management cops.

In this research, we study antiterror police and criminal investigation police in Norway. We have formulated the following research question: *How does police culture differ in antiterror vs. criminal investigation police?*

This research is important, as leadership approaches in police management is dependent on insights into the occupational culture of police officers. If, for example, the culture is focused on time constraints rather than work quality, then leadership might be effective if work performance is monitored by the time factor.

In this section, we compare the occupational culture of the antiterror police with the occupational culture of the criminal investigation service in Norway. We conducted surveys in both organizations. The questionnaire had 18 scales to measure occupational culture.

Survey results are listed in Figure 6. Each scale had two extremes, at 1 and 7, respectively. For example, one scale said that time is firm or time floats. Police officers in the antiterror organization find that time is firm (1.83), while police officers in the criminal investigation service finds that time floats (5.06).

Figure 6. Statistics for the comparison of occupational culture between antiterror police and criminal investigation police in Norway (Likert scale 1 to 7)

#	Item	Anti-Terror	Criminal	Significance
1	Time firm vs. time floats	1,83	5,06	123,633***
2	Legality vs. effective	1,71	3,13	26,701***
3	Direct vs. indirect	2,54	4,06	22,366***
4	Open vs. closed	2,52	4,06	20,924***
5	Informal vs. formal	2,33	3,63	15,256***
6	Equality vs. hierarchy	2,38	3,75	14,296***
7	Safe vs. challenge	2,40	3,53	13,361**
8	Change vs. tradition	3,33	4,56	11,925***
9	Applied vs. theoretical	2,14	3,06	10,430**
10	Liberty vs. control	3,19	4,25	9,502**
11	Individualism vs. cooperation	5,44	4,56	7,042**
12	Privacy vs. openness	5,31	4,69	4,283*
13	Competition vs. cooperation	4,81	5,25	1,814
14	Task vs. relationship	3,31	3,63	1,087
15	Firm leader vs. individual	3,73	4,06	,799
16	Work vs. balance	4,35	4,00	,692
17	Short term vs. long term	4,38	4,56	,175
18	Act vs. plan	3,85	4,00	,169

Note: The statistical significance of the t-values is *** for $p < .001$, ** for $p < .01$, and * for $p < .05$

The most significant difference in occupational culture is found on the scale from time firm vs. time floats, as illustrated in Figure 6. Police officers in the antiterror police find that time schedules, deadlines, and speed are important in their job. On the other hand, police officers in the criminal investigation police find sufficient time and not being run by the watch are important in their job.

The second most significant difference in occupational culture is found on the scale from legality vs. effective. Police officers in the antiterror police find it very important to follow laws, regulations, guidelines, and instructions in doing the job. On the other hand, police officers in the criminal investigation police find it just as important to be effective and efficient by demonstrating a willingness to fight serious crimes, without necessarily exactly following laws and instructions.

Differences in occupational culture can be explained by organization, structure, and task. While the antiterror unit has to react quickly and precisely in an emergency situation, criminal investigators have to spend time to organize and carry out the investigation. The time frame for an antiterror police officer to act can be extremely short, while criminal investigation can go on for quite some time. Therefore, it comes as no surprise that the scale time firm vs. time floats receives very different scores in the two organizations.

The second most significant difference in occupational culture is a little surprising. It might seem that criminal investigators can ignore the law as long as they are effective and efficient in their investigations. However, we have to remind ourselves of the scale here, running from 1 to 7. An average score of 3.13 is slightly closer to following the letter of the law than to following free initiatives.

We find many similar culture dimensions. For example, both prefer to work long term rather than short term. A longtime perspective implies a thorough decision-making process, and an ability to sustain relationships over long periods of time.

Overall, the antiterror police officers have the highest average score on the scale from individualism to cooperation, where the average score is 5.44. This implies that the group's needs are put first, and that each officer takes responsibility for the group's actions.

Similarly, the criminal investigators have the highest average score on the scale from competition to cooperation, where the average score is 5.25. This implies that the internal cooperation in the organization has priority.

This section documents both similarities and differences in the Norwegian police. Both antiterror police and criminal investigators find cooperation important. The antiterror police officers are concerned with fixed time limits, while criminal investigators consider time to be flexible. This section illustrates the importance of understanding both similarities and differences for leadership in large organizations such as the police.

Criminal Investigations as Value Shop

Based on a literature review, this section suggests potential determinants of police performance in the value shop. Determinants include occupational culture, knowledge sharing, leadership roles, and stages of information technology. Because the pilot study of police investigation officers had a limited sample, hypotheses could not be tested. However, statistical results from the study provide interesting insights into both the dependent variable (value shop) and the independent variables (occupational culture, knowledge sharing, leadership roles, and knowledge management technology).

At a seminar for criminal investigators, a questionnaire was handed out to measure the extent to which the participants found that they were performing the tasks in each primary activity. Results are listed in Figure 7.

The self-reporting suggests good performance with slight variation, as illustrated in Figure 8 with average responses at or above 5.0 on a scale from 1 to 7. Figure 8 investigates whether there are significant differences in performance between primary activities.

Figure 8 shows significantly lower performance for the final primary activity. Evaluation of the implementation and learning received significantly lower score. This might imply that police officers find that evaluation activities have the greatest potential for improvement.

At the seminar for criminal investigators, a questionnaire was handed out to measure occupational culture. Results are listed in Figure 9. As listed in the table, the culture is characterized by cooperation rather than individualism (4.6) and competition (5.3).

At the seminar for criminal investigators, the questionnaire also measured knowledge sharing. The multiple item scale from Hunter et al. (Hunter, Beaumont, & Lee, 2002) was applied. In this pilot study, the scale achieved an acceptable reliability of .85. The average score was 4.5.

Figure 7. Performance in primary activities of the value shop (1=little extent, 7=great extent)

#	Primary activities in the value shop	Scale items	Scale reliability	Scale average
1	Problem understanding and diagnosis	7 (none deleted to improve reliability)	.70	5.5
2	Alternative solutions to the problem solutions	6 (none deleted to improve reliability)	.72	5.4
3	Choice of best solution to the problem	9 (none deleted to improve reliability)	.79	5.4
4	Implementation of best solution to the problem	8 (two deleted to improve reliability)	.71	5.9
5	Evaluation of the implementation and learning	9 (none deleted to improve reliability)	.84	5.0

Figure 8. Statistical test for significant performance differences

#	Primary activities in the value shop	1	2	3	4	5
1	Problem understanding and diagnosis		.406	.482	-1.594	4.383**
2	Alternative solutions to the problem solutions			.541	-2.336*	3.890**
3	Choice of best solution to the problem				-2.907*	2.435*
4	Implementation of best solution to the problem					4.163**
5	Evaluation of the implementation and learning					

Note: The statistical significance of the t-values is *** for p < .001, ** for p < .01, and * for p < .05

Figure 9. Statistical results for culture concepts

#	Item	Mean	Std. deviation
1	Time firm vs. time floats	5,1	1,06
2	Change vs. tradition	4,6	1,63
3	Individualism vs. cooperation	4,6	1,41
4	Liberty vs. control	4,3	1,20
5	Privacy vs. openness	4,7	0,79
6	Informal vs. formal	3,6	1,41
7	Competition vs. cooperation	5,3	1,06
8	Equality vs. hierarchy	3,8	1,48
9	Short term vs. long term	4,6	1,21
10	Work vs. balance	4,0	1,21
11	Task vs. relationship	3,6	1,09
12	Direct vs. indirect	4,1	1,18
13	Act vs. plan	4,0	1,59
14	Applied vs. theoretical	3,1	1,18
15	Safe vs. challenge	3,5	1,30
16	Legality vs. effective	3,1	1,45
17	Firm leader vs. individual	4,1	1,18
18	Open vs. closed	4,1	1,73

Results from the pilot study are listed in Figure 10. The entrepreneur role achieves the highest score of 6.1, followed by both personnel leader and monitor.

Figure 10. Statistical results for leadership roles

Leadership role	Mean	Std. deviation	Significant difference
Personnel leader	5,6	1,1	More important than spokesman
Resource allocator	5,3	1,7	Less important than entrepreneur
Spokesperson	4,9	1,4	Less important than entrepreneur
Entrepreneur	6,1	0,7	More important than liaison
Monitor	5,6	1,2	
Liaison	5,0	1,8	

In the pilot study of police investigators, IT support was measured according to value shop activities, as listed in Figure 11. The most extensive use of information technology in police investigations is found in the second primary activity of alternative solutions to the problem, and in the fourth of implementation of best solution to the problem.

From a statistical point of view, the use of IT in the second activity is significantly higher than in the third and fifth activities.

This section defined police investigation in terms of value shop activities. The performance of the value shop is influenced by determinants such as occupational culture, knowledge sharing, leadership roles, and the use of knowledge management technology. With a limited sample from a pilot study, no regression analyses for hypothesis testing could be carried out. However, the pilot study data provided some insight into both the dependent variable (value shop) and independent variables (occupational culture, knowledge sharing, leadership roles, information technology).

Figure 11. Performance in primary activities of the value shop (1=little extent, 7=great extent)

#	Information technology support for primary activities	Items	Scale reliability	Scale average
1	IT in problem understanding and diagnosis	4	.78	3.9
2	IT in alternative solutions to the problem	4	.83	4.0
3	IT in choice of best solution to the problem	4	.74	3.5
4	IT in implementation of best solution to the problem	4	.89	4.0
5	IT in evaluation of the implementation and learning	4	.86	3.3

Systems for Homicide Investigation

A survey of urban police departments concerning automated information systems for homicide investigations was conducted by Sidrow (1999). While many respondents indicated that they had some form of automated system for their work as detectives, Sidrow's (1999) study focused on the systems that are commonly used to support local homicide investigations. These can be grouped into three major types of systems: unit systems, departmental systems, and remote information analysis services (RIAS). The RIAS systems can further be divided into regional and federal systems.

Sidrow (1999) found a positive relationship between computer use and homicide clearance rates. Police departments that reported high-clearance rates (80-100%) had the highest percentage of users (85%) using RIAS systems. Generally, she found that as the use of computer systems increases, homicide clearance rates decrease. Departments with clearance rates below 60% were usually in very large metropolitan areas that witness a high number of stranger-to-stranger homicides.

Survey respondents reported poor or nonexistent documentation for unit-developed systems. They called that a major reason for the short life cycle of unit-level systems (except where the developer remained on staff). System documentation, including user guides, data dictionaries, and maintenance manuals, were better for departmental and regional systems that offered the added benefit of facilitating information sharing (Sidrow, 1999).

Value Shop and Stages

Police investigations are a complex undertaking that have both reactive and proactive dimensions to them. The knowledge required to effectively carry out an investigation is built upon "three pillars," a term employed by the Singapore Police Force, that are forensics, intelligence, and interviews.

A well-grounded forensic understanding of a crime scene is the foundation of any investigation. Intelligence gathering is a crucial activity for an investigation, particularly so for proactive investigations into organized crime and/or terrorist-related operations. As regards interviews, the ability to derive relevant information from people through effective interviewing is seen by police as an essential activity in any investigation. Hence, as Chen et al. (2002) point out, police investigation units represent a knowledge-intensive and time-critical environment. The primary mission of any police force in the world is to protect life and property, preserve law and order, and prevent and detect crime (Luen & Al-Hawamdeh, 2001).

We treat police investigation as value-shop activities. As can be seen on Figure 12, these five activities are interlocking and while they follow a logical sequence, much like the management of any project, the difference from a knowledge management perspective is the way in which knowledge is used as a resource to create "value" for the organization. Hence, the logic of the five interlocking "value shop" activities in this example is of a police organization and how it engages in its core business of conducting reactive and proactive investigations.

Also noted on Figure 12 is how, in practice, these five sequential activities tend to overlap and link back to earlier activities, especially in relation to activity 5

Figure 12. Knowledge-managed police investigations in the value shop

'Value Shop' Activities of Knowledge-Managed Police Investigations

Key Task - assign competent person (s) eg. In a serious, complex crime/operation an SIO (Senior Investigating Officer) will head an investigation team of several experienced detectives/investigators.

Key Task - discuss approaches to investigation (e.g., initial brainstorming sessions occur to look at the crime/operation from all angles.)

1: Activity - Problem finding and acquisition

2: Activity - Problem solving

An organisation creates 'value' by solving problems through the management of its knowledge

3: Activity - Choice of solution to problem

5: Activity - Control and evaluation

4: Activity - Execution of solution

Key Task - decide on investigation approach (e.g., based on the most promising investigative leads a focus and direction is decided on to pursue the investigation.)

Key Task - evaluate investigation (e.g., SIO monitors the investigation and evaluates evidence to determine offender(s) if possible and ability to prosecute.)

Key Task - implement investigation approach (e.g., SIO directs the lines of enquiry and establishes the elimination criteria for suspects.)

Secondary Activities in the Value Shop
Infrastructure: use of police intranet for internal communications   Technology: image processing
Human Resources: use of police intranet for competence building   Procurement: use of public agreements

Figure 13. Stages-of-growth model for police knowledge work

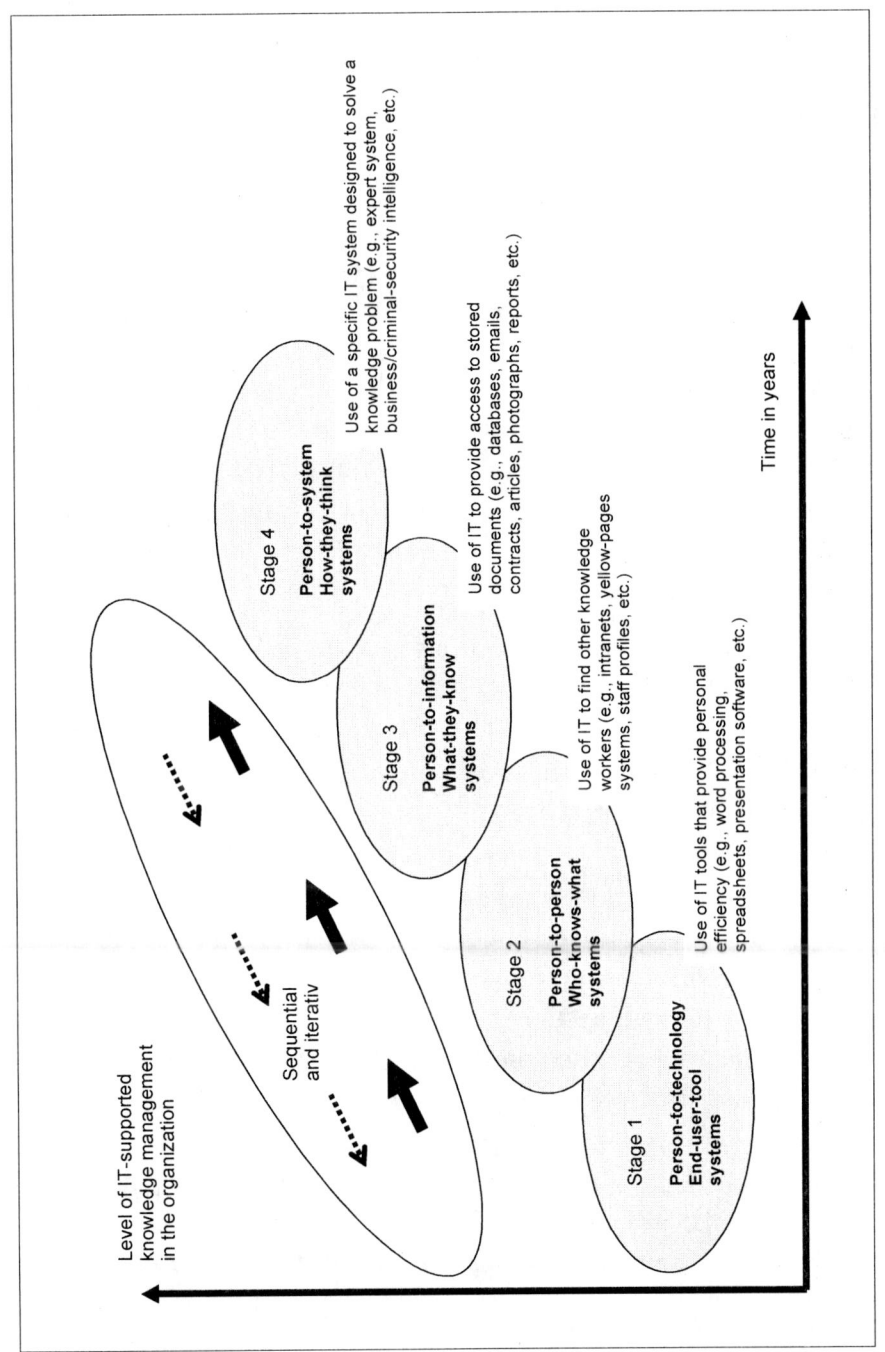

(control and evaluation) in police organizations, when the need for control and command structures are a daily necessity because of the legal obligations that police authority entails. Hence, the diagram on Chapter VIII's Figure 13 is meant to illustrate the reiterative and cyclical nature of these five primary activities for managing the knowledge collected during, and applied to a specific police investigation in a value-shop manner.

Moreover, the basic requirements needed to develop a knowledge management system with the appropriate level of IT support are shown in the box at the bottom of Figure 12. In this regard, it is worth noting that research by Adhami and Browne (1996) into the possibility of developing a knowledge based system for sexually oriented child homicides in England found that the infrastructure of the HOLMES (home office large major enquiry system) database could be used to structure and store such crime-specific information that would greatly assist detectives in investigating this type of crime.

Briefly, these five activities in relation to a police investigation unit can be outlined as:

1. **Problem finding and acquisition** involves working with parties to determine the exact nature of the crime. It involves deciding on the overall approach to police work for the case.

2. **Problem solving** is the actual generation of ideas and action plans for the investigation.

3. **Choice** represents the decision of choosing between alternatives. While the least important primary activity of the value shop in terms of time and effort, it is also the most important in terms of customer value. In this case, trying to ensure as far as is possible that what is decided on to do is the best option to follow to get an effective investigative result.

4. **Execution**, as the name implies, represents communication, organizing, investigating, and implementing decisions.

5. **Control and evaluation activities** involve monitoring and measurement of how well the solution solved the original problem or met the original need. As noted previously, this is where the command and control chain of authority comes into play for police organizations.

The use of knowledge management systems has the potential of improving all of the five primary activities. However, based on the previous discussion of police investigations, we argue that the greatest potential is found in the second phase of problem solving.

Nested within this proposition, that police research efforts should be focused on developing knowledge management systems that concentrate on enhancing the activity of how "problem solving" takes place within investigations, is a second proposition based on the empirical research by Dean (2000) that identified four qualitatively different thinking styles (method-challenge-skill-risk) that investigators rely upon to guide them in solving crimes. The proposition is that knowledge management systems are more important in the thinking styles of method and skill than in the thinking styles of challenge and risk

As Dean (2005) notes in police investigations, the experience of investigation begins for detectives when they are given a crime to solve. When handed a case, detectives apply methods they were trained in. Often, they follow a set of five basic procedural steps: collecting, checking, considering, connecting, and constructing.

Dean (1995) argues that essentially, investigation is a mind game. When it comes to solving a crime, a detective's ability to think as an investigator is everything. Hence, the value of the four distinctively different ways of thinking, as noted previously: investigation as method, investigation as challenge, investigation as skill, and investigation as risk. All four ways of describing a criminal investigation can be seen as more or less partial understandings of the whole phenomenon of investigation.

The ambition level using knowledge management systems can again be defined in terms of stages of knowledge management technology as illustrated in Figure 13.

We argue that a police investigation will find greater support in their work at higher stages of the growth model for knowledge management technology. This proposition is also congruent with the first proposition about the importance of knowledge management systems for police investigations being focused on the problem-solving activity. Clearly, problem solving is a higher order thinking skill and therefore, as the figure indicates, a matching up of a Stage 4 "how-they-think" KM system is required at this level in the investigation.

With regard to the focus of this chapter on police investigations, knowledge is the most important strategic resource that police, as a "firm," use to solve their particular crime problems. If police fail to fully utilize this resource, then their return-on-the-investigative investment will be lower. Therefore, we believe that police investigation success is positively related to the extent of access to strategic knowledge resources.

References

Adhami, E., & Browne, D. (1996). *Major crime enquiries: Improving expert support for detectives* (Special Interest Series, Paper 9). London: Home Office Police Research Group.

Ashby, D. I., & Longley, P. A. (2005). Geocomputation, geodemographics and resource allocation for local policing. *Transactions in GIS, 9*(1), 53-72.

Brehm, J., & Gates, S. (1993). Donut shops and speed traps: Evaluating models of supervision on police behavior. *American Journal of Political Science, 37*(2), 555-581.

Chan, J. B. L. (2001), The technological game: How information technology is transforming police practice. *Criminal Justice, 1*(2), 139-159.

Chen, H., Schroeder, J., Hauck, R. V., Ridgeway, L., Atabakhsh, H., Gupta, H., et al. (2002). COPLINK Connect: Information and knowledge management for law enforcement. *Decision Support Systems, 34*, 271-285.

Chen, H., Zheng, D., Atabakhsh, H., Wyzga, W., & Schroeder, J. (2003). COPLINK—managing law enforcement data and knowledge. *Communications of the ACM, 46*(1), 28-34.

Christensen, W., & Crank, J.P. (2001). Police work and culture in a nonurban setting: An ethnographic analysis. *Police Quarterly, 4*(1), 69-98.

Dean, G. (1995). Police reform: Rethinking operational policing. *American Journal of Criminal Justice, 23*(4), 337-347.

Dean, G. (2000). *The experience of investigation for detectives*. Unpublished PhD thesis, Queensland University of Technology, Brisbane, Australia.

Dean, G. (2005). *The cognitive psychology of police investigators*. Conference paper, School of Justice Studies, Faculty of Law, Queensland University of Technology, Brisbane, Australia.

Ekman, G. (1999). *Från text til batong. Om poliser, busar og svennar*. PhD doctoral dissertaion. Stockholm, Sweden: Ekonomiska Forskningsinstitutet, Handelshøgskolan i Stockholm, School of Business. Sweden: Stockholm.

Fahsing, I. (2002). *The man behind the mask: An archival study of 250 eyewitness statements in 48 cases of armed robbery.* Master of Science thesis, University of Leicester, UK.

Fielding, N. (1984). Police socialization and police competence. *The British Journal of Sociology, 35*(4), 568-590.

Glomseth, R. (2004). Norway. In *World police encyclopedia.* New York: Garland Publishing.

Holgersson, S. (2005). *Yrke: POLIS—yrkeskunnskap, motivasjon, IT-system og andre forutsetninger for politiarbeide.* PhD doctoral dissertation, Institutionen för datavetenskap, Linköpings universitet, Sweden.

Hunter, L., Beaumont, P., & Lee, M. (2002). Knowledge management practice in Scottish law firms. *Human Resource Management Journal, 12*(2), 4-21.

Kahana, E. (2001). Mossad-CIA cooperation. *International Journal of Intelligence and CounterIntelligence, 14,* 409-420.

Kiely, J. A., & Peek, G. S. (2002). The culture of the British police: Views of police officers. *The Service Industries Journal, 22*(1), 167-183.

Lahneman, W. J. (2004). Knowledge-sharing in the intelligence community after 9/11. *International Journal of Intelligence and Counterintelligence, 17,* 614-633.

Luen, T. W., & Al-Hawamdeh, S. (2001). Knowledge management in the public sector: Principles and practices in police work. *Journal of Information Science, 27*(5), 311-318.

Norconsult. (2005). *Evaluering av Politireform 2000—publikums vurdering av polititjenesten. Veien videre for politireformen.* Politidirektoratet, Oslo, Norway: The Police Directorate.

Reuss-Ianni, E. (1993). *Two cultures of policing: Street cops and management cops.* New Brunswick, NJ: Transaction Publishers.

Sidrow, C. L. (1999). *Automated information systems for homicide investigation: A survey of urban police departments.* Washington, DC: Police Executive Research Forum.

Stedje, S. (2004), *The man in the street, or the man in the suite: An evaluation of the effectiveness in the detection of money laundering in Norway.* Master of Arts thesis, University of Manchester, Social Sciences and law, UK.

Stortingsmelding. (2000). *Politireform 2000—et tryggere samfunn.* Stortingsmelding nr. 22, Det kongelige justis- og politidepartement, Parliament report no. 22 from the Department of Justice and Police.

Zamanou, S., & Glaser, S. R. (1994). Moving toward participation and involvement. *Group & Organization Management, 19*(4), 475-502.

Conclusion

In this book, we have proposed that police investigation success is positively related to team climate, knowledge sharing perceptions, and stage of knowledge management technology. Furthermore, we propose that police investigation success is more positively related to the spokesman role than to other leadership roles for the team manager. These four research propositions for determinants of police investigation success should be empirically explored in future research.

Some of the important causal influences between knowledge management and police investigations are mapped in the causal loop diagram in Figure 1. Causal loop diagramming is described by Sterman (2000), and presented as a tool by http://www.vensim.com.

As illustrated in Figure 1, police investigation success is dependent on knowledge sharing, leadership roles, and organizational culture, in addition to crime complexity. When crime complexity increases, resource mobilization increases, leading to more knowledge management technology that improves knowledge sharing, leading to higher level of investigation success.

One positive feedback loop in Figure 1 is illustrated in Figure 2. When knowledge sharing increases, investigation success rises; as a consequence, management takes on leadership roles that further encourage knowledge sharing.

Figure 1. Causal loop diagram for knowledge management in police investigations

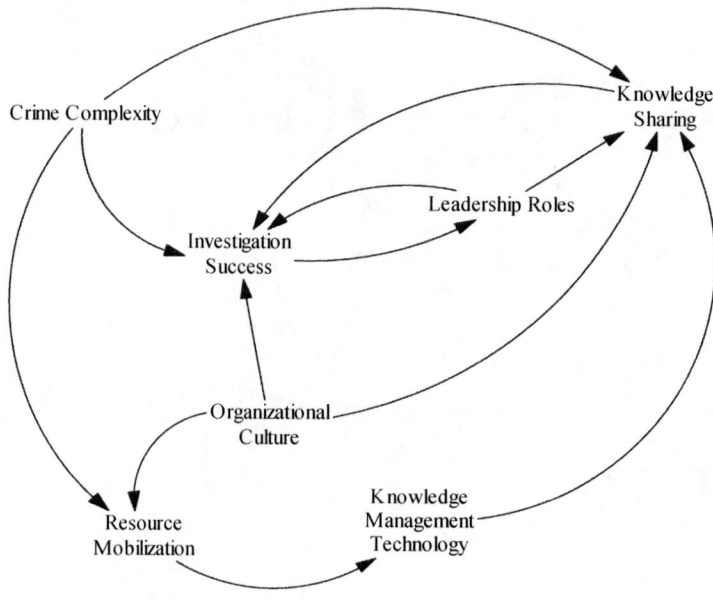

Figure 2. Positive feedback loop in the causal loop diagram

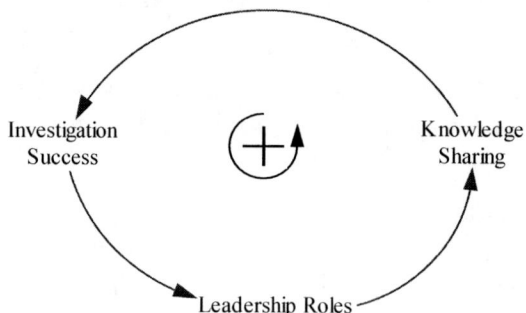

Information technology has become an integral part of police life. Information technology has redefined the value of communicative and technical resources, institutionalized accountability through built-in formats and procedures of reporting, and restructured the daily routines of operational policing. These changes in the field of policing have led to some changes in the habitus. For example, information technology has allowed police procedures to be more transparent at the level of "customer interface," and this transparency has become accepted as an indicator of good police service. Similarly, officers are beginning to appreciate the value of using technology-generated information for tactical and strategic purposes such as crime prevention, problem solving, and resource allocation. Nevertheless, the dominance of traditional policing styles and values remains. Although information technology has given police the capacity to follow a "smarter" or more problem-oriented style of policing, this capacity has not been fully utilized. Even where technology facilitated proactive police work such as the checking of outstanding warrants, it has been used mainly to support a traditional law enforcement style of policing focused on clear-up rates. The cultural suspicion and cynicism against management and external watchdogs is still very much alive, but this has been channeled into hostility towards the organization's "obsession" with risk management, and external agencies' demand for data and accountability (Chan, 2001).

As an organizing framework for this book, the stages of growth model for knowledge management technology was applied to both police investigations and law firm work. When lawyers and detectives communicate and exchange knowledge, we see more and more information technology applied in the information exchange. However, the use of information technology to support interorganizational knowledge exchange between police organizations and law firms is dependent upon the availability of similar infrastructure services and applications. This might require that both police and firm are at the same stage of growth in the stage model in the future.

References

Chan, J. B. L. (2001), The technological game: How information technology is transforming police practice. *Criminal Justice, 1*(2), 139-159.

Sterman, J. D. (2000). *Business dynamics: Systems thinking and modeling for a complex world*. Boston: McGraw-Hill.

About the Author

Dr. Petter Gottschalk is a professor of information and knowledge management in the Department of Leadership and Organizational Management at the Norwegian School of Management in Oslo. His executive experience includes positions of CIO at ABB Norway, and CEO at ABB Datacables and at the Norwegian Computing Center. He earned his MBA in Germany, MSc in the U.S., and DBA in the UK.

*   *   *

Anne Puonti, PhD, is the head of administration at the National Bureau of Investigation, Finland. She finished her doctoral dissertation at the University of Helsinki in spring 2004. Her dissertation is called *Learning to Work Together: Collaboration Between Authorities in Economic-Crime Investigation*. Her current interests include the development of an information management system for the NBI. Previously, Puonti has worked as a forensic expert at the National Bureau of Investigation (1991-1998), as a researcher at the University of Helsinki (1999-2002), and as a development manager at the NBI (2003-2004).

Index

A

administrative knowledge 40, 168,
    177, 257
advocate 254
agency theory 13
AICAMS 100, 193, 210
analytic technology 107
analytical knowledge 40, 168
antiterror police 306, 309, 313
application service provider (ASP)
    278, 280
Armed Robbery Eidetic Suspect
    Typing (AREST) 208
artificial intelligence (AI) 100, 191,
    199, 205, 279
Association of Chief Police Officers
    14, 151
Atlassian's JIRA 89
automated fingerprint identification
    system (AFIS) 107

B

ba 50
barrister 254
best practice 66, 267
Blue Flag 279
Boston Police Department 107
Bugge Arentz-Hansen Rasmussen
    (BA-HR) 264

C

case development 227, 238
chief executive officer (CEO) 255
chief knowledge officer (CKO)
    46, 82
CIA 12
CIO 256
CKO 46, 82, 256
closed-circuit television (CCTV) 97
cognitive interview (CI) 146
Comanche County Sheriff's Depart-
    ment 208

Thommessen Krefting Greve Lund
 (TKGL) 264
training technology 106
transformative technology 106
Tucson Police Department 98

V

value chain 63, 214, 219
value network 214

value shop 214, 221, 238, 315
Vanguard Software Corporation 89
virtual space 50
virus 109

W

wisdom 27
Word 89
worm 109

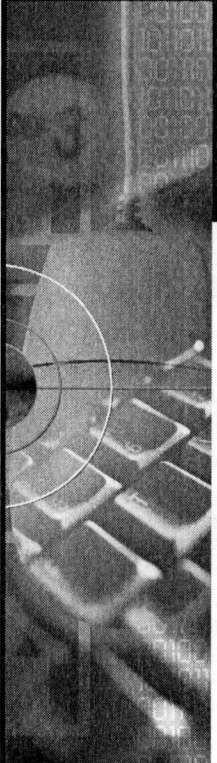